Sixties Going on Seventies

A Volume in the Series

PERSPECTIVES ON THE SIXTIES

Edited by Barbara L. Tischler

Sixties
Going On Seventies

Revised Edition

Nora Sayre

Rutgers University Press
New Brunswick, New Jersey

Library of Congress Cataloging-in-Publication Data
Sayre, Nora.
Sixties going on seventies / Nora Sayre.
p.   cm. — (Perspectives on the sixties)
ISBN 0–8135–2274–9 (alk. paper)
1. United States—Politics and government—1945–1989.   2. United
States—Civilization—1945–   I. Title.   II. Series.
E839.4.S29   1996
973.9—dc20   95–42680   CIP

British Cataloging-in-Publication information available

"Marching," "Black Panthers and White Radicals," and "Shoot-
ing Revolution" were first published in *Esquire* . "Five Years After
Kent State" was published in *Ms*. "The John Birch Society" and
"Strike and Lulls: Harvard" are reprinted by permission of *The
Village Voice*, Copyright by The Village Voice, Inc., 1971, 1973.
The Progressive, the *New Statesman* and *London Magazine* are
thanked for permission to reprint material that first appeared in
their pages, often in a different form.

This Edition is for

Toni Willison   *Martha Huggins*   *Malcolm Willison*

Contents

PART II   UTOPIA AND INFERNO

PART III   NEW YORK FOR NATIVES

PART IV   THEATER AND A COUPLE OF MOVIES

PART V   CONTRADICTING THE CONVENTIONS

Acknowledgments

Many of the chapters expanded for this book first appeared in the *New Statesman*, and I thank Paul Johnson—who was the editor from 1965 to 1970—for the literary and political freedom I enjoyed in writing for the magazine. Both were scarce among New York publications at that time.

I adapted some of my *New Statesman* pieces for *The Progressive;* I remember the editors Mary Sheridan and Morris Rubin and Erwin Knoll with gratitude—their concern for writers was unique. And I was fortunate to work with Alice Glaser at *Esquire.*

I thank Leslie Mitchner of Rutgers University Press for the exhilarating opportunity to revise and update this edition.

Introduction

1995

In the early Seventies many kept remarking that a year seemed like a decade, or a decade like a century. And it appeared that there was an acute hunger for quite recent history. A writer who had been immersed in the era was constantly asked to pull out facts and events from 1967 or to go all the way back to 1965. Few seemed nostalgic about the Sixties, but many wanted to examine the sequences, the details: to see how they did or didn't play into the present. Here I was reminded of the famous computer which was given "Out of sight, out of mind." The answer was "invisible idiot." Perhaps some feared becoming invisible idiots—if they didn't continually try to understand what was occurring around them in those years of flux.

This was and is a book of changes. Writing about the period meant recording contradictions and shifting alliances, watching the tides move in and out, searching the sands to see what was left behind. Sometimes the task was being clear about confusion. Or—when a movement was still very fluid, like the early New Left—one had to be careful not to freeze it prematurely, to stress that it was still altering.

From 1965 to 1970 I was the New York correspondent of the *New Statesman,* which gave me enormous editorial freedom; also part of the pleasure was being a foreign correspondent in the city where I was raised. Many of the chapters published here appeared in somewhat different form in that magazine. For this book I added a great deal of new material; some of it came from consulting my original sources or reviving common memories among longtime friends. When writing for the *Statesman* and *Esquire* or others, I chose subjects I thought were endowed with enduring interest: historical moments which would be worth revisiting a decade or two later. I began as a reporter and a critic; by 1968 I was feeling rather like a war correspondent, a sensation I could never have foreseen. As many topics became political or racial, the arts and some of the most casual conversations mirrored those themes. A New York editor said to me, "You can't even talk about sex without ending up with Vietnam!"

Most of the book was written while the war was still on. The people quoted here had no idea when or how it might end, and Vietnam seemed like a permanent part of our cultural landscape. As I plunge into the period once again, I can hear Phil Ochs singing "I Declare the War is Over," Simon and Garfunkel's "7 O'clock News/Silent Night," Melanie's "Peace will Come (According to Plan)," smell the pot smoked at the end of some antiwar marches, recall pungent scenes from Barbara Garson's *Macbird!* and Jules Feiffer's *The White House Murder Case*. The songs and the plays kept reminding us that our government was lying to us: about body counts, about the successes of American troops, about the waning strength of the North Vietnamese.

Our most powerful politicians were still clinging to the domino theory inherited from the Eisenhower regime: if South Vietnam were conquered by the Vietnamese Communists, the rest of Southeast Asia would follow, then possibly India, Burma, and the Philippines, maybe even Japan. Russia and China would control more and more of the globe, imperiling all of Western civilization. In 1967 and 1968 some national leaders, who told each other and the public that they were preventing World War III, began to doubt that the Vietnam war could be won—as former Secretary of Defense Robert McNamara informed us in his rueful memoirs. More than fifty-eight thousand Americans and three million Vietnamese were killed while—as McNamara wrote—some members of the administration came to think that the antiwarriors were right. But Lyndon Johnson and then Richard Nixon kept insisting that the dissidents were prolonging the war.

Watching old footage of Mississippi 1964, I remember how people were losing their lives in the civil rights movement while others died in Vietnam. So many blacks in the Deep South had been murdered for trying to register to vote, for being seen with white visitors from SNCC or CORE, or just because they were black. In the North we were still naive in the early Sixties; we didn't know that racism was endemic to all parts of the country, nor how dangerous it was to work for desegregation in the South. After Andrew Goodman, James Chaney, and Michael Schwerner were shot dead by Klansmen, the search for their bodies turned up unexpected black corpses in the Mississippi Klan's dumping grounds: the woods, swamps, and rivers of Neshoba County; some were found with their hands or feet tied together and their heads cut off.

During Johnson's 1964 campaign he sought to make the issue of poverty important to voters and said he wanted to end "poverty as we know it." In August 1965 he increased our involvement in Vietnam just as the bills enacting portions of his Great Society program were passing through Congress. Because of the war, the administration was never able to fund the domestic programs as had been planned; the amount of money decreased each year as more was pumped into the war. The Office of Economic Opportunity was badly administered by Sargent Shriver and the White House became alarmed by the community participation of the poor, which the OEO had initially encouraged. But it was apparent that parts of the War on Poverty started well, as I witnessed when I spent weeks visiting the Job Corps and two Head Start centers—and later saw what ground was lost when the funds were diminished. Johnson's earlier focus on poverty had caught the sympathies of a good many middle income Americans who had lived through the Depression or heard about it from their parents or grandparents—hence they could still identify with the poor, as many born after 1960 did not.

In 1968 Nixon's "Southern strategy" was most effective: declaring that busing "would only destroy" school children, denouncing the OEO, he won white votes by asserting that his party had none of the Democrats' reputed allegiance to civil rights. Black activists were becoming members of Congress and mayors, but it was plain that the path to equality would be a long one. Still, for radicals and certain liberals, the determination to fight racism, to change laws and enforce the new legislation, surged through the mainstream of the Sixties. It would have seemed unimaginable that many solid gains would crumble in the Seventies and beyond.

When I was writing about the Sixties during that decade, I especially wanted to portray the (very) American experience of those years: people of different backgrounds discovering what each other's experiences were. I thought that was the nature of the period. Of course it was mainly the middle class which was educated. But a number of rather comfortable persons began to learn about the experiences of the poor; whites learned what black Americans were thinking; some GIs learned what the Vietnamese were living through; older people perceived what the young were feeling. Many on the left learned from and about the right: what George Wallace's constituency was experiencing. A spell of heightened sensitivity? Yet it seemed that much of what was absorbed was fairly soon forgotten—as after a cram course during a reading period. But for a few years it appeared that quite a bit of experience was shared, when many were exposed to one another.

As a writer I've passed through so many people's lives, have seen them surface in new incarnations. In the beginning of 1966 I spent some time down at the Free University of New York (long defunct), where I met a few of the Weatherfolk of the future. FU was one of the first counter-universities; it aimed to provide "a substantial socialist education of high quality" while "combating mindless activism" and there were some good courses, ranging from "Rebellions That Failed" to "Revolution in Latin America." The faculty commented on the students' lack of preparation; in the seminars I attended, some seemed to have difficulty in understanding the concept of "sponteneity," and they were flummoxed by such questions as, "What would you do if you were Poland in 1945?" One woman, a sober, reserved graduate student who taught a course in nineteenth-century Russian literature, later reappeared as one of the Crazies in 1968; naked, she offered a pig's head to the supporters

of Hubert Humphrey and Edmund Muskie. In December 1970 she was arrested (and convicted) as one of a group who were trying to firebomb a bank
in my street. It was the anniversary of the murder of Black Panther Fred
Hampton; the city detectives, pretending to be drunks, closed in and invited
the technicians to a party while they were arranging their containers of gas
and benzine outside the bank. Others I knew in denim turned up in dark
suits and conventional jobs, droning away about their real estate. And some
who thought they were apolitical found that they weren't; sometimes an event,
like the massacre of Vietnamese civilians in My Lai in 1968 or that year's
Democratic convention in Chicago, revealed their own views to them; others
made the discovery gradually, as their surroundings seeped in on them. Yet
others recoiled from those they were working with, finding that they couldn't
accept the final product—whether it was supposed to be revolution or a
hairspray, a new business venture or a polygamous commune. Some switched
their sex. A number disappeared. A few died young.

I think the era showed that one had no right to be surprised by the reincarnations. But because the Sixties demanded definite commitments, the
reversals were more conspicuous than they might have been at other times.

Amid the dilemmas of the left and the momentum of the right, the shattering of cities, utopias gone awry, the revolts of blacks, women, and the very
young, I was obsessed with voices—in choruses or solos. Since I put all these
chapters together, I see that the voices restate a loathing of institutions, even
more so than I realized at the time. And the voices—mounting and muttering and shouting and accusing and even agreeing: the voices yield the period. They were also a writer's reward.

$\sim$

Amid the Sixties rebellions, one of the most striking was the revolt of many
young people against consumerism and the money culture. Some of the talk
about capitalism was fuzzy, but the disrespect for acquiring objects appeared
to be sincere. Of course what did seem worth owning was often affordable—
new albums or tape recorders—and naturally the young were enjoying their
costumes, apart from jeans: the flock velvets, the silver bell bottoms and feather
vests, minis and tie-dies, chain belts and Nehru jackets. People under thirty-
five mainly wanted what was portable: paperback books, paper dresses, pais-
ley floor cushions and Art Nouveau or Op Art posters, bead curtains. Rejecting
commercialism bestowed a perceptible high, and refusing to enter the establishment could be a playful act as well as a moral stance.

Just as the finest and worst aspects of our society were conspicuous in the
Sixties, the images from those years are both heartening and painful. Pictures retained on my interior screen: the colossal black and white crowds
marching on Washington in 1963, singing and fanning themselves in the
August heat, waiting to hear Martin Luther King; the Saigon police chief

lifting his pistol to the head of a young North Vietnamese in a plaid shirt—he will fall dead in a minute; the astonished upturned faces of dealers and clerks on the floor of the New York Stock Exchange as they watch dollar bills flung from the gallery by laughing Diggers who are mocking the world of finance; police dogs springing at black civil rights marchers in Birmingham, Alabama.

It appeared that the Sixties ended in about October 1970. But the largely conservative and cautious times that soon followed were no less violent, no more secure. Although urban riots declined, it looked as though even more individuals were being killed, whether in New York or Southeast Asia. And as I allowed the images of the Seventies to pile up and seize me, they weren't soothing. On the eve of Nixon's departure to China, I read that the presidential plane was carrying lots of blood and champagne. There was "an adequate supply" of Nixon's blood type—in the likelihood of attempted assassination—and cases of American champagne for toasting his hosts at a reciprocal banquet. That vast jet, pounding through the skies full of blood and bubbly, stayed with me as a symbol for peace-keeping in 1972. The hijacker who dropped his ransom money while bailing out seemed like a creature of the period, and so did the demonstrators who learned to wear their lawyers' names inked on their wrists. Also another hijacker whose bombs turned out to be a few large lemons wrapped in tinfoil. In those days I collected headlines, especially from the *Times,* and I had a wallfull of choice ones: "War and People Called Hazards to Civilization"; "Touch of Humor in Science Urged"; "President Says His Mind is Open"; "VD Upsurge Tied to Pace of Living"; "Slumming in Harlem is Passé."

When you entered the Harvard Bureau of Study Counsel, the first thing you saw was a huge gleaming box on the water cooler, labeled SURVIVAL RATION CRACKERS. Its metal flanks were dense with printed instructions, such as how many crackers a "Normal Adult" should eat. The thing appeared to be a piece of fallout-shelter equipment from the early Sixties. A member of the bureau said it had turned up at a white elephant gift party; she added that it was puzzling that the box had never been opened or thrown away.

∾

In the Sixties you kept hearing that reporting was the new art form. While that was beguiling, I felt that not enough was said about how complex it had become. First, you struggled with the facts you knew and couldn't print—since you didn't want to send certain people to jail or to be subpoenaed for your confidential sources. Second, many were afraid to talk to you, fearing that they would be quoted accurately—just as much as they feared misquotation. (Valid fears.) Third, although you deplored the traditional media's distortions and felt you must correct the straight press, honesty often demanded that you report bad news from your own side. (A Black Panther said about a white radical who wrote a complimentary account of a black conference which ended poorly, "Now that really *is* paternalism.") You might appreciate the ideas of different radical groups while worrying about how they were being applied, and that double bind had to be recorded. Throughout this book, I retained the dilemmas that many radicals had in common: about the uses of force.

Meanwhile your own skepticism grew fiercer: apart from those who lied to you, or pretended to be what they were not (as in 1969, when both the Progressive Labor Party and the FBI were claiming to be members of SDS), or told you four-fifths of the truth (when you happened to know the other fifth—which altered everything), or needed days or weeks of acquaintance before they could trust you, by which time you didn't trust them—aside from all these bear traps, it was sometimes very difficult to know what was true, what actually occurred. (I doubt that we'll ever know all the facts about the death of George Jackson in San Quentin.) You also met people who didn't seem to believe what they themselves were saying: I especially encountered that in California. And I found it hard to forgive reporters who invented a single quote or character. The groggy public no longer knew what to believe, and I thought the mistrust would last for a lifetime. But fact was also a victim of disbelief: ugly news which happened to be true became easier to ignore.

These were a few of the problems which plagued writers in the Sixties. But what I particularly like about reporting is that it requires you to lead so many different lives in the course of one year or several weeks or months—while you sink yourself as deeply as possible into the subjects or ideas you're writing about. Yet I was also at odds with the era because it was a time when contempt for the past was paramount. Those of us who choose to preserve the present—in order to study it as it quickly becomes the past—still stubbornly believe in history: we want to see how the events of this season will look in the future.

In the "Hindsights" I wished to be rather informal: to talk with the reader about the past, or to relay new information—before hurtling into the next crisis or set of concepts. Throughout I decided to take the reader back and forth in time, not only out of respect for Kurt Vonnegut's *Slaughterhouse Five,* but because the years between 1965 and 1974 were divided by Chicago 1968, and I thought it was good exercise to keep reliving what happened before and after that summer. Many of the original hindsights were written in 1972, but I've updated them and some come up to 1995.

In 1972 (MORE), the New York journalism review, held a counter-convention of the press. Many of the panels discussed the scarcity of editorial freedom in the major media, and *New York Times* columnist Tom Wicker spoke of the deadening forms and "molds" imposed on writers: "But each story dictates the *way* it ought to be told." I tried to follow that dictation: the demands that every subject made on the narration. Researching each chapter, I also valued the incongruities which couldn't be squeezed into any generalization, and it seemed essential to include them too. So the forms varied—because they had to. When I wrote about my own city, my priority was to make New York sound like New York. Some of those chapters are short documentaries, designed to give the tang of the time and the events, or the moment when we were first aware of a new notion. Those who hate cities and those who like them often responded rather violently. Again the readers' own experiences were involved. Because no one ever feels neutral about New York.

In fact I didn't find much neutral territory—maybe most of it evaporated or disappeared, as some like to vow that New York will. But here is a series of way stations where many kinds of Americans spent their time; some of them were trying to make a different sort of history than what they'd already known. They didn't fully succeed, but they did make certain changes—and some of those changes have lasted past expectations. Yet other changes were temporary, swept away during the Reagan–Bush years or vehemently assaulted by Newt Gingrich and his followers. Some activists from the Sixties looked back and agreed that they had won many battles—which would have to be waged all over again in the future.

Part I

Exercises in Upheaval

Democratic Death-In
Chicago August 1968

Such blood: released from bruised and broken veins, from foreheads, scalps, and mouths, from eyesockets, shattered wrists, and skulls. Broad bloodstreaks on the pavements showed where bodies had been dragged. We all bleed inwardly from the particular atrocities we witnessed. I saw seven policemen beating one young woman—long after she had fallen; a row of sitting singers whose heads were cracked open by a charge of running cops; a photographer's camera smashed thoroughly into his eyes. Each day scores staggered bleeding through the streets and parks, reeling or dropping, their faces glistening with vaseline—for Mace. Gas rinses your lungs with the lash of iodine and vinegar: your own breath burns your throat.

Outside the Hilton, a little old woman patted a rebel on the chest, murmuring, "Knock the socks off them." I said to her, "Funny how the police seem rather powerless right now." Then she and I were suddenly hurled against the wall when some hundred policemen seized their blue wooden barricades to ram the crowd (mainly onlookers and press) against the building with such force that many next to me, including the old woman, were thrust through the hotel's plate glass windows. ("For no reason that could be immediately determined": *New York Times*.) The police then spilled through the smashed window and clubbed both those who'd gone through it and some of the drinkers at the bar. Outside, people sobbed with pain as their ribs snapped from being crushed against each other. (My ribs were protected by an unknown man's magnificently fat, soft back. All praise to Fat Power.) Soon a line of stick-whipping cops swung in on us. Voiceless from gas, I feebly waved my credentials, and the warrior who was about to hit me said, "Oops, press." He let me limp into the hotel, where people were being pummelled into the red carpet while free Pepsi was timidly offered on the sidelines.

Since delegates, newsmen, and spectators were thrashed along with the demonstrators, many learned what blacks have always known: that the democracy of savagery makes no distinctions—everyone's guilty for his mere presence or existence. The Chicago cops taught us that we were rubble with no protection or defense. In future we can understand the ghettos' rage: without uncoiling any imagination. Later, as I watched the beatings and gassings from a second-floor McCarthy room, twelve policemen surged in, slammed down the windows, drew the curtains, and told us to turn away and watch the TV set, where Humphrey was starting to speak—"And that's an order." The Chicago cops, whose trucks advise "Reach Out and Grab the Greatest Summer Ever," rarely speak, not even when asked for street directions, and they direct traffic as though they were flogging invisible bodies. A veteran Chicago reporter said the cops are extremely afraid of the local blacks. Hence they took a special revenge on the August marchers, primarily because the police failed to subdue the ghetto's April riots after Martin Luther King was killed. Yet even Humphrey has defended them—"I was targeted by an assassination team and supposedly to be taken care of. . . . We had intelligence information from the . . . police department and the FBI of planned assassination"—and a recent poll suggests that 71.4 percent of queried citizens thought the actions of the Chicago police were "justified."

Thus it's difficult to determine what the protest accomplished. True, the liberal press and all free minds throbbed with a communal concussion. But as James Reston noted, the young, the poor, the black, and the intelligent "have the fewest votes," and the demonstrations were probably deplored by the voting majority. Still, "voting with bodies" wasn't bootless. Tom Hayden wrote, "We are coming to Chicago to vomit on 'the politics of joy' "—indeed they did, and the image was distilled by a stinkbomb at the Hilton, which smelled as though hundreds of gorges had risen. Rennie Davis said the motto would be: "There can be no peace in the U.S. until there is peace in Vietnam"—and there won't be. At a Panther rally, young white militants vowed "to join the blacks—by putting ourselves in the same grists that blacks are in. We'll take the same risks. Cops who beat on them must beat on us." Yet few whites seem able to realize that they can never fully share the black experience. A black militant replied, "The strongest weapon we have is all of us. United black-white opposition." It looked as though some liberals became radicals, and some dissenters began to talk about revolution. But the most moral point came from Dick Gregory: "Had there been a bunch of young people who challenged Hitler the way you challenged Mayor Daley, there might be a *whole* lot of Jews alive today."

Many have observed that large groups often behave like the worst persons among them. But I felt that the Chicago crowd reflected its best members— who were also the majority. The aims are simple: peace, liberation for blacks, an America where property is less valuable than human life. These goals must be constantly repeated because the tactics confuse older—often sympathetic— people. (A seasoned, oldstyle liberal reporter, watching the mayhem from the Hilton, asked me in real bewilderment, "What do those people want?") But the movement seethes with such contradictions about method and leadership that when Humphrey said it was "programmed," one only wished that he were right.

A few leaders were lavishly irresponsible: they excited the most naive—teen-agers and hippies—who didn't know that the mild term "personal risk" could mean getting killed or maimed. These gentle waifs, plus a few glittering hysterics, usually rushed to the front; at moments one feared they would be used as fodder. Two young brothers—both tripping on acid and eager to tell me how their "really hip mother" had given them a hookah for Christmas, inscribed as "a *joint* present! Haw!"—were ecstatic when they misheard directions which came over the mike to go to the Limits Garage—to lend support to the striking black bus drivers "He says we should *go the limits!*" one boy cried. Thinking that their heads were more vulnerable than some, I dragged them off to see Pigasus, the pig who was running for president on a platform of garbage. But they were ideal fodder.

SDS and the Mobilization Committee had had some disagreements about tactics before the convention. SDS—which decided that "mass confrontations don't effect constituencies"—didn't actually demonstrate; instead it worked to organize and protect the marchers. One SDSer said, "We don't believe that a bop on the head is more educative than a pamphlet." But some MOBE workers generated a tension that split bones instead of hairs. Different leaders springing to the microphones instructed the crowd to be cool, to get hot, that they were helpless, that they were powerful, to go home, to gather, to disperse into small groups, to mass for a huge nonviolent march—in which other speakers warned that they'd be trapped. (And they were.) Many marchers were too inexperienced to choose clearly. Despite MOBE's love of spontaneity, the need for organization was as desperate as the ache for peace.

You come lurching out of these vast fleshpacks with a reeking dilemma about violence—which is now a suitcase word for assassinations, student protests, ghetto revolts, mugging, and nut crimes. For the right these are indistinguishable. For some members of SDS, violence means wrecking Selective Service files or bombing a draft board—at night, when there's no one there to be hurt. One said, "We're *not* nonviolent; we'd like to take over the city. But we can't. So we'll use long-range political organization. We're ready to use force to achieve a political end. The question is whether it *does* achieve that end?" For others, "Revolution is a form of self-defense . . . since our society is already founded on force."

For one who has never accepted violence and has always believed in working through the political process, Dick Gregory's words kept echoing, underlining the realization that the threat of black violence has become a useful tool for black people. (A Watts militant told me: "Perhaps the *threat* of violence is even more important than violence itself.") And of course the cold war mentality has educated all of us about the international use of threats. Yet how do you draw a dotted line between street fights and killing, between "good" and "bad" violence? Any brand of violence is contagious, as this land of assassination knows. Moreover, since madness seems to be the country's most pungent odor, more people may become violent merely to be heard: "Just to be taken seriously," as one calm man said. Many of us are wrestling with evaluations of the fact of force. If violence in the United States could result in peace in Vietnam, then I would support it—with a ravaging disgust at a society which forces anyone to make such a choice. I haven't the physical courage to fight in the streets, but in Chicago I respected those who did. A white Chicago clergyman said he felt the same. He added that the church hadn't yet decided its own position: "Listen, we've been holding seminars on violence *ourselves*. Because we don't know what to say to our parishioners about it—we no longer feel able to tell them that they must be nonviolent. Because we know that no social change has ever occurred without violence." But the very new "revolutionaries" will never remold America on their own. And at moments some sound like the general who said he had to destroy a Vietnamese village in order to save it. But perhaps their momentary power could be a partial fuel for change—if a right-wing renascence doesn't stifle us all. That possibility hums in every wire of the mind. Chicago taught us what law and order can mean. After all, these protestors were not violent. The streets were dangerous because of the police.

The images of Chicago come crowding in thicker now. The bravery of TV crews at night: their clumsy trucks lumber after the crowd that the cops have driven behind a screen of trees; their floodlights offer a little—but not much— protection. Two vast black men in Levi's, dancing lightly on their sneakered toes, almost waltzing in anticipation, who tell me: "The brothers are coming. It's going to be beautiful." But it doesn't happen—later that night I see them both in different (daytime) clothes. Jean Genet's sweet pink smile in a dimpling Santa Claus face, as he tells the crowd that they're "very pretty and beautiful," but—pointing at the nearby policemen—"The ones I love most are those with the blue helmets who dress unconventionally also." Allen Ginsberg omming like a death rattle, his voice ravaged by the days of Hindu chants and gas. William Burroughs's incredibly white face beneath a gray fedora; although some students urge him not to march out front, he says that he and Genet must keep their promise to do so. The two rather sadly smell some bunches of flowers that were given them. A young man riding the statue of General John Logan, the Civil War hero, until the police drag him down and fracture his arm. At four and five o'clock each morning, as the hotel clerk gives me the key to my room, he cackles, "Hah! We really give it to them didn't we! Fix them dirty hippies! Wait until tomorrow!" An ice cream truck, weaving slowly through a frightened crowd, is cheered, and the driver's fingers split in the forked peace sign. Old reporters frozen on the sidewalks, goggling in disbelief at the clubbing, saying things like, "But this is *America!* This can't be hap—"

As the press stands ringed by National Guardsmen, an NBC cameraman points out that those who are supposed to be protecting us are aiming their rifles right at us and at the Hilton. One promptly drops his weapon. *"Jesus, that's dangerous, he's very green."* Before the convention, *Newsweek* said that Chicago's manhole covers were sealed up with tar so that no one could hide beneath them. The only story that makes people smile: when some reporters were picking up their credentials, they saw an old man in a baseball cap shouting, "But you *must* have press tags for me, I'm Walter Winchell! I'm Walter Winchell!" Wandering into the crowds each day, I'm nearly always joined by a couple of men: priests or blacks, students or photographers. One said, "I'm scared stiff, but would you like a little *psychological* protection?" I run whenever I want to and usually find my bodyguards on my heels. With two doctors I walk five blocks ahead of the group that Dick Gregory is leading to the Amphitheatre; we see the tank with the machine gun that awaits them. We turn back to tell them, discovering that the empty alleys—where we'd planned to disappear if necessary—are now crammed with police and Guardsmen. None who want to disperse will get away. One of the wounded says, "Now we know how the Vietnamese must feel—we never knew we'd end by fighting our own people."

Peter and Mary sing "If I Had a Hammer," and a scowling Chicagoan says, "They have the filthiest mouths." Angry cars in a traffic jam honk like panic—then finally pound their horns to the rhythm of "Hell-No, We-Won't-Go." Even an ice cream mixer in a drugstore sounds like a siren. When the chairman of the New Hampshire delegation, who was arrested, jailed, and accused of biting a policeman, says on TV, "I swear that I have never bitten anyone," a gathering of students whoops at the level to which the convention has fallen. . . .

At LBJ's antibirthday party, which Ed Sanders of the Fugs said was mainly inspired by Lewis Carroll, there was music by the Conquering Worm and the Holocaust. Dick Gregory mused about the Prague citizens who had been pasting swastikas on the Russian tanks: "Just you try that *here*." He added, "Can you believe, this country is so insane that LBJ don't trust *you*?" And, "If you knew Daley's record down through the years, you'd know that this week he is on his best behavior." Finally, "If democracy is as good as we tell you it is, why the hell do we have to go all over this world, ramming it down people's throats with a gun." The audience cheered and cheered when he read them part of the Declaration of Independence—"Whenever black folks burn up and sack a town, I read this"—concluding with, " . . . whenever any Form of Government becomes destructive of these ends, it is the Right of the People to alter or abolish it . . . "

Mixed media: leaving the gassy streets again, to watch from the Hilton's twenty-third floor: Humphrey's voice chattering from the haunted fish tank in the background: " . . . it is the special genius of the Democratic party that it welcomes change . . . " Below, the police slice savagely into the crowd, while beside me a man with a walkie-talkie warns the crowd that fifty National Guard jeeps are arriving. My notes are little newsreels: "bayonets fixed now . . . doctors try to reach wounded . . . cops won't let them. . . . New marchers coming . . . but they're trapped." *Walkie-talkie:* "You're about to be gassed from the left." *Humphrey:* "We are and we must be one nation, united by liberty and justice for all. . . . " *Crowd in Street:* "Pigs! Pigs! Pigs! *Oink! Oink! Oink!*" (The frantic chorus bursts when anyone's arrested.) McCarthy-workers to Humphrey delegates in lobby, on *walkie-talkie:* "*You* killed the party! *You* killed the party!" Humphrey asks the young "to join us . . . Never were you needed so much . . . " The police are smashing heads more swiftly now. The crowd sings, "Where have all the flowers gone?" More have fallen who don't get up. Others shout, "Daley Sucks! Hump the Hump!" *Walkie-talkie:* "Look, I don't care if the Guard *has* brought bazookas inside the Hilton. They won't use them—it's a *very* impractical weapon for a hotel lobby. See, they need a long firing range, or they'll blow up everyone *behind* them." *Crowd:* "Peace . . . Now . . . Peace . . . Now." *Humphrey:* "I do not intend to appeal to frustration, but rather to your faith."

It all blows the mind farther than any discothèque hinged for destruction. Bombarded senses don't make succulent sense. Cosmic irony tinges many details; earlier, David Dellinger was interviewed by a TV network: as he said that technology was "looting the universe," both camera and sound kept breaking down. "Would you mind repeating that?" "Technology is . . . " "Oh dear. This isn't working again."

It's reported that the Hilton management is very angry because sheets were torn up to make bandages in the McCarthy headquarters.

Back in the street again. Speakers ask those who support them to blink lamps in the hotel's windows: the Hilton prickles with blurts of light. Rolls of toilet paper fall unwinding from above. The crowd's character has changed in five days: the hippies with flutes and recorders and finger cymbals have been joined by more conscious radicals, students, clergymen, numerous older people, girls with long earrings labeled EUGENE swinging from their pearly lobes, many costumes of propriety, plus all the bandaged heads. Many keep repeating that they used to be middle class before they left the system. And the innocents are still there. Tête-à-tête: "We pool our money and buy one of those small independent islands in the Pacific, and have our own government." Sad reply: "But then won't Washington bomb us?" Tourists of violence prowl past, loving the nerve-splitting agony. The crowd shouts "Shaft the draft!" A few dance before the National Guard. "PEACE." A CBS man says the police are outraged by the Guard's presence—they say it's hurt their pride. Crowd: "*Sieg heil! Sieg heil!*" Then they sing, "This land is made for you and me."

Hindsight: There was a shred of comfort when the Walker Report to the National Commission on the Causes and Prevention of Violence, headed by

Milton Eisenhower, defined the events at the convention as "a police riot." But some history had been lost in the tumult. Many in Chicago were not aware that the black delegates of the Mississippi Freedom Democratic Party— refused proper credentials at the Democrats' 1964 convention—were seated in 1968; it was a symbolic civil rights victory after the MFDP's rejection by Lyndon Johnson, who had claimed to fear losing white Southern votes if he had allowed black Mississippians a place in the Atlantic City convention hall.

~

I spent my first evening home from Chicago in the Manhattan Criminal Court. My apartment had been broken into a few hours before I returned. But a neighbor called the cops and they found a young man with my typewriter in his hand. He was a pusher who had jumped bail several times, though he had no record as an addict. It's awkward meeting your own burglar—we traded defensive stares in court—but I didn't have to press charges, only to say that he wasn't an old friend who was free to remove my lock and my Smith-Corona.

Then the cops arrested my typewriter. They said they'd have to keep it for a couple of months as evidence for the trial. I had a ferocious deadline, it was Labor Day weekend, and it would be almost impossible to borrow anyone's machine. So I threw a fit, purposely blowing all the cool I'd tried to maintain in Chicago. I punished the New York cops as though they were responsible for the whole convention, insulting them as brutally as possible, while the very nice officer who'd nabbed the burglar pleaded with the D.A. to return "the tools of her trade—why, this is like taking a doctor's bag, or a taxi-driver's cab!" So I stopped hating all policemen, even though I didn't get the typewriter.

It did seem healthy that Chicago had served to shock so many spectators about the state of their own country. But like lots of others, I didn't sleep for weeks afterwards. I kept having documentaries instead of dreams. Each night was full of the same footage: people bleeding and weeping and running.

I kept playing Phil Ochs's song from 1966, "Miranda." There was a verse which seemed to express the mounting lunacies around us:

> The sunburned skin is peeling
> On the doctors who are healing
> And the license-plates are laughing on the cars . . .

In a jolly voice Ochs sang that "the dice of death are calling," and "the Howard Johnson food is made of fear." The rickytick accompaniment grows gayer: "The arguments are clashing/While commercial planes are crashing, /And the music of the evening is so sweet . . . "

Years afterward the sense-memories are just as alive as ever—the terrible creak of breaking glass as bodies burst through it, or the thick rim of the

china cupful of bourbon which was offered as an antidote to gas—but some
of the emotions seem distant. Fright of course is easily relived. But that sense
of confidence which came out of Chicago—that momentary hope that a number of people could possibly begin to change their society—feels remote. In
1968 it would have seemed incredible that some could flee to Vermont to
construct a way of life that would take all their time: hours to bake the perfect
loaf of health bread, days to build a bed, weeks to dig a well.

By the summer of 1971 I'd had wailing calls from all over New England
about carrots that didn't come up, or how sick a cow had become: the old
comedy of intensely urban people expecting that farming would be easy. And
some couples used rural settings to escape the whole issue of feminism:
through a way of life which required both sexes to be home-makers all day
long.

In 1972, although we saw many young people working for McGovern, few
of his supporters whom I knew were the radicals of the late Sixties. Many of
those who were proud of revealing the hypocrisies of the Chicago convention have since been unable to back any candidate. The scar of Chicago may
be cynicism, along with the curious exhilaration of a grim memory: indeed
the ugliness of national power was exposed, and its institutions could never
quite claim purity again. Of course others responded with the determination
to strengthen those institutions, in hopes that those who marched in Chicago couldn't ever act so freely or so wildly in the future. The fact that they
were reflecting their own society was incomprehensible to some—whose understanding probably continued to diminish.

Marching
1969-1972

Fear can start in the scalp, which may sweat at the first soft splat of gas gre-
nades, at the mere sight of nightsticks raised. The head may be suddenly
wet before the knees or wrists dissolve and the feet move. It's a reflex for
many—since Chicago, marching or voting with bodies will never be quite the
same: that old confidence in one's rights was punctured along with some
lungs and kidneys and snapped ribs on Michigan Avenue. The fear can be
unjustified: in the dustups after the November 15 Moratorium in Washing-

ton the police were indeed controlled; marchers were gassed only for decid-
ing to be in a certain place at a particular time: risk was choice. Still, while
jittering with cold or apprehension, the memory of other demonstrations
made one marvel at how easy it all used to be: before the symbols congealed,
when the styles of conviction were unperilous. Free in fact.

Today a reporter needs several bodies at once to experience and register
the varieties within one fleshpack. You hardly know what to do with your only
body, since it becomes a participant, a witness, a recording device, a piece of
crowd: a range of schizophrenia is required.

Demonstrations have changed, both in style and purpose. It's not frivolous to weigh the behavior of protestors; if they act stupidly, the press and the
opposition can ridicule their beliefs. Hence it's ironic that the (magnificent)
character of the November mass left it oddly vulnerable afterward. The *Washington Post* described the event as an amiable binge for "youth culture": "a
happening at which nothing happened." Many who scorn marches simply as
a form of expression were especially caustic—"all those nice little people with
candles"—as well as disgusted with those who were aggressive at Dupont Circle
and at the Department of Justice. Now, if marchers are orderly, they're derided. And peacefulness in the cause of peace is patronized.

Of course no single protest accomplishes its purpose; it's the accumula-
tion of demonstrations that can finally slam a point home. Some think that
the November Moratorium may be the last of the big tranquil marches. Having marched for ten years, I have fresh doubts about demos, yet see no alternative to intensifying them.

Aldermaston, Easter 1959: streaming in a vast, jubilant throng into Trafalgar
Square, fighting with a brilliant ten-year-old boy (later a radical student) about
the future of the Labour party, heaving with reluctant laughter at his jokes
while struggling to maintain the dignity essential to one of eight Americans
walking behind the U.S. sign. There were hoots from some Empire Loyalists
while the pigeons wheeled around Nelson, and everyone gleefully hailed their
friends. In London there are no strangers: all who tangle with politics or the
arts are ghoulishly well acquainted, to the extent that one luminary groaned,
"Oh God, isn't there *any*one on this march whom I don't know?" But the
exhilaration was unique: for many it was the first sense of strength in numbers. The initial intention was to force the Labour party to stop dithering
about disarmament: it was an appeal to politicians from their own constituents. Naturally it was also an attempt to put the squeeze on the Tory government. Before long, as a former activist recalls, "We were trumpeting to
everyone who would listen—to the U.S. too—to try to educate them about a
new horror." The movement very nearly converted the Labour party to uni-
lateral nuclear disarmament, but Hugh Gaitskill finally fought it off. In the
early Sixties the Campaign for Nuclear Disarmament was shattered from
within, and there's still a bomb to ban. But CND alumni feel they helped to

create the atmosphere of opinion which made the Test Ban Treaty possible: the revulsion at nuclear weapons which soon swam through many bloodstreams.

After the tidal crowds from Aldermaston it was odd to stroll slowly within the mild little cluster which picketed the White House on Easter 1960. While Ike played golf in Georgia, some of us carried signs protesting research on nerve gas and germ warfare (especially pneumonic plague), while students from Amherst, Williams, Trinity, and Wesleyan marched to support black sit-ins at southern lunch counters. A small unit called the Peacemakers vowed not to pay taxes for any kind of war, and one man hoisted a huge placard opposing Celestial Annexation. It was all very balmy and leafy, passive and pastoral—also very amusing for spectators. I shoved a cop's hat off with my clumsy sign and we both apologized eagerly. I came away feeling that demonstrations were useless in this country: the effort was put down as a whimsical eccentricity; the impact was nil.

Before the March in Washington in 1963, the press was almost as alarmist as it was before the November Moratorium. (It's worth remembering that JFK didn't want the March, although he finally played at being a benefactor.) Editorials promised that "tomorrow may be a day of tragedy." A helpful friend said, "Holy shithead, you'll all be immolated. Be sure to crawl out quickly when the bus begins to burn." Buying Sara Lee pecan rings and hard cheese the night before (we'd been warned against liquids and runny foods), I did quail at the ravenish croaks from liberals. However on CORE's bus, morale was restored by a *Newsweek* cover story on the March, which was dated September 2. It was read aloud on August 28th by those who hadn't yet marched. *Newsweek*'s deadline crunched the event into the past tense: "Who were the marchers?" "Certainly, the ingredients of trouble were there . . . " Whoops restored our queasy confidence.

Perhaps it was the only demonstration that ever made a lot of people happy. Some thought it accomplished little else. (A derisive observer said, "It proved Negroes' ability to stand quietly and patiently on street corners, which I've known about for several hundred years.") How many remember that it was a march "for jobs and freedom?" One black man, repeatedly jailed in Danville, Virginia, told me, "This isn't a protest. It's to show the numbers who agree about one thing. Also a ceremony of a sort. And—as the newspapers *don't* report—it's also a memorial for Medgar Evers and two others who were murdered." Black leaders also intended the March to show support for President Kennedy's civil rights bill, which was meeting resistance in Congress.

Afterward most of the press praised the acute degree of dignity and cheer as though it were a new brand of fudge ripple ice cream: sweet, soft, digestible—but hardly part of anyone's regular diet. (The fish-fry, *Green Pastures* theme stressed by many papers was a parody of logic: we'd been told to bring our lunches, and of course we sat upon the grass.) All that docility seems extraordinary after the mire and fury at Ole Miss in the fall of 1962, plus the infinite cattle prods and dogs already used on nonviolent marchers in the South, and the punctual beatings and gassings (of blacks) which fired far less indignation than the clubbings (of whites) in Chicago 1968. The line that still echoed from Ole Miss was a student's remark, widely quoted in the press, about James Meredith: "I'm a broad-minded individual, but he just isn't a good nigger."

Meanwhile most northerners still refused to realize that their territory was as ugly as the South, in terms of that fingertip phrase of 1963, "the racial problem." Only four I knew from New York went to Washington. The liberal response was remote and marching wasn't yet fashionable. Some shrugged; whose problem? Others thought it hilarious. Others analyzed at length the recent self-discovery of prejudice (as it was called), for psychological reasons: an early spanking by a black maid, being beaten up on the way to school at the age of eight. Others jumped hard on culture: why was there no Negro Shakespeare, no black Mozart? But most hastily added that of course the educated Negro is just like anyone else. A British visitor asked for a comparison between the class system in England and racism in America. I found myself saying, you don't kill people to keep them out of Eton. Returning on the train from Washington, someone said, "It is *the* moral issue of this country." At that time it was possible to believe that the civil rights movement was going to succeed, above all because the cause was just. In the months that followed, some came to feel the March itself was almost a betrayal: a substitute for concrete action. But eventually many thought that crowd of over a quarter million—a third of them white—had helped to create the climate that produced the Civil Rights Act of 1964. As the civil rights legislation of the Sixties developed, no one I knew dared to use the word "progress": the beatings and murders continued. But having heard Martin Luther King's speech in the midst of those hopeful multitudes was a memory to be prized among the waves of tragedy that followed.

In the next few years we marched in Harlem and elsewhere to reinforce those who were marching in the South, went on sympathy marches for civil rights workers who were killed or children bombed in churches, while the antiwar marches began. All those I took part in were calm and deeply serious: the style was still that of 1963 and the marchers were dressed for the office. But a new angry response was erupting. Early in 1965, as a silent line of high school students and clergymen trickled down Lexington Avenue, carrying signs that merely read "Negotiate," I heard two bald men—clearly strangers— stirring themselves into frenzies on the curb. "If *I* had a boy in that group," one said, "*I'd* break his jaw for him, *I'd* make him crawl—" "So would I. I'd stop his allowance, I'd take away his car . . . " And so on. They agreed that their sons would have to enlist—immediately. Finally one growled, "Got any kids?" "No," snarled the other. "Huh. Neither have I." Suddenly awkward, they separated: two neat, embarrassed men, perhaps startled by their own ferocity as they waited for the traffic lights to change.

Styles of dissent had altered lavishly by April 15, 1967. Central Park blossomed with a giant be-in, a merry day for exchanging daffodils and pot and buttons saying "Puppies For Peace," parading new Day-Glo ponchos and glistening jumpsuits, necking in the streets, body paint, rock bands, and chanting "Flow-er Pow-er." A counter-demonstrator's sign read, "Dr. Spock Smokes Bananas." Although the smoke from burning draft cards curled up through wet spring leaves, the big pâpier-maché yellow submarine float was a more valid image for the day. A new arrival said, "There are sure to be some groovy people here, and I want to make the scene." I was angry at parts of the crowd for being so blithe and careless: many seemed to have forgotten that Martin Luther King was waiting to speak outside the UN: to declare that the war was as destructive to the ghetto as to the Vietnamese. The idea was thought dreadfully controversial: the press rebuked him for daring to connect the war with poverty at home. However editorials soon began to echo his convictions, tinged with the smugness of their own originality. But that April march was a fun fest: the participants disregarded the purpose of the demonstration and the style contradicted the intentions.

A month later an enormous pro-war parade—organized by a captain in the New York Fire Department, which contributed some engines—gathered in my street in the East Nineties for eight uproarious hours. PEACE was a large, loose-bellied doll, footless from being dragged behind the jeep to which it was tied: the cross-eyed face was painted to look insane. A young boy dressed as Uncle Sam nervously fingered his decomposing cotton beard as he slumped in the jeep's front seat. Signs read, "Eradicate RED CANCER," "Bong the Cong," "Death to Pink Finks." Two parachutists decked with flags landed in Central Park, and were arrested (it's illegal to jump on New York). Later a spectator was beaten, tarred, and feathered by thirty marchers because of his sandals and long hair. The crowd alternated funeral dirges with Broadway tunes, yelling and stamping in and out of the battered Third Avenue bars, banging beer cans into the gutters. Less silent than in Nixon's dreams, they also seemed far more confident than many flights of doves.

Soon desperation about the war exploded into more desperate shapes of protest. By late 1967 the demonstrations began to resemble boils breaking out all over one vast sickened body. Wildness replaced the serene or celebratory styles: the word was "force," not yet "violence." At the Pentagon many in the front ranks seemed to have brought their own private neuroses to mingle with their loathing of the war. That was a far more bitter, much older crowd than the one at the November Moratorium. Heading for the Pentagon, many constantly disobeyed their own leaders, surging ahead when asked to wait for traffic. Screaming "Mother-fuckers!" at the stationary soldiers, some even pressed their chests close to the bayonets—as though on a dare—while others peed on the Pentagon. (Beforehand, when a human chain around the Pentagon was planned, some said that they were going to masturbate—but I couldn't see how, not if everyone was holding hands.) Many mouths were ringed with the white crusts of dried spit. Late in the afternoon I became a marshal, one arm trussed up in baby-blue satin—the color that one now associates with the Chicago police. The main assignment was to get slabs of the crowd along the rope ringing the Pentagon to sit down so that those who wanted to walk across it and be arrested could make that choice, without forcing others to be shoved forward by the bodies behind them. Now and then I was able to persuade about thirty to crouch down together; then one small man would leap to his feet, yelling "Only chickens sit, only chickens shit!" and the group would spring up again. Many appeared to feel that their personal courage was being tested or insulted. While some aspects of the grotesque were appropriate, those of us who didn't believe in rioting for peace were slightly depressed. And many of us were losing faith in demos: it seemed as though the participants merely discharged their own energies and then felt virtuous. While the war went on.

By early 1968, many were wrestling with notions of violence, kindled by the response to black revolts, plus the awareness that profound social change rarely occurs without violence. But the word "revolution" still sounded silly in Manhattan, especially tripping off the lips of editors and sociologists. Hence it was staggering to be in Paris in late May where, at the doors of the Odéon, students searched all purses and satchels for bombs, and then kissed those who carried none. (Among the wall posters, my favorite was *Attention! Attention! Les oreilles ont des murs.*) The elation of an uprising that nearly worked ebbed swiftly. Most radicals knew that the Communists didn't want a revolution, and agreed that they themselves could achieve nothing without a party of their own. In early June I joined a tremendous *manifestation* which strode from Montparnasse to the Gare d'Austerlitz. Those who firmly chanted, "*Ce n'est qu'un de'but / Continuons le combat!*" would then turn aside to explain that they knew they had lost, but that they must still turn out to show that their beliefs were as unshakable as ever, and that de Gaulle's claim to restored national unity was a lie. Workers and students greeted each other affectionately in the streets. The rebels had no program and they hadn't "looked toward Moscow"; even so, tricolors were torn in thirds to make red flags. Many praised Cohn-Bendit for his instructions on how to restrain violence, how to preserve lives. Then they would shout with the same sturdiness, "*Nous sommes plus en plus enragés!*" and "*Elections-trahison!*" Between slogans, they remained equally positive, practical, and sad: "It's all over now, we've had it—*Ce n'est qu'un début . . .* " That night someone said that Russia would hate to see France go Communist, because the national frivolity and sensuality would set a bad example for other Communist countries.

October 15, 1969: PEACE drifting down Manhattan avenues: sky writing.

Once again thousands used their bodies because others hadn't used their heads. During the large Wall Street rallies, a publisher said, "Businessmen used to pick up phones and punch out ticker tape when they wanted something done. Now they also take to the streets. . . . Maybe business isn't so big anymore in decision making. Perhaps it's become a submanagement of the new state management within the Department of Defense." No generation gap: at a high school students' rally, teen-aged speakers urged seniors threatened with the draft to "talk to your parents—tell them to work legally against your going. Try to educate them if they don't yet understand." The participation of middle-class and professional people—many of whom had never demonstrated before—displeased some of the Left. There were jealous snorts about "co-optation," even an unwillingness to share a condemnation of the war. Jerry Rubin later complained in Washington, "It's like peace is becoming respectable." In the age of paradox, even the antiwar movement can lament its own success. Rubin himself came on like a camp counselor, leading chants, toasting the marshmallows of his thought. It seemed that many had bypassed him.

By November 1969 it was conspicuous that feelings against the war had flared in three distinct stages. In 1965 there was the response to the suffering of Vietnamese civilians, women or children maimed or dead. In 1967 Dr. King unleashed the consciousness of what the war was inflicting on the ghetto: suffering at home. By early 1969 there was a fresh burst of outrage at the killing of soldiers on both sides—such sympathy for the U.S. military had hardly existed before. When protesters in Washington walked across Arlington Memorial Bridge, wearing placards with the names of the dead, it was an attempt to restore each man's individuality—to show that casualties were creatures, not mere numbers. There was almost an atmosphere of resurrection: an effort to revive particular persons. The names came with all the diversity of the continent: Glenn Nobuyki Nichizaura, Jimmy Lee Cook, Manuel G. Yberra, Arie Terry. Walking alone and far apart stressed the singleness of the dead, their isolation. Candles glimmered through cupped hands as in the seventeenth-century paintings of Georges de la Tour; shadowed faces were lit from below. Some looked rather haunted, as though briefly possessed by those whom they symbolized. Warren O. Kneppery. Balades David Zalada. Roy Smith. Perfecto M. Lorez. Albert Glanton. As Murray Kempton said, many of the Wasp names probably belonged to blacks: the descendents of slaves who were given their owner's names. Mine was Ronald Powers. Wearing the name made one wonder what he was like, what he looked forward to. Passing the White House at night, power has never seemed so blinding: for "security," the lawn floodlights were reversed so that the building was almost unseeable— it was hard to imagine that it was actually there. Dropping the names into the coffins to the recurrent drumroll, watching the steady line of candles still approaching: that was as repetitive as death itself.

Of course some of the young men marching were also making a plea for their own lives. Although many cheered up later—"See you at the big cock" (the new name for the Washington Monument)—some appeared as bleak as the candles which had been extinguished by the wind.

Trust is so lacerated and suspicion is so lavish that if there had been rain throughout the Moratorium, it would have been tempting to deduce that Nixon had seeded the clouds. (During one downpour, a man in a drugstore said, "He's taking care of those dirty hippies out there." God or the President?) But by asserting that violence would occur, the administration tried to frighten away some of the potential demonstrators and also issued an invitation to possible psychotics.

During the Chicago convention, two sixteen-year-old waifs and I foolishly accepted a lift from a crew-cut stranger, a professional ballplayer from Florida. (There was a bus strike and a taxi shortage, hence many were offering rides.) Ignoring the boys' street directions, he drove us further and further into the deserted outskirts of the city and then stopped speaking to us altogether. At that point we noticed his stunning resemblance to Richard Speck, the mass murderer. We asked to get out, but he wouldn't stop or reply. Really alarmed by his silence, the boys asked him how long he'd been in the movement. "I'm not in any movement," he hissed, "I'm here for the action, for kicks, like anyone else." We spilled from the car at the next red light. "Man!" said one boy. "That was really feeling like croaksville."

At any rate there could have been a few like him in the herd that played games around Dupont Circle and the South Vietnamese Embassy in Washington. Also the crowd may have contained some provocateurs, fulfilling prophecies for Agnew. Many seemed propelled just by curiosity. Others kept losing their affinity groups. But it was the only truly provocative group I've seen. Just as those in the front ranks stood nose-to-nose with the police, a man offered some of us poppers from a paper bag: "You want some courage?" Afterward some were brave enough to trash the windows of parked cars or small shops. Later two cackling Weatherwomen described how the wicked pigs had been gassing innocents. They failed to arouse a resentful audience of over a thousand marchers. There was also a man who claimed to be a Panther from the New York chapter. I doubted it because I knew that group fairly well at the time, and because he got a lot of the Panthers' ideology and slogans wrong. But he was urging his hearers to "bring it all down tomorrow."

Despite the debates about violence that were continuing among militants, many agreed that November 15th was the wrong time for it. Then the most pungent way to defy the administration was to be peaceful. But some Weathermen hadn't combed out the difference between thrills and results. The issues got lost. If you kick a cop and he kicks back, you're a hero and he's a villain. Many black people know it's not that simple. In October Fred Hampton, the chairman of the Illinois Panther party (who was killed by police in

December), called the Weathermen "anarchistic, adventuristic, chauvinistic, masochistic, and Custeristic," adding, "We don't dig confrontations that lead people into struggles they're not ready for."

Obviously no street event is worth an ounce of the persistent long-range organizing for change in specific areas, from the military to the ghetto, in schools or throughout the whole system. Yet demonstrations do tend to commit those who have been present. Still, while swaying within the Moratorium mass to "Give Peace a Chance," sharing tangerines, cigarettes, Hershey bars, blankets, and gum, warmed by hugs and smiles, the whole experience made many of us feel more helpless than ever about Vietnam. Futility filtered through the sunlight: some later agreed that the sensation of being in that crowd was to be invisible—along with a multitude. Few could agree with Howard Samuels that the Moratorium was "more consistent with the American tradition" than the war was. But trying to catch Nixon's attention or concern was like waving at a drunk across a canyon. What someone called "the flexibility gap" appeared to yawn wider than ever: the grin of a dying dog.

~

On April 15, 1970 there was another modest Moratorium which ended up behind the New York Public Library, where a couple of small groups seized the microphone from one another. I saw only one person I knew—Dwight Macdonald—and we wandered about rather sadly, agreeing that when antiwar demonstrations were held, we would continue to join them for the old reason of increasing the numbers. I felt that the attitude toward the war had subtly changed. Quite a few seemed able to live with it, even though it still gnawed at them—rather like a person who's learned that he has an incurable disease which isn't going to kill him.

~

One of the most radical events I've covered was the Gay Liberation march of June, 1970. Striding up Sixth Avenue: thousands of young people, many in plain jeans and work-shirts, flourishing their fists, marching with a determination that had been scarce in recent peace demonstrations. Spectators squinted for clues; another Panther rally? A draft protest? Then they heard the rousing chants: "Gimme me a G! Gimme an A! Gimme a Y! . . . GAY POWER"; "Less pop-u-lation/More de-via-tion!," and "Ho-ho-ho-mosexual!" Agog and aghast, the faces on the sidewalk curdled as they saw placards reading "Sappho Was A Right-On Woman" and "Release Oscar Wilde." A boy on the pavement gasped, "There's my *mother! Marching!*" As they surged into Central Park for a vast Gay-In, many wished each other "Happy Birthday." Visiting heterosexuals worried that they might not be recognized as such; in much of that crowd it was impossible to tell who was gay and who was straight. A news photographer murmured, "Everyone looks so . . . normal." In that long afternoon, lots of labels got lost and it appeared that the gay community was over-riding a history of self-dislike and fear.

I was also impressed by the way that gay men sympathized with women: for the inadequacy that both have been made to feel. (At that particular period, the lesbian groups were wary of talking to a straight reporter, but some of the men were very open.) One said, "While homosexual oppression is different for men and women—we can also oppress each other! Gay men have many of the habits of straight men: we talk abstractly, argue competitively." He described a meeting where a gay woman kept banging the floor with a baseball bat; he told her the bat symbolized oppression to him—all the sports that had dogged his childhood. She replied that it meant liberation to her—since she'd never been allowed to be aggressive. But they combed it out.

The feminist march of August 1970 bestowed confidence to some who were fairly new to the women's movement. It also inspired the most hostile crowd reactions I've ever seen. Yelling and jeering from the sidelines—all the way from 59th Street to Bryant Park—were a mixture of hard hats and men in neckties who'd just emerged from their offices, plus many women, their faces knotted with contempt. "You should all have been aborted!" was a recurrent cry. The counter-demonstrators from MOM—"Men Our Masters"—absentmindedly held a lot of their signs upside down, reading WOW. It also looked as though the 42nd Street skin-flicks had shooed their audiences out to watch us: there were some spastic faces among the spectators which appeared to be waiting for titillation.

Walking slowly down Fifth Avenue, I thought about my lateness in realizing that I was part of the women's movement. I'd been tardy for several reasons. First, I'd felt that feminism distracted people from the facts of racism, which I'd been concentrating on almost exclusively for more than five years. I was also influenced by a few militant black women who—in the late Sixties— thought sexual politics was apt to obscure most others. Second, I come from quite a liberated family; all the women in the last three generations had worked, so I'd assumed that women had won their rights well before I was born. My male relatives took a very dim view of women who expected to be supported; I'd been raised knowing I would have to earn as soon as I finished college. But I'd failed to evaluate all the poor salaries I'd been offered, or the frowns and sighs and little headshakes I got when I asked for a raise.

The second stage in my education occurred when I talked with a number of women and men at *Newsweek* and Time Inc. for a piece about women's jobs in the media. From amiable male editors I learned why women can't write: it's because they get cramps. ("Oh, I'm sure *you* don't"—an outsider is no threat—"But you know, sometimes lots of them have it at once.") So Mark Twain's definition of women as "beautiful creatures with pains in their backs" helped to perpetuate the nurse-and-surgeon mentality of *Time* and others.

By 1970 women were weary of hearing that they were irrational and

unreliable—while being told that they were also more stable and less sensitive than men. Meanwhile the wit of decades continued to decorate the magazine researchers' role: there was a senior editor at *Newsweek* who affectionately
addressed the researchers as harlots, sluts, broads, and little bitches. He had
a favorite joke about "greasing the researcher." First you strip the researcher,
then you grease her (like a pig), run her down the hall, and whoever catches
her can have her for the night. My father contributed a Time Inc. belly-breaker
of the Forties: at *Life* the researchers sleep with the writers; at *Fortune* the
researchers sleep with one another; at *Time* no man would ever sleep with a
researcher—because they're all so ugly and intense. As a *Newsweek* woman
said bleakly, "The assumptions are rather hard to change." A woman editor
at *Esquire* quoted a male colleague's remark from an editorial meeting about
women's liberation: "Give them some dildoes and they'll shut up."

Next I read some recent issues of the *Ladies' Home Journal*, having been
rather surprised that Media Women had selected it as the magazine most
degrading to women. But they were right. Many articles and ads evoked life
as a perpetual apology: for being inefficient, helpless, thick-headed, or charm-
ingly incompetent—for making a mess. In 1970 *The Journal's* typical protago-
nist was apt to burn the roast, dent the fenders while backing the car into the
garage, fudge the income tax, blow the budget, or dye her hair the wrong
color. You could easily imagine her losing her children in a tornado, setting
the house on fire, or starting an avalanche. Hence "salvation through house-
work"—the only way to ask for your husband's forgiveness. You feed him
Baked Alaska because you fused the new power lawnmower or scorched all
his shirts. This relates to the psychiatric columns on "what to do with your
husband's ego," how to build him up (after you've broken everything in
sight?). And *The Journal's* "Newsletter of Involvement" was far from liberating: "Across the nation, women are rolling up their sleeves to get at society's
laundry list of urgent problems."

Many women in the antiwar and civil rights movements had been repeating that their male colleagues expected them to limit their political commitments to mailing, filing, and stapling—along with some dusting and coupling.
One young woman said, "Licking stamps began to feel like licking boots."
Because Power to the People did not include both sexes, contradictions about
the nature of Peoplehood impelled some women radicals to try to make radical changes for all kinds of women.

As the backlash grew fiercer throughout the Seventies—when many large
firms resisted giving equal pay and class action suits proliferated at such institutions as NBC, CBS, the *New York Times,* and *Reader's Digest*—it seemed that
some male executives were even greater victims of machismo than many
women. Hortense Calisher wrote in her 1971 novel, *Queenie,* "It's you men
who envy penises. The one you can never be sure is there. Till it's there. Then
of course you admire it . . . And pretend we do. Penis envy is really *male.*" And

from the women's movement I came to understand my own loathing of violence—while continuing to believe that this country brings violence upon itself.

Hindsight: During the years of opposing the war in Vietnam, we need not have felt useless as we wore out so many pairs of boots and sneakers. Eventually we learned that Nixon had been planning a gargantuan bombing of Vietnam for the fall of 1969—but was deterred by "all the protests and the [November] Moratorium," according to his memoirs. Watergate taught us that the President had been listening after all. Deeply upset by the demonstrations, he allowed paranoia to drive him to the illegalities which finally forced him out of office, while car horns bleated outside the White House in response to signs reading HONK FOR IMPEACHMENT. On the day of Nixon's resignation, an antiwarrior said to me, "We all had a hand in it." Later we would be told that the ex-President considered himself a casualty of Vietnam.

~

A vast pink triangle flapping over the entrance of the New York Public Library; a mile-long, thirty-foot wide banner carried along First Avenue, its rainbow stripes an emblem of gay and lesbian unity; fifty thousand spectators at Yankee Stadium for the Gay Games: the twenty-fifth anniversary of the 1969 Stonewall rebellion—when crowds of gay men and drag queens fought the police for five days—was celebrated all over New York in 1994. Mayor Rudolph Giuliani marched near the front of the joyful June parade. Ten thousand athletes performed, and the events received ample and friendly coverage by the traditional media. The Empire State building shone with a lavender light. From the softball teams to the powerlifters and the hockey matches on Coney Island (won by the Toronto Mighty Dykes), the athletes reveled in their sexuality and their audiences turned out in silver lamé, military uniforms, tiaras and satin gowns, leather and chains, chiffon, nipple rings, minidresses with anklets and pumps, overalls, beehive wigs, spandex, and lots of shorts and T-shirts—a range of costumes that soared far beyond the denims of 1970. And it seemed that the gay community had gone through more stages than some of its counterparts.

There had been conflicts between generations. In 1970, listening to some male workshops organized by the Gay Liberation Front, I heard camping denigrated as Uncle Tomming: a way of masking pain, acting out a defensive stereotype as a wistful bid for acceptance. It was said that older homosexuals shouldn't be derided for camping, but their juniors weren't going to flounce or caricature themselves. The young gay men of 1970 also repeated that they didn't want to be viewed solely as sexual beings: "that kind of role-playing oppresses both those who are attractive and those who aren't." But the work-shop participants were hardly puritanical; before AIDS was identified in 1981, freewheeling polygamy was equated with liberation and gay sex was seen as a political act. Displaying their roots in the New Left of the Sixties, some spoke out against consumerism and "the capitalist trap," noting that ads had begun to beckon to chic single men who could afford the latest styles in cashmere or coffee tables. The hippie sensibility of the acid rock era disdained posses-sions, and few would have guessed that many gays of the next decade would be charmed by acquiring waterbeds and carousel horses, Victorian wicker fantasies and miles of track lighting.

In 1968, a year before Stonewall, Mart Crowley's *The Boys in the Band* was hailed as the first openly gay play to win a large audience. When the film version opened in 1970, it was denounced by young gays because—despite many deft and witty jokes—it showed male homosexuals as miserable. The lines frequently quoted were: "If we could just *learn* not to hate ourselves quite so very much" and "Who was it that used to always say, 'You show me a happy homosexual and I'll show you a gay corpse.' " Although camp dimin-ished in the Seventies, when many gays dressed like truck drivers or dockhands, it was back in the Nineties, when I heard gay Texan teenagers calling one another "Miss Thing." Camp had become a form of defiance: a (sometimes playful) challenge to straights, a demand for recognition. In 1994 Terrence McNally's *Love! Valour! Compassion!* seemed like a direct but respectful answer to *The Boys in the Band:* another group of gay men who camped and pranced—most of whom were able to love each other and like themselves, although AIDS loomed over them and two were infected.

Even before AIDS entered the gay world, gay male culture had entered the mainstream, as when Andy Warhol's images became ubiquitous and gay Pop artists promoted parody, when gay disco clubs in New York in the Seven-ties set the style for their straight equivalents around the country, and hetero-sexual couples danced to a beat that had first exhilarated shirtless men stoned on poppers under flickering red and orange lights. David Bowie's "Changes" and the Village People's songs, especially "Macho Man" and "YMCA," were as popular with straights as Liberace was at an earlier time—though many may not have realized that the singers were gay.

Homophobia and violence against gays didn't abate, but that did not seem to drive people back into the closet. The gay presence was asserted through-out the nation; in Columbus, Ohio, I witnessed a huge Gay Pride parade of the Eighties: pink and mauve balloons were released while speakers thanked the police for protecting them from raging "Bible-bangers" along the route. The AIDS movie *Philadelphia* was the first box office hit of 1994; big Broadway audiences cheered at the end of McNally's play and gave nightly ovations to Tony Kushner's *Angels in America;* an opera about the murdered gay politi-cian Harvey Milk had productions from coast to coast. Lesbian experiences and perspectives didn't seem to reach as much of the public; quite a few lesbian novelists received fine reviews but their fiction appeared to be somewhat ghettoized, perhaps because publishers marketed it mainly for lesbian readers. Possibly gay male writers and artists drew a wider audience because AIDS had caused all sorts of Americans to face questions about love and death and the linkage between them. Foreign wars—in Vietnam, Central America, Bosnia—had made many of us vividly aware of death: bloody deaths in other countries. AIDS brought death to the center of our culture: a war we were losing on our own turf.

~

The media published so many obituaries for the women's movement that feminism would have had to be reborn almost monthly in order to die so often. For many women there was "no turning back" as countless voices sang or chanted. Despite all the passionate opposition—male and female— feminism had altered the way that innumerable women looked at themselves, at politicians and employers, at schools and universities, at medicine, at movies. There would always be fiery conflicts and there would be lacerating battles about abortion, sexual harassment, and affirmative action. But the self-reliance that numerous women gained after 1970 wasn't going to dissolve. Not even a sea of hostility could drown it.

Conversations in Watts
January 1968

You cannot leave Watts regretting that there was a riot. The visiting radical or liberal departs with the donation that Watts forces on an outsider: a new moral teething ring, plus the sensation of swallowing your own blood while trying to learn how to use it. You are not allowed to regret that in August 1965, there was killing and burning and thirty-four people dead. Some nine hundred were reported injured. But it's ridiculous to claim that the firestorm "helped" in a tangible sense. As so many have noted, the "war on poverty" has hardly made a dent in the ghetto; Paul Jacobs wrote in *Prelude to a Riot* that "the amount of money spent thus far has been less than $100 per poor person in the country and a sizable percentage of that has gone to administrators." (LBJ's 1968 State of the Union message contained exactly one sentence about civil rights, and it got no applause. But he was cheered for his "anticrime legislation," which is especially aimed at rioters.) Yet Watts gained by "the Revolt," as it's called there: there's a new energy and confidence, combined with self-determination and outrage, and the revelation that black Americans do, after all, have a weapon. Many don't want to use it: the older people, the educated, the employed. But they of course are a shred of a minority. And so many speak of the Revolt with pride; they ask, Where were you when it happened? Did you understand the news?

The young militants stress that patience, reason, and nonviolence did nothing whatsoever for blacks—and no one can disagree. There's no way to refute Ron Karenga's remark: "Only thing nonviolence proved was how savage whites were." Yet if you deplore killing in Vietnam, you can't sanction it in American streets. And having appreciated what the last rebellion did for Watts, you dread the next: which is very frankly expected. You can agonize over the shattered skulls or spines, each body on the pavement, the bullet in any inch of flesh, down to the pain of a broken leg. But you can't call black riots unreasonable. Meanwhile no one—black or white—can pretend to discuss them unemotionally. So you end by supporting what the militants say and fearing what they will do—while remembering that their own death will come sooner than yours. You don't want to share their fatalism—yet you can't unfurl resounding alternatives. So the teething ring grows bloodier as you chew, while you talk to yourself about programs . . . solutions . . . and all the words that failed to become facts.

Beginning with a guided tour of Watts, you visit job-training courses, where sewing is called Garment Technology and typing is Secretarial Science; some private and public agencies that appear to be well run; and an impressive new health center. A series of solid programs, administrated by blacks who explain all of the possibilities—and then burst into cases about funds that haven't arrived, the snarl of conflicting outside interests, the paralysis of liberals' "research." People have learned new professional skills, but employment is brutally sparse. Typically one program trained a hundred workers, but had only twenty-five jobs to fill. Many projects weren't refunded after ten or sixteen months of work, and many who'd been hired were back on welfare. One young politician said, "Why is that fellow back standing on the corner? He *had* a job, he learned how. But it's over. He's got nowhere to go. He can't even go home. Mom's watching *Peyton Place* on TV in the living room, where he sleeps. He doesn't have a room of his own. Doesn't want to see *Peyton Place* or Mom. Doesn't want to stand on the street corner. He's feeling very sore."

And the theme expands. The Office of Economic Opportunity—"*Hah!*"— gives only year-to-year commitments. No housing has been built since 1965, although there are plenty of plans on paper. Public transport hardly existed, now it's been slightly increased—"But have you ever *seen* the bus?" No. "See, we got an *imaginary* bus. Or maybe invisible." (The nearest hospital is twelve miles away. Anyone with a job outside Watts would have to walk to it—for several hours.) Even the new health center, with all its fine facilities, may not fully serve Watts in the long run, since in two years it will be administered by the University of Southern California, a private and conservative university outside the area. Some fear that it will then be used for research rather than for curing local patients. Currently it's the main center in the country where black physicians can get experience. But it will be very difficult to keep it that way.

Community involvement has been attempted on all of the programs. The participation of the poor is still the most important—and the most controversial—concept that arose from the poverty program. The Watts boards of citizens have been carefully chosen as cross sections from young and old, moderates and militants, men and women. One administrator said, "My board is pretty rough. All the emotions of the whole country bust out when these people sit down together. Sometimes I wonder if they were chosen *because* they could never agree." And certain boards have only notional power: for example, they may not be able to fire an outsider they find useless. And, as one young black official said, "Community action *must* be based on aggressive saneness. Yet how can you balance sanity and aggression over a *long* period of time?" He added that his board is so shot with internal combat that "some feel that community action is just a frustrating thing designed to wear you out." Then he magnified another point that echoes through Watts: that the battles of the sexes and the generations are also raging there—and that these are related to many aspects of the racial war.

A black man of about fifty said: "Two revolutions are needed: racial *and* sexual." He and other men spoke volubly and bitterly about matriarchy—referring to the days when female slaves worked in the house and slept with their white masters, while their husbands worked in the fields. "The black woman is killing the black man," a man repeated—looking straight at a black woman who neither flinched nor replied. He added that equal numbers of men and women on one community board resulted in the women "shouting the men down and chasing them off the board—so you got a ladies' majority." While 63 percent of Watts's population is twenty-four and under, "Women over fifty have too much power here." He noted that the young nationalists are "teaching their women to sit back." Ron Karenga, the local nationalist leader of US—a separatist group that rewrites most of its maxims from Malcolm—instructs that the black woman should be "submissive." Karenga's followers are told that "Male Supremacy" is natural, and that "Equality is false; it's the devil's concept." Women have two rights: "consultation and separation." At Karenga's headquarters you see quiet young wives in floor-length African print gowns; their appearance, at least, is meek. Most of the older blacks are still cautious and timid about challenging whites: "They want their social security and their retirement pay." But they are scorned by the young, who condemn their parents for "sandpapering their feet and scratching their heads."

After a general tour it's possible to persuade your hosts to introduce you to the militants. Accents thicken ironically to inform you that Watts has been "*researched*" and "*evaluated*" by thousands of sociologists, writers, planners, and meddlers. "We're still the basic test tube, the ghetto *laboratory*." "Yeah, we get a lot of visitors with plantations in their heads. You know, the Albert Schweitzer complex. They say, 'Let's all be brothers—and I'll be the oldest!' " The Sons of Watts and the Young Men for Total Democracy and SLANT (Self-Leadership for All Nationalities Today) are sick of talking to strangers, and a few of them sometimes charge a fee—usually about $100. (I'd certainly do the same if I lived there.) One group told me that they captured NBC's camera—until they were paid to return it. The idea of expenses diminishes later, eased by conversation itself. Of course you expect to feel hostility against whites directed personally at you. But I never did, although naturally I heard it—including the jokes about whites "who think they're doctors of nigger-ology." But everyone I saw was cordial and very ready to answer questions.

The cordiality increased when I ran out of cash and had to borrow $15 from a white woman. A militant was appalled: "*What* kind of magazine do you write for, anyway?" He urged that I apply for a job at *Time* or *Life:* "Now *there's* the bread." I explained my own notion of editorial freedom, which brought snorts of laughter and the indulgent pronouncement of "Crazy." Naturally the choice of earning less than you *can* sounds mad to those who are hardly yet allowed to earn at all.

False promises made the poison. "After the Revolt, they came in and filled people with hope—hope up to here. Now that hope's run out." There will be another Revolt because "Hope's made things worse." As well as the discontin-ued programs, there are jobs that need to be done now: which are not filled. But the young men don't froth when they talk about killing. They are the same local leaders who meet to discuss highway and transit systems and ur-ban renewal, who have run summer work programs for teen-age gangs (who cleaned lots and were not allowed to fight), who think that the Job Corps is a good idea but that it needs detailed revising—especially that it should in-clude camp counselors from their own neighborhood. Veterans of many beat-ings by the police and some jail terms, they still talk about "being involved in your community" and say that a new city could be built in seven or ten years. They've been using sensitivity sessions to heighten and test their blackness, and sometimes to confront whites. They have the certainty that their elders lack, plus guns.

When you think of the false promises, it's odd to see all the childrens' paintings of Jack Kennedy displayed in the health center, including many bitter pastels of the assassination: Kennedy as a felled tree or a lost sailor. Again and again the Statue of Liberty crumbles or collapses in the background.

The refrain is "Peace and equality by any means necessary." Everyone knows that different groups are arming themselves and that they keep meeting to discuss some kind of revolution. (Here the nationalists, who study Swahili and shave their heads "in mourning for the black living dead," stress the need for an independent Afro-American culture, while the militants appear to want advancement as Americans—theirs seems to be a very Yankee determination.) A fledgling riot was suppressed by some militants last summer: because they "still had hopes of the promises that had been made." Now they speak about choosing "the right time." "But we would stop any outburst if it happened at the *wrong* time." Laughing, one said, "The most beautiful thing the government did was to take our fellows to Vietnam and train them and bring them back. Now they're skilled at guerrilla warfare, and they know the area."

The concept of revolution is in a wingless, larval state; most of those who discuss it are talking well into the future. And you have to remember that overstatement is not only the language of the ghetto but of this whole country, from our ads to our politicians' speeches. Still, Ron Karenga has his lively moments: "When the word is given we'll see how tough you are. When it's 'burn,' let's see how much you can burn. When it's 'kill,' let's see how much you kill. . . . And when it's 'take that white girl's head too,' we'll really see how tough you are."

The militants say that some of the middle-class blacks who came from outside Watts to run the stillborn programs will be erased in the next Revolt. When they repeat that "our next one will be against the middle-class *Nee-grow*," you feel that black people are still the victims of divide and conquer. "It's the Toms who sold us out They helped themselves: they took all the gravy off the top. They come back with meringue around their mouths, and we say, "Where's the pie?' And they say, 'It's *alllll* gone.' " These "house niggers," accused of "lipping the songs," are also called "hat-trick men" and "Whip-Me's." Contempt and fury erupt when they're mentioned. The 1963 March on Washington is known as "The Sell-Out." Militants add that "slatting up against liberals" is worse than dealing with racists—"who don't feed you a lot of songs. At least they're straight." But, "We'll accept whites' support— *anyone's* support."

Wrath against the system coincides with a desire "to be part of the structure—while keeping your identity with blacks." Perhaps the moral—and the discussion does become very moral here—is that a black who makes personal progress in Watts should continue to keep battling on behalf of those who haven't yet made it, should "bring back what he acquired from the system." One man said, "I want what's mine here." The point is "here": in his own town, not in some "better" neighborhood.

One young activist who guided me through Watts, scolded me like an indignant nursemaid when I wandered away from him to buy cigarettes. "You want smokes, you say so, we'll go get them. But if you're on your own, suppose some eleven-year-old kid throws a rock at you, and another does, and the cops come, they use gas. That's how shooting starts and our people get killed. So we're having no riots *today*." Because he didn't want to be seen too long in the company of a white woman, we sat talking for hours in a parked car in a burnt-out lot. I asked what he did during the Revolt, and he heaved a huge laugh out the window. "I made twenty-seven thousand dollars!" He picked up a lot of color TV sets—"and I know where to sell them quick, because I used to be a hustler. Any man who didn't take advantage of the Revolt I feel sorry for. You had Mom out there looting too—got herself half a cow from the supermarket. What's to be afraid? Everyone you know is on the street. Then a lot of us took trucks—we just blocked traffic and made the drivers get out. You had to have a truck to move all your stuff."

Fatalism about dying alternates with the talk about what *could* be done for Watts, with the angry amusement at "liberal" mediators, with the advantage of having your own car. Death seems to be accepted as a matter of timing: "No one's running from death. You say, Well, I guess this is my time." Those already killed "were there at the wrong time. That's the breaks, Jake." In a society of hoaxes, put-ons, lies, public relations, imagery, and political cha- rades, you feel that the Watts militants mean what they say. These are private citizens—unlike the public revolutionaries who enjoy raising the rhubarb on TV. But these young men's feelings about death should be believed: it is the measure of their seriousness, the proof that life in Watts is as intolerable as ever.

After talking about violence for over an hour, my guide in the car sighed deeply and said, "Perhaps, perhaps the *threat* of violence is even more impor- tant than violence itself." He felt that the threat could be used as a substitute: "If only people could fear what we *might* do—enough to make things better for Watts—then we could really save some lives, instead of risking them." But Washington's reply is new police weapons and "riot control," fuelled by what Dr. Kenneth B. Clark has called "the democracy of American racism, which includes *all* Negroes." The level of national comprehension seems equal to that of a Californian diet specialist, who deduced that everyone in Watts eats "hostile foods." She offered to change their nutrition and their emotions through a program of "neutral foods."

Hindsight: By late 1970 the press reported that unemployment among blacks in Watts had increased by 61 percent between August 1965 and the end of 1969. Still, in April 1972 Watts got its first hospital, which the *New York Times* called "a most imposing response to the riots of 1965."

January 1968 was still pre-Panther time, even though the Panthers had been formed in Oakland in the fall of 1966. They were hardly mentioned when I visited Watts, beyond a couple of admiring references to the occasion in May 1967 when twenty-five armed Panthers made a visit to the California State Legislature in Sacramento. But the themes of this ghetto showed how many were going to listen to the Panthers.

In 1968 and 1969 one lived with an apprehension of summer—for those who might suffer in their own neighborhoods. But one administrator in the Watts health center very firmly predicted that the next confrontations would be on campuses, not in ghettos. By late 1968 community control was more than ever a theme; Tommy Jacquette, the head of SLANT in Watts, said, "The brother is too busy getting his thing together to think about riots. But Whitey's funny; he worries like hell when we riot and he worries like hell when we don't."

The press continued to focus on new "nonlethal weapons," including "instant banana peel," a substance to make streets slick. A Los Angeles police chief warned his staff: "Don't throw your guns away. Let us not be seduced by the naive philosophy that foam dispensers or slippery substances can summarily pacify rioters, looters, and arsonists." In 1969 Julian Bond was still trying patiently to explain that "what you have now is a conflict between black people and white institutions." But by late 1970 my anthology of white supremacies included this remark from Major General Walter Johnson, commander of the Mississippi National Guard, in his testimony before the White House State panel that investigated the two killings at Jackson State: "There is a difference between stealing watermelons and stealing color television sets."

One of the lessons from my visit to Watts was the way that things had been structured to turn black people against one another: the economic classes and the age groups and the sexes. I heard far more anger of blacks against blacks than against whites. Our institutions, like OEO, have a talent for perpetuating systems which force people to deeply disagree and then to fight one another. And of course the spectacle of divided blacks satisfies many whites—it's even better than when radicals or women battle among themselves.

Starting in 1968, until about the midsummer of 1970, I heard some white activists say that they were ready and willing to die. I didn't believe most of them for a moment. But in Watts the discussions of death were undramatic, very quiet. Death as a fact of life.

∾

On the tenth and twentieth anniversaries of the Watts rebellion, the media noted that the area had a new bus service, two new shopping centers and two banks, that a park had replaced Charcoal Alley, where the fiercest fighting had erupted—and that unemployment and poverty had expanded further than ever. "Conscience money" had evaporated in the early Seventies; in 1985, after all the emphasis on the desperate need for job-training programs, Watts had none at all. To the young, drug-dealing seemed to be the only reliable way of earning a living. Among the local gang wars and drive-by shootings, paralyzed young men in wheelchairs became a familiar sight throughout the neighborhood.

Watts is part of South-Central Los Angeles, where the riots of May 1992 left fifty-eight people dead. After an all-white jury acquitted four white policemen on trial for the beating of black motorist Rodney King, flames engulfed even more buildings than in 1965. The verdict appeared to justify the beating. The looting seemed more calculated this time: Koreans were often the targets of blacks, Hispanics looted black stores. As President Bush gave a speech calling for law and order, he seemed bewildered by the results of twelve years of federal neglect of poverty and civil rights. Soon thereafter White House spokesman Marlin Fitzwater blamed the riots on the "destructive" social programs of the Sixties.

Touring the ashy streets and ruined blocks, the President inspected shattered storefronts and murmured "Unbelievable, unbelievable." In a Los Angeles hospital, visiting a firefighter who had been shot in the neck and was unable to speak, Bush gave out tie pins and told the young man's wife that his family estate in Kennebunkport, Maine, had been badly damaged by a storm. He promised aid for Los Angeles and momentarily halted his habitual requests for reducing welfare benefits. Then Vice President Quayle claimed that the riots were caused by a "poverty of family values" and denounced the television serial *Murphy Brown,* where an unmarried woman had a child (many voices reminded him that her alternative was an abortion). White House officials said the administration was not planning "dramatic" spending to rebuild South-Central.

Right after the acquittal, city-dwellers all over the country feared violence from black citizens. In New York the United Nations sent its staff home and was closed for perhaps the first time in its history, although its offices in Bosnia remained open. On the radio I heard black Americans in different states repeating that they had lost all confidence in the criminal justice system.

Black Panthers and White Radicals
Oakland July 1969

During those July days of the Moon and the Pond, the lunar dust and the bubbles from Ted Kennedy's car, "the astro-pigs and all that moonshit" and one politician's panic were ignored by some three thousand people, who were attending the Black Panthers' conference for "a United Front Against Fascism" in Oakland, California. The conference was neither a failure nor a success, as varying voices pronounced it.

Contrary to the Panthers' intentions, those three days of forty-five speeches and panels didn't establish a new party of blacks, browns, Third World forces, and whites. But it tried to be "a preface," as Chairman Bobby Seale called it. He welcomed the audience to a "mass workshop," stressing that "You came here because of heads bleeding . . . you came because you related to the reality that people suffer." In a period when dissent is as diffuse as frog spawn, the need for unity is so acute that each attempt raises momentary hopes.

Clearly the Panthers were determined to forestall the types of tumult which dismembered the SDS June convention in Chicago, when the Progressive Labor party was expelled and Weatherman was founded; in Oakland you felt the influence of that frenzied prelude. Hence debate or even discussion of ideology were not allowed on the platform—which distressed a good deal of the audience. (Elsewhere the Panthers have been clear in their conviction that capitalism and democracy cannot coexist, and that the poor are the victims of class as much as race. But many at this conference knew very little about the Panthers' ideas.) Seale made the mistake of equating rhetoric and ideology: "When you start a united front, you do not start with some jive ideological struggle." But he and others did unleash enough rhetoric to kindle a longing for more theory behind the action—as well as an ex-minister's remark that "We're all in the movement. But any movement without thinking and a program is a *bowel* movement!" After all the species of shit that had been mentioned, many gasped at this image and a lot of shoulders heaved.

The emphasis was on practical action which people could take in their own neighborhoods, in labor unions, church groups, in dealing with the law and with hospitals. The aim was to provide the poor with information that could help them to help themselves. This plan reflected the Panthers' efforts to be "a service organization to the community," which they would like to extend well beyond the ghetto to include Puerto Ricans, Indians, Mexicans, and poor whites, as well as working people throughout the United States. (Although it's probably too late, some do wish to reach Wallace's audience.) It was repeated that many people are treated as objects—that valid modern terror which strikes even the middle class—as well as those robbed of hope or dignity by racism and poverty.

During one panel, Andy Chavez of the Farm Workers' Union, condemned the Defense Department's doubled purchase of grapes for soldiers in Vietnam, and urged a boycott on Safeway Stores, which still market California grapes. He remained committed to "militant nonviolence," even though his co-workers have been beaten and sprayed with insecticides in the fields. Other speakers called for strikes in plants that contribute in any way to the Vietnam war. A white man from the Chicago branch of the United Auto Workers said white workers in skilled jobs must realize that "sweetheart agreements" (which exclude blacks in unskilled work) with employers will only result in "being tied to *and* screwed by the union boss. . . . You're with the boss or with the black worker. There's no third path."

A good 80 percent of those present were white; there were many of the same faces I've seen in Chicago, at the Pentagon, on peace marches: those who were already converted. Quite a few tend to spin fantasies around the Panthers, evoking them as pagan animal deities in male or female form— excitingly nonhuman. Jungle thrills tinged with mysticism allowed some to forget the issues. Others were huffy about having to listen to people less educated than themselves. And some were privileged, querulous innocents, who, as one observer grimly remarked, "wouldn't recognize a worker if it came and peed on their leg." Not that they should have stayed away. But their presence underscored the absence of working people and the poor, and above all the scarcity of blacks who weren't Panthers. It was odd to hear so many speeches about the community—when the community wasn't there.

Despite the Panthers' breakfasts for children, their programs to inform welfare clients of their rights, their advice on dealing with bad landlords, it looks as though they may have lost the neighborhood support they had in Oakland until recently. Several rueful militants said that perhaps the Panthers are forfeiting the trust of impoverished blacks because of the collaboration with whites. This is Stokely Carmichael's charge. In his July letter of resignation from the party, Carmichael wrote, "Any premature alliance with white radicals has led to complete subversion of the blacks by the whites." Yet this hasn't happened to the Panthers. Since they reject black separatism, the Panthers may be the last black organization willing to work with whites. Bobby Seale said, "We're setting examples: that's why we're so hard on black groups that are racist." But if the white backing that the Panthers have received is hurting them, if the best aid that radical whites can offer them is withdrawal, then many white conservatives will be delighted. Yet the white left may have to accept a period of black separatism—without wounded resentment.

While some of the recent altercations between the Panthers and the cultural nationalists have been magnified by the press, one clash did result in two murders. In January 1969 two of Ron Karenga's US group shot and killed two Panthers at UCLA. (One of the dead was John Huggins, whose widow, Ericka, was later acquitted in the New Haven Panther trial. The two accused members of US gave themselves up to the police soon after the UCLA killings.) The January dispute hinged on whether the Panthers or Karenga's group would run the black studies department at UCLA. If Karenga had been in charge, only blacks would have been hired; the Panthers were expected to employ a range of colors. The Panthers accused Karenga of being a capitalist and of "enslaving" the women of US. (Years afterward FBI files revealed that the bureau had inflamed the rival groups against each other.)

Few black militants are eager to discuss the pros and cons of nationalism; one quoted Malcolm X: "When you have problems in the family, solve them indoors." Cultural nationalism, which is still in a liquid state, is apolitical—nor is there any radical demand for a restructured society. So far it plays into the hands of white conservatism: by implying that dashikis, black theaters, Afro jewelry, and some tom-toms are all that's needed to satisfy black discontent. Sometimes it looks as though black art is in danger of being used as a hush-puppy. Last spring a young Atlanta activist told a reporter that he didn't wear Afro clothes—"the beads and bones"—because "it costs more to dress for the revolution than to run it."

Culture was hardly mentioned at the Panther conference, where the liveliest session analyzed the abuses of medicine. A group of radical doctors assailed their own profession. They stressed that a lot of medical care is hardly intended as a cure, since symptoms are often treated without much probing for their cause—a practice which plumps up profit. One doctor said, "Illness is one of the most lucrative products of this country. . . . Every health professional can be paid by propagating your suffering. . . . We've been carefully groomed *not* to relate to people or to suffering, but to meat—to carnage." (He was talking about the tendency to experiment on the poor.) He added that "the health industry creates the *shame* of illness"—which so many do feel, due to the cost that sickness wrings from their families, as well as the sense of personal humiliation that some of our public hospitals administer along with the brutality of their treatment. This doctor and others urged a "demystification" of the industry, announcing that they want to teach the poor how to look after themselves, and about their own bodies. A very graphic pamphlet on diseases, injuries, and short-term remedies was given out. The pamphlet, which explained medical rights in hospital and in jail, treatment for bleeding and shock, lacerations and bruises, also contained a section on different tear gases, nausea and blister gases, and Mace. For nausea gas, "masks are dangerous . . . as the gas is absorbed in the skin . . . and you can choke in your own puke." Reading the pamphlet in a sunny Oakland park, surrounded by teenagers nibbling bright green sherbet, I was reminded that this was the neighborhood where such information had already been needed.

A psychiatrist gave his views on mental health and capitalism: "Depression and neurosis often occur because of the oppression that people are living under. This runs through our whole society, and includes the rich and even the oppressor—he gets ugly in the head. . . . Emotional illness can come from being fucked over by the system." He described his very poor patients, who have just lost their jobs or have been thrown off welfare. Naturally they are depressed, and many assume that they're worthless—since that's what they've been told by the ethic that surrounds them. "The idea that some people are better than others" is quite literally sickening. He denounced much of the "mental health industry" as "a pacifying program—to get people to adjust" to abnormal conditions, and he cited the expanding desire to believe that social rebellion is caused by emotional illness.

A lawyer's panel explained some of the legal rights which many do not know they possess. William Kunstler also declared that bearing arms is the only way to keep the police from savaging the ghetto: that the fear of retaliation is the only protection. "If you have the power to defend yourselves by weapons that are legal, then you have the power to rid the ghettos of the paralyzing fear that invites repression." He said that he hoped that retaliation would not be needed. However, "if you [tell] the power structure that they need not fear you, [then you] open up the whole sad trail of misery and depredation that has characterized life on this continent for so many years."

Later a band of rebel clergymen attacked the corruptions of the church, including its loss of moral and ethical values, and insisted that the public must help to reform it—"especially through your concern for others than yourself." There was lavish disgust at the churches' economic greed; one ex-minister cried, "I didn't leave the church, the fucking church left me!" Several expressed the dilemma which has racked many churchmen in the past year: the use of violence. Quite a few priests have found it impossible to instruct their congregations just to go home and be quiet. One said, "God gave us all life, and life exists primarily to be preserved. When you see a pig moving toward you, I can't tell you to get down on your knees and ask God what to do. . . . The best prayer I can suggest is: to defend yourself!" Throughout the clergymen demanded that life on earth must be salvaged; none even mentioned the afterlife. For them Christianity means serving and protecting other people—immediately.

Indeed despite the infinite confusions, fragmentations, vicious or silly feuds, and all the gargle within the movement, you feel that its members do have one thing in common: an awareness of suffering, in the ghetto, in Vietnam, next door or in Prague, in the subway or the laundry—a painful consciousness that won't relent.

Still, the Panthers' conference had its frustrations—which may have left some groups farther divided than ever. While almost everyone agrees on the goals—peace abroad and equality at home—few can harmonize about tactics or priorities, and the alliances keep dissolving. (Currently you cannot summarize the convictions of SDS, since so many within it are denouncing each other's beliefs.) Since the movement is deeply anti-individualistic, many of its members do try to eschew ego trips, and attempt to submerge themselves in their groups. But groups can fight with the same gusto as individuals: the result is just like a collision between warring personalities.

So I could see why the Panthers feared that ideological battles would dilute or destroy the drive for unity. However many found them far too authoritarian. The Progressive Labor Party—which was barred from the conference due to their denunciation of the Panthers as "bourgeois nationalists"—tried to distribute leaflets and were beaten up for it. PL members also slugged some of the SDS. And one random incident confused witnesses about the nature of brotherhood. Toward the end of one panel, a middle-aged man who seemed rather drunk kept asking in Spanish and English why there weren't more Mexican-Americans at the conference—as had been announced. Panther officials told him to stop interrupting, and advised him to go consult Bobby Seale. The man mumbled, "I've tried to—but I can't find the mother-fucker." "WHO you calling mother-fucker!": five Panthers hit him until he fell crashing among the folding chairs. The term, uttered every few minutes by many speakers, couldn't be used casually by an outsider. A friend of mine caught the man's watch as it sailed through the air, but when we gave it to him, he was still muttering, bloody and groggy, "I just want to talk to the motherffff—."

The conference yielded some other distressing lessons. After all, dodging ideology hurls you back to the stock responses to rhetoric and clichés. Deadened language is dangerous and corrupting because it makes perfectly good words and phrases meaningless—with the consequence that the ideas behind the words can seem to weaken. When the word "revolution" is flying around like an old frisbee, when "fascism" twangs like a wornout rubber band, even "racism" may become too familiar—a word and a concept that may already have ceased to shock a numbed society. (Since both SDS and PL delegates shrieked "Racist!" at each other in Chicago, what new term can emerge?) This fascist tablecloth, that racist tree, those imperialist soap flakes— you start entreating others in the movement to preserve their ammunition, to allow language to keep its force. Even "violence" is a furry notion, befuzzed by more than leagues of eager cops. We're still far from a revolution—when so few have untangled the nursery tales about "good" and "bad" violence. For example, how provocative are you going to be in order to stimulate suppression—simply to prove that suppression exists? And how do you know how you will react when the moment comes? After the ferocious police siege at People's Park in Berkeley, a former civil rights worker told me that some of those who had been shouting "revolution" all winter were the first to run away, while he, who had always been nonviolent, found himself picking up a rock and belting someone.

Yet the Panthers seem to know the dangers of thoughtless action; as many Californians keep saying, Oakland itself was expected to explode long ago. The Panthers have worked to prevent this; they stress that the local police would welcome an excuse to move on them. On several occasions Panther leaders have told black high school students to cool it, and many have mentioned how they warned the young against rioting after the murder of Martin Luther King. But some of their white fans are still very naive; the notion that "the blueprint will grow out of the struggle" has kept some on what's called "the praxis axis." How often I've heard lines like: "The thing to do is to break down old forms and not worry about coming up with new ones."

Another confusion that needs flushing is the association of "life styles" with revolution or even reform. Drugs and flowers and fun and beads and horoscopes have been grafted onto rebellion—mainly by overnight hippies. (They weren't at the conference, but they scramble into activism at Berkeley and elsewhere.) None of the charms of stylistic experiment has any kinship to politics. When protest means nudity, social criticism sags. (No one needs to write satire now. Especially in California, it writes itself.) A woman who had been one of the early Panthers told me that she thought the party was fading— not only because of the FBI's harassment or because most of the leadership was in jail—but also because style had become too important: from the shiny black jackets to the slogans. She said she and Huey Newton had originally agreed that style was useful in appealing to the young, "But now the Panthers are holding press conferences, getting into public relations—so much is getting lost in the image." Other concerned leaders groaned when black students at Merritt College used time and energy to win the right to black vanilla ice cream in the cafeteria—"all that jive *licorice*"—or when women's groups fought for two days about what to wear to the demonstrations at People's Park: overalls? red stockings? (Finally it was decided that everyone could wear what she wished.) When I was at Berkeley there was a "militant fly-in" to defy the banning of frisbees on campus: about a hundred protested what their leaflets called "another attempt to repress . . . our youth culture in general."

Among all the muddles about relevancy, the Panthers' conference showed that women were hardly included in any revolution. On the first night, a women's panel was unexpectedly postponed by a long, old-fashioned speech by Herbert Aptheker (who probably had no idea of the evening's agenda). During his talk, some women—who feared that their speeches would be eliminated altogether—stood up in protest; others clapped. Masai Hewitt, the Panthers' Minister of Education, warned the women: "You want to act bad, you get treated bad," and told them they were "pigs and provocateurs." Some walked out.

Some women Panthers were very frank about the sexual strife within their own party. In his lectures of 1968, Eldridge Cleaver praised "pussy power," announcing that "political power grows out of the lips of the pussy. Ladies constitute a strategic reserve for the revolution." He urged women to "cut off the sugar" from reactionary or uncommitted men. "If you're part of the solution, how can you justify laying up with part of the problem? You're giving aid and comfort to the enemy when you lay up with one of those chumps." He added that, for women who did reject men with lame politics, "there are plenty of us who will come to aid you in your hour of need."

Cleaver made both sexes laugh, and—since he was mainly talking about who *not* to ball—many missed the point that radical women would be pressured to hit the sheets with any man who called himself a brother. Soon other Panthers' reiterations about pussy power made black women extremely angry, since the theme developed to that famous line, "The only position for a woman in a revolution is on her back." One young woman Panther said, "The brothers expect us to stick to typing and cleaning the office and all that shit. They forget that lots of the sisters can shoot as well as they can."

On the last night of the conference, Bobby Seale and a white lawyer tried to outline a plan for community control of the police to a weary audience of a few hundred—the remains of the three thousand who had originally attended. Many white radicals associate police brutality with simply being hassled by narcs—just as some assume that freedom means legalizing drugs and some don't yet seem to understand what cops do in ghettos. But Seale was a weak and rambling speaker, and he couldn't hold the tired listeners who kept straggling out. (It's said around Berkeley that he was always a good organizer, but was never meant to be a public figure—that was left to Newton and Cleaver.) When the evening ended, a few dozen Panthers—waving their red books and stamping their feet in rhythm, swaying and bobbing—chanted "*Pow*-er-to-the-*peo*-ple, *Pow*-er-to-the-*peo*-ple . . . *Pow*-er . . . *Pow*-er," and I thought I'd rarely seen people look so powerless.

If the movement sometimes resembles an overturned basket of marbles that are rolling apart or away, the upheaval may partly result from the concept of polarization—a word that's already so mossy that it needs more than a good shave. Sometimes both the left and the right seem to be trying to create one another—in order to sculpture their own identities. I've met some militants who said they voted for Goldwater or Nixon; others have even said how splendid it would be if the United States made a disastrous invasion in Latin America. The theory is that if the forces of conservatism grow uglier, then the left will finally organize itself—that everyone will line up. (Few who think this way remember that the left could also be a pushover.) On the right, certain professors seemed truly disappointed that last spring's campus revolts were not bloodier: there was the desire to point at smoking ruins, to affirm that the moment for galloping suppression had arrived. On both sides the occasional longing for violence is also due to the tension of waiting; it's rather like the agonized impatience of a body that must vomit. And it's human enough to love being right: all factions agree that the country's in an appalling state and that *something* is going to happen.

And maybe it isn't. Some of the most committed black and white radicals feel that this is a time for temporary withdrawal: to rethink, to regroup later—and certainly to stop fighting those who are supposed to work together. One said, "*If* there were a revolutionary party, I would join it. . . . " Those in retreat concentrate on tangible actions: tutoring poor children, organizing tenants' groups, starting a cooperative store, helping with the Panthers' hot breakfasts, trying to reach those in their own block or neighborhood. They agree that it's not enough. But some still express a hope that there's a new awareness of need and "the meaning of pain" that has never quite existed before.

Black Panthers and White Radicals
Philadelphia September 1970

The exhaust fumes from the Mister Softee truck mingled with the baby-powder smell of the creamy cones, while bongo drums thudded throughout the crowd of ten thousand waiting to hear Huey Newton speak at Philadelphia's Temple University—a crowd throbbing with suspense, elated by anticipating their own celebrity. Political proximity has a new tang now: sniffing Softee, I remembered inhaling the mixture of tear gas and maple syrup that suffused a Washington waffle shop near the Department of Justice in November 1969, where some of us raced for shelter. But one of the points of the plenary session of the Revolutionary People's Constitutional Convention—which was sponsored by the Black Panthers and other black groups in September 1970—was the absence of CS gas or violence. And when an excited young group from North Philadelphia's ghetto started to march toward City Hall, the Panthers stopped them and made them go home. Just as they had been relentless peacekeepers on Yale's Mayday—when fights began on the New Haven green, while the Yale radio station repeated "The Panthers ask you to go to your rooms"—so the Panthers used their authority in Philadelphia. When it came to the crunch they saved skulls: to the astonishment of some Philadelphians, who later said that they'd been "sure of" a riot. The Panthers' military discipline, which is very disturbing to their white supporters, is certainly respected by many of the ghettos' young, and even by the white revolutionary trippers who appear half-stoned at Panther conferences.

In the week before the Philadelphia convention, one policeman was killed and three were wounded. After five suspects from a group called "The Revolutionaries" were arrested, they were shown to be unconnected with the Panthers. Still, these events inspired a raid on the Panther headquarters. (A former Philadelphia policeman told me, "The best publicity any police department can have is a dead cop.") After a shootout the police made fourteen Panthers strip naked against a wall and spread the cheeks of their buttocks so that "body cavities" could be thoroughly searched for weapons and explosives. Bail was set at $100,000 apiece, as "preventive medicine," but it was soon lowered to $2,500 and much less. Police commissioner Frank Rizzo, who at first referred to the Panthers as "yellow dogs" (because they submitted to the search) later tried to retract this image. He did say, "Imagine the big Black Panthers with their pants down!"

The savagery of Rizzo's troops had already generated a lot of neighborhood support for the Philadelphia Panthers, which had been one of the Party's weakest chapters in the country. The dean of Temple's School of Social Administration said the raids were in response to dissent, rather than a reaction to any activities of the Panthers. One U.S. district judge issued a very unusual temporary order restraining the police—announcing that "a madman out of control shooting policemen is not much more dangerous to the community than a policeman who loses control and goes shooting up people's houses and raiding them"—while a black judge, long known as a moderate, called the raids "outrageous," also "totally unnecessary, uncalled for and really improper." He added that white Philadelphians "were hopeful of violence [during the Convention, so] they could retaliate."

As a New Yorker I found Philadelphia so jammed with hostilities and hatreds that Manhattan seems gentle and pastoral in comparison to the police-camp vibes which shiver through Philadelphia or Chicago. (Rizzo: "The only thing we can do now is buy tanks and start mounting machine guns.") During the convention no white Philadelphian would give me street or bus directions to the ghetto; most just turned away, shrugging or scowling, though one cab driver said, "You want to see stabbings and killings?" In fact the only violence I saw was in the dining room of the Benjamin Franklin Hotel, where one middle-aged man began to slug another in the belly and the throat, finally pounding his head against the table. As they pummeled each other toward the doorway, a waiter said, "They're only brothers," and the audience of diners seemed relieved.

During the unviolent convention, the Panther speeches—although pruned of much of last year's rhetoric—weren't lamblike. Michael Tabor (of the New York Panther 21, an ex-addict who later jumped bail and joined Cleaver in Algeria) and Newton sounded as disgusted as William Lloyd Garrison must

have been when he called the U.S. Constitution "a covenant with death, and
an agreement with hell" which "should be immediately abolished"—because
the document which gave whites their human rights excluded blacks. Both
Newton and Tabor quoted the Declaration of Independence, including the
ever more popular passage about "the Right of the People to alter or abolish"
a government which is destructive to their rights, "and to provide new guards
for their future security." Tabor, who spoke for over two hours, viewed the
Nixon Administration as part of the native tradition: "what they're doing is
the natural outgrowth" of our history and its Constitution. "The Founding
Fathers started this show. . . . [Genocide has continued] since 1607 when those
racist bandits landed on that rock." Moreover, "Nixon ain't in control of this
government . . . he's just a paranoid with a loser's complex." He piled contempt on the Pentagon, corporations and their directors—"They're the true
dope fiends—hopelessly addicted to money"—white and black capitalists, denounced all "murder on an international level," and said of Vietnam: "That
war is over. It's over. It's over. The Vietnamese have won. So why is fighting
still going on? Why? Because here in America, we have not done our job. . . . "

He said that "a lot of people are confused about the whole issue of self-
defense." He cautioned that an unarmed man can't protect himself against a
cop who menaces him at noon. "But, come sundown, come sundown, when
the streets are dark and deserted, and you go up on the roof, and you take
your action out, fix up your sights, put your index finger on that trigger, and
you pull that trigger—that's self-defense, that's self-defense. Because if you
don't get *him,* he's gonna get *you* the next day." (Roars of delight from the
crowd.) He continued, "We have enemies who are dedicated to killing us, to
offing us. If you're a masochist, then you'll just allow your life to be snuffed
out. . . . History will look at you not as a martyr, but as a goddam foooooll."
He added that violence or nonviolence isn't the issue: "The issue is whether
we want to live or we want to die. We're all here today because we want to
live."

"America today has one foot in the graveyard and the other foot on a
banana peel, and they're slipping fast, fast. . . . " (Cheers.) "Lots of people
think they're going to get through this by playing cool. . . . But the name of
the game in America is tag. And specifically, black people is *It.* . . . But I also
think Kent State was It. . . . They have turned on their own sons and daughters." He repeated the Panther commitment to class struggle as an alternative to racial war, and the need for a socialist government. (Actually the
Panthers' brand of socialism sounds quite similar to that of Clement Attlee
after World War II.)

Among the later responses to Tabor's speech, some thought that he referred to shooting *only* cops who had attacked you: others felt that the whole
sundown passage was a fantasy. I was less concerned with his intentions than
with the question of who was listening—especially the handful of spaced-out

teen-agers who nodded through most of the program, but would jerk awake
to cheer at the most dramatic moments.

After Tabor finished, two tear-gas canisters were found near the speakers'
platform: they could have sent five thousand people stampeding up the
wooden bleachers of Temple's gym—an ideal scenario for broken legs. Many
had complained of the Panthers' stern security measures: all the frisking and
"patting"—"You been patted yet?"—required before anyone entered the gym.
Yet the canisters had slid through; later we were told that there had been two
telephoned threats on Newton's life. Still, much of the crowd was unnerved
by the searching; a jittering matron yelped at a boy behind her, "You blew on
my neck!" When he apologized, she said indignantly, "I don't let even my
husband do that." Otherwise the waiting crowd was cheerful and friendly,
although there were little clusters of racial shyness. About half the mass was
white. But the neighboring ghettos turned out more fully than for any Panther gathering I've seen.

The press was closed out of the hall for Newton's speech. Crammed up
against a huge glass doorway, reporters rumbled with resentment and one
man began to mutter, "Press—op*press*ed, de*press*ed, sup*press*ed." In the past,
the Panthers I've seen have been helpful to reporters. But now all journalists
are associated with the distortions of all the media. And I can't be totally
indignant—since I've seen how often the Panthers (and most dissidents) have
been wildly misrepresented. (WBAI titles some of its reports, "Forgive Us
Our Press-Passes.") In Philadelphia many of us wanted to disassociate ourselves from the rest of the press; not wanting to be lumped with media pollution, we sometimes behaved as though the others had contagious cancer or
inflammable VD. (After two days of walking freely in and out of the Church
of the Advocate, the convention's information center, I was banished simply
for standing next to two black reporters from the *New York Times*.) Later we
were told that Newton was displeased at our exclusion from his speech, supposedly due to "a mix-up with security." We also heard rumors that CBS—
and perhaps ABC—had had a rumpus with the convention's sponsors (which
included the Muslims, African Unity, the Nationalist Separatist Front, the
Black Vanguard, and others besides the Panthers) over the question of paying $25,000 for exclusive coverage. It was said that the sponsors had argued
about the possible shakedown until Newton began his talk, and that the networks had refused to deliver the sum.

For the next session we were assured that we'd all get in; then told that
only one reporter would be allowed; then that we ourselves must choose ten
representatives—out of thirty. Soon some of us loathed each other: it was a
fine case of divide and conquer. Finally everyone was admitted, after being
made to march rapidly, two abreast, from one locked door to another, circling the building several times, yielding "anything sharp," such as a nailfile.
One reporter asked forlornly, "Can I keep my ballpoint pen?" In some ways

the hassle was a healthy reproof to those who control the established press: to the arrogance which has betrayed facts for so long. ("My editor rewrote it" gets no forgiveness now. Reporters who can't be responsible for their published pieces will soon find all doors closed.) Still, as some of the Panthers became more dictatorial, a sentence from Daniel Berrigan kept swimming through my head: "A revolution is interesting insofar as it avoids like the plague the plague it promised to heal." Eldridge Cleaver said in a speech in 1968, "People are so confused nowadays that they don't know who their enemies are and they don't know who their friends are." Philadelphia reflected that confusion.

So we heard Newton on tapes and read his speech. His style was far cooler than Tabor's. He said that "a nation conceived in liberty and dedicated to life, liberty, and the pursuit of happiness has in its maturity become an imperialist power dedicated to death, oppression, and pursuit of profits." (Cataracts of applause.) " . . . we will not be blinded by small changes in form which lack any change in the substance of imperialist expansion. Our suffering has been too long, our sacrifices have been too great, and our human dignity is too strong for us to be prudent any longer." ("RIGHT ON!") He stressed that the Constitutional Convention should produce "rational and positive alternatives." As for self-defense: "People are never violent . . . until they are aggressed."

Afterward the big crowd surged to the streets around the Church of the Advocate. In this ghetto the gashed sidewalks sparkle with broken glass—it's not yet paved with diamonds by the OEO. Standing on a ravaged curb, I learned from a former Urban Coalition staffer that this was a Model Cities area, where $25 million had already been spent, too much of it on office space and salaries. He described job programs which allowed participants to earn less than welfare recipients—"people working for their poverty"—and said that the techniques of "trying to create a golden ghetto" only intensified segregation; the housing plan ties residents to dwellings they can't afford to leave, while the jobs which would pay them better are in the suburbs, remote from local transit systems. Around us the packed streets seethed with the hope that Newton would appear; he didn't, and it was then that the Panthers prevented a possible explosion.

Each of the next day's fifteen workshops produced a paper which would serve as a recommendation for the final draft of the new constitution. The two sessions I attended—on "the Distribution of Political Power" and "Control and Use of the Educational System"—kept breaking into smaller groups. Many delegates were haunted by the question of whether any eventual government could be trusted, and whether there's any alternative to voting: "Isn't it worse if we never vote at *all?*" Later I heard that some other workshops came close to punch-ups. But the proposals were finally thrashed out and were then read aloud to all the delegates.

The recurrent themes were decentralization and self-government for numerous groups. Self-determination for women and homosexuals was a very new position for the Panthers, who until recently had derided both. (Many of us who were moved by much of *Soul on Ice* had also been disgusted by the attack on James Baldwin.) But Newton wrote a supportive statement for both women's and gay liberation, admitting that "sometimes our first instinct is to want to hit a homosexual in the mouth and [to] want a woman to be quiet. We want to hit the homosexual . . . because we're afraid we might be homosexual; and we want to hit the woman or shut her up because we're afraid she might castrate us, or take the nuts we might not have to start with." (He added, "Friends are allowed to make mistakes"—a notion that's scarce among revolutionaries.) From several workshops, there were repeated demands for community control of the police; others focused on the military ("No genocidal weapons shall be manufactured or used"), the legal system, environment, religion, drugs and health, and "internationalism—relations with liberation struggles around the world." An ovation burst for "a redistribution of America's wealth to the have-not nations of the world . . . and acceptance of a more modest standard of living that such a move would require." Many papers leaned on the phrase "*after* the revolution." The street people's paper stated that acid, mescaline, and grass "are instrumental in developing the revolutionary consciousness." The crowd whooped until the ceiling rang. However, "*after* revolutionary consciousness has been achieved, these drugs may become a burden." Small response.

The next morning, while crowds swirled around the Church of the Advocate, I listened to Charles X Kenyatta—who was once Malcolm X's bodyguard and was very active in helping to calm Harlem streets after Martin Luther King was murdered, when he volunteered to man a sound truck—describing the international Congress of African People in Atlanta, which had taken place on the same September weekend. The congress, which included such diverse speakers as Whitney Young, Imamu Baraka (Leroi Jones), and Roy Innis, largely favored black separatism ("White cooperation is white cooptation"), the use of the existing political system (by running more black candidates), and nonviolence. Kenyatta said the Atlanta audience was professional and middle class in contrast to the Philadelphia convention, which had drawn so many from the streets. He expressed his own doubts about black-white coalitions; he felt that the priorities are too far apart. "The black radical is fighting for his freedom, while the white radical is fighting for power. The white's free already. So they don't really need the same things."

At this point a Philadelphia TV crew started to interview Kenyatta. He said he didn't believe in the gun, although he would defend anyone's right to have it. He added that he was worried about "diffuse hatred"—and he should know, since he was gunned down and badly wounded by unidentified blacks a year before. Just as he began to say that the one thing he can't forgive whites is their ability to make blacks turn against each other, two teen-aged

Panthers stopped the interview, by making it clear that they would hit him if he went on talking. They told the rest of us, "Don't listen to him, he's been purged from the party." Kenyatta told me later that he'd never been a member, that he'd always differed with the Panthers and had often told them so.

Next I talked with a Panther who said that the party was trying to establish some "unofficial alliances" with separatists and cultural nationalists, despite all the disagreements. Newton had told the Liberation News Service that "blacks have a moral right to separate," but that separatism was a poor "political strategy." Later a young Panther said to me, "We're just as alien to African culture as the Atlantic is to the Pacific)"—but someone down the block shouted, "Pigs are beating the sisters!" Warning the crowd to say put, he and other Panthers dashed to the corner and learned that the police had merely answered a house call from the neighbors of a brawling couple. The Panthers quickly killed the rumors that were rippling through the neighborhood. Once again they proved that they knew how to avert violence, just as they knew how their own aura of violence gave them an authority which awed their adherents—and made the police of many cities feel justified in further assaults on the ghettos.

Hindsight: Looking back on the Panthers' early years, I still think they were useful in many ways, even though some of the local chapters were destructive. But the main spokesmen did provide an amazing amount of public education: about racism, about unjust trials for black people, about the problems shared by the poor of any race. At a meeting of the poor during the 1969 Washington conference on hunger, the blacks, whites, and Mexicans all withdrew and caucused. Finally the blacks produced a list of demands, the whites had a list of goals, and the Mexicans presented grievances. The lists turned out to be very similar. That was the kind of point the Panthers were trying to make.

The Panthers arrived after liberalism had come to mean hypocrisy to many Americans—the promises of "economic advancement" that weren't refunded, plus the notion that the Vietnam war was a moral exercise, and above all the habit of rationalizing: "seeing all sides of the question, and then walking away." (One Panther told me, "The liberal really is a threat—because he can rationalize *anything*, like overkill.") It also appeared that the Panthers were one of the few groups in the country which reached both educated and uneducated people. In the midst of a fairly horrified reaction from the press, the *Wall Street Journal* ran a lengthy, carefully researched piece which described the respect the Panthers drew from the ghettos—especially because of their efforts against hard drugs—and many white-collar blacks said the Panthers were expressing things that they themselves had often wanted to say.

So . . . the language of violence. Throughout the late Sixties I continued to think that threats were quite valuable as a substitute for violence itself.

And as the language grew fiercer, more and more black faces appeared on TV, in offices, in schools and universities, in ads—the hasty but much wider tokenism in hiring appeared to be a direct response to militancy. (But it benefited only the middle-class, professional, already well-educated blacks—not the ghetto, where most of the threats were made.) And of course the threats soon became dangerous to those who made them and hastened them to jail. James Baldwin offered a helpful reminder in one speech: "White people seem to think that when any black cat says woof, he hates you. But he wants a job, a roof, a raise, to breathe." Baldwin had also written, "When white men rise up against oppression, they are heroes: when black men rise, they have reverted to their native savagery."

Yet it grew harder to know what was really meant by some statements. In 1968 and 1969, when I saw quite a bit of the New York Panthers, including some of the eventual 21, some of them stressed that guns were merely for self defense. Numbers of black moderates said they agreed that the ghetto needed such protection against assaults by the police. And others talked about offing or icing the pig so casually that it sounded like a form of shuffleboard. Meanwhile nonverbal actions accelerated. Pickets, marches, and seizing buildings had been symbolic speeches—which were noticed less and less as the press and the public became accustomed to them. In April 1969, the eighty-year-old Arnold Toynbee said in an interview how much he deplored violence, and: "You have to shoot somebody, burn yourself alive, do something violent, in order to get any attention at all, however good your cause or causes, however patient you have been, however well you have put your case. There is an absolute stone wall of indifference. All over the world."

The theme was changing from defense to the possibilities of attack. But if you argued that the innocent would suffer, you were reminded that they were suffering already, from malnutrition to murder, from the diseases of poverty to the black babies who die at six times the rate of white ones, from lead poisoning in slum tenements to the throngs of blacks who die from the nature of ghetto life. If you objected that devastating retaliations would overwhelm any shape of organized revolt, you were told that "more people will join in as blacks are killed off. They won't just stand back and watch it happen." (That wistful argument was very common.) Some accused the Panthers of romanticism, and others angrily charged that the Panthers' young white supporters were being romantic about black people getting killed At the same time you heard middle-aged and even elderly white speakers telling students that they must be prepared to die, "ready to go to the wall," and that "you may ultimately be bathed in blood"—always "you"—an easy shove from those who'd already had some fifty years of life. Many were reasonably confused by the death talk—it was difficult to untangle image from fact.

By 1970 Cleaver, in his Algerian sanctuary, was openly encouraging people to kill cops, and many who had respected him earlier had to write him off.

Long after their split with Cleaver, Newton and Seale were still denouncing him and repeating that they'd "rejected the rhetoric of the gun." But the battles within the Panther party later provoked James Forman to quote an African proverb: "When two elephants fight, only the grass gets hurt." The reputation of poor or militant black people was damaged when the Panthers fought each other—since much of the white world was waiting to hear the worst about all of them.

The Panthers' macho, which suited the Sixties—when I heard a man chide his wife for being "a sissy about violence"—was unacceptable by the end of 1970. The irony was that the Panthers functioned very well as policemen—at the moments when certain communities needed cooling—and at other times they maddened their supporters by policing *them.* Also when most of the Panthers I met talked exactly alike, in identical slogans, I wondered if that extreme effort to suppress all individuality wouldn't result in an almost inhuman experience—as it did for quite a few whites in the movement. (Hence by 1971 the acute introspection among many who were once so doctrinaire. It seemed an inevitable reaction for some who'd tried to have no character at all for a few years.)

During 1970 Tom Wolfe's famous Bernstein piece frightened away much of the support that had been building—even though most book reviewers subsequently knocked Wolfe sharply for obscuring the issues of racism and preventive detention. (Later someone remarked that since the Bernstein guests had been doing a worthy thing—i.e., raising bail—that it was natural that sophisticates would be ridiculed for an activity that was so *un*chic.) When the remains of the New York 21 were acquitted after two years in jail, the case had become an embarrassment to many who'd seemed roused by their arrest, and Bobby Seale's release in New Haven was barely noticed. The murder of Alex Rackley, and later, of several Panthers caught between the Newton-Cleaver factions, seemed to echo Fanon's thesis that "oppressed people . . . kill each other all the time"—expressing what they'd like to do to their oppressors. But those who preferred to see blacks fighting were rather smug about the murders; some even talked as though they were social gaffes on the level of Leonard Bernstein's. And the Panther leaders' own discovery that quite a few hoods and crazies had entered their ranks came far too late.

Throughout, some whites had expected the Panthers to be morally superior (also forgetting that most of the chapters were staffed with very young kids). This tied into the old American notion that people are ennobled by being oppressed. Hence the shock and dismay when the Panthers made many mistakes—which made their documentation of racism easier to forget, or so it seemed.

~

We should have realized that the guns were much more than symbols. And as the Eighties progressed we saw the difference between "madness" and madness: as Eldridge Cleaver declared himself a born-again Christian, then a Moonie, tried to enter the fashion industry by designing men's pants with codpieces, extolled the CIA, backed Ronald Reagan in 1980, and ran for the Senate as a Republican, some of his old associates began to speak of schizophrenia. Later he was arrested several times for possession of drugs. In the meantime Huey Newton had succumbed to cognac, cocaine, and paranoia before he was shot to death on an Oakland street by a young black drug dealer in 1989. No one could guess when either man had lost his balance. But the habits of violence with which they grew up had not receded while the Panthers were administering the community service programs of the late Sixties and early Seventies: the hot breakfasts for children, an accredited elementary school, free legal aid and health clinics, escorts for elderly persons depositing or cashing Social Security checks, free roach and rat control. (Early on, young black men calling themselves Panthers hurt the Party's reputation as they flashed their weapons, conned money from white liberals, or held up stores.) In the Nineties, books by former Panthers Elaine Brown and David Hilliard reported that Newton and other officials had inflicted savage beatings on their followers as well as their enemies, that rabid sexual abuse of women was frequent, that the Panthers were reputed to be extortionists among the black businessmen of Oakland. When Newton and Cleaver loyalists killed one another, outsiders could no longer tell what the party was meant to represent.

Yet perhaps the Panthers' self-destructiveness was outdistanced by the FBI's mammoth campaign against them—which included letters with forged signatures calculated to turn the leaders against one another, hate mail and obscene cartoons which seemed to be exchanges between the Panthers and Ron Karenga's US, and many other actions in keeping with J. Edgar Hoover's intention to "expose, disrupt, misdirect, discredit, and otherwise neutralize the activities" of black radical organizations. Hoover also called the Panthers "the greatest threat to the internal security of the country," and their phones were tapped so faithfully that some experimented with not paying their bills— to discover that the FBI continued to pay them. The bureau alleged that certain Panthers were spies for the FBI or the CIA (at least two suspects were executed by the party), while planting informers and provocateurs in different Panther chapters. The FBI's anonymous missives made both Newton and Cleaver think the other planned to have him assassinated. The sudden raids on Panther offices, the shootouts with policemen or the FBI, and the murder of Fred Hampton by Chicago police: the sense of persecution that afflicted Newton and Cleaver wasn't rooted in fantasy.

Although the Panthers' experiences did seem to imperil sanity, Bobby Seale retained his. Having founded the party in 1966 with Newton (who expelled him in the Seventies), Seale shelved the beret and the black leather and ran for Mayor of Oakland—losing by a slim margin—wrote a barbecue cookbook, became an advocate of gun control and a community organizer affiliated with Temple University in Philadelphia. In 1994 I heard him referring proudly to the party's early years, when its "basic principle" was "crossing racial lines." That brought back memories of the rapport between the races which the Panthers encouraged, along with their attention to history: they used to repeat that racism began as an economic program, starting with the profits made from selling slaves as well as from the tobacco, rice, and cotton crops produced by unpaid field hands, and that slaves freed after the Civil War provided cheap labor once they ceased to be property. Listening to Seale describing the "working coalitions" of the past, I remembered a bail-raising dinner of 1969, when I asked a New York Panther if I could talk with him later, when he was free. "When I'm *what?*" he cried, unleashing a large laugh from several of us as our plates were heaped with soul food.

Shooting Revolution
January 1970

Like some hapless Victorian waif, ripe for rape, the left has rarely been lucky in its allies. Besieged from right and center, punctually lacerated from within, the movement faces yet another problem: how are you going to make a revolution when your enemies keep joining it? Industry has long been into revolution, which has already lost some of its language to ads for lipsticks and vaginal sprays, while Bergdorf Goodman and Kenneth have announced "Right On" styles for next fall. And Hollywood—equally inspired and unnerved by the success of *Easy Rider*—is producing "Now movies" by making films about "campus disorders." M-G-M has filmed James Kunen's *The Strawberry Statement* and has bought Abbie Hoffman's *Revolution for the Hell of It*. Elliott Gould has just made *Getting Straight*, Stanley Kramer is producing and directing *R.P.M.*, footage has been shot for a movie on the Chicago Seven, and others are being packaged with a haste that's almost outpacing the politics of genuine protest. Deputy Attorney General Richard Kleindienst has announced that "While Nixon is President, random civil disorder will not be seen in America." But it will be seen in many movies.

However, as an independent film maker admits, "The trouble with Now movies is that they're often Then movies." What may happen on the campus or in the streets before a picture's released may worry the publicists as much as it worries Martha Mitchell. How can your product maintain its appeal for those who provide the material? Only fest films, like *Woodstock,* seem safe in this sphere, since culture isn't changing quite as rapidly as politics.

But some of the current styles of movie making still seem influenced by the techniques of promotion. As many have noticed, parts of *Easy Rider* resembled TV commercials: filming attractive bodies within nature at its nicest suggests the hint of menthol or seems to advertise the way of life that's depicted. And although *Easy Rider* was the ultimate Now movie of 1969, a few have remarked that it seems at least ten years old—a nostalgic belch from the Beats and *On the Road.* But the moral stance for filming revolution will be slippery: are you trying to sell it outright, or must the conclusion be an awful warning? (Of course good intentions can't validate any movie: as an English critic said of Antonioni's *Blow-Up,* that wopsided view of London, "He got it all so *sensitively* wrong.") Meanwhile young film makers are being hired to help the industry to reach the audience which it's trying to portray. As Graham Greene wrote in 1935, "There's always money to be picked up in a revolution."

One movie that's braving these problems is Stanley Kramer's *R.P.M.,* starring Anthony Quinn and Ann-Margret. The confrontation scenes were filmed at the University of the Pacific in Stockton, California—it's one of the few universities which will permit the miming of revolution on campus.

Like a professional army, the crew and twelve hundred extras—including many real students from Stockton—stand about on location, where the bushes around the college buildings have been sprayed with yellow paint to make December look like fall. A chorus of responses punctuates the shooting. "Quinn's finished. They knocked him down and they've been kicking him in the head."

"Were there some nice kicks?"

"Yeah."

Policemen scrape dirt and leaves from their uniforms, rub their sore ribs and knees, compare shattered visors and broken clubs; students press icebags against bruised faces, share bloodied bits of Kleenex for cut lips. Some pat each others' backs or shoulders, others scowl. All wade in succulent mud that clutches their boots and streaks their thighs. One says, "The vibes are getting ungood." Two crewmen recall the styles of riot control they once saw in Italy: "We should have the kind of equipment they have. They squirt guns full of red stuff all over the leaders, the inciters—it dyes their skin. Then it's easy to arrest them later."

"That's good. Not messy, you know what I mean?"

The *R.P.M.* script is by Erich Segal. Anthony Quinn plays the acting college president: one of the world's most distinguished sociologists, author of

Studies in Alienation. A radical in his fifties, he has been chosen by the students to replace the president they've forced out. (The faculty agreed to his appointment, since the other choices were Che and Eldridge Cleaver. And at least some of them are flexible: one professor admits, "We've been absentee slumlords in the ghetto of the mind.") Stanley Kramer, who cheerfully refers to himself as "a discarded liberal," focuses the movie on the aging rebel who's racked by conflicts of responsibility when the younger militants outdistance him. At one point, the Quinn-president protests, "I marched for the Textile Workers' Union! I fought against Franco. . . . I spoke out *against* McCarthy. . . . " (Throughout he gets limited comfort from Ann-Margret, cast as a student body, whom he urges to "Read Talcott Parsons . . . *and put on a bra!*") He does satisfy most of the radicals' demands, but balks when they insist on hiring and firing faculty and abolishing formal courses. So they threaten to wreck a two-million-dollar computer in the building they've occupied. Quinn accuses the white student leader of having "a pathological need to destroy." But the latter's unmoved by Quinn's earlier defense of private property; the student replies, "Private property is the jockstrap of the American conscience." The anguished president orders a friendly police chief to clear the building, stressing that there must be no violence. But as the students are gassed out, a psychotic badmouth woman activist attacks a cop and inspires a bloodbath. After a giant bust, the president is hissed, booed, and pronounced "Pig!" by even the moderate students, who continue to jeer as he walks away. . . .

Filming is slow because the weather's unreliable. Someone says, "It's all in the lap of the gods."

"Yup. And sometimes the gods stand up."

∽

Sweating beside a swimming pool before Christmas, drenched in steam and cooked by lights: they're shooting an earlier scene in which Quinn mingles with the students just after his appointment. "You gotta look radical," a makeup man says, pasting sideburns and a moustache on a sulky extra. "Yeh, like one of those goddam hippies." The one-line actors explain that they were cast as left or right according to their looks.

"Oh, but I was left yesterday and right today."

"Well, I was left in my last picture." Then they talk about the word faggot, its multiple meanings, and what it stems from.

Blue lights are arranged to shine on Quinn's scene with the right; later a red glow bathes his consultation with the left. The two groups assemble at opposite ends of the pool. The conservative students keep telling Quinn that they deplore the left's tactics, that the university should stay the way it is. One actor keeps fluffing "Maoist" for "Marxist"—a slip of the Sixties.

Just before I came to Stockton, a couple of young New York militants were disturbed to hear that such a movie was being made at all. One said, "That really hurts. What will they make of us? Brutes or clowns?"

Disgusted with the right, Quinn dives and swims down the pool to the left. They keep telling him, "You're beautiful." The president basks in their admiration.

Then they say, "No more classes!"

"Unstructured things, no tightness."

"No more goddam science requirement."

"Science is killing Vietnamese children."

Quinn says, "It also cured polio, guys."

They tell him, "Back to nature!"

"Let the flowers grow straight and tall!"

He mildly defends classes, but they explain, "The important thing is communication. . . . *We* are the only subject. We've got to relate to each other."

"No more classes."

"No more ghettos."

"No more wars."

Quinn surfaces from the pool between takes, shaking himself and scattering water like a formidable sea god, shedding the kind of charm that makes the soles of your feet sting. No wonder he has eight children. It's nice to hear him speak without an accent, after all those life-affirming Mediterranean roles.

As a tenth-grade dropout, he describes preparing for this film. "I really crammed—I've read forty books for this part. I even read Abbie Hoffman and those dirty newspapers at Berkeley." He and Stanley Kramer visited universities, questioned many students, attended classes. He says that the theme of *R.P.M.* is "Where does permissiveness end and authority begin? There comes a point when you have to say, Here's the line. Right, dad, it stops here." (He doesn't think highly of Dr. Spock. "I think he was well-meaning, like Emily Post—but so many sins have been perpetrated in his name. I just bought his book in Italian and threw it down the toilet.") He praises students for their instincts and their ideals, but he considers the rebellion to be psychological rather than political. And yet he hopes that a third political party will come out of the student movement. "If the students could ever unite, they could put this country on its ass economically. . . . I don't think a lot of them are morally against the Vietnam war; instead, they know they're being exploited as slave labor. But nowadays you don't need kids to fight a war—you can have old men pushing buttons. If my generation wants this war, let *them* fight it. With their buttons."

He says that he refuses "to do anything outside the system." Still, he was recently touched when the Brown Berets asked him to be a spokesman for them (he tells me he's a Mexican Indian). He visited the Indians who were occupying Alcatraz, has given speeches on their behalf, and was chided by George Murphy for his efforts.

Quinn says he and his family came to Stockton from Mexico when he was
a boy, and that they were migrant fruit pickers, traveling in cattle cars with
wooden slats. At first they didn't know that the California workers were on
strike, that they themselves were being used as scabs. Now, he says he's left of
center, although "my son thinks I'm one step behind Nixon. . . . But don't
make me sound like one of those far-out leftists." And yet: "The public doesn't
do shit. . . . If tomorrow a shooting war started, we'd all run and hide." Suddenly, he's furious: "We've reached the same point that Nazi Germany reached
when they were killing the Jews!" He's fiercer than I've seen him on the screen.
Then he shakes his big head; there's a pause; the outrage subsides. He talks
quietly about the power of economic boycotts: "A twenty-five-million Negro
boycott would really hurt. . . . But I still wonder how far the balloon can
stretch—like a balloon, you've got to say, This is all the air I can take. You've
got to stay within the balloon, within the system."

He takes off his robe, stretches, swats his toes, prepares to dive for a re-
take. "Some people are buying good will from the students by saying Go! Go!
Go! kids. I don't agree with that."

He swims off; soon the radicals who will later defy him are repeating that
he's beautiful.

~

Stanley Kramer, whose productions include *Home of the Brave, The Men, High
Noon,* and *The Wild One,* and who has directed *Judgment at Nuremberg, It's a
Mad, Mad, Mad, Mad World, Ship of Fools,* and *Guess Who's Coming to Dinner?,*
among others, says that he'd like to be "a leader of the counterrevolution"—
which means "hope against frustration. Life against death. Many of the films
of the moment have a death-in-life motif." He emphasized that *R.P.M.*'s student revolutionaries "must appear pure and idealistic. I take very seriously
the responsibility of having people understand them. I dig the activists. If I
were black I'd be a militant now. And I also think that tyranny is worse than
anarchy." But he feels that some students have carried their tactics too far.
He's already been attacked by some: "I told them, 'I've been fighting the
establishment for thirty years, and I can't find out what it is.' And they said,
'Because you're it.' " To refute them, he cites some of his earlier films that
were considered radical. The Navy objected that *The Caine Mutiny* was anti-
American; they protested that the character of Captain Queeg gave them a
bad image and that they'd never had a mutiny. The government refused to
lend him a nuclear sub for *On the Beach,* and he had to defend himself before
a congressional committee concerning "world guilt" about nuclear weapons.

Stressing that no single movie "can tell the whole truth," he underlines his
identification with the college president played by Quinn. "Yet I'm part of
the system that's financing me." He looks momentarily wistful. "Isn't it possible to be someone who has a little compassion and awareness—and work in

your own area? Isn't it possible to wait a little while, until things become clear? Before you choose sides?"

$\sim$

I'm up against the wall, standing with my back to a college building: the police are about to charge. That sickening suspense—of waiting to see if and how the cops will move—uncoils from the experience of Chicago, Paris, even Washington: from covering many confrontations of the past two years. Now, as the sun winks on visors and helmets and the revolving red lights of police cars, I shrink as the uniforms and boots hurtle toward me and past me. But it's only a rehearsal; those who practice tussling with each other have to be reminded not to laugh. "*Please! No* more laughing!" Smoke billows from the windows: it does look exactly like tear gas, and dispels a mildly unpleasant stink of inner tube. I remember how gas can make you hate your own lungs, detest your throat.

Two young cops twirl their rubber guns, fencing lightly with their plastic clubs. One, mishearing directions says, "Hey, the riot starts now!"

"No, we don't get to be violent until after Christmas."

Most of the cops are from UOP's student football team. The black football instructor and the president of the Black Students' Union tell me that UOP is very conservative, very expensive, and that many undergraduates are still apolitical. Atmospherically the Stockton campus seems a solar distance from most impassioned universities—few of the student extras seem to have many feelings about the war or the draft. However when the BSU demanded a number of scholarships for minority students, the administration granted more than they asked for. Still, verbal agreements have outstripped concrete action. The football instructor talks about white activists; he says "their main project is to get rid of football; they forget that it gives scholarships to blacks." He adds that whites at many universities are especially isolated from politics due to their recent discovery of drugs, which absorb so much of their time. "Drugs have done a flip-flop. They were a black thing for years. Now they're white." He and I share a queasy sensation that this movie's being filmed far from the experiences on most campuses. Yet my own actuality bump is dissolving: at moments the movie jolts into what one knows so well—at others it jars because it's so remote. Sometimes the *R.P.M.* company seems to distill most of the opinions and quandaries of the whole country, with all of the contradictions which are thickening up around us. Only one ingredient is missing: militants.

Now they're making some close shots of the left. I chat with an amiable old woman from Stockton who enjoys watching the shooting. She has a library face, haloed with the transparent Martian pleats of a rain hood. Apropos of nothing, she asks if I believe in giving eighteen-year-olds the vote. I say yes, and she says, "But look at the kind of people they turn into! *Look* what they did to Sharon Tate." She points at the college building, occupied by actors and some extras, who are leaning out of the windows for a close-up. "You never know," she says, "they might do anything."

Rap groups tend to form around Gary Lockwood, of *2001* and the TV series, *The Lieutenant;* he plays *R.P.M.*'s leading white revolutionary. Young actors and extras close around him, arguing, asking questions. He talks about redneck California, the world he grew up in, which is now hostile to the abundance of his (not very long) hair. (Thus the problems of hitchhiking: "You can't get a ride with long hair. But you can't get a free bed on the other end with *short* hair." "So go buy a hair piece.") Shaggy Californians are used to being called dirty faggot hippies, but mere insults in the East can be threats fulfilled in the West. Although *Easy Rider* isn't Lockwood's favorite movie, he and others agree on the validity of the theme: you really can get killed for the way you look. He's regretfully giving up his place on the Colorado River "because of the polarization": those who yell at him when they drive past his house could one day start shooting. Of course the police are equally suspicious at the sight of him; he describes being frisked at gunpoint by a cop who snatched a small brown box out of his pocket. "What's *this?*"

With his hands over his head, Lockwood meekly replied, "That's my electric garage opener."

"Your *what?*"

"You press that little button on and off and you can dig my garage door going up and down."

Still, he was held for several hours at the police station, where a boy who was descending from acid was weeping and rolling on the floor. Lockwood mimics the two cops who bent over the writhing boy: "*Seeing a lotta monsters,* huh? Having a *bad trip,* aren't you?" Yet he has a rueful sympathy for tough, rural whites—after all he was one.

Two crewmen disagree about Vietnam; both fought heavily in World War II. One says we should withdraw. The other insists that we've got to stay. Someone asks him why. "Because of the minerals."

The local police of Stockton, who patrol the location, are very friendly to the company; they admire the professionalism of Stanley Kramer's staff. They snort with disgust in referring to M-G-M's *The Strawberry Statement,* which was filmed very freely in Stockton a month ago—the police call it "Fruit's Delight." "Those hippies were so disorganized, and they used four-letter words that were eighteen inches high." The City Hall was used as an administration building, and the city manager was staggered to find his office being occupied by extras. He said that he had to get into his desk, but they said, "We're making a movie, daddy!" (The bona fide policeman loves imitating them; he switches his hips and snaps his fingers.) "And *he* said, 'Let me in or I'll call the *real* cops!' Ha!"

One theme that drifts around the lot is the plight of the huge Hollywood studios. Many have been bought up by corporations attracted by the vaults of old movies which are rented to TV, and the profit from selling the valuable property the studios own. Bob Yaeger, the unit publicist for *R.P.M.* (to be released through Columbia), remembers the lush years of Hollywood, "when the golden goose was erupting eggs from its backside." Of the takeovers he says, "There are more laughs in a heart transplant." He describes Paramount trying to endure: "like a convict under water breathing through a reed while the dogs are after him." Others repeat that the businessmen who now dictate to film makers are crushing the chance for experiment or change. "All they want is to make money. They bring in their IBM machines and their MIT graduates in tight-ass dark suits. But they don't know anything about pictures." It's stressed that big business is strangling big business. But when the voices of seasoned Hollywood protest, they may not realize that they sound rather like student radicals deploring capitalism.

Anthony Quinn thinks the movie business has been its own worst enemy: by pandering to popular taste. "They want fucking—so we'll give them fucking! There's this twelve-year-old girl, we'll have her fucked by a horse. . . . It's our own fault that people don't accept movies as an art form." Younger actors love listening to him—they nudge each other's ribs when he roars with disapproval. (He detested *Oh! Calcutta!*)

The extras even repented having to shove him off his feet. "He *is* beautiful. He's much too good for lots of his crappy parts."

Gary Lockwood is having another rap group. Someone's talking about survival. He says, "You dig plants?"

"Uh?"

"Man, plants are outtasight! Say you've got a sick plant—he's got so many ways of trying to tell you. He puts out tendrils all over the house, his leaves will change color or droop in a certain direction. If he can't make it—if you don't understand his signals—he just dies. But the plant that survives! He's stronger than any of the others. Sometimes you even have to starve them to make them strong."

Someone objects that starvation isn't equally good for humans.

Lockwood doesn't fight it. "Look, man, all I mean is that you've got a very complex society—it's like onions growing under roses. . . . You can't store apples and potatoes in the same cellar: they don't like each other. I do think there's a weird connection between people and plants. But I don't think people are really into people yet. . . . "

On the set of *R.P.M.* an echo steadily recurs: so many kinds of Americans can no longer stomach living with each other. Later several crewmen reminisce about "how the boys who came home from the war cleaned out the zoot-suiters in two weeks—they strung them up and had them hanging from the lampposts in L.A."

"Oh, I don't think they actually *hung* them."

"Well, anyway, they got rid of them."

Bob Yaeger says, "Well, time's scythe has reaped another day."

∽

Gentle and cordial, Ann-Margret is reflective when asked for her views on revolution. "I've never been in a riot," she says, "I'm not an intellectual." But she's sympathetic to student protest—"I think it's very healthy." Still, "I find so many of the kids so mixed up, they don't know what, because the world is going so fast. I wish there were more leaders than followers. The leaders know exactly what they're doing, and sometimes they're doing wrong.

"You get a sixteen- or a seventeen-year-old kid, seeing their parents into the martinis and sleeping around, they tell them not to smoke pot, you know, blah, blah, blah, they're so confused, they'll grasp at anything. Some of them find it.

"Lord knows it's ten thousand times harder to go to college now than it was for me." (She went to Northwestern's School of Speech.) "I don't know how the kids remain sane. And some don't, and we know that some freak out, and some are unsanitary. They've got to have something, or else they'll go completely out of your mind."

∽

The film company grows restless during its week on location in Stockton. Someone says, "This is a one-horse town. And they castrated the horse."

Mounting toward the confrontation, a female militant, played by Linda Meiklejohn, yells at the police chief who has ordered the students to clear the building: "Thanks to you, and to our *noble* president, maybe our citizens who are so unmoved by our use of force overseas and in our own cities will wake up when they see hobnailed boots in the Garden of Eden . . . "

Between takes, Graham Jarvis, of Elaine May's *Adaptation* and her movie, *The New Leaf,* tells me he initially hesitated about playing the police chief. He accepted the role when Stanley Kramer assured him that the students "would not appear in a bad light." It does seem likely that the audience may leave the theater thinking the rebels are sick adventurists. I know that Stanley Kramer doesn't intend this. But Jarvis and I talk about how easy it is to play into the hands of the right. After all this subject is in the public domain—it merely belongs to everyone in the country.

ABC-TV is filming the filming; Gary Lockwood makes some shots with his hand-held camera; a still photographer snaps pictures of Lockwood and ABC filming the filming. Bob Yaeger says, "So this is not just for The B'nai B'rith Bugle."

∾

Teda Bracci is setting her hair for tomorrow's confrontation. She plays the ferocious activist who mauls a cop, shouting "Pig bastard!" and thereby touching off "the riot." She loves her part. Her eyes glow and her excitement kindles as she anticipates the shooting—she throbs like a Tolstoyan heroine looking forward to her first ball or National Velvet before the great steeplechase. Her bony face ripples with a flurry of rapturous smiles; she has the kind of ripe, husky voice that can slide from a whoop to a croon. Meanwhile Audrey Hepburn is having nun's trouble on TV. Teda says, "I mustn't have any breakfast, or there'll be something *else* all over the ground." Audrey Hepburn says, "How can I be a good nun if I cannot get the Congo out of my blood?"

∾

Agitation rustles through the location, despite the fiberglass vests and shin guards and the plastic skullcaps which some stunt men wear beneath hairy wigs. Waiting for planned chaos pinches some nerves and mouths, tautens the skin stretched over cheeks and around nostrils.

Teda Bracci kicks her cop's feet out from under him, flinging him prone. She's a magnificent fighter; someone says, "She knows where a man's castanets are." Hundreds race and leap to beat each other's heads against the ground, to wrestle in a mud-rich fleshpack that grows angrier every hour. Arms, legs, fists, knees, clubs reassemble again and again to punish one another. When the action's cut off by the bark of a gun, they stand panting and gasping and glaring. After all the rehearsals, the preparation, the choreography with stunt men, much of the crowd starts punching from the heart. Later it was discovered that some who swung hardest weren't even student extras, but were unpaid visitors simply fighting for free.

Many grudges build up through the reshooting: "*Next* time, I'll get *him*." A cop slams a student hard against a car; a student knees a cop repeatedly; many skulls are cracked together; one policeman socks a student six times after a take is finished. The casualty list swells. Blurts of blood glisten through the glycerine and the red paint, and lots complain of having been bitten.

Older professionals talk indulgently about "body contact": they think that's what makes the crowd grow wilder. But it's also the period: by December 1969, the real students who play students can't help reacting against the symbols embodied by their classmates who play police. And the latter do hate being called pigs. One says he'd *never* join the force: "like it changes you." Another adds, "I used to wonder why they called cops pigs, and now I know why." A shortish boy in uniform has been jumped five times by the same group. Another extra tells me that he overheard them saying, "Let's get him— he's in ROTC, and that's Communist, you know!" (Gary Lockwood unpicks the initials: Russian . . . Oppressive . . . Terroristic . . . Communists.) Lockwood's astonished by receiving his first mouse: he was doing elaborate flips and rolls with a stunt man, when a student ran up and belted him in the eye. "Man, I've been in at least five hundred fights and never had a mouse!"

A black student playing a cop says happily, "Pig hit a pig." He explains that a few of the students are actually police trainees, and two have just accidentally clobbered one another. Two of the fledgling cops recall the flaming ping-pong balls they encountered on a stretch of duty in Washington after Martin Luther King was murdered. "They're worse than Molotov cocktails. You take a hypodermic needle and inject the ball with fire-lighting fluid. After it's lit, you can bat it through a window with a tennis racket."

"It's not just an amateur thing."

A cop and a student—who have been pounding each other into the mud—spring up beaming, and slap each other's palms. At least a few remember that this is a movie. But as the days of shooting have accumulated, many have started weighing the issues that *R.P.M.* has shoved at them. Some seem to have acquired more respect for student revolt: "They're trying to tell us something, but nobody listens, so the next time they try harder. What else can they do?"

Gary Lockwood says, "If enough people are okay financially, there won't be a revolution. And if enough *aren't,* there will be." He talks about ghettos: "Like I'm glad I'm not sort of black, man." Since he was poor for years, he's personally irritated by those who call him a copout because he now earns well: "They attack my eighty-dollar desk. But why shouldn't I groove on my own?" I press him about student revolution. "Man, I *gotta* be for it! I just *have* to think it's good. But there's a lot of . . . elements I don't go along with. If you go ripping down the street with your bayonet, chanting from Mao, that's cool, but don't come yelling to me if you get shot. . . . But if this white conservative middle class doesn't come around, then it looks like we're moving toward civil war, man. Sometimes it seems inevitable. But I don't want all those people killed, or the rest of us. I like my old lady, I like my dog, I like me. And I'd like to be seventy, man."

Someone else says, "But what do we *do?*"

Small arguments continue about violence and repression, plus the likelihood that both will ripen soon. But there are others—including some high school students—who gleam with the sheer exhilaration of the fighting. "We're going to miss this when it's over."

"Man, we've never had such fun."

One murmurs, "Right on," as though he's never said it before.

Later I learn that it cost over half a million to film the confrontation—including the price of keeping the company at a motel for twenty-six days.

The flesh pile is heaving and hurting again. Paul Winfield—who plays the key black militant—and I compare our confrontations: he was in the antiwar crowd that was savaged by blue power at the Century Plaza Hotel when LBJ visited Los Angeles in 1967. While we agree that most of *R.P.M.*'s combat scenes are painfully accurate, we're startled when many students jump on cops' backs and send them rolling over and over on the ground. We've never seen anyone attack the police so blithely, nor cops who are so easy to knock down. But today's action is being shot in blur and slow motion, so perhaps the fuzz won't look like such a pushover.

Winfield, who grew up in Watts, describes being shot to death in his last picture, *The Lost Man.* Pellets of pseudo-blood and gunpowder were taped to his body beneath his clothes; when an electric switch was pressed, blood and smoke stains burst through his shirt. He says it wasn't unpleasant, although the electrical aspect did make him uneasy beforehand. (In 1978 Winfield would play Martin Luther King in the television series "King"; filming the assassination scene was painful beyond all expectations.)

The last gun is fired to end the shooting. Teda Bracci lies on the ground with a cop in her arms, patting the back of the man she's been kicking.

The real Stockton police produce a huge cake with blue icing, inscribed To the *R.P.M.* Crew/From the Boys in Blue.

Bob Yaeger gazes benignly around the location. "Well, as they say in the hardware business, God bless 'em and screw 'em."

Hindsight: For me the filming of this movie characterized the end of the Sixties. A few young actors on the set had just been at the Rolling Stones' concert at Altamont, where the murder confirmed their impression that it was all coming down, that the ordinary life they knew might be over very soon. There was a sense of inevitability about violence—but none of them liked it. Some tried to ignore what was happening outside the movies, but they didn't succeed very well.

When the revolutionary movies were released, almost all of them had deservedly poor reviews. As was predictable, the filmmakers had known far too little about their subject. *R.P.M.*'s reviews were perhaps the worst, but *The Strawberry Statement*'s were dreadful and many found *Getting Straight* the most offensive: revolution as a real gas—where all involved were stupid or crazy. *R.P.M.* was more respectful of students than those other pictures, and the silliest lines I quoted were cut from the final version, as was the swimming pool scene.

These conversations on the set of *R.P.M.* seem fairly amazing in retrospect, muddled as many of them were. In 1969 it seemed that few could escape the questions of the country, not even movie extras or movie stars.

Voices From The GI Movement
February 1971

Heavy peace rings worn like brass knuckles; military bases where STOP signs have been repainted to read STOP WAR; young officers' cars bristling with antiwar stickers. "Dissent? It's more like contempt. Dig it: disgust." For many, loathing their personal experience within the military is the first step toward deploring what it represents; the next stage means rejecting U.S. foreign policy and its kinship with racism and poverty at home. Desertions and AWOLs are up as never before; reenlistment is at its lowest since 1955. Many refuse to carry out orders; a Vietnam returnee can't stop laughing as he describes how often his team neglected to set up ambushes in the jungle, and just blew grass for hours while they radioed back false information about their activities and their locations. You even hear about pilots who drop their ammunition in unpopulated areas, far from their targets. Members of the GI movement agree that they're still a minority—"But how we're growing! Just since early in '69." Until a couple of years ago, the civilian peace movement concentrated on draft resisters and tended to ignore or scorn those who were already in the service. "People weren't upset back in '63—when only Green Berets were getting croaked. The hollering didn't start until lots of draftees were killed." Today Vietnam vets and returnees are the marrow of the GI movement. Hence those about to leave Vietnam are kept apart from "the new meat," since their views are "bad for morale and discipline."

The antiwar GIs I met weren't drafted campus radicals. Most were the sons of hardhats or blue collars or random hair-haters. Few had been to college. Among those who said that they'd grown up apolitical or reactionary were an ex-biker from the Boston Hell's Angels with an Elvis ducktail of the Fifties, who did five years in jail before his induction; a forlorn welder who reenlisted only because of the job shortage in his home town; a trainer of horses and grade-riders who went to a Seventh-Day Adventist school and was once the 4-H Canning Boy of the Year; a cross-country wheat harvester and street chemist; a deepfreeze salesman; the son of a policeman. Most remarked how the military had exposed them to their own racism, which had altered when they discovered that black and white GIs have the same problems: "only the black dudes get even more shit from the lifers than we do." Lately the GI papers have carried detailed reporting on labor news, strikes, and unemployment, since so many of their readers come from or will return to the realm of unions.

The papers also aim at educating GIs about their legal rights and pool bad information about the military. "See, the army's the tie that binds—because it's so goddamn stupid."

~

What turned you against the war? Or changed your politics?

Bill (enlisted, reenlisted; 4 years): "You shoot a little gook kid and they give you a medal. I've got the Good Conduct Medal, the Bronze Star, two Purple Hearts, and some other shit too. I was very gung-ho in basic, fight for the flag and kill-kill-kill and all that."

Tom (enlisted, reenlisted; 4 years): "When I got back from Nam, I was a plans clerk for the 301st ASA Battalion, during August and September '69, and I worked at writing invasion plans for more than seventy countries—all for the 18th Airborne Corps. We're ready to go to *any* country in Africa, every country in Central and South America, and part of Europe—like Germany and East Europe. And there's a plan for the Middle East crisis now: we're fully ready to support either side. . . . I was always antiwar, but that's what made me revolutionary. It's amazing what the army does to nonviolent people like me."

Buckwheate (drafted, reenlisted; 4 years): "The way guys collect souvenirs in Nam. Trophies like heads or breasts or ears. We had Head-Hunters painted on the nose of our chopper. And cutting off the penis and shoving it in the mouth. I saw that five times. The sixth time, I pulled a Thompson machine gun on a guy who said, 'I think I'll cut me some nuts.' I said, 'You start cuttin' and I start shootin'.' There weren't any more mutilations while I was around."

Paul (enlisted; 2 years): "At first I dug the excitement. I'd been in my unit fifteen minutes when we went into contact; since I was a cherry—after I'd made a kill—the guys stood around in a circle while I took the ear, and they said, 'That's the way we like to break them in.' That first time it made me feel queasy, but I didn't later, the army does wonders. We used to do it all the time and laugh about it. That was in the Boogaloo Renegade Rat Control—Second Platoon, E Troop, 17th Cav. I didn't get my head changed until it happened to one of my buddies—what we did to gooks all the time. They cut off his fingers and ears and wrote Ho-ho-ho across his chest with a knife. At first I wanted to go out and kill all the gooks I could find. Then I realized they're human, like I'm human. . . . How come? Well, when I was ghosting, I had a house in Ben Cao, I'd like to be there now, it was so nice. The Viet navy used to take me out in their PT boats, or I'd float around in the sampans; a kid would paddle me on the river. I used to leave my weapon behind, or give it to the mama-san; she looked after my billfold when I was all fucked up on dope. I knew I could trust her. When they started liking me, they just gave me my dope free—when they could have made money off me. So I started selling their dope at camp and bringing the money back to her. She had old Beatles records, and what I used to dig was doing dope during the monsoon and listening to the rain on the roof. I'd get stoned and swim and listen to music. It was so nice."

Jake (enlisted; 2 years): "Blood on my clothes, on the walls, on my hands. Not my blood. It was when I was flying Medevacs, picking up wounded guys. Their blood would be sloshing all over the chopper by the end of the day."

George (enlisted, reenlisted twice; 6 years): "All the lies on TV. They said there would be no troops in Laos, but—being in the military—we *knew* there were. Last June or July 1970, hearing some senator say the 82nd *wasn't* on alert for the Middle East—when we knew we were. Everybody's lying, the president's lying, it blows your mind, if you've still got one."

~

Again and again you hear the rebellion against treating people as objects— GIs refer to this as often as feminists do. After all it's how the army treats them—and how they're told to treat the Vietnamese. "You're always hearing: 'They're not people, they're just fucking gooks.' Your platoon leader will tell you that if you hit one with a truck or a jeep, you should back up and hit it again—to make sure it's dead. Otherwise, it'll sue the American government, and maybe sue you too."

A few said their hatred of the war was fueled by the kinds of weapons we use; several had researched the weapons outlawed by the Geneva Convention of 1954—which the U.S. didn't sign. "In Nam, you see people literally nailed to trees by fleschettes—those are beehive artillery rounds. That's definitely against the Geneva Convention. So is Napalm B: that bursting white phosphorous which we use all the time. It sticks to the skin more than the old types of napalm. Oh man, they've got a lot of neat things. Let's see, other goodies: the army says a flamethrower is humane because you only die of suffocation, not burning. That's true if you're in a bunker. But if you're outside, the body fats burn, it cooks you alive. Nothing like being a torch."

"You know how they kept saying we found such big munitions caches? Well, in Cambodia the enemy had old rusty weapons—which the Vietnamese had already replaced. The only weapons I found were useless to the Cambodians."

"What gets me down: my parents treat me like a big shot because I've been in the war. But I know I'm just a big shit."

Another Vietnam returnee said that U.S. card companies send whole decks of the ace of spades to Vietnam. "Dudes tuck them in the camouflage bands of their steel pots. When they kill a VC, they nail the ace of spades to his forehead." Discussing the constant mutilation of the Vietnamese dead by American GIs, one returnee said, "We were fed a whole lot of propaganda about its having such a terrible psychological effect on Charlie. In their religion, if the body's mutilated, the soul can't get to heaven or something like that. But lots of guys do it just to do it."

"And revenge. Because you hear it's done a lot to Americans—although I personally never saw an American body that had been mutilated."

"I was there in '66, when helicopter crews were pushing Viets out of choppers. They took one prisoner and dangled him from a fifty-foot rope from a chopper and dragged him through the trees. It was strictly Americans doing this: the 326 Engineers, attached to the A Company 327th Infantry. When I first got there, I thought that was how war had to be fought."

"I wonder what our psychiatric wards will be like a few years from now?"

~

In Haymarket Square, the movement coffeehouse near Fort Bragg, in North Carolina, table after table was awash with notes by GIs who were filling out their applications as conscientious objectors—some for the second time. Many were recently back from Vietnam. Some tablehopped to advise others about the procedures for CO. A white captain and a black first lieutenant—both members of the Concerned Officers' Movement—were also applying. A few weeks later the lieutenant received an honorable discharge; he was the first West Point graduate to get CO. The captain, a dentist who wore a vast mushroom felt sombrero and loops of brown glass beads, had already been reprimanded for talking politics while his patients' mouths were jammed with metal—"I just lay some antiwar rap on them when they can't answer back." Among those rustling through their notes, there was some outraged talk about army chaplains, who are said to be most unhelpful to potential COs. "Those old rinkydink chaplains—they shock the shit out of you because they still think Christianity is the tool for fighting communism."

"Yes, and they tell you it's OK to burn babies with napalm because it keeps them from burning in hell later—because dying keeps them from sinning, and all Vietnamese are sinners anyway."

"Ahhhhh, Churchianity is just a capitalistic plot."

Some of those applying for CO said they'd split if they were turned down. In California a lawyer told me that some GIs who work in offices (especially in Germany) have become expert at writing discharges for one another: "And by the time the brass wakes up, all the files on those guys have disappeared!" One of the nimblest forgers was finally detected, so he wrote emergency leave orders for himself, boarded a military plane, and is still enjoying his freedom.

You hear about a galaxy of actions against the military, from numerous groups of GIs who file petitions to have their officers replaced (an Article 138 gets an officer investigated), to some who try to have their officers court-martialed for charges like "communicating a threat," or assault and battery, plus all the fragging in Vietnam. Thus, from the flight line at Quan Loi in late 1969, in the Bravo First Squadron 9th Cavalry, the First Air Cavalry Division: "Once we were pulling inspections at night and we all had our various means of relieving tension. A CID man saw us smoking; he whipped out his badge and said, 'You're all busted!' And those were the last words he *ever* spoke. Three guys fired on him at the same time."

"Fragging used to be mainly for racism, or too much harassment. But it's up a lot now—guys do it to almost anybody they don't like. After you've been in Nam a while, it's not too hard at *all*."

"I had a section sergeant in Camp Holloway, in Pleiku, who gave us twenty-hour workdays, seven days a week. He was found from the waist down."

There were also references to putting prices on officers' heads. Someone with a private income may offer $1,000, "plus legal fees if necessary," or a group will take up a collection. The Fort Bragg GIs told me about two officers who are said to have expensive heads; one is a general in Vietnam who "initiated the policy that enlisted men who failed to salute officers were sent to the forward firebase"; another is a major at Bragg who's considered "big on racist repression." Someone added that the price on officer removal is rising due to inflation.

It was mentioned that some buildings at Fort Bragg were nearly burned in the summer of 1970: "It was close. Guys were coming back from Nam, realizing they were being used here just as they were used there, hating the war, hating the army." Last year two mess-halls in the Special Processing Detachment at Fort Ord, California, were burned down. (SPD is used for pretrial and posttrial confinement, and is usually crammed with AWOLs.) This account comes from a civilian who visited the SPD about an hour after the fire: "That night, an MP busted one guy for not wearing a hat, and another for keeping his hands in his pockets. So about twenty stoned the pig car and demanded that both men be released. Then about a hundred and fifty guys smashed up the cage—that's the only locked part of SPD, where the new arrivals are kept—and sprang them. After they burned the messhalls, they decided to burn the dayrooms, but they didn't want to burn up the pool table, and it was too big to carry through the door. . . . Well, the brass got wiggy after the torching, and some discharges were speeded up, especially for political types."

Mutiny?

"It's hard to have a mutiny in Nam. When guys are over there for only a year, they just cover their ass and wait for the time to be over. But you could have strikes in the form of massive sick calls. And you could organize sympathy strikes back here. The real test will come for a lot of bases when guys are ordered out for riot control duty or told to break up a labor strike."

Some at Fort Bragg told me that they would refuse riot duty. They praised the forty-three black GIs at Fort Hood, Texas, who refused to be sent to the Chicago Democratic Convention of 1968.

"I'd love to get orders to fight my brothers. It would be so easy to fuck up riot control!"

"If there's riot duty, there are some of us who'd like to keep some units here—if only because the brass is worried about what *might* happen. If we keep them here through rumors, that's cool too. Anything's possible, but it's up to the brass to find out the differences between plans and rumors."

From the alumni of any base, there are many accounts of low-level sabotage. Sugar or mothballs often appear in officers' gas tanks, with certain regional variations: maple syrup is popular with New Englanders, but Southerners favor molasses. I learned that "peanut butter saturated with gas explodes, although you need a cap to set it off." At Bragg the technicians were very explicit. "Sabotage—oh wow! Every time my unit goes into the field, the machines are in perfect running order. In five miles, they break down. Turning the ignition on and off blows pistons out nicely. You can take the spark-plugs out and bang them with a hammer. There are other neat things, like not putting the lug nuts on tight, so that the wheels fall off, or loosening the bolt in the steering wheel. What else is cool: broken bottles beneath the back wheels of two-ton trucks."

"Take the air inlets in the cheeks of army gas masks—if they get wet, the mask is useless."

"I used to work at the airport, but now they've decided they can't have me around half-a-million dollar aircraft."

"In Nam, when you hear there's going to be a bad mission, you can say there's something wrong with the bird. Then you make it wrong. Put a scratch on a rotor blade, or scrape the insulation off the wiring, or loosen the fuel lines, or spray oil on the engine so it looks like it's leaking."

"See, we're just using intelligence that the army taught us."

A statue of a World War II paratrooper, known as Iron Mike, is rather wistfully mentioned as a symbolic target.

But there are many other GIs who think that further revolutionary actions within the military "would only result in sheer terrorism." One militant added, "You've got a lot of dudes who are into any kind of violence. Sure, that's how the army schooled them. But luckily, they haven't done much about it yet, because the targets they'd choose would be the wrong ones." A spokesman for the GI movement said, "Some of us find it difficult to decry sabotage, because we know that GIs have no political power. But we also tend to discourage it because it won't build a wider GI movement. . . . Still, the result of fragging in Vietnam is that guys aren't ordered into a combat situation. So maybe fragging's a form of pacifism?"

∼

"You know how the brass uses racism? It's a way of keeping people in line: by turning them against each other. Last Halloween, at Fort Ord, the army tried to provoke a race riot in SPD. The black GIs were told that if there was another riot, blacks would be thrown in the stockade, but not whites. There were rumors that whites would burn the place down, and rumors that blacks would beat on them if they did. But nothing happened." From those who've been in the stockade, there are recurrent reports that guards threaten blacks with punishment for what the whites might do—which increases the possibility that blacks may attack whites and vice versa.

Although black GIs get most of the worst jobs and much of the fiercest combat duty overseas, you're told that "Black guys really have it together in Nam," where many officers look the other way when blacks "give dap" (the power shake); however many have been hassled for flashing the fist on bases at home. A number have faced court martials rather than trim their Afros. In October 1970, a black GI at Fort Lewis was given three years' hard labor and forfeiture of all pay for refusing to part with his Afro and his beard. A few months earlier, some white Marine reservists who wouldn't cut their hair received fourteen days' hard labor. All in all it's unstartling to hear that "Some black guys are joining the marines to get training for the war. Not the Vietnam war."

Racism in the military surfaced like a sperm whale at the Alameda Naval Air Station in California, where a white staff sergeant produced, dittoed, and distributed a drawing of a naked black man tied to a stake, his penis bound by a string attached to a pistol pointed at his head. A naked white woman crouches in front of him: when he has an erection, his brains will be blown out. The drawing is titled "HOW TO ELIMINATE THE NEGRO PROBLEM!" Several white NCOs helped to circulate the drawing in the fall of 1970. A black lance corporal took it to a lawyer and they filed a writ of habeas corpus for the lance corporal's release from the marines—on the grounds of the racist nature of the military. More than two-thirds of the petitioner's detachment of some hundred and fifty men signed a solidarity statement concerning the case—and only seven of these were black. But the judge dismissed the case.

~

During my first evening's conversation with GIs at Fort Bragg, I was staggered to hear four of them contemptuously referring to some others in their unit as sexist pigs. Almost all the antiwar GIs I met were stronger supporters of the women's movement than many civilian radicals, perhaps because GIs are beginning to rebel against their own experience with machismo. One huge crop-headed GI, just back from Vietnam, said, "Macho is still the army's biggest drawing card for enlistment—it's even more powerful than patriotism or opportunism. So many of us have been programmed to this compulsion: it's what sucked us into the military. There's got to be a way for young men to learn that they don't need the army to make them feel worthwhile—the army's still capitalizing on their insecurity. So I think civilians and women's liberation groups can help GIs a lot: by continuing to expose the absurdity of the male role."

"Right on!" came from the GIs in earshot—to my astonishment. (And I didn't bring the subject up; they did.) They went on to stress how badly the army treats WACs and army wives: "WACs are just supposed to be a handy lay." Distilling the army's attitude toward women, someone mentioned a friend who had refused to wring a chicken's neck during survival training in basic; his colonel had shouted, "If you can't strangle a chicken, how can you ever make love to a woman?"

Two WACs later told me that their daily assignments were pointless "jerk-off stuff that's too dumb for GIs to do." Their bubble gum popped softly as they angrily snapped and shuffled a deck of cards. "If they need us in the army, they better give us some goddam work. We're supposed to look busy in the office, but I don't even have a goddam desk—I'm supposed to look busy standing up?" Their descriptions of army life sounded like a caricature of a 19th-century girls' boarding school, stiff with humiliations and "piss-poor morale." They added that their major keeps a baseball bat by her desk, and their first sergeant has a billy club in her in-tray.

I also learned that homosexual GIs are discussing the possibilities of gay liberation groups on several bases. "At induction centers, you can tell them you're gay and you'll still be drafted. So if you're gay, you're going to Nam—and lifers'll tell you that you're going as a lay." Although homosexuality can mean a dishonorable discharge, some are convinced that coming out will be useful in further weakening the army's reliance on macho: "The last stereo-type to fall could *really* fall!"

As for wives, the military sometimes tries to use them as a conservative force—in hopes that they'll pressure their husbands to stop their antiwar activities. The most political GIs are fined repeatedly for indirect reasons, such as untidy lockers or lateness for formations. (Fines are taken out of the paychecks, hence the married are particularly vulnerable. And families are easily divided.) One black army wife of twenty-two years—"I am now violently against the war"—told me she would like to organize GI wives around the issues of peace and pollution. "But they threaten you with your husband's rank. If you do anything they don't like, they *suggest* that he won't get pro-moted." Her own husband is now in Vietnam for the third time, he also spent eighteen months in Santo Domingo, and has been wounded on three differ-ent occasions. Half in tears but trying to stifle them: "God forbid that it should happen, but if my husband is killed—and I really mean this—I feel he will have died for nothing if he dies for this country. And if they give me that flag and those medals—they pin those medals on you and I'll rip them off my chest, and I'll tell them to send that stuff to Nixon and tell him to *shove* it . . . "

～

The notion of liberalization unleashes a series of hoots and snorts; *Time*'s December cover story, "The Military Goes Mod", brought some gut-spilling laughs from a number of GIs—especially because the "people programs" described have no relation to their hostility to war. Longer hair and rock and beer in the barracks hung with psychedelic posters don't make them more eager to fight: "Raising a 'fro is supposed to make me dig Waste-More-Land?" Many are very cynical about the Enlisted Men's Councils, which allow them to "voice grievances," but give them no authority. At Fort Carson some GIs yelled "Safety-valve!" and "Pacifier!" at officers who were offering them culture in hopes of making them fonder of the army. At Fort Bragg, which is supposed to be a liberal base, GIs say their NCOs often fail to carry out "all that public relations crap that the brass dishes up. So they've abolished reveille—and our field first sergeant keeps threatening us with a 5:30 A.M. *work assemblage*. Haw."

Quite a few said they'd reenlisted just to get out of Bragg. "After a year or eighteen months in Nam, you can't stand the way you're hassled here." And the living conditions for GIs aren't as swinging as the media suggests: some showed me the broken windows—long unrepaired—which makes their temporary World War II troops barracks so cold that ice forms overnight in the water cans they use as ashtrays. Ravaged boilers and toilets often stay that way. Bragg is so blanketed with coal dust that many who blow their noses on awakening complain of having black snot.

"I lived so much better in Nam than I do here."

"Well, at least it's warm in Nam."

Within the bleary glare of Fayetteville, N.C., a town of no character, which is merely a strip of rip-off stores and drive-ins to tempt GIs, plus eateries and topless Live Entertainment, signs winking "YALL COME HEAH," the Pop-a-Top Lounge and the Pink Pussycat, John Wayne or skin-flicks, bleak trailer camps filled with Mobile Unit Homes, lunch counters, where, "If you're with a black dude, they fix you food to go," and the juicer-joints disdained by the grass generation, a GI called the antiwar coffeehouse "an oasis of enforced peace." At Haymarket, posters announce "GULF KILLS" and "This vacation visit beautiful VIETNAM," bulletin boards report the latest in lettuce boycotts and officers who demand war crimes inquiries; sweatshirts are stenciled with the Statue of Liberty looking rather like Che and giving the fist, and buttons support Nat Turner or Tom Paine. While the Nitty Gritty Dirt Band or the Youngbloods or Led Zepplin get some assistance from twanging Jews' harps, and "The Sounds of Silence" begins to sound like the national anthem, GIs can buy or browse through I. F. Stone, Fanon, Leroi Jones, Mao, and Juan Bosch, or "Cuba for Beginners" or "The Myth of the Vaginal Orgasm," or chalk up more graffiti on the black walls: "I am a captain in the U.S. army and I think it sucks;" "They put in my mind the ways of truth—in my hands the weapons of war!! Then they take my sanity!!"; "My country right or wrong, but right the wrong in my country." And everywhere there are signs forbidding the use, possession, or dealing of dope.

~

"Listen, that whole war's being fought on dope!"

"To stop dope, you'd have to jail the whole army."

"For a while, I thought I'd stay in Nam—just sitting back and getting stoned. I could dig being over there now for a lot of that cheeeeap grass, and those sweet little vials of liquid dex."

"On patrols, we used to carry speed right in the kit."

"The day I reenlisted, I was skagging so much I was nodding, but they managed not to notice."

"In Nam, our CO told us, 'I don't care what you use as long as you get the job done.' "

"I wasn't doping much in Nam—it's mainly since I came back here."

"I was. That's the main reason I went to Nam."

Despite billows of puffery—about burning occasional fields of marijuana in Vietnam or opening drug centers on bases—it's obvious that the military has indeed been permissive about drugs, as the Defense Department has openly admitted. But GIs say their COs have been reluctant to confront the subject, since the evidence of drugs will blacken their own records. "But the brass is getting scared now. They're striking out sporadically, here and there, which makes people schizzy. But they'd rather have guys around on dope than going AWOL to look for it—they'd rather have them stoned than screaming. In Nam—where so many start doing smack in the combat zone—there's very little real effort to unhook them. The army knows that smack-heads can function on heavy drugs for a year—which is all that's needed."

"I worked in a clinic in Nam, and I saw the same thing happen over and over: when guys came in and smack was proven—unless they were withdrawing and *had* to go to the hospital—they were sent right back to their units, where they got more smack and went right on."

"Sure, the army lets H happen—to keep people quiet. If they *really* wanted to bust the dealers, then they would."

It's steadily repeated that many become addicted to hard (or robust) drugs in Vietnam. Black-market speed comes from Vietnamese pharmacies; one favorite is known as "mop juice," since "mop" is the Vietnamese name for fat, and the product (Obisotol) is used for dieting. "Number tens" or "BTs" (binactols) are also popular: "They're superdowners, it's just like being drunk. They appeal to juice-freaks who want to get into the dope scene. BTs make you very hostile: they get you into the guerrilla bag."

It's said that quite a bit of heroin comes from the Thai troops. Also: "We wonder how much money the Saigon government is making on dope. Air America, that CIA airline, flies opium—from the Meo tribes' crops. The U.S. Air Force supplies planes to fly it when Air America can't. We have armed guards protecting opium fields in Laos and Cambodia during the harvest—

especially Laos. We heard this a lot from our friends in the Special Forces; they said the guards were sometimes discharged Special Forces guys."

"And I've heard that our planes have even destroyed a competitor's aircraft—like Air Vietnam or the Cambodian Air Force—so the product can't get to market."

References of this sort have been trickling into the press for a couple of years. In a speech by Representative (now Senator) John Tunney of California on March 24, 1970, there were charges that "We are . . . engaged in a secret war in Laos, a tribal war in which the CIA has committed the United States to support a faction of Meo tribesmen led by General Vang Pao whose sole function is to dominate other factions of this opium-producing Meo tribe through northern Laos. . . . The Administration has deliberately veiled in secrecy our deepening involvement in an opium tribal war . . . clandestine yet official operations of the United States Government could be aiding and abetting heroin traffic here at home."

At Fort Bragg heroin usage increased so much in 1970—mainly due to Vietnam returnees—that Bragg is now called the second largest heroin market in America, after New York City. Quite a few GIs told me they often see others shooting up in their barracks. But Bragg's much-publicized drug-treatment center, Operation Awareness, was derided as "a farce." "Officially, no one's a doper if he's been in there. But they're just barely rehabilitating guys so that they don't have to be immediately discharged from the army."

One ex-addict—who said he'd finally gone cold turkey in a friend's apartment while on leave—gave this account of Operation Awareness: "First you rap to a bunch of shrinks. Then you start earning points, like a little kid at camp. More points get you out sooner, and patients even get points for telling other people on post that the program is good. That's lying, man. Then you go to the shoot-up room" (where emetics are injected) "and puke your guts out. And you get some Methadone: I was really stoned on that. But some guys are bigger junkies when they leave than when they go in—smack's so easy to get from the corpsmen. One dude I knew came in with a twenty-dollar-a-day habit, and he left with a forty-dollar-a-day habit. So you just puke and earn points and don't get cured. I think the whole setup is only political propaganda. They just want the public to think they're trying."

The most political GIs stress that they're "very down on dope," and some said they had given up hallucinogens "for political reasons." They said they try to tell others, "Skag wastes you worse than it wastes the army," and they continually warned them to keep any kind of dope away from Haymarket. But several admitted that it's tricky to put down psychedelics without turning off their audience. "Yes, grass and acid can be radicalizing—to start with. But how can we tell people to stop after a little?"

"The biggest problem I have rapping to the guys is that they're too stoned to hear me."

~

Naturally political dissent within the military means lots of assignments for agents—either federal or military, as well as the GIs who are busted for pot and told, "Be nice, inform a little, and we'll take the heat off you." Traditionally, drugs, or planted drugs, or those where "the flakes were lost in analysis," yield the most convenient charges against an individual or an organization. "Outside agents used to be the easiest to spot, because they offer you some grass right away and offer to blow up a building for you at once."

During the week when I visited Haymarket, the civilian staff was acutely worried that the coffeehouse might be closed. They expelled all known dealers, held an antidope panel, and distributed warning leaflets. Someone wistfully suggested building stocks and a pillory. But since the Fayetteville police had shut off the local park a few months before, contacts and dealing had accelerated in bars and coffee joints all over town. High school students especially liked to go to Haymarket. Therefore new dealers (who aren't old friends of FDR) kept wandering in. Most were strung-out teen-agers in velvet jeans or fringes or capes; some twirled their rolled-up umbrellas far too casually on their way to and from the bathrooms—while the staff grimly wondered what kinds of agents might be watching.

So it was helpful when a federal narcotics agent introduced himself to me. On learning that I was a writer, he asked to see my credentials and then unbosomed himself. I think his motive was simple megalomania: he kept saying how professionally expert he was, what a lot he earned, how much he knew—the power glands were buzzing. He was almost romantic about the perils of his job, and told me, "There's nothing like the touch of cold steel." Throughout our talk he constantly pointed at himself: he kept tapping his chest, where his notebook of dealers was, tapping his leg to indicate one gun, jabbing at his jacket for the other. (He was indignant because I initially thought he was an army narc: "No, no, the *Federal* Bureau.") He had fake army ID and looked like a basic trainee: his reddish hair was strikingly short, his moustache very small, and his fatigue jacket was well pressed. So his appearance would have jarred within any Aquarian landscape; however he had the virtue of being inconspicuous, except for flyaway ears. He repeated that he was a good actor, which I doubted. Nor was he likely to blow dope with his suspects, as many agents do; he said he'd had one joint in his life—by accident, when he was drunk.

Wagging his head, he promised that Haymarket would soon be closed and the staff busted: "It'll just be a matter of time." He insisted that two members of the staff were dealers who were making a lush profit on the coffeehouse. He then named two Fayetteville natives who I knew weren't on the staff, but he wouldn't believe me. While he explained the ultraviolet test for the strength of acid, and documented the range of drugs which he said dealers had offered him on the premises, I realized that his was a rum blend of efficiency and sloppiness. He didn't know any of the staff members' names or that they lived in a collective, or even that they had a policy against dope. And it wasn't very bright to talk to a writer.

He was very vindictive about all drug users, and spoke scornfully of the organizations that work with heroin addicts—"They only try to *help* them, I'd jail them for ninety-nine years"—but occasionally he tried to sound like the movement: "See, I just don't want my brothers and sisters out there to get hooked." He added that his stint at agenting was a substitute for military service, and that he'd done "big jobs" in New York and Oregon. He mentioned a vast supply of heroin he expected to arrive in Fayetteville in three days. Although he had recently fingered one civilian for an acid bust, he said it was worth waiting for more detailed information on dealers and suppliers, so he was ready to let the heroin reach its source—the microboppers or GIs who would be easy to arrest later. All in all he couldn't separate the politics of the GI movement from the presence of teen-age dopers.

When I told the staff about him, they were distressed but took it calmly. Some considered asking him if he was an agent—if he denied it, he could still arrange arrests, but wouldn't be able to give evidence in court. (I was touched when he was referred to as "Nora's pig.") But they finally agreed that "It's better to deal with a narc you know" than with a stranger, and that it would be useful to note whom he talked to, since they would then know who to toss out. On the next night the agent left the coffeehouse after a brief visit, and a member of the staff followed him. The agent went to a phone booth and made a call. He didn't return, but soon three policemen strode through Haymarket and then frisked three civilians who had just gone to a car outside. They were clean and had to be released.

A few weeks later the staff reported that the agent had widely admitted his identity, that he'd told them he liked Haymarket, but was still repeating, "Just a matter of time." Not long after, he suddenly claimed that "his head had changed and that he didn't want to be a pig anymore"—and pointed out four others he said were agents. The staff, which couldn't believe he'd flip-flopped, thought he was probably trying to ingratiate himself and to learn more about them—since he'd already blown his own cover.

There are plenty of other places in Fayetteville where dealing and contacting are the norm. But military and federal authorities are naturally eager to eliminate the actual locations where GIs can talk freely about the war and the government. There have been (unsuccessful) efforts to close the Oleo Strut at Fort Hood and the Shelter Half at Fort Lewis; the UFO in Columbia, South Carolina, has been shut down. Yet antiwar groups like GIs United and MDM (Movement for a Democratic Military) continue to expand. The civilian tax-exempt United States Servicemen's Fund and similar nontax-exempt organizations, such as Support Our Soldiers, help to support some twenty projects by providing money for educational materials, lawyers, and speakers, and also finance the largest of the seventy-five GI newspapers.

At Haymarket I was told that pro-war GIs also make visits: "They fall by to argue. It's the usual stuff—either, 'You fight a war to win,' or 'If you don't stop communism in Asia, we'll have it in Brooklyn!' So we try to make them aware of facts, to give a direction—rather than impose an opinion."

Early in 1971 quite a few at Bragg were wondering if they were going to be sent to Jordan on an alert. "They're building up troops to full strength now—why? And we're being trained in desert-type tanks. Jordan's been mentioned quite a bit, and they keep pounding it into us that it's not just Nam anymore."

"If we ever get out of Nam and Laos, I wonder what'll be next? Bolivia?"

"Chile?"

"Peru?"

Hindsight: Since Vietnam was bombed more heavily in 1971 than during any previous year of the war, and since more GIs in Vietnam freely expressed their astonishment to the press when they heard that they were no longer in combat but merely in a " 'defensive' position," Washington's insistence that the war was winding down meant little to those in the military. It was also discovered that while the heroin in America is of about 5 percent purity, the heroin available in Vietnam is of about 95 percent strength.

In early 1972 some of the "liberalization" programs in basic training were discontinued, the beer machines were removed from the barracks, private cubicles were abolished, and the new recruits received a 30 to 40 percent increase in physical training. On some bases, the "people programs" persisted, while others pushed for a tougher army.

Within the year following my visit to Fort Bragg, the Haymarket staff shut down their own coffeehouse because the drug problem was inescapable throughout Fayetteville. They opened a bookstore that served as a meeting place for GIs and offered counseling and legal services. The location chosen was outside the town but still near the base. Other coffeehouses have gone through a similar transformation, and legal counseling accelerated.

In 1972 activities increased in the navy and part of the air force. There have been Stop Our Ship campaigns. In April 1972 seven crew members of the U.S.S. *Nitro* jumped overboard when the munitions ship pulled out of New Jersey; they were cheered by forty-five demonstrators who were paddling canoes and lifeboats near the ship. Those concerned said they wanted to prevent the ship from delivering ammunition to aircraft carriers in Vietnam. In October 1971 eight sailors from the U.S.S. *Constellation* refused to sail to Vietnam with their ship; they took sanctuary at Christ the King Catholic Church in San Diego, California. (They later received "general discharges under honorable conditions" from the navy.) Some on the U.S.S. *Rush—*

which left Newport, R.I., for "a friendly tour" of Angola and Mozambique—
sent petitions to Congress protesting these trips to colonies of the Portuguese regime. And there were vigils at air force bases in Idaho and Texas.

Amid all the stories of defiance and the tough talk I heard at Bragg, one of
the sturdiest GIs I met left me with an image that won't retreat. When he was
in Sydney, Australia, on leave after combat duty in Vietnam, he decided to
treat himself to a fine dinner to celebrate his first night away from the war.
Perusing the menu in a posh restaurant, he ordered Steak Diane, not knowing what it was. The waiter brought a dish to the table, poured on some fluid,
and the thing went up in flames. "I jumped back and crashed into the wall. It
looked just like napalm. I couldn't stop shaking—and I don't usually shake."
He paused. "You know what the steak reminded me of."

Frank Rizzo and Philadelphia
June 1971

B abies for Rizzo: blond and bald and rosy brunette, dribbling or chuckling,
babies studded with Rizzo buttons, which click and clank whenever they
move, even when a deep breath's drawn. The babies cry when the pins prick
them. All the mothers and daughters and fathers wear so many buttons that
three or four buttonless visitors are stared at with suspicion; those who don't
accept buttons must be creeps. Chesty teen-aged boys and youngish jocks
strut about in lemony, grape, or lime pastel T-shirts stenciled with RIZZO RIGHT
NOW—surely a mating of Right On and Peace Now—at this backyard rally in
Richmond, where some hundred and fifty people sip soda and munch a frank
for Frank, while the crewcut guitarist gives them "Jailhouse Rock" and "All I
Have To Offer You Is Me." Rizzo's own small band sinks the singer's voice
with "O Dem Golden Slippers," and a few older women in smocks and spoolies
twirl each other around in the sunlight, laughing a little when their buttons
clack. Rizzo, like most behemoths, looks ready to burst his suit, but he signs
autographs and then nods quite amiably when a small, neat, middle-aged
housewife calls out that she has a question for him. Suddenly, two Right Now
sweatshirts grab her and haul her away, she shouts "*Hellllpp*" while the drums
crash louder and Rizzo begins a speech about creeps who don't get up until
three in the afternoon, bums who don't work like the rest of us, and the
woman gets the bums' rush because this is private property.

Trembling on the sidewalk, she explains that she wants to ask Rizzo what he will do about drugs when he is mayor—what methods will he use which weren't employed when he was police commissioner? She says that as the mother of a fourteen-year-old son, she's terribly worried about drugs in schools. Two weeks ago she waited outside Sears Roebuck to ask Rizzo the same question. But his staff wouldn't let her near him, and one man put on a gefilte-fish accent and said, "Vot are you doing here, Mrs. *Cohen?* Vy don't you go away?" She objected to his inflection, but he said that his name was Weinberg, so how could he be anti-Semitic? (Rizzo's assistant campaign manager was Martin Weinberg.) Then a young Rizzo staffer asked her, "Do you want the Zulus to take over the city?" and his female colleague added some remarks about niggers, and the woman was ordered to leave.

On her second appearance, Rizzo's campaign workers recognize her and make certain that she won't be able to speak to him. Still on the pavement, she repeats, "Why can't I ask a candidate a question? What's happening in this city? If you can't ask a question?" Several young boys look disturbed and say she's right, it's true, there's a lot more drugs at school this year. She rubs her cheek with a hand that still shakes: "So why can't I just ask a question?" To avert this danger, Rizzo is filtered out through another entrance, while a few goons chortle at her and say, "Have some nickel-bags"—"Yeah, have some"— and they tell her to beat it, don't make trouble, stay away.

~

In Philadelphia these days, much can depend on who looks guilty. Last winter, near Society Hill, the neighborhood was intrigued by seeing a couple on a rooftop in the early morning: the woman wore a nightgown, and the man was naked. Police cars hurtled to the spot, and Rizzo himself rushed inside the house. The couple had actually been threatened by a man with a gun— before they'd dressed for the day—and had rushed to their own roof in fright. The assailant was still walking around in the streets, openly carrying his weapon, but the police didn't notice him or nab him. A neighbor said that— in Philadelphia's current mood—a gunman wouldn't attract attention: the guilty person must be the naked one.

~

Philadelphia: a town of harmless drunks and mean old women in information booths who give you the wrong information; the lacy, flowing script of compulsive young black graffiti artists—Cornbread, Chewy, Kool Kev, Tity, and Kleptokid, who proclaim themselves King of the Walls or paint crowns over their names (the fiercest graffiti I saw were WATCH MY SMOKE, and in the ghetto, Irish Power Is Boss, chalked in letters that grew smaller and smaller); soft pretzels—"there's a lot of crooked dough in this town"—and news features on Princess Grace's "Fifteen Years of Serenity." A city where the words "gorilla" and "guerrilla" fly around so fast that it's hard to distinguish them (even though gorilla means right and guerrilla means left), of shining shelves and floors and banisters and glistening oilcloths on tables in ultraclean Italian homes; sequestered nuns in shocking-pink floor-length habits rollerskating behind their convent; where a man in drag won the "best life-style expression prize" in 1971's Easter Parade, and mud-brown skirts droop over the shins in Bonwit's windows, while a Presbyterian church announced its Sunday sermon: "The Importance of Being Properly Dressed."

A very puzzling town for a New Yorker. The city's brave enough to number the thirteenth floors in many buildings, but—against a new guest's pillow—hotels prop cards reading CAUTION (Please Turn Thumb Bolt, Also Attach Chain). Poe drafted *The Raven* in Philadelphia, Zelda Fitzgerald took dancing lessons there, Pound went to Penn and later wrote the alumnae secretary, "All the U. of P . . . does . . . for a man of letters is to ask him to go away without breaking the silence"; Eddie Fisher and Mario Lanza and Frankie Avalon and Fabian all came singing out of South Philadelphia. They have one of the world's best zoos, plus something called a Sinatrarama.

Many old houses have slanted, reflecting mirrors on upper floors, which enable house owners to see who's at the front door. These are called *busybodies,* which seems appropriate for a town of intense gossip: everyone tells everybody everything, and most of it is at least two-thirds true. Not lies, not malice; what you hear may be merely incomplete. And you're sure to get the story again soon: the source may be next door or across the room.(You also hear correct accounts of what appeared in the press—where the facts were fudged.) So you learn who had shad for lunch yesterday at which Bookbinder's, who was (or wasn't) a bagman for the Mafia in Seattle, who has just switched laundries (and why), and that Cornbread is dead (he isn't). There are various versions of who punched who among those who are working for the same political party, and lots of recycled jokes about piles, since both Rizzo and retiring Mayor James H. J. Tate had operations described as "their lobotomies. We call this our hemorrhoid administration." (Mayor Tate, said to have "delusions of mediocrity," was mainly reelected because of Rizzo, who ran his department as "a private army" and was answerable to no one.) And there are endless discussions about Rizzo's youthful case of diabetes, which got him an honorable discharge from the navy in 1939. He explodes when questioned about his war service, and has asked the Navy Department that no information be given about his record—which is now in the Pentagon's file of "prominent persons." Eager reporters keep trying to trace the men who served as Rizzo's shipmates on the U.S.S. *Houston*—in hopes that a few of them can clarify whatever he seeks to hide. But his supporters say that his hysteria about the discharge is merely due to the shame of not having fought "a man's war." The gossiping Philadelphians also tell you where sheets and towels are on sale.

In the Philadelphia evenings I go back to my hotel, where Dutch Schultz is dying on TV and a cop fires shots into a muffler, hyping Lead-Free Amoco, and read Chrisopher Morley's *Kitty Foyle:* "Philly doesn't want to feel things unless they've had a careful okay from yesterday." William Holden and Clifton Webb appear in dog collars, coping with the Chinese; one of them says, "Now they're spreading disease along with their propaganda." Kitty Foyle says, "I suppose Philly is the last place in America where it still matters to be a gentleman." The Warwick Hotel recoils from my Master Charge card, calls my editors, then says accusingly, "They say you're not there." "No, I'm here." Then they call my New York answering service: "They say you're here." "Yes, I know I am." But they insist that the N.Y. phone company has never heard of me: "You have no number." "But you just talked to it." After yards of Pinterish dialogue they announce that I'm here, but since they don't know me, they might have had to lock me out of my room. It makes me happy to say that I would have called the police if they had, and I switch to the Bellevue-Stratford, where the toilet flushes by itself so often—and especially when I'm phoning—that someone kindly suggests that the room is bugged. "Maybe it flushes when the tape is changed." But the Bellevue-Stratford, unlike much of Philadelphia, doesn't seem suspicious of strangers and is willing to let them pay to stay there.

By this time I'm ready to let Philadelphians tell me that they're masochists: some really boast about it. A native dwells delightedly on the subway system: "We're packed into cattle cars by conductors trained in Auschwitz—if we get home alive, we're pleased. A city that can elect Tate twice has to be willing to tolerate *anything*." (Rizzo disclaimed responsibility for safety on the subway; he said that was up to the transit authorities.) Another added, "Philadelphians love to wear the hairshirt and beat themselves," love hearing bad stories about the city, constantly cite the paint-spray amendments to the Schuylkill Expressway billboard—"Philadelphia Isn't as Bad as Philadelphians Say It is/NO, IT'S WORSE"—and seem proud that Lincoln Steffens's phrase, "corrupt and contented," was invented about their town. (In 1903 Steffens discovered that Philadelphia's votes were padded with the names of dead dogs as well as those of small children and imaginary persons. A native told him, "At least you must admit that our machine is the best you have ever seen.") Today you hear lots of bleak bragging about graft and payoffs and deals: "Suppose you wanted to support motherhood or to give City Hall $50,000—they'd still say, 'Now wait, we have to make a deal.' " Some stress that docility, torpor, and indifference are intensely Philadelphian traits, which serve as fertilizer for many seething local problems.

After all the triumphant put-downs, you rather desperately ask what natives like about the city. They talk about intimacy, easy mobility, also a security in the notion that nothing will change—unlike the headlong New York temperament that clamors for changes (and helps to keep New York exhilarating and destructive). But Philadelphians cherish their own territory, and you can quickly appreciate the charm of small, leafy side streets and envy the modest rates for renting or buying homes. In fact the possibility of liking where you live and being able to afford it is astounding to a New Yorker. (How many New Yorkers apologize before letting you into their apartments for the first time, explaining, "My place isn't me.") Since Philadelphia's property taxes are low and it's cheaper to buy than to rent, natives can even afford to embellish their dwellings, paint their front doors, buy trestle tables and embroidered donkey bell covers and wrought iron twisted to their taste, and can actually expect their surroundings to reflect them. When Philadelphians want to offer you something very nice, they take you home; it's also their way of showing why they do like Philadelphia.

The city is run by neighborhoods; natives really have the decentralization which some other cities (think they) want. And it all comes down to possessing your own turf: the discreet liberal watering his own lawn in Society Hill or planting his tulips seems to have much the same feeling as the teen-aged gangs do about their own blocks of the ghetto, where young boys have been killing each other at the rate of 158 in the last four years. (There some graffiti read DTK, meaning Down To Kill, if you set foot in our nabe. Others elaborate: DTKLMF . . . like a mother-fucker.) The old liberals buy guns and Mace and pens with tear gas, and the kids croak one another, especially because the presence of a stranger seems so threatening. (Even the most impeccable outsiders are unwelcome; Richardson Dilworth told me that he was called a carpetbagger when he first ran for mayor in 1947—because he came from Pittsburgh.) Meanwhile unwanted change accelerates: no city I've seen changes so rapidly from block to block, from white prosperity to black poverty to the modest, gleaming lower-middle-income areas, where residents hose their pavements daily, polish their brass, and go up the wall when newcomers don't do the same. The traditions of solidity and serenity continue to amaze a visitor: our battered national landscape reveals few pockets that appear so comfortable or confident.

And Philadelphia is also the most frightened city I've ever seen. Fear in the air: trickling and leaking across sidewalks, under doorsills, between the buttons of many suits, crawling up sleeves. Reasonable persons tell you that they've given up the movies or the ballet, that they mustn't leave home at night. At midday, walking for several blocks behind a severely limping black man who was shabby but not ragged, I noticed the twitches of fright in most of the white faces coming toward him—their eyes flew to the fact that one hand was in his pocket; they clearly imagined a gun. (Since his limp was so bad, I wondered if he was holding onto his wallet.) Sometimes you feel that you're wading in Philadelphian fear: knee-high, waist-deep, finally eye-level fear. Although—as in most cities—a majority of the most serious crimes occur in the ghetto, inflicted by blacks on blacks, many white Philadelphians seem convinced that the youthful gangs are going to carve their giblets out in center city. At moments there seems to be a whiff of voluptuousness in some Philadelphians' dread—perhaps it's more of the local masochism.

The task is to comb out the difference between rational and irrational fear. Just before leaving New York I was prepared for Philadelphia by being held up on my doorstep by a small addict with a chisel. Our conversation—"You're gonna give me all your money!" "*Damn*"—cost me six dollars, but I've had worse for free. All my neighbors said it was my fault for walking home after midnight, hence none were alarmed. During my first three days in Philadelphia, a nine-year-old was shot dead while playing in the street, and a man—whose sixteen-year-old son was killed by a policeman who now faces manslaughter charges—lost an eye defending his own windshield; both were victims of rival gangs. Both were neighborhood crimes, in North Philadelphia, where many citizens are very bitter about the lack of protection. (As one said, "Law and order *only* means keeping black crime from spilling into white neighborhoods.") Although most of the gang killings have been solved, Rizzo and his troops haven't reduced the murders. For him punishment takes a huge priority over prevention. In 1970 he and Mayor Tate rechanneled $400,000 which the City Council had marked for gang control into police overtime and armored police buses. (The city has 93 gangs and about 40 men in the gang control unit.) A popular technique for dealing with gangs occurs when the cops catch a boy outside his turf; they deposit him in a rival gang's area and suggest that he won't get home alive.

∾

So you can slice Philadelphia like a four-layer cake: it's a terrified city, but is supposed to have the lowest crime rate among the ten largest cities in the United States; while some calm citizens repeat that much of the city is quite safe, many have lately questioned the official crime statistics—on the suspicion that adequate figures aren't given. According to the FBI, Philadelphia rose from 126th to 58th place among all U.S. cities in the realm of major crimes during Rizzo's years as commissioner (1967–1970). Concerned Philadelphians emphasize that despite the folklore, Rizzo has not been effective when it comes to reducing crime. Yet you also hear: "Frank's kept the lid on and kept *them* in their place." Some Philadelphians, including many cops, refer to the ghetto as "the jungle," and insist that "they" drum on cars and garbage cans whenever a stranger comes near: a percussion that no one I met had ever heard. Those who know North Philadelphia well stress the general passivity—even the conservatism—of its majority. The Panther convention of 1970 drew most of its leadership from other parts of the country.

With all these contradictions afoot, Rizzo and Mayor Tate have been deft at manipulating the fears of all kinds of Philadelphians. This city is the place to study the political use of fear, the value of scare tactics. In 1969 Rizzo said,

"Look at the city after dark. Grown men walking down the middle of the street. Women afraid to venture out of their homes. You leave your children out at night, you're frightened to death until they come home." In 1970 he evoked Philadelphia as a vast combat zone: "It's exactly what it is . . . a war. Almost as severe as the war that's going on in Vietnam. We've run a comparison a couple of weekends in our city against the casualties in Vietnam. And, surprisingly, we had more homicides and deaths and casualties than they did in Vietnam."

Aside from those who live in rugged neighborhoods, it's Rizzo's liberal supporters who are the most intriguing. Many consider him a practical (not an admirable) choice: "Frank's the man for the times. Normally I wouldn't vote for him, but kids are breaking windshields." These can be the same people who want an end to the war, support equal opportunities, study ecology. One said pensively, "Philadelphia used to have good race relations: due to the Quaker tradition of tolerance. The whites were content to be on the top, and the blacks were content to be on the bottom." He referred to the "hopelessness" of trying to educate some black children: "Maybe we should do what they do in Spain: let kids drop out at eight or nine, since they're uneducable."

Suddenly you realize that visiting Philadelphia means time-traveling: you're back in the Fifties, even racially and socially, when upper-middle-class whites talk about self-improvement for black or poor people, and shy, formal, middle-aged men peer bleakly down women's dresses while making awkward cocktail conversation. Few in Philadelphia seem to have discovered that the word liberal isn't lovely anymore, or that it's come to mean hypocrite—when it doesn't mean Communist. Those who want to stop gang wars or expand education are still talking about charter reform. Alvin Echols, director of the North City Congress, a community action group, observed that most liberals are still hung up on the notion of a fair chance, assuming that if people work hard and save, they'll earn well—whereas, "You're always going to have poor people; you mustn't tell them that they'll never be poor again." As one who believes in supplementary payments to those who work but can't ever earn enough, as well as direct incomes for those who can't get jobs, he agrees that this defies the whole American ethic: that effort's certain to put you ahead. Hence "giving direct dollars will upset the liberal bag." Meanwhile "Liberals think, 'Well, a *little* repression right now wouldn't be too bad,'" since Rizzo is focusing on the white fear of black militancy and the black hatred of white recalcitrance." There are also ex-liberals, some of whom are Jewish; they vibrate easily to the anti-Semitic statements of young blacks. You also feel that some in Philadelphia are withholding their full opinions. Perhaps women with glass fingernails and Pucci dresses, wearing peace buttons and crying "Right on!" for Rizzo's opponents, may finally be willing to sacrifice civil liberties in order to think they can walk down the street.

~

Outgoing Mayor Tate, who naturally backed Rizzo, may be one of the most unpopular mayors in the U.S.; "incompetent old-time party hack" is one of the kindest terms you hear applied to him. Elected in 1962, Tate is said to have been "sucked to the top by the vacuum"—a seasoned Philadelphia joke. However, from 1951 to 1962, Philadelphia had a reform government under Democratic Mayors Joseph Clark and Richardson Dilworth. Many Philadelphians explain Tate's election as part of the inevitable political cycle; they feel the reform movement had run its course and that the reformers lacked professional political staying power. As the likeliest supporters for liberal government moved in greater numbers to Philadelphia's suburbs, the city became more and more the province of conservative working people who voted for Tate or Rizzo.

While kids turned the *z*'s in Rizzo's name into swastikas, and revived old Goldwater rhymes—"In your guts you know he's nuts"—some of his most dedicated opponents stressed that his personality was less important than the likelihood that he would perpetuate the Tate machine. Also many mused on the fact that a man from the extreme right of the Republican party would represent the Democrats.

Black Philadelphians who detest Rizzo agree that he's not anti-black—despite his often overheard remarks about niggers, and his famous cry of "Get their black asses!" to his men when black high school students demonstrated outside the Board of Education on November 17, 1967. (Heard on TV and by many individuals, the blackness of the asses has often been denied, and it's said that the TV prints were destroyed.) Witnesses stressed that the demo was disorderly but under control and that the cops themselves were restrained until Rizzo appeared and whipped up the police. Richardson Dilworth charged that the police "provoked" the rampage that followed, which scattered students all over the city, where they did beat up some whites. A few weeks later a group of white South Philadelphian housewives demonstrated in the same place, to protest busing; they pushed and tore the clothes of some school board aides, while the cops stood by and did nothing.

Despite Rizzo's 1967 statement on black power—"The only thing they understand is force, and they have to be crushed before they destroy the community"—one black writer said, "No, Rizzo's not a racist—he's a sadist." Although the police are at their fiercest in the ghetto, many Philadelphians repeat that Rizzo has been just as ready to savage whites as blacks. In 1957, when he was still a captain, he blinded a white Italian in one eye and fractured his jaw with a nightstick—for not moving his car at Rizzo's request. The case is often mentioned as proof that Rizzo treats all races equally.

Creeps, kooks, liberals, phonies, fags, ultraliberals, lefties, hoodlums, and bums—Rizzo's morality dictates that he must save his city from the shaggy perverts whose politics or culture spread like dandruff. In 1959, when he was captain, his raids on some six new coffeehouses inspired cops to rip Vivaldi off the hi-fis, drag away bearded chess players and espresso-heads, and book them at the police station. Although Rizzo insisted that drugs and homosexual solicitation were flourishing in these dens of poetry reading, not a single conviction resulted. Still, it was Rizzo's obsession that the coffeehouses thrived on immoral profits, since they made so little money. (He is frantic on the subject of homosexuals; almost anyone he dislikes gets called a fag.) Richardson Dilworth, who was then mayor, says in retrospect that those who lived nearby were indeed alarmed by the coffeehouses—since Philadelphia had never had an equivalent to Greenwich Village—and that many were outraged by the intrusion into their own neighborhoods. In 1969 Rizzo told the owner of the Electric Factory, Philadelphia's first rock club, "You brought these people to Philadelphia and you're going to pay for it. I'm gonna make a parking lot out of this place." Precisely one patron in over 100,000 was convicted on a narcotics charge. After terrorizing visitors with onslaughts of cops, Rizzo had the Factory closed because of "the rise and fall of sounds."

Known as a puritan—"I never saw my mother or father without their clothes on. My children never saw me without mine on. What are these kooks trying to do?"—Rizzo still felt free to call his primary opponent Bill Green "a fucking bum" in front of reporters, and to joke winsomely about the photographs which show his nightstick rising out of (or "protruding from" or "jammed into") his cummerbund. Many Philadelphians call it the phantom phallus. But his morality demanded that the Playboy Club mustn't open in Philadelphia—although many observed that the bar investments of Rizzo's friend Frank Palumbo would have suffered from the Playboy Club's competition, as well as some of the profits to Palumbo's associates. For years Palumbo supplied enormous organizational help to the Democrats in South Philadelphia, hence most politicians have been cautious with him.

The clip joints along Locust Street, which Rizzo raided enthusiastically when he was a captain, have been thriving since he was appointed commissioner. Philadelphians believe that most of these bars are owned by the local Cosa Nostra, which Rizzo appears to tolerate. Since the bars are distinguished for prostitution, watered drinks, serving minors, and other violations of the liquor code, many natives suspect payoffs at the lower levels plus accommodation at the top. Some forty to fifty policemen are quietly fired each year for graft, but it's assumed that many cops earn well on the side. (It's also said that prostitution doesn't perturb Rizzo, although he thinks that most women should stay home and bake.) Yet his morality can sometimes peak to a passion that starts him talking in the third person. "Ask Frank Rizzo if he's ever hit anyone with a pipe to take his money. Never did that. Ask Frank Rizzo if he ever took a gun and shot someone else . . . to rob him. Never did that. Ask Frank Rizzo if he ever burglarized someone else's home . . . or took someone else's belongings, that didn't belong to him. Never did that. So if this is the standard that we're going to measure any individual by, I say that's the proper standard."

The moralist has files on some eighteen hundred persons he disapproves of; reporters have heard him repeat, "Get me their weakness" to detectives, who then research a man's tendency toward booze, women, drugs, fags, peace demos, or past charges. (A few young men were arrested for "conspiring to commit litter"—putting up posters which criticized the police.) After the 1967 school board explosion, he told the Board of Education, "I have a file on every one of you," and also boasted to the press that he had "something on" all the other candidates running against him in the 1971 primaries.

Rizzo's campaign manager, Albert Gaudiosi, who has defined Rizzo as "a big cuddly bear," wrote a series of pieces with Bayard Brunt called "The New Revolutionaries" while Gaudiosi was still at the *Evening Bulletin*. Despite the searing implications that "fragmented" Marxist groups were preparing to bring the country to its knees, the revelations were modest, reporting that one *Philadelphia Free Press* staffer "is very domineering . . . and her 'bag' is opposing male chauvinism"—and that her three-year-old son "has been known to shout obscenities and epithets at the police." In the "Pepperpot" section of *Philadelphia* magazine, an editor questioned whether Brunt and Gaudiosi had ever interviewed a single "revolutionary," adding, "the core of the information obviously came from the files of the Philadelphia Police Department and the FBI." Rizzo has denied this. But as a result of the series, the *Free Press* was closed. All in all there's an extra tang of fear in Philadelphia, even among very moderate dissenters: fear of the police. Some of Rizzo's power rests on "the *uncertainty* of what he'll do": no one knows when or if he might be followed, suddenly arrested for an unpaid parking ticket, beaten, charged with resisting an officer, or whether drugs might be "found on his premises."

~

As the ACLU has noted, Rizzo "has a long history of publicly accusing organizations of criminal activities, but failing to produce evidence that results in convictions." Some dud stories received huge initial coverage, although charges later had to be abandoned and sometimes no one was even brought to trial. The ACLU's report added, "The media bear a heavy brunt of the blame for playing the police game." But the newspapers are understandably reluctant to expose these fluff-outs, since such an admission would reveal their own distortions.

On November 30, 1970 Philadelphians read about a plot to kidnap Rizzo and hold him as a hostage for Angela Davis—with the alternate possibility of using him for "target practice" by black militants. Bombings of two police buildings were supposed to bracket these events. A "People's Liberation Army" was held responsible, and the press coverage was meaty.

In April 1971 a very different kind of story was released. An Alaskan-born Asian called Sulieman, who said he was an agent sent by Mao and claimed that he had fought with Che and with the NLF in Vietnam, had conned a group of young blacks into believing that the U.S. government had a plan to provoke ghetto riots and to put black people into concentration camps and to exterminate them. (Most of the revolutionary warriors of November were characterized by the *Bulletin* in April as "not militant . . . ordinary wage-earners . . . middle class types.") Sulieman persuaded his young listeners that they must prepare to defend "the helpless people of the ghettos" against "the King Alfred Plan," which he said Chinese Communists had stolen from Washington. Arms were collected and suddenly two members of the group were shot dead because Sulieman decided that they'd betrayed him. Over a month later, another member discovered that the King Alfred Plan was lifted from page 306 of the novel *The Man Who Cried I Am* by John A. Williams (published by Little, Brown), and he told the FBI about Sulieman, who had already disappeared. In the long run the Angela Davis kidnap plot was discounted as "wild talk" of Sulieman's, even by the police who investigated the case. But the public mainly remembered the alleged threats to Rizzo. The national atmosphere, which suggests to impoverished blacks that whites may suddenly overwhelm them, and which made Sulieman's manipulations possible, wasn't really acknowledged. One of Sulieman's eighteen-year-old followers later said that Sulieman's style was hypnotic, and added, "He played on all our fears." In Philadelphia you feel that dangerous fantasies or accusations can be accepted with more ease than in some other towns—whether they come from gifted con artists or from the police.

~

The Philadelphia Police Department is acknowledged as one of the most efficient in the country. Their communications, mobility, and command systems enable them to respond to emergencies far more quickly than the police in most other cities. Although Rizzo absorbs the credit, many Philadelphians say that it should go to his predecessor, Howard Leary, who initiated the rapid communications. (Leary headed New York's Police Department from 1966 to 1970.) Rizzo despised Leary's restrained methods, and often called him "a weakling." Newsmen reminisce about the time when Rizzo was chasing a boy and Leary intervened—and got socked by Rizzo. Rizzo told the press it was an accident.

Even Rizzo's critics agree that he is a quick learner. For example, he has not allowed his men to freely maul demonstrators since the 1967 outbreak at the Board of Education. But some Philadelphians are increasingly worried about police actions against individuals—especially against any black persons found walking after sundown in prosperous white neighborhoods. The phrase "unnecessary shooting" recurs. Rizzo's own favorite unit is the highway patrol, known as "The Boots"; clad in shiny black leather jackets and crushed hats, they're assigned to holdups and shootings. They're also the shock troops who ignite much community outrage. "Even the other police hate them," said an expert.

Rizzo loves arriving at the scene of action—the press constantly repeats "Rizzo was there"—and has been photographed dismantling a bomb with his bare hands. But he skirts the issue of organized crime in Philadelphia, and has said that Angelo Bruno, who is considered to be the head of the local Cosa Nostra, has been properly questioned and has denied ever bribing a cop. One student of Philadelphia rackets mused, "We have a very peculiar Mafia here—like the rest of Philly, it's dull." Bruno doesn't believe in violence, and there hasn't been a gang killing in Philadelphia for years; he prefers legitimate business. Bruno's interests include John's Vending Machine Co., and his wife owns the Miami Pest Control Co., plus a couple of other outfits in Florida. Rumors concerning Bruno's other holdings could make a book the length of *The Sot-Weed Factor,* but the complexities of nailing him down are distilled by this excerpt from the Philadelphia Police Department's interrogation of Bruno in 1957:

Q.: Tell us how much money you made last year from the ironing board cover business?

A.: What?

Q.: Ironing board covers.

A.: I don't even know what you're talking about, chief.

Q.: You know what we're talking about.

A.: Ironing boards?

Q.: The cover a woman uses to cover an ironing board when she irons.

A.: I don't know what you're talking about, chief. Are you serious?

Q.: Yes, we are serious.

A.: Do you mean something else or do you really mean ironing board covers?

Q.: Ironing board covers.

A.: That's a new one. Am I supposed to be in that business?

Q.: You tell us.

Q.: I told you we are not particularly interested in . . . gambling and any income tax . . .

A.: I know that.

Q.: We are interested in major crime. We are interested in homicide.

A.: That's out of my line.

Some years later it appeared that heavy investigations of the Mafia were out of the police department's line; what the *New York Times* calls "reputed rackets chiefs" have gone generally unmolested. While Philadelphia's heroin scene isn't as ferocious as New York's—"But just give us another six months"— many natives have been staggered by Rizzo's observation that drug traffic isn't connected with organized crime, and that drugs haven't really increased in Philadelphia.

Although policemen pursue grass users and small-time peddlers, and are said to hassle addicts outside clinics, there are few arrests of professional suppliers or dealers. At 17th Street and Norris, quite close to the local police station—in an area saturated with police cars—pushers operated freely until the *Bulletin* published pictures of their transactions; only then did the police make arrests. As many say, the police reflect Rizzo's indifference toward the problem: "*Either* he doesn't give a damn, *or* the cops are paid off and he doesn't want to upset them. But you have to hold him responsible: because the cops take their coloration from the top, as they do in any city." (Rizzo complains that "soft" judges should be blamed for the narcotics trade, and he has threatened to campaign against certain judges before elections.) Witnesses say some Philadelphia bars are supported by drugs—that you can sip a beer and buy stuff under the counter—and that much of the numbers profit now goes into drugs. Yet some shapes of public tolerance persist; one moderate Rizzo supporter said, "Maybe heroin isn't that bad: it might keep them quiet. In a permissive society, you give everyone what they want, and perhaps it'll keep them off each other's throats."

⌐∽

Famous for fresh shirts and for redying his hair once a year, Rizzo usually sits with his back to the wall, like someone expecting to be shot. His hands often open and close while he talks. Ham and beef are mentioned when his fists, face, or torso are described. During the Democratic primaries, which he won with a 40 percent plurality, he was about as available for interviews as Huey P. Newton was after his release from jail. As a primary candidate Rizzo made few statements beyond observing that lots of air pollution comes from the suburbs, not just from cities. But he used to shower editors and reporters with wallets and police lieutenants' badges, and take his favorites, like Walter Annenberg, for rides. (Since most fledgling reporters in Philadelphia begin by covering the police, favors win over many at the beginning of their careers.) He made it easy for his friends in the press to get gun permits quickly—"You have a problem? Just come in"—although he fought hard for gun control a few years ago, with the implication that students would arm themselves. Rizzo has a habit of ringing reporters and asking, "Is it going to be a good story or a bad story?" At times he practically assaulted those who were questioning him—springing up behind his desk and jabbing his finger at their chests, turning maroon while yelling about his own integrity. He responds to tape recorders the way Dracula responds to the cross, and often tries to retract some of his wildest statements or actions. In 1970, after the celebrated stripping of the Panthers, the assistant DA told the press that the Panthers had stripped themselves—"to have a case against the police."

When Rizzo learned that a *Daily News* reporter was consulting some of his critics, as well as his admirers, for a series of articles, Rizzo demanded to know why he was talking to "those creeps." The reporter replied that he wished to be fair to all sides. Rizzo said, "Fuck this fair bullshit. If you were to find yourself in jail, I'd be more than fair. I'd violate my oath and let you out." The management at the *Bulletin* has always been tender of Rizzo; as long as Annenberg owned the *News* and the *Inquirer*, there were few anti-Rizzo stories. Now, although all three papers have run unflattering pieces and editorials about him, their coverage is still mild. Some reporters complain that references to Rizzo have been constantly cut from their columns and that they've been taken off assignments that would concern him or transferred to harmless topics. Even so, some of his fans were indignant when a couple of papers ran photos which rather resembled Mussolini. The intimacy of Philadelphia seems to feed inertia: some reporters don't want to raise dust, let alone rake muck, or to ask questions that would disturb him. Others are just intimidated. But he has been very pleased with a few articles which actually put him down—since he was proud that they made him sound tough.

Hindsight: Throughout Rizzo's eight years as mayor, many of his supporters and opponents expected him to become a national figure: a senator or a governor who would inherit George Wallace's constituency. But after he took office, the press published many articles that criticized him. During his two terms, Rizzo—charged with trying to bribe a colleague—failed a lie detector test, employed a secret police squad to investigate his political adversaries, bought a $400,000 house on a $40,000-a-year salary, and permitted the offices of the *Inquirer* to be blockaded because he was enraged by a satirical column about him (the staff couldn't enter the building and the paper did not function for ten hours). Crime rates rose and the city came close to bankruptcy.

More than 200,000 people signed a petition demanding a special election to remove Rizzo from office in 1976, but his board of elections declared that many of the signatures were invalid. Under President Jimmy Carter, the Justice Department filed a most unusual lawsuit accusing the Philadelphia police department of violence, racism, extreme brutality, and many illegalities while Rizzo was police commissioner. It was the first federal suit against a whole police force and was signed by Attorney General Griffin Bell. Eager for a third term and predicting his "greatest victory," Rizzo urged Philadelphians to "Vote White" in 1978. But they voted overwhelmingly against changing the city charter to allow him to run immediately after his second term. In 1987 he became a Republican candidate for mayor and was defeated by incumbent W. Wilson Goode, the city's first black mayor.

Angelo Bruno, known as "the docile don," was shot dead in 1980, reportedly because he didn't permit his crime family much involvement in the drug trade or to fight over the turf of New York gangsters at a gambling casino in Atlantic City; younger mobsters were determined to seize those profits. Killings soared among competing criminals, and Rizzo's adherents claimed that he would have curbed the mob if he were still mayor; his critics said he had been permissive toward the Philadelphia Cosa Nostra since the Sixties.

Rizzo died of a sudden heart attack at the age of seventy, just a few months after winning a Republican mayoral primary in 1991. The political pundits of his city doubted that he would be re-elected. But thousands lined the streets to watch his funeral procession circling City Hall, and his hearse was decorated with red carnations reading "Frank Forever."

The John Birch Society
The 9th New England Rally for God, Family and Country July 1971

Blue flames bursting through the darkness, jouncing to the beat of "Hey, Look Me Over": held high over waiters' heads, fifty bombs of baked Alaska speed to our tables while everybody cheers. When the lights go on, the snowy crewcut on my right says, "Pass the Rockefeller cream." He explains that the food business is part of the Conspiracy: the communists are weakening and starving our bodies so that we'll knuckle under more easily. That filthy socialist Rockefeller controls the milk industry, and he uses that foundation of his to research formulas for polluting dairy products. "Not *poison*," he grunts, holding up the cream, "*Just weak*." We compare our tastes in salads. It's easy to talk with Birchers and their friends: you befoul Nelson Rockefeller, praise watercress and radishes, agree that Washington's gone bananas, and curse inflation. The doctor across the table repeats, "Nixon should be tried for treason." Here in the Boston Statler-Hilton's ballroom, when the swing band plays each state's song. Ohioans or Rhode Islanders or Virginians whip to their feet and whirl their yellow napkins in wide circles at the ceiling (as usual, most New Yorkers fudge that line about "Me and Mamie O'Rourke" from "East Side, West Side"). After "Dixie," the rebel yell sounds very much like the cry of the Algerian women or the Yip whoop—perhaps because most larynxes are withered or worn.

For five days I've been clutching my collarbone to pledge allegiance and jumping up to sing the national anthem again and again, or bowing my head for benedictions. (The only way to report on the John Birch Society is to be invisible and follow the crowd.) Hence it's soothing to sit still and hear Art Smith sing "The Hawk and the Dove"—"They're two different birds, / They'll never make love"—and the evening's most popular song, "Accentuate the Positive," which makes me hope for "Celery Stalks at Midnight" or "Fry Me Cookie with a Can of Lard." But we never get beyond "Don't mess with Mister in between." At Smith's request, we all hold hands around the table while he sings "A Closer Walk with Thee." There are little yuks about sensitivity training, which the Birchers deplore, and a murmur of distress when he says that a song was inspired by Plato ("That homo, Socrates"), but Smith is far better received than Rudy Vallee, who doesn't seem to understand his audience. He carries a plumber's friend—"Is he going to clean up the cesspool?"—tells dozens of drunk-jokes, ("After the Taj Mahal cocktail, ya won't know what got India"), shocks his listeners by saying that he campaigned for Nixon, and confuses them with "The Whiffenpoof Song" and "Winchester Cathedral."

Therefore my table is grateful when conversation can be resumed. Still, the man on my left maintains a nervy silence, aside from saying that he's heard there are a lot of patriots in Florida. (Some Birchers immediately tell you that they're members, while others never do—they just talk about patriots.) The rather charming elderly Bostonian describes how she tried to prevent a college scholarship from being given to the son of an Italian workman in her family's granite business. "His father has $187 take-home pay a week. For only five people! Scholarship indeed." So she gave the boy a bad reference. The old man beside me asserts that some public figure will be assassinated this year: the communists—in league with part of the establishment—will kill someone *in order* to make the public clamor for gun control. Then everyone will have to register their guns, and "they'll know who and where we are." The sole point of the assassination will be the identification of the Birchers, since they're such a threat to the Conspiracy. Hawaii may be used as a refuge for "some of the big boys—to sit it out until the shooting war is over."

The Conspiracy may sound like a boutique to you, but it's plasma to the

Birchers. Basically much of the U.S. federal government and the rich are plotting to bring about world government, which will eventually mean communism—which has *always* been financed by "the international bankers." In a wonderful lecture by G. Edward Griffin, slides and diagrams of triangles and arrows and circles show how the Conspiracy learned its techniques from the 18th-century Freemasons of Europe. Those at the center control the dupes or lackeys in the outer rings. After references to the Warburgs and the Rothschilds, accompanied by drawings of dusky, shifty-eyed men whispering behind their hands, I thought the Anti-Defamation League would have some fresh ammunition. However, "*not* all international bankers are Jewish." Our politicians have had a secret agreement with the "private banking dynasties," hence "the total control of the nation's money fell into private hands." Suddenly the name of RUSKIN! flashed across the screen. Ruskin's "ruling class ideas" influenced Cecil Rhodes, whose secret society was inherited by Lord Alfred Milner. In the U.S. this pattern is imitated by the Council on Foreign Relations, which is a front for J. P. Morgan and Co. While the Council isn't the absolute center of the Conspiracy, it "governs the country" through its control of education and the media. But some of the Council's own members don't realize that it's a front.

Those who plan a "world superstate" pay and incite left-wing groups to start confrontations—so that the terrified public will accept a police state, martial rule, and a larger government. In fact world government will be offered as the only alternative to violence. The Birchers don't seem much alarmed by the New Left, since it's just a tool of the establishment—which "needs chaos and crime in the streets and the threat of nuclear war."

The Strawberry Statement was cited as an example of "an intelligent programmed mind thinking it's acting against the establishment." Stokely Carmichael was respectfully quoted as saying that the Morgan Guaranty Trust and the Chase Bank "own most of the mortgages in Harlem," and Griffin suggested that Carmichael was expelled from SNCC and the Panthers because he knew "the truth." (The Birchers would loathe those rumors about Carmichael being a CIA agent.) So "the establishment publicly condemns but privately supports the revolution." And the communists are secretly encouraged because the Conspiracy "needs a huge foe." (My neighbor crooned the Birch bumper slogan: "Get the U.S. out of the UN and the UN out of the U.S.") Griffin urged his audience to "challenge the establishment's candidates," and "to return government to the hands of the people." He added, "Is it possible that the communist and capitalist conspiracies have one more inner circle? We don't know, but it seems likely." My neighbor sighed, "One ball of wax." Griffin concluded by quoting Looney Tunes, "That's all, folks!"

During long days of staring at liver spots on the backs of bald heads, and wondering where the men found those old seersucker jackets of the Fifties, I unwound by chatting with a very pleasant judo instructor in the hotel's basement, where he taught self-defense to children and adults throughout the rally. Small Birchers tumbled in cartwheels around his knees while he explained to me that it takes only three pounds of pressure to break someone's finger. Few at the rally looked younger than fifty; a trickle of teen-agers had clearly been brought by their parents. They had discussions about "whether rock music is part of the Conspiracy," and practiced singing "Gobless America" for the final dinner.

Quite a few Birchers dozed or took little naps as soon as the speeches began; others applauded at the wrong moments and were gently reproached by the speakers. With nine hours of lectures a day, many seemed quite exhausted and they wandered off to the exhibition halls where booths were staffed by sympathetic organizations. (The rally is said to be sponsored by "a coalition" of conservative groups, but the Boston press sets it firmly in Birchdom.) The bazaar of Birch-related products ranged from alfalfa sprouts and little dishes of seeds, which you should grow and can to become SHELF-SUFFICIENT—as riots, pollution, and strikes increase, you won't be able to leave your house and the supermarkets will be empty—to rhinestone flag pins or an LP on "The Child Seducers" narrated by John Carradine, pamphlets on "Freedom's Judas-Goat" (Fulbright, sometimes called Fooldull), bumper stickers—MY GOD IS ALIVE, SORRY ABOUT YOURS; SHOOT LOOTERS; SEE AMERICA FIRST, IT'S A RIOT!—or Orwell's *Animal Farm,* a great favorite of the Birchers.

Spooning up wet cold beans and apple mush dispensed by the Hippocrates Health Society, you could watch Devin-Adair Garrity presiding benignly over Devin-Adair books, while Taylor Caldwell autographed her latest, or read the riveting hand-outs on devil worship in America. At the Birch Society's own tables, *Teddy Bare,* a rightwing analysis of Chappaquiddick, was this year's best seller. The usual Birch front groups offered their regular literature: TACT (Truth About Civil Turmoil), which connects black groups with the communists; TRAIN (To Restore American Independence Now), which belts the UN and the peacemongers; SYLP (Support Your Local Police); and MOTOREDE (The Movement to Restore Decency), which fights sex education, birth control, and abortion. These organizations recruit citizens who may not realize that they're halfway into the Birch Society. There wasn't much evidence of SHAME (Stop Helping America's Marxist Enemies). They recommend boycotting stores which sell Polish hams, Czech toys, also Camel, Winston, and Salem cigarettes—which are supposed to be made with Yugoslavian tobacco. In the past SHAME has intimidated even Sears Roebuck, Woolworth, and Kresge out of selling products from East Europe.

You can easily predict what Birchers hate: disarmament, socialized medicine, busing, programs to aid Appalachia, the *New York Times,* taxes, John Dewey (who is still being "exposed"), and of course any Kennedy. Throughout we were swimming in Chappaquiddick jokes: "Teddyboy laid down his friends for his life"; the races run by the Kennedys include "the race to get out of a submerged automobile"; the Democrats, who will definitely nominate him, "can swallow a bridge or two"; "Some condemned Teddy for wearing his neck brace to the Kopechne funeral. But he needed it: to hold his head up." (These are in keeping with the Birchers' old gags about JFK's funeral: "Jackie got a Jack-in-the-box.") Only Pat Nixon escaped: "Isn't it nice to have a *lady* in the White House again." (Timid applause.) Certain names are magic: Bernadette Devlin, "who won't know the *color* of her child—black, white, or Red," Jane Fonda, Walter Lippmann. But only Sammy Davis, Jr., got hissed.

At other moments, when the Birchers repeat: the government's lying to us! the media distorts! public schools are disintegrating, the establishment is exploiting us all . . . you wonder if you ever left home. The Birchers are fascinating because they're half right on some points, also because they're fueled by a period in which it's often hard to know what's true or crazy. They dislike the CIA, the AMA, the National Council of Churches, and "capitalists"—meaning "rich socialists" who don't practice free enterprise. They're not a bit fond of John Mitchell, and even Agnew (who was hardly mentioned) is understood to be a "phony conservative"—a front for the left-wing government we actually have. As for the Silent Majority, it "never saved any nation," and it stood back while Jesus was crucified: "the Silent Majority is yellow and always has been."

It's beguiling to hear the Birchers use certain phrases when they're obviously innocent of the source: the AMA and other medical organizations which deny individuals their rights are "*not* part of the *solution*, but part of the *problem*"; what the U.S. needs is "people power"; those who are ruining America should be lined "*up against the wall*" (before a firing squad.) At times I felt as though I was again covering the Panther conventions of the last two years.

The Birchers naturally uphold the Vietnam war—but they don't love it. Robert Scott, the retired brigadier general, author of *God Is My Co-Pilot* and its recent sequel, *God Is Still My Co-Pilot*, survivor of 388 combat missions in World War II, mentioned that Douglas MacArthur and others advised against a land war in Vietnam, and added, "then we sent our sons away to do the dirtiest job in the world." Lecturing on "The Poison of 'Peace,'" he said that "our carefully planned failures" were conceived by "very intelligent men"; again, they're part of the Conspiracy "to unite with Soviet Russia." (Birchers refer to Russia much oftener than to China.) God willed us to have the atomic bomb—not only to win World War II, but for peacekeeping. However we've been sold out by the Conspiracy. Scott blamed the military's drug problem— "if there is one"—on letting the war "get boring." Also, "the uniform has lost its glamour." Proudly he said, "I was as much a murderer as ten Calleys." But his home town gave him a hero's parade and even rented a water buffalo— "at great expense"—for him to ride on.

The Birchers cherish their weapons for self-defense: "Take up a relevant sport—target practice." Although the speakers weren't inciteful, a couple of men in the audience chuckled over the possibility that Mike Mansfield might get shot during the next hunting season in Montana: "He better stay out of the woods." Patriotism may indeed mean risking life. But the U.S. itself is "underarmed." William McBirnie, the executive director of "the Voice of Americanism," urged his audience to press their congressmen for the rapid development of "exotic weapons," such as more bacteriological warfare and the neutron bomb, which is "destructive to human tissue," but leaves most buildings standing. It removes people, not cities, and "doesn't make rubble out of the land."

Nixon? Some were hopeful at his election, but he's now despised as "the liberal he always was." And "trading LBJ for Nixon is sort of like getting custody of your ex-wife's parents." Nixon was used by the Conspiracy during the Hiss case, when "only *one* communist was exposed, and the public was placated." After many sneers at Keynes' homosexuality, plus references to Keynes's "*dear* friend, FDR," it was stressed that "Franklin Delano Nixon" has finally "confessed that he's a Keynesian—though that doesn't mean he's a homosexual." Nixon, like the CIA—and its employee Daniel Ellsberg—feeds the Conspiracy. "Let's fly above those silly Pentagon Papers"—which were leaked by the government to make the public demand peace, which means defeat.

Birch buffs say that many who embraced the Conspiracy theory used to be openly anti-Semitic, despite Robert Welch's efforts to keep racism at bay. (Welch has written that anti-Semitism is a weapon of the communists. Others have claimed that the Birch Society has been plagued by "anti-Semitic infiltrators.") So most Birchers are extremely cautious now. They even produced a couple of black speakers. One, named Charles E. Smith, who edits and publishes the *Voice of Watts,* explained that employers who wouldn't hire blacks were "sitting on the boards of the NAACP and the Urban League"; the same people "were making the problem and financing the protest." Later I questioned him during a whispery rap session in the hall, while square dancers in mammoth crinolines thundered by. He confirmed that "colored people" and whites can get along—it's only "planned class warfare that makes them fight." He referred to "those Hollywood movies that make colored people look dumb—and on the boards of those movie companies, you'll find the NAACP and the Urban League." In fact "civil rights leaders" really deprive other blacks of their rights.

The square dance caller shouted "Do-si-do!" The black Bircher began to weave a wild parallel between the United States and medieval Europe: "See, the squires finked on their own families, to get themselves up the ladder—"

"Allemande left!"

"And the fiefs—"

"Swing your partner!"

"What's Queen Elizabeth ever done against the communists? Nothing. They help to keep her in power."

"Do-si-do!"

"Shoot a leader—like Joe Columbo or Martin Luther King—and you solidify the people. They think there's a plot against them—so they're ready to fight other races."

"Now I want to see a graaaaannnd chaaaaaaiinn."

At a reception for some hoop-skirted women, who'd dressed themselves and a collection of dolls in the style of Godey's Ladies, an exercise which was somehow plugged into "the priceless heritage of being an American woman," it was repeated that "the Alabama Negroes love Governor Wallace." The Birchers paid tribute to "predominantly Negro" colleges; Daniel Payne College is one of the few in America "that's never had any violence on campus." Moreover the aim of integrated schools is "*not* to educate Negroes but to keep whites ignorant." The "purpose of keeping people ignorant is to make them more malleable, easier to lead."

Beneath the emblem of a broken hammer and sickle, superimposed by a sword-tipped cross and flag, speech after speech confirmed the Birchers' beliefs. "The poor of America own more cars than *all* the people in Russia." Hence "Mostly, poverty is a state of mind. . . . Money and education cannot end poverty." Higher education is "the most overrated thing since Jackie Kennedy." (Cheers.) There is no population explosion, so there's no excuse for birth control; also, "Have you noticed that those who support abortion are against capital punishment?" Sex education is designed simply to distract children from learning anything else. Students take drugs "because someone wanted it that way, and industriously promoted it." All drug users should be jailed. This may be the age of Aquarius, but the water in that sign "isn't being used for purification, but for *brainwashing* our youth." Modern women are "immodest and unclean." The churches could have prevented the communist takeover; instead they promoted it. And the "pagan" peace symbol is an inverted crucifix, designed by Nero, and was originally used for crucifying St. Peter and others upside-down. It has also been identified as "the witches foot" of the Middle Ages and "a symbol of the anti-Christ" used by Satanists. Throughout "You can't play down the possibility that the same group may be running the capitalists and the communists."

Although "We depend on the press for information as a child depends on its mother's breast for milk," all publications which aren't produced by the Birch Society are toxic. One white reporter was forced to leave the rally when he tried to cover it for the *Boston Herald Traveler,* and was threatened with "personal assault" if he returned. A black cameraman who had the Society's permission to film the rally for a Boston TV station was kicked, kneed, and carried out by a group of men who didn't want their pictures taken. He reported that one of his thirty or forty attackers said he hit him "because I am a patriot."

The Birchers are anarchists—if only they knew it. They detest most professional politicians, except for Wallace, and they don't seem to like any form of government. "Our authority is *not* the President, but the Constitution . . . anyone who sabotages the Constitution should be resisted"—like Richard Nixon. The audience loved a story from ancient Greece: "When a senator made a proposal, he stood on a box with a rope around his neck. If the people liked the proposal, they took away the rope. If they didn't, they kicked away the box." Huge applause.

Any kind of liberal should be flattered to learn that the Conspiracy is brilliantly organized, and that its members have been very well "*trained.*" The world is laced with corridors and wings: FDR was "waiting in the corridor"; communists "always have a student waiting in the wings." But the Birchers' strength springs from their knowledge: again and again speakers told them: You *know* so much, you're the only ones who know what's going on in this country. Hence their sense of superiority. Certain as any astrologer that he knows what lies ahead, the Bircher feels a titanic responsibility: to tell others about the Conspiracy. "It's *our duty* to inform them, and to *name* the culprits."

There's great emphasis on organizing in your own community to fight the local Job Corps or the school board or the library or fluoridation, or to harry the sponsors of TV and radio stations who finance unpatriotic programs. Speakers stress that "We have *only fourteen months* in which to do something for America" (convince students to vote against Ted Kennedy); "we have *only thirty-six months*" before the Russians "force a confrontation in the Middle East." Yet they know that many Americans will ignore or try to suppress them. "If there's a murderer *crawling* into your bedroom at night, and your dog barks in the yard, you have two problems: discomfort at being awakened"—and the suspicion that "something's wrong with the dog." But if you shoot the dog, you've lost your protection from the murderer. And that's how the spiritual watchdogs of the Birch Society feel they're treated today.

Aside from the ego biscuits, part of the Society's spell may be cast by the vagueness and the rambling contradictions of the speakers. The polite audience sighs or gasps in response to passwords like Conspiracy or fluoridation, but few can explain the concepts to you. (Does the Conspiracy direct the communists, or vice versa? You hear it both ways.) Most of the Birchers I met were doctors and teachers and small businessmen; all were from the professional classes, and there was no mention of Middle America. Yet unlike the yelling mobs I've seen at Wallace rallies or the smug "realists" who turn out for Ayn Rand, many Birchers seemed quite forlorn or weary people. The hatred and rage they were known for in the past may have ebbed, although many are very bitter indeed and their jokes have a queasy malice. But they didn't gleam with the confidence you see at most rallies—that exhilaration which often peaks when any kind of faithful get together.

Last year even the Young Americans for Freedom broke with the Birchers and denounced Lester Maddox, their prime speaker, for his racism. Empty of all political sophistication, they seem unable to capitalize on most conservative sentiments in the country now. Yet I'm sure they can still exert furious pressure in their own small towns or neighborhoods. It was said that some three thousand registered for the rally, and officials claimed that it was the largest they'd ever had. After all those long and boring speeches, many kept saying what fun the rally had been, how lovely it was to see each other again, and how much they looked forward to meeting next year—if only the Conspiracy doesn't kill a lot of us off, if only we can work fast enough to prevent it.

Strikes and Lulls

Harvard July 1972

"Si, si, Sihanouk!
Rotcee's building's gonna cook.
Workers, yes! Harvard, no!
Racist Rotcee's got to go."
—*April 1970*

I covered the Harvard strike in 1969 and the Yale strike in 1970, and wrote rather hopeful pieces about both. At each university the issues seemed very clear—although many commentators insisted that the upheaval was psychological, not political or social. (There was a lot of palaver about sons battling fathers, and one Harvard dean even had a biological interpretation: he declared that student protest was engineered by "the sons of communists.") At both universities I was heartened by the fact that those who disagreed were still talking with one another, still arguing and listening. By early 1969 that had almost ceased in New York; a tired satirist said, "If we don't confront our polarizations, we'll have to polarize our confrontations—*then* maybe we can have a dialogue."

Despite the nationwide lull that followed the university strikes after October 1970, it was plain that some students' convictions hadn't changed, even though the campuses were hushed. (Also, as one of my friends said, "Whoever expected a revolution from the children of the ruling class?") But in 1971 I even heard old-style liberal professors—who had hated the strikes—contemptuously putting down their own students for being "docile."

In May and June of 1972 I returned to Cambridge and New Haven to ask a lot of people what they thought about their strikes in retrospect. The seniors of '72 were the freshmen of '69: the last Harvard class to have lived through the strike. What direct or indirect results did they see? Or side effects?

Near Harvard Square, where many used to try to sell you dope, people were pushing kittens—little, mewing bundles were thrust at me while I read the sign on the Unitarian church: "It Is as Much a Sin to Take Offense as to Give it." And the voices of Harvard rose to battle with each other:

"The strike changed everything!"

"*Nothing's* changed."

"So you give the ruling class a heart attack. Then it recovers."

"Dig it, the war's not over. But people grew a lot in awareness."

"Five or six years ago, radicals were a fringe group. Now they're the mainstream."

"There's a new course in revolution, which is terrible."

"I have a really rough time thinking about bombing. I don't want anyone hurt. But I was glad to see the bomb in the Pentagon. But I do know that bombing's a male chauvinist pig fantasy."

"So what's new? Harvard still houses Handlin, Skinner, Bell, and all those end-of-ideology creeps from the Fifties."

"I think—at its best—our generation is the conscience of the country. And we'll *never* be the same as we were before the strike."

"People offed LBJ. Then they found you could change the person but not the system. From Pusey to Bok: the only change is style."

"The peace movement picked up again, then it died, then it picked up, then it died."

"There are some people it's still hard to speak to—it's been like the aftermath of a civil war."

So as a Radcliffe graduate from the Fifties, I did a bit of time-tripping: in 1969, when one of my favorite professors asked me what kind of piece I was writing about the strike, I said it was a term paper which would please no one: neither students nor faculty, not moderates or militants. I added, "Pleasing no one was exactly what you taught us to do up here." He snorted and agreed. I also remembered the experience of majoring in English: they told us that generalizations were evil—sloppy and perilous—and then they asked us to make them, demanded the very thing we'd been warned against. So I'm always uneasy around Harvard: what's required is also what's despised. Uneasy and also scornful: an institution which teaches you to be so critical can't ask for much respect in return. (There used to be a dredging firm near Harvard called the Veritas Sludge Company, which pleased a lot of students.) And yet I've a reluctant soft spot for the old dinosaur: I liked what they gave me to read, liked many people who are still my friends, am grateful for the skepticism it bred. I also think that part of the Harvard-Radcliffe education means disliking the university itself. That was true for many I knew in the apolitical Fifties—even though we didn't know the facts which students do today.

In 1972 almost all the undergraduates I met said the strike had been a major part of their education—except for a few who sounded rather as though they'd once performed in a school play. (One said, "It made everybody try out radical politics to see if they liked them. Lots *didn't* like them.") But those who still felt that the strike had been valuable spoke of the lessons about power and how it operates: "having the university exposed as the monster it is." Another said, "When I came here, I had no use for the government, for Washington. But I did think the one thing you could trust was the university. Now I know you can't." And another: "When Mother Nature turns out to be an old bitch—that really hurts. But it's useful to know it."

Throughout, the discoveries about Harvard were mentioned in a positive way: as a preparation for a society which can't be trusted and should be changed. An alumna of the graduate school said, "The strike changed the administration's behavior. Now, all their stalling mechanisms are finely honed. They've resorted to so many Nixonish techniques, like the stalling, or saying they'll do things which they don't. It's like saying you'll end the war—and you don't. They say, 'Sure, We'll hire more blacks'—and they don't. Yet I still feel I have to try to change things, even though—as a *non*politico—I feel it's all rather hopeless. But I can't be passive any more. The strike did that for a lot of us: and that's a *huge difference.*"

The same person reflected on Harvard's resistance to reforms: "When you take these things on, you feel angry all the time . . . Harvard's so cynical. For example, the Design School has listed one black Mexican woman three times—as though she fulfilled three different categories! She's listed in the percentages of women, blacks, and 'other minorities' enrolled in the school. So many of us feel we're insulted *all the time* with these tactics. Do they think we're so stupid that we don't *know* what's happening?"

Trust has disintegrated like an old shower curtain—the one you bought at Korvette's seven years ago. Almost none of the professors I saw really trusts the administration; some said they didn't trust students either. The three words I heard oftenest in Cambridge were "impotent," "nefarious," and "manipulative." ("Impotent" came up in nearly every conversation; it was always used socially, not sexually, and was uttered by as many women as men, equally among faculty and students. I wondered why they didn't say helpless or powerless. Perhaps a number have been reading Wilhelm Reich.) One professor believes that the strike has meant long-range disappointment for everyone: "For the administration, because they couldn't control the students. For the students, because they didn't change the administration. For the faculty, because they felt they couldn't affect either the administration *or* the students." He and other professors (including some who aren't political) agreed that one prime result of the strike was that the administration swiftly became more conservative than ever, also more bureaucratic. One added, "My students don't yet know that counter-revolutions happen oftener than revolutions. Life is so *much* messier than they realize."

From the faculty to the graduating seniors, many suspect that the admissions department has been screening students for potential radicals—although this will always be denied. But many remarked on the degree of squareness in the recent freshman and sophomore classes (1974 and 1975). Bridge is back and so is booze; jocks are conspicuous, you hear the word "dating"; there was even a formal last year, also a panty-raid. One instructor referred to the freshman class she was teaching in the fall of 1970: "The culture shock of who I was talking to! They weren't with me at all when I mentioned Cambodia. They came from very unaware families—I think some were admitted for their backgrounds."

Although it can never be proved, some students believe that there's a profile of "the radical troublemaker": an Easterner who's often from New York, probably Jewish, apt to major in Social Studies or History and Lit., a likely candidate for a magna. In January 1971 Chase Peterson (then the dean of admissions) met with a group of Jewish faculty who felt that Harvard was taking fewer Jews. (It didn't appear that they were inquiring about radicals.) Peterson said it was his "impression" that Harvard was simply admitting fewer applicants from "the doughnuts around the big cities"—meaning the suburbs. He referred to students with good grades from local high schools. One professor retorted, "Dr. Peterson, those aren't doughnuts, they're bagels." The doughnuts-and-bagels are mentioned when Harvard indicates that it has an obligation to educate the elite. "Look, Harvard could go into the subway and choose twelve hundred people and they'd *become* the elite."

∽

These were the themes which swirled forward when I asked about the aftermath of the strike. Quite often I had to keep pulling the conversation back to politics, or to some of the main demands of 1969. ROTC has been abolished; its former building is now a day-care center. But there's no applause, since some think it may return—as is being considered at Dartmouth and Brown. Army ROTC has been reinstated at Princeton (without the naval and air force programs). Many are convinced that intelligence-related research still continues, along with investments in "pig products." As for the university's expansion into the poorer communities, no one seems really sure of what Harvard has or hasn't done. Harvard did donate a small lot—for ninety-nine years—on which some housing for the elderly was built with federal money. Some feel that this would not have happened before the strike.

Expansion was an impassioned issue in 1969, but few seem interested now. Yet I also found many individuals—at both Yale and Harvard—who'd gone off to work in neighboring community projects such as women's health collectives, tenants' organizing groups, or welfare rights. One instructor added, "But you can have people in tenants' groups who aren't interested in welfare; too many are isolated with their own issues and don't realize that it's all related." Another added, "You can be *into* day care or *into* food co-ops, to the exclusion of other things: including human pain."

Which brings us to the collapse of the movement—not merely on campuses, but throughout the country. (Enquiring after one radical of 1969: "Jack? Oh, he's into primal scream now.") A librarian said, "Kids are aware of their limitations now—as they weren't before. Some students feel very threatened by the possibility of big political reinvolvement. So they try to develop healthy interests—like suburban husbands doing woodwork—such as working for McGovern." One senior said, "Now that Nixon's changed the draft laws, men are dropping out like flies again. For some, the war is really over." He and others spoke rather sternly about "instant gratification": wanting immediate results from any protest. Another senior said, "This place is screamingly apolitical. It's a point of honor that *one* does not get involved in political issues. After the Cambodia actions, it was a disaster here. When the government didn't crumble to its knees in ten days, lots of people threw up their hands and said: 'I can do nothing.' Cambodia helped students to construct a very sophisticated defense against *any more* antiwar activity."

In 1969 I wrote: "Anyone who has seen (or shared in) some fighting and bleeding and weeping cannot escape the issues that began it. Romanticism ebbs; sore heads and soreheads have to consider what has hurt them." I now see that I was wrong; many want to forget the varieties of hurt and some issues were partially obscured by pain.

A Radcliffe junior, who had taken one year out, was eloquent about dwelling amid the conflicts: "When I came back last fall, I was grateful for the apathy because it allowed me to immerse myself in work. And people are much more into personal relationships." (Others said they'd had no personal life at all when they were spending ten hours a day in meetings. Harvard's health and psychiatric services reported that fewer students sought aid throughout the strike.) "Because of '69 and Cambodia in '70, people have come to feel that they can't change all the shit around them, so they might as well have full private lives. They won't listen to the news or read the papers— they know it's all there, it won't go away. But the feeling is *impotence.*

"After '69 and '70, I felt all that euphoria was a dirty trick, somebody's dirty trick. After Cambodia, when we felt *some* feedback—some reaction from Washington—it was so brief. So temporary.

"The atmosphere for head-changing isn't what it was two years ago. Then you had to talk about the issues."

Not now?

"You don't *have* to talk politics now. But the trouble with that is—when Nixon decides to bomb Vietnam again, people say: Oh hell, it's one more thing.

"Cynicism really runs counter to the undergraduate experience. If you're cynical—as many were after 1970—you can't relate to Plato or Ibsen. You can't study if you're cynical." (She referred to the numbers she thought had dropped out for that reason.) "A lot of people feel they can have some power over their lives—in terms of this place—I think that's an illusion.

"Listen, the strike made Harvard a better place *and* a deader place. It opened things up, academically and between people. It was even a stab at community democracy. And it was ultimately deadening *and* liberating."

All the students to whom I quoted her views agreed. One said, "No wonder I've been feeling funny."

∾

And a few are still nostalgic about the strike.

At the height of the 1969 bust in University Hall, one student saw a friend of his being badly beaten in the Yard. "That set something off inside me, so I jumped the cop. He beat on my back. Then I broke away. Every moment of fury and rage I've ever felt in my whole life was concentrated in my body at that moment. I felt completely impotent, I didn't know what to do, I threw rocks: from a pile of dirt from some construction work. Then the cops bore down, and I ran, I tripped over that same pile of dirt—which may say something psychological about me. They ripped my jacket and I slipped out of it. . . . Afterward l was in a state of shock, I just walked around, glaring at the deans and wishing them all good morning. For an hour after the bust, *no* one was in charge of Harvard—not SDS, not the administration. *Anything* could have happened, but no one had prepared for that moment.

"For seven days, anyone could walk into the Yard and communicate intensely with anyone—on politics *or* personal things. That never happened again.

"But I think it was the taste of what a revolution could mean. 'The transformation of everyday life.' "

∾

Behind Widener Library, I heard two middle-aged white men—neatly buttoned into their jackets—chatting about "the brothers."

"How are the brothers doing?"

"Oh, the brothers are doing fine." Somewhat startled by their apparent concern for black militants, I eavesdropped until I discovered that they were talking about Brooks Brothers. One was worried that the firm might be bruised by recession.

Among the white undergraduates and teachers I saw, almost none knew any black students. They referred to the strong black separatist movement at Harvard: "Blacks make you feel that you mustn't intrude on them." Some sounded rather forlorn about having no black friends—especially those who'd had a number in high school. Some said that individual blacks might mix with whites when they were on their own, but would not do so in front of other blacks. One instructor described a paper written by one of her black freshmen: about continuing to mingle with whites while experiencing the scorn and anger of his black classmates. Certainly not all black students are separatists, but it appears as though they have to make a choice when they arrive at Harvard. A black man with a white woman will probably be ostracized.

White students spoke respectfully of the separatism; they said it was clearly a source of strength and reinforcement. A black faculty member who is close to black students explained: "If a white wants to be liberal, he has to accept black separatism. Sure, it makes whites uptight—but they've got to realize that it's not animosity toward them: it's solidarity for us. But we can't have our causes co-opted by theirs, we can't have our minds infiltrated by their issues; we've got to work full-time for ourselves. And we've learned that it's possible to survive without sharing white values. You learn you don't need white people! Because of their mutual support, I think the black students' morale is better than the whites'. Also, because the Afro Department was established in 1969: black students got more out of the strike.

"I feel that most of the faculty don't know anything about black people— and they don't bother to learn. Many black students feel that they're here for the *benefit* of white students—to broaden their horizons."

There are some four hundred black students at Harvard now. The few I did meet were enthusiastic about being there. One said, "It's easy to become a black activist here—this place does heighten *all* the contradictions." But he and others kept stressing that they enjoyed the university's variety: "Where else would I find so many kinds of cats? Even the ones who are into the conservative bag—I won't come down on them. That's what's solid about Harvard: you can have both radicals and conservatives here." ("*Solid*" seems to be replacing "Right on," at least around Boston.)

In April President Derek Bok announced that Harvard wasn't going to sell its 683,000 shares of Gulf Oil stock—as had been demanded by the Pan African Liberation Committee (PALC) and the Harvard-Radcliffe Association of African and Afro-American Students (Afro): in their protest against Gulf's involvement with the Portuguese colonial regime in Angola. The future president of Afro told me that black students had been working on the issue since September 1971, that they had steadily sent petitions to Bok, but were unable to see much of him. They'd asked for a decision on Gulf, and when they got it, about thirty-five occupied Massachusetts Hall where Bok and his administration have their offices. The blacks held Mass Hall for six days. Bok did not call the cops. Instead he obtained a court injunction which meant that if the occupiers did not leave, they could have been sentenced to six months in jail for contempt of court. During the occupation there was a supportive picket line outside the building; at times it reached a thousand.

The PALC and Afro tactics, which impressed many white students, were carefully considered. There were different roles for different temperaments. Some of the most militant blacks occupied the building; others helped to organize the pickets, delivered food, or gave information to the press. "It would be ridiculous to force someone to occupy the building if he didn't want to. But he can do other things. . . . We do encourage white support—we couldn't have succeeded without it. But when SDS wanted to take over another building, we asked them not to. We didn't want occupying buildings to be the issue—*Gulf* was the issue." There was a five-day strike by some white students—against the renewed bombing in Vietnam, as well as in support of the Gulf action. However this strike wasn't directed against Harvard itself. On quite a few campuses, the university is less of a target than it was three years ago.

In 1969 the issue of black studies was initially separate from the general strike. But when black students learned that the proposed program might be merely a "Committee on Degrees," which would offer only tutorials, and would have given degrees only to students who had fulfilled the requirements of one of the other departments, they joined the strike and won their demand for a full academic department. Three years later professors in Afro-American Studies say there have been growing pains—in part because the program was assembled so hastily; also because Harvard has been careless in its requirements; for example, African languages aren't required to teach African history—"But would Harvard hire someone to teach German or Asian history if he didn't know the language?" And some feel that outsiders, including one black professor, have sought to damage the department. Also: "Afro Studies are a threat to professors in established fields, like history and economics. They should have done their homework, but they say, 'We haven't had the facilities.' So it makes them uneasy that the department even exists." Obviously no outsider can judge the department. But the black students I saw were keen on their Afro courses, especially literature and languages.

&

When you pursue the current weaknesses of SDS—which at Harvard is dominated by the Progressive Labor Party—you hear a lot of grunts and sighs from former members, as well as from independent radicals or moderates. Of course the 1969 split in SDS—when Weatherman was formed and others were left to fight one another—was permanently crippling. Some feel that PL was never serious about the war: "Sure, they surface at antiwar demonstrations. But people who care about the war just can't make it with PL." Many repeat that SDS and the movement fell apart because there never was a blueprint. "If you think the world is ending in three weeks, you can't plan a movement. But many *wanted* to think there was a very short deadline—because that was the only way to keep up the pressure."

And SDS developed a talent for picking the wrong issues. Garrett Epps, president of the *Crimson* from 1971 to 1972, wrote in 1971, "As the bombs dropped on North Vietnam, SDS held a demonstration against Harvard's system of parking fees for workers; as crowds marched to Boston Common to protest the invasion of Laos, SDS demonstrated at Holyoke Center against Harvard's apprenticeship program." SDS still attracts a small new membership; one activist explained, "If there's no doctor, you take the guy who has a Band-Aid."

But manipulation is the theme that recurs again and again: from those who feel that SDS and PL were able to tyrannize others by denouncing them as ideological scum or political pukes—including many in the movement, who were working on the same issues. The rigidity of PL—with its assumption of moral superiority—drove away some with deep political convictions; the style was far too authoritarian to build a "mass base." One veteran of 1969 said, "There was the pressure to have a total analysis of *everything*. Your intuitions weren't trusted or valid unless they related to politics. You were being *judged* all the time. You'd say something, anything, and then the counterattack would begin: they'd say '*That's not clear,*' and then they'd rip you apart. A lot of people couldn't deal with that. . . . Once I was taking half an hour off, listening to The Band and loving it, and I was told that it was capitalistic, rock revisionist music. I was *really* shamefaced. I got so I didn't want others to hear me hearing it."

Did the standards seem inhuman?

"Yes. People are reading a lot of Orwell now. He said that zealots or purists are always in danger of changing into their opposites—because they've let go of human values.

"Weatherman was the logical extension. Because you've been raised in a sick society, blah, blah, blah, you have to smash yourself. Weatherman said: Okay, we're going to be *perfect*. We're going to smash bourgeois experience. But most people can't keep that up. And they can't be perfect."

I've always felt that Harvard teaches self-doubt. Along with recurrent dissent—the carping and the sneering and the most valuable dogfights—searing self-criticism makes many far too skillful at putting themselves down. Truly scorning the self can follow easily. (Again I can vouch for the Fifties.) And I've felt that many alumni were hampered by this; quite a few I know have large egos but very little confidence. It's the mark of our common schooling and I can often recognize it in strangers. So I can well understand those who were vulnerable—in 1969 or 1970—when told that they were lousy. One student who said the movement had made him feel that he ought to "negate or dissolve" himself—that he should "abdicate" his judgment to his superiors, "destroy your own identity to serve others"—gave me this description of street fighting in the Square in April 1970: "I loved it, I thought it was great, that kind of chaos. I ran back and forth, though I didn't throw rocks. It was danger and chaos and everything being transformed—like the streets you know. It was a form of self-obliteration. No thought. I wasn't frightened at all. Maybe because I placed a low value upon myself."

What else did you like about it?

"The feeling that you are out of yourself, your revolting, imperfect . . . corrupt . . . self—and you're into something that requires no decision. You're part of the flow. A feeling of transcendence—transcending yourself, transcending reality. I think I was basically out of my head—on adrenalin. . . . Placing no value on yourself—the way Harvard makes you feel."

We chewed that over, and he went on: "The distrust of yourself that is taught here—I bought the whole thing. My freshman year, I'd start reading—it didn't matter what it was—and I'd feel too ignorant to understand it. To read a piece of literature, I'd feel I needed to understand economics, linguistics. Before I read Chaucer, I'd have to know Latin and Greek. I felt like an idiot, more and more."

Another student said, "Yes, that's where Harvard still destroys people. Meanwhile everybody here is used to being told they're Number One—but they know that's phony! Although they may look good in the eyes of other people—outside Harvard—they know that's just bullshit."

Some in the movement who were reviled by their own classmates have rebelled against that abasement. A radical senior's summation: "People here never learned from SDS, and SDS never learned from the people here, so everyone stayed stupid."

≈

"Hey, I'll tell you one result of the strike. You haven't heard anyone mention a 'generation gap' up here. Right?" (Right. Not a word.) "Because the Sixties are over! We all passed through them together—parents and children. Now, due to the sad facts of the economy, kids are understanding what their parents went through—how they compromised." An alumna said, "The strike blotted out a lot of generational differences. Because people divided politically. And that was the only thing that mattered." In 1969 I heard about a student who accused his parents of "knuckling under to the Depression." But in 1972 I heard no one knocked for being a parent—or for being any age.

≈

One senior looked back to 1969: "Everyone was talking solidarity. That was a party line that no one could live up to. So it just produced more loneliness. People tried so hard to merge with the group, then they felt *more* isolated than ever."

At the end of 1970, at a Yippie workshop which was expected to be totally political, I was astounded when the theme became "cultivating personal relationships"—though none I questioned had heard of Bloomsbury. In universities many have withdrawn to lead acutely private, often introspective, lives. It's the revival of individualism that you see everywhere, and I'm sure it's a reaction against the conviction of the late Sixties that ego is ugly: from SDS to Timothy Leary, you heard that the sense of self must be ditched. In the name of politics or acid, many Aquarians tried so hard to suppress their selfhood. Now it seems as though many egos have sprung up like toast from a toaster.

Some of the more political students in Cambridge are impatient with others who have been lulled with life styles. "You know the old one: that society can be changed with life styles. But the relation between smoking a joint and stopping the war is just too tenuous!" Another said, "There's lots of consumerism. Buying expensive hiking boots. Fancy dope—being a connoisseur: like winesmanship. Waterbeds. The basic thing that Harvard runs on is that people here deserve to earn a lot of money. And so a lot of my classmates will go on to perpetuate the system; they'll be doctors and lawyers, and they'll say: I'm going to do a lot of good things for other people, radical things, but I must be well paid for it. Lots of people live with accepted schizophrenia: they know the system is shit, but the sugar at the end of the trail is just too sweet: the promises of jobs and money."

The puritanism of some of the left has abated. "I expect to be a radical all my life—but not to give up going to the movies." Although the general morale at Harvard seems very low, you also hear quite a lot about "the quality of life" from political animals. "I began to realize that radical politics wasn't just SDS screaming about imperialism, but that politics related to personal experience and daily living." And I met quite a few who aim to stay outside the system. Planning to live cheaply—while running small summer camps or play groups, being a carpenter or driving a taxi—but hoping to earn just enough to travel, to explore. Of course the groundnote is freedom—especially from a deadening high-powered job which gives no nourishment to the self. My Fifties concept of freedom was quite similar, except that it hung on a compulsion *to be grown up:* to be treated as an equal by adults, to pass as one of them—which sounds hilarious to students now.

"People are willing not to have much security. Desire for success? No, not much, we know that what the employer wants is bullshit. But there's a desire for a *niche.* To be in your own place, to be with friends. Who wants to go up some ladder? *Less* desire for fame—not wanting to go out and beat T. S. Eliot or Albert Einstein." (That was a Fifties hangup at Harvard: some fledgling writers would measure themselves against Proust or Dostoevsky or Melville and then despair.) "Trying not to be part of the economy, still living the student life style: in small towns, communes, not big cities. I'll get a room in someone's house for ten dollars a week, spend ten dollars for food. We'll live on the underbelly of society."

A senior said, "I look around me and I don't see anybody doing anything

I want to do. So I'm going to spend a few years being a bum." She and her friends kept razzing each other about not being "directed." One punctuated the conversation with "That's *irrelevant*" while she doodled on a paper napkin.

A young man said, "I thought of teaching in public high school. But I hear the kids just sit there and stare at the teachers. They know they won't learn anything. They know what the school system is doing to them."

"I'm going to work with a group that's organizing sharecroppers in Louisiana. But I think doing one thing for a whole lifetime is ridiculous."

"I had a summer job in Washington with Nader. I'm not sure muckraking is useful, but I enjoyed it."

"You're not directed!"

"Who is?"

"That's *irrelevant*."

"You see, Harvard's standards have lost their legitimacy: in terms of what they expect of graduates. Or Harvard's idea of success."

"That's irrelevant too."

Another disagreed. "Harvard just wants you to be good at what you do—whatever it is."

"Like being a good Panther?"

Many expressed disgust because they feel that Harvard trains students only for academic work—"And many think that's not worthwhile. So what you've been trained for you don't believe in."

"I've talked to professors who say their profession is bankrupt."

"We're trained for nothing. We have twenty-thousand-dollar BAs, and magnas, and no skills, just a lot of nothing."

∿

Ex-President Nathan Pusey, who had outraged so many when he called the police to clear University Hall in 1969, got a standing ovation when he received an honorary degree at commencement in June of 1972.

Strikes and Lulls
Yale May 1970 and June 1972

"Fuck *Dick*, fuck Spiro!
Bobby *Seale's* the people's hero!"

The bus driver spat out the window as we approached the New Haven Green, where crowds were massing for the Mayday rally in support of the nine Panthers going on trial for the murder of Panther Alex Rackley. The driver said, "At least they're mostly white. But it's gonna be disgusting." The bus rumbled with agreement. The fourteen passengers were so nervous that they kept talking compulsively to one another: as though words could ward off the menace of the next few hours. An old woman jabbered: "I wish I had a penny for every mile I've walked my dog. She's six years old." Someone said, "I wish I had my dog with me right now." "Oh, dogs are the best protection." The woman hardly heard them: "These days, dogs don't have a chance. The way people want them policed—tied up." The driver growled like a mastiff—"Look at that crowd"—while her voice spun faster: "You must always talk to your dog. That's how you educate them. They like to be treated human."

I went to New Haven a week before Mayday, just after some undergraduates began carting their stereos out of their rooms and leaving town. Local shops had boarded up their windows; all over the plywood, students had stenciled WHY BE AFRAID? (On one, someone had written, "But what about Alex Rackley?") A truck carrying 280 weapons—including riot guns with fixed bayonets—was stolen in New Haven and found empty in New York; a fire in the Law School Library burned $2,500 worth of books; fires in abandoned buildings in the ghetto have caused the police and the Panthers to accuse one another, while some in the neighborhood suspected right-wing arsonists. A lot of liquid mercury, which can be used in making bombs, had been swiped from the chemistry lab; it was found in the apartment of a revolutionary dropout. There were rumors that the Gutenberg Bible would be stolen, replaced by a fake, and that the original would be sold and the money given to the poor. There were even more rumors about white vigilantes and Weatherpersons and Hell's Angels and out-of-town adventurists arriving. It was said that certain outsiders—who later preached nonviolence in New Haven—had invited large audiences in Boston to come and help trash Yale. Some felt that others had decided that the Revolution would start on May 1st in New Haven, Connecticut.

Medical centers were ready to go on full-time alert: they especially prepared for head injuries. Volunteers were organized to drive ambulances or station wagons to collect the wounded. Some prepared water bombs to be dropped from roofs to extinguish Molotov cocktails. There was also talk of "comfort stations," where medical students would soothe those who had witnessed bloodshed but had not been badly hurt. The police and the National Guard would be backed up by some four thousand army paratroopers and marines, which Connecticut's Governor John Dempsey had requested from John Mitchell as "a precautionary measure." Many felt that their presence would be highly provocative.

In late April, walking through New Haven, I looked at all that brick and stone and glass and saw how perishable that stern New England permanence might be. (A new sensation for an American; one that older Europeans would understand.) I also saw some haughty faces that looked as though they'd been dropped from a great height; those faces appeared as though they'd been certain of their superiority—until about five minutes ago. And yet the town's terrors seemed irrational; it was easy for a visitor to think that many middle-class natives were overreacting. (Regrettably I now know that the dangers were greater than they seemed at the time: in terms of what a few hoped they could make happen.) Still, Harvard Square had been severely trashed the week before.

Yale's neighboring black communities had a reasonable dread that if there was an explosion, their own teen-agers might get excited and involved, the police would chase them back to their own turf, and a real battle might begin. There police violence was greatly feared. A middle-class black, who was far from radical, told a friend of mine: "If there's a white riot—if *they* start it, *we're* going to finish it. If it means going to the barricades, then we're going for the last time." Meaning that he and others would fight to defend their children if they were incited by revolutionary gamesters and then shot at by the cops.

There was the sense of being on a conveyor belt; as the whole town was tugged toward a date which threatened to extinguish the issues, some worked hard to keep the priorities clear. Yale was less on strike than in the midst of a vast moratorium. (One activist told me, "Basically, most of us like Yale. We're not interested in hustling deans out of their offices or destroying files.") The black faculty had asked for "the suspension of normal academic functions" as an acknowledgment of the oppression of the Panthers and of all black Americans. President Kingman Brewster helped to reword the proposal to "normal academic expectations" being "modified." "FUCK NORMAL EXPECTATIONS" became a slogan.

Many (but not all) classes were suspended in support of a fair trial for the Panthers, with particular concern for Bobby Seale, who had been charged with ordering the execution of Rackley. (It seemed more than forlorn that the dead, illiterate young man in his early twenties, whose torture-scarred corpse had led to the shutdown of Yale, was rarely mentioned.) But there was solid alarm because George Sams, one of the chief witnesses for the prosecution, was "an alleged dangerous mental defective" who had spent four years in institutions. Sams alone had accused Seale of ordering the murder. Out of twenty grand jurors, twelve were friends of the county sheriff's, who had chosen them, along with his barber and the barber's landlord. By early 1970 many middle-class Americans were aware that the trials of dissidents or black militants should be viewed with the famous "skepticism" which President Brewster voiced. Some students doubted his sincerity when he said in a speech at a faculty meeting on April 23rd, "I personally want to say that I am appalled and ashamed that things should have come to such a pass that I am skeptical of the ability of black revolutionaries to achieve a fair trial anywhere in the United States." There were students who called him a shrewd hypocrite. But even cynics seemed glad of his support.

Most of the Yale students I met were moderates who were worried about civil liberties; only a few radicals demanded that the Panthers be freed. Throughout, the long-term abuse of black defendants by American courts was analyzed. Novelist John Hersey (then the master of Pierson College) and some distinguished New Haven attorneys set up a trust fund to defray the costs of the trial, including witness and subpoena fees, special investigators, transcripts, research, and attorneys' fees.

Many white students were perplexed by the Panthers' rhetoric and assumed that the Panthers' language was responsible for their being jailed. Some black professors and students replied that the Panthers were repressed for being black and for challenging the system. One thesis, restated from Eldridge Cleaver, emerged in many discussions: if whites didn't commit themselves to working for change, then black people would be left on their own, and then the country could have a racial war. It was repeated that the choice was up to whites.

But it wasn't clear what the Panthers specifically wanted of Yale students in the spring of 1970. (To me the campus seemed like 1966; despite the strike, many undergraduates appeared to have missed the late Sixties.) David Hilliard, the Panthers' national chief of staff, had turned off an audience of some forty-five hundred when he told them "There ain't nothing wrong with taking the life of a mother-fucking pig." Some booed him; he said, "I knew you mother-fuckers were racist," and the boos grew louder as he denounced them. Then he added, "Although you don't agree with what I have to say, you should be intelligent enough to tolerate that rather than boo me." Eventually: "Now you got me talking like a crazy nigger. . . . And I want to compound my sin by calling you long-haired hippie Yale mother-fuckers. Fuck you." Hilliard then said he would "take it all back . . . On the grounds that you all repudiate your boos." People sprang to their feet and applauded, holding their fists high. At an earlier meeting students cheered nonviolent speeches, cheered those who attacked nonviolence, then booed and cheered some speeches favoring violence. Sometimes mass emotions seemed to be whirling in a giant centrifuge.

The theme at Yale was Either/Or: as many buttons announced. It was understood as a statement from black people: either you're with us or against us—for or against equality. (It came from Cleaver's motto of 1968: "Either you're part of the solution or part of the problem.") No one was supposed to be able to escape taking sides. Later Tom Hayden envisioned a day when Nixon and Agnew would move heavily on Brewster: "He and other people like himself are caught in the middle when the middle is disappearing." But Yale without a middle is impossible to imagine. Some also wondered if Either/Or meant: either you pick up the gun or you get shot down. So the Panthers had the (reluctant) support of many—who wanted a fair trial but couldn't swallow the notion of guns.

There was (or seemed to be) an equal focus on Yale's relationship with New Haven's black community: the land-grabbing which occurred as the university enlarged and the false hopes raised among black citizens. In May 1968, Yale did give an $111,000 grant to the Black Coalition, which represents over thirty groups in New Haven. But Brewster had given the impression that he would help raise $1 million a year for ten years for the coalition, and that money had not materialized. (That was known as "the $10 million misunderstanding.") Also a health center which the university had initiated was desperately low in funds, since the federal money which began it had dried up, and Yale had not assumed the responsibility for continuing it. Yale's administrators argued that for legal reasons they could not give university money which is tax deductible for education—although they repeated that they were ready to help black groups gather money through grants. But many felt that Yale had planted seeds it refused to water. "The community is tired of having programs come and go at the whim of Yale." Some felt that there was no way for Yale to be neutral: "Just being here is a promise."

The other demands of 1970 were that the proposed Social Sciences Center should not be built (since the money could be spent in better ways), that day-care centers should be set up for the community, that Yale provide unemployment compensation for its own employees, and that low- and moderate-income housing should be subsidized by Yale. Many felt that the ghetto had too long been used as a laboratory for Yale's "research." As someone said, "Privacy is the only luxury of the poor."

Kenneth Mills, the black Assistant Professor of Philosophy, born in Trinidad and educated at Oxford, who was one of the main forces behind the strike, said in a speech at the Yale Medical School: "Yale symbolizes—and is—the contradiction that plagues our society today: the elite and the oppressed." He developed the theme of "people living in an enclave of privilege, surrounded by those who are suffering." In another speech he called Yale "a jewel in a swamp." Like many others, he stressed that the black community would suffer most if Mayday was violent, and that New Haven should be a better—not a worse—place for them to live after May 1st. (On Mayday itself, he said, "The determination to be nonviolent is the determination to be militant." Many also realized that a savage Mayday would be damaging for the Panther defendants.) In conversations and teach-ins, the question expanded to what the rich should do for those who have nothing—or what comfortable whites owe to besieged black people. Momentarily Yale seemed like a giant membrane through which a lot of social change might be passing. And it was said that the black faculty wanted "to defend Yale by reforming it."

As the university prepared to open its colleges to house and feed the arriving crowds, solidarity sweatshirts—stenciled with a bulldog and a Panther—appeared, along with signs like THE BLACK PANTHERS' RIGHTS ARE YOUR RIGHTS TOO. While fear kept quivering through the spring daylight, I heard many amplifiers playing "Here Comes the Sun" again and again: like an incantation or a spell cast against destruction, almost a prayer: "It's all right . . . *it's all right.*"

The black students I talked to were very dubious about Yale's concern for the community or for the Panthers. They thought their white classmates were naive, and they were certain that any commitment to the black or the poor would vanish rapidly. "It's just self-interest, they don't want their dorms blown up. The weekend *ought* to be a small bead on a very long chain. But it'll be like a big stone dropped in a pond: it'll sink out of sight." And: "Sure, Yale realizes its debt to the community. But Yale will try to fulfill it as little as possible. . . . People *are* wide awake—and looking in the wrong direction. They know what the facts are, but they don't want to see them." A group of black students stressed that so much of their experience is inaccessible to whites. One senior described being jumped by two cops when he was unlocking his parked car in order to remove his camera—which he thought might be stolen if he left it there. It took a long time to convince the police that it was his car and his camera. "We're all supposed to be Yalies. But a black person here has no immunity. Two feet off campus, we're treated like criminals."

Yale opened its colleges not only in self-defense, but also because some were determined to build a base of protection for the Panthers, so that the police wouldn't feel as free to raid their headquarters as they had in cities across the country, as well as in Chicago, where Fred Hampton and Mark Clark were shot and killed. "The People's Yale," as some renamed it, echoed with rock bands in the college yards and oozed with Familia. (After tasting the stuff, one New York Panther remarked that it could be used to provoke a riot, since it was "subpoverty level.") The fact that the weekend itself was quiet was a poke in the snoot for Agnew, who had called for Brewster's resignation. After that statement, Yale students collected fifteen hundred signatures in an hour in support of Brewster. (When these were presented to him outside the administration building, applause rose even from passers-by in the street. Brewster was slumped with fatigue and hardly seemed able to respond.) After the big rallies, the crowds drifted calmly away, some picking up papers and a few playing leap-frog. It was apparent that black families had kept their teen-agers at home; there were very few in sight.

Cambodia had just been invaded. But there wasn't a great deal of reaction—perhaps because the weekend had absorbed so many energies.

On the morning of Mayday, Jerry Rubin told an audience in Woolsey Hall that the most oppressed people in America were the white middle-class young—more so than blacks in the ghetto. He said that schools and colleges were simply "an advanced form of toilet training. . . . Number One on the Yippie Program is kill your parents . . . they're dictators, teaching you to be a capitalist, a consumer—school is a concentration camp! . . . Parents eat their children—it's a children-for-breakfast program." He shouted that the only reason that "fancy liberals" are against the war "is because we're losing. If we were winning, they'd be standing right behind the flag." And: "Everything comes out of the university—Che was killed by university research." He referred to the case where a vice-president of the *Reader's Digest*—who had been lecturing around the country about the necessity of taking the young in hand—was stabbed severely by his teen-age son, who punctured his lung but did not kill him. "Our parents kill *us* at birth—we've got death-before-life, we've got to be reborn again." The crowd whooped and roared. Later: "It's the fucking alcoholics who are putting the pot smokers in jail! Alcohol is a part of capitalism—it makes you aggressive, makes you beat your wife. . . . Arresting us for smoking dope is like arresting Jews for eating Matzohs." He told an old Ted Kennedy joke (about crossing that bridge when we come to it), adding: "If Bobby Seale had been in that car with Mary Jo, he'd be hanging from a tree, he'd be lynched!" His hearers began to bang the wooden armrests of their chairs and stamp their feet until there was an ovation.

That night I listened to Tom Hayden in a Yale courtyard. He asked for a show of hands among the group of several hundred to determine where they came from: there were many from New York and Boston, but fairly few from Yale. He told them: "It's possible for us to go beyond spontaneous action: we had a peaceful rally that was not a copout." However: "If Yale shelters those who want to do something about Bobby, the government will move on Yale the way it moved on Cambodia." He stressed that May 1st was "the beginning of a struggle, so I'm not disappointed that more didn't happen here today." Some of his listeners shouted "Co-optation!" and tried to goad him into telling them to bring it all down—which he refused to do. Adding that sporadic busts and gassings make it difficult to sustain radical programs, he emphasized the value of teach-ins—because many are still politically confused—and expressed the hope that a new strategy for change was developing at Yale.

Hayden said New Haven could become a sanctuary for the movement, that students should remain in the summer and that outsiders must return, and urged that Bobby Seale Brigades should be formed throughout New England, in order to mass at the trial. "There's no contradiction between trying to organize people and—or—getting into heavy shit." He recommended the formation of an underground railway. Moreover: "We're divided unnecessarily about tactical issues." He said there was a valid reason for staying in school, stemming from Castro's idea of organizing cultural guerrillas. "Consciousness is to us what hunger is to the Third World—momentum." (A friend stirred uneasily beside me at that last point: "*That* sounds pampered.") Hayden said, "It's the fault of the left—not society—that the left hasn't worked yet." Stressing the need for discipline, he went through a self-criticism passage about male chauvinism, individualism, and public figures: "No movement should be organized around media freaks like ourselves."

Later a sham Panther borrowed Jerry Rubin's microphone while Rubin was speaking at Branford College, and untruthfully announced that Panthers were being arrested on the Green. Rubin cautioned people against going. But some of the hot white blood on hand strode off for some senseless (but not drastic) scuffles with the National Guard. An outsider explained, "I'm here to *free* this place, man." The Panthers—who didn't know the provocateur—were so helpful in crowd-cooling that Brewster praised them afterward. They shouted through bullhorns and loudspeakers and worked to head the mainly white crowd away from the Green. That night three bombs went off in Ingalls Rink, but there were no serious casualties. The police later indicated that a right-wing group was responsible. Kurt Schmoke, a member of the Black Student Alliance at Yale, who was active in the strike and skilled at calming volatile crowds, thought the May 1st rally was useful because it showed that many people had come to demand justice at the Panther trial—but that the clowning of Abbie Hoffman and his playmates obscured the political purpose of the demonstration. (Schmoke would become the Mayor of Baltimore in 1987.)

The next day on the Green, Hayden blew many minds, including mine, when he announced that "Facts are . . . irrelevant in this case." All my writer's cells protested, aided by my recurrent anger at those chunks of the press which betray facts in a way that helps the public to believe lies. But I also remember an elderly woman from Boston mentioning the fights she'd had with her older relatives about Sacco and Vanzetti. She'd told them it didn't matter whether the two were guilty or not (she was sure they weren't, but was even more concerned with the larger questions of justice). So I could see what Hayden was probably trying to express: that the overwhelming existence of racism was far more important than the question of who killed Alex Rackley. But I thought he'd unintentionally confused a lot of people more than ever; others had so firmly insisted on the Panthers' total innocence that few could deal with the notion that Rackley had died at their hands—not those of the police.

Returning from New York to New Haven, I was writing about Yale when the news of the killing of four students at Kent State came through. That and Cambodia made the New Haven weekend seem like a festival. Only three weeks before, some NYU students—who were supporting a cafeteria workers' wildcat strike—had liberated some frozen steaks from the faculty club kitchen and had gleefully given them away in the streets. Games with steaks now seemed as remote as the swallowed goldfish of the Thirties; bombings, which had been deplored as "the politics of despair," began to seem almost inevitable to some who hated them. The anguish of that spring of 1970, after two students were shot dead and twelve were wounded at Jackson State, and the killings abroad accelerated, and more bombs flared across this country, made many feel that there was very little time to turn around in.

Hindsight: When I revisited Yale in November 1970, it seemed as though there had never been a strike; one day-care center had resulted from that tumultuous spring. When a *New York Times* reporter, who had been covering Panther Lonnie McLucas's trial, came to talk to students about the case, not many showed up, and they had few questions. Those I met recoiled mildly from the subject.

∿

When I'm around Yale, I begin with the illusion that I'm in a familiar place; since I know Harvard well, it always takes me a few hours to discover that the references don't apply. (Lifting a glass in a master's lodge, I read Lux et Varitas and am startled that Veritas has been improved on. Somehow light does sound more like luxury in New Haven.) But what amazes me most is the real affection that so many express for Yale—as they did even during the strike. I've rarely heard such sentiments in Cambridge. I'm accustomed to Harvard's sour energy, the perpetual bad-tempered Yankee griping, the capacity for indignation that was taught us—until we learned to level it against Harvard itself. This education for malcontents has produced constructive rebels, snarling conservatives, reformers, and bad losers. (Dissent at Harvard dates from 1776, over the issue of rancid butter: "Behold our butter stinketh!") Students and teachers, stamping across the buckling brick sidewalks of Cambridge, have been denouncing the university, its practices, and each other for decades. That's my idea of normal college life. So I'm astounded by all the good manners I encounter at Yale and the apparent self-confidence of the students, and the scarcity of strong criticism. I find it all very pleasant and at times I wonder: what are they taking up here? There must be lullabies in the water supply.

Since being deeply fond of your university is incomprehensible to me, I'm further amazed that everyone seems to agree about the reasons: they mention the intimacy of the college system, which means that students live much more closely with their teachers than they do elsewhere, and that their faculty are also their administrators—there's no loathed impenetrable bureaucracy, as there is at Harvard. Yale also has fewer deans; the administration has been kept small and supple: "When the kids want walls to break down, they find we have no walls!" I found no shortage of trust in New Haven and no one seemed to think that applicants were screened for their politics.

In June of 1972 the signs on the churches near the Green were hearty: the United Church asked, "Is Your Religion A Spectator Sport?" and the Methodist Church was almost hysterically jolly:

> YES TO STRIVING
>
> YES TO HOPING
>
> YES TO LIFE!

The latter reminded me that Yale students may have the illusion of having more power than they actually do.

Many seemed glad to talk about the strike and a few students said it was still very important to them, especially because it had influenced their choice of work for the future. Some black students felt the strike had succeeded in its purpose of drawing attention to the trials of black militants: "Without all that exposure and pressure, Bobby Seale and Ericka Huggins and the Soledad Brothers and Angela might not have had the just trials that freed them."

But the word I heard oftenest from white undergraduates was "embarrassed." One said, "*Somebody* killed Alex Rackley. We thought the Panthers were framed—we didn't look any further than that." But there was no evidence to convict Seale. Didn't it help that he and Huggins were released, that the others—most of whom were very young—were judged to have been terrorized into the murder by George Sams, and that their sentences were comparatively light? "Not really. I still feel embarrassed." And the concern for the black community? "Next to nothing. The impact was zero." Yet Yale did receive an anonymous gift of $1 million to be used for economic development programs in the community.

A faculty member said, "You don't hear boo from the black community now." He added, "Many students truly feared that Yale would be damaged. The more upset they got, the more they wanted Yale to be an agency of social reform—they wanted it to be an instrument of change *in order* to save it. . . . Protecting the university was protecting themselves. The colleges are their homes, we're like their family, and who wants his own home trashed? Holding certain social opinions—for three or four weeks—was in many cases sincere. Their concern was honest, but it had no staying power. As the black students were right to perceive."

A black administrator described the meetings held by the black community about a possible explosion on Mayday. "*They* drew the line, and they told white kids and Black Panthers not to step over it. They said: Hey, you cats are having a circus. But you better keep that crap downtown and not bring it into our neighborhood." He and many others spoke of how sternly the black population had warned outsiders against disrupting their lives.

One master rather ruefully called the strike "a catharsis that didn't work." Afterward: "Many felt that a breach had been made in the stone wall, but that the wall was rebuilt brick by brick." He compared the Harvard students' occupation of University Hall in 1969 to the general use of Yale's buildings in 1970: "There, they claimed a piece of territory. Here they were *given* it—and discovered that they weren't well organized. There's no reason why students shouldn't take over everything. But they find they can't sustain it. They learned a lesson in their own incompetence. Which is sad."

A dean said, "In 1970, there was the notion that the nation would listen to Yale. That the country would follow the elite. The touching naiveté of the students: they despised elitism and yet partook of it."

A woman graduate, now a teacher who plans to become a therapist, and who was deeply affected by the strike, recalled: "A lot of very repressed students had a chance to throw shit at society. You don't get into Yale without having worked hard, or having been quite intense. *Then* you become disenchanted with American politics, with the university—you feel you're being lead by the nose, as tenderly as any ass. . . . For many of us—for people who were stifled and resentful against society—it was a *huge* release. Yet I'm embarrassed, by some things I rejected at the time."

How so?

"I thought it was a confrontation between good and evil. We wouldn't listen to anyone. We were dangerous in our idealism, I think. Now it's hard to tell who was good or bad. We thought one significant encounter between right and wrong was going to change society. . . . Yet I might do it all again."

She and others spoke of the Kent State murders, which followed the Mayday weekend by half a day. (A dean said, "Yes, that was very instructive to students.") A black male student remembered: "In 1970 people didn't know they were going to get croaked. After Kent State, they said: *Goddam!* I could get killed doing this! . . . Maybe it was the first time an American government has taken a part of its population and said: We gonna bust their ass." The same woman described the signs that read "Four of Us Died Today." The number was crossed out to read "Six" after Jackson State. "Everything we thought and feared had come true. It felt like us against them—a personal attack on students and nonconformists. It showed that they were going to shoot us down if we got in the way."

She mused on the outcome of the strike: "Then, realizing that the world won't change, you ask: how am I going to dig my feet in and keep struggling?

I still believe you must be on the right side. Even though I don't believe in progress. I think there's just an exchange of problems. Some people said fuck it altogether. Others flooded the Med School and the Law School.

"The strike gave some of us the feeling that no work or job could be good or untainted. Teachers still oppress children, most industries make products that oppress people. There was *nothing* that *wasn't* part of the problem. So some went to Vermont and baked bread—because that was untainted.

"Perhaps there's no way? To be part of the system and maintain yourself."

Then you and your friends are extraordinarily different from Yale graduates of the past.

"Listen: this is very important: we thought we bore more guilt than others for being the leaders of a society that's morally bankrupt."

How do you feel now about politics?

"My radical sense says that it doesn't matter who's president. Maybe it's better to have Nixon, because he makes the static. But—even though I can't believe it will work—I think McGovern would make people's lives better. Then people tell me I'm a liberal, not a radical. The strike gave me a terror of being called a liberal."

She spoke of "looking for a middle way that's all right." (This theme recurred with almost everyone I saw.) "Two years ago, they said: You'll change your mind. We said: *Never*. But we've changed a little and it's not so bad.

"Someone made a good movie, which juxtaposed scenes of the strike with the reunions. I thought it was a stunning put-down of reunions: grown-ups acting like children—their funny handshakes.

"Later I saw the movie again. It seemed different. The students looked as ridiculous as the alumni. I was suddenly frightened by it—had there been wool over my eyes?

"The strike seemed simpler than it does now. . . . I was willing to let blacks get away with a lot more shit then." (She referred to some rough experiences working in a community project in the summer.) "They're *not* morally superior, they don't need a revolution *more* than anyone else. They should be able to see that women and homosexuals are oppressed too. . . . We're all capable of these big guilt-trips about blacks: like the strike. But I have no truck with blacks who just want a middle-class life."

~

I have to keep remembering that there was no bust during the Yale strike. Listening to a live recording made in Harvard's University Hall at the peak of police violence—the cries, the crash of battering rams, the scared narrator's cracking voice—a cheerful child asked me, "How many people were killed in this?" I said none. "Oh. Then what was it for?"

∽

A black Yale graduate, a former radical who was particularly active in 1970, said, "The thing was storybook for so many people to begin with. A play thing. With white students, it was a freedom-justice-and-*equality* thing. You had kids running around like they were ten years old. For the blacks: we were here with the Panthers. Some of them tried to push us around. But we refused. We watched those cats every day. I knew who the jive Panthers were and who the righteous ones were."

Yale and the community?

"I'll be cautious, but I think some good and quiet things are going to be done. Not flamboyant. Maybe we *need* more flamboyance. I don't know if Yale will ever give night courses for the people of this town." (Some feel that Yale could best serve the community by establishing more educational programs.) "But Yale won't face the question of open admissions. This is Ivy League, man." He and other black students agreed that there wasn't much separatism, although there are black entryways and floors for those who want them. "Some don't talk to whites, but most do." There are about three hundred black students: "The morale goes up and down. Some play supernigger, and others bite on the Protestant ethic. A lot find the experience of Yale was hip *after* they've finished. But we're the first generation of blacks here—we're told we're the cream, and that's a burden!"

He doubted that black Yale students would care much about Yale owning Gulf stocks: "Everybody here makes their money off somebody's back. People say: let's take care of ourselves for a while before we go out to change the world."

He said of the strike: "I believed in it then, and I believe in it now. But . . . " But? "I'm a cynicist. But I *was* a politico. I nearly went nuts. Finally, one day I stopped. Went back to my music, tried to get my head together for a while." Why nuts? "You carry the weight of the world on your shoulders, you gotta go nuts. That's true for whites, but even more so for blacks. . . . "

Are drugs decreasing, as some think?

"Here, we've got *quiet* junkies—they're studying. Not flashy junkies, like Harvard. . . . There are going to be a lot more crazy white boys. Blacks who strive hard to come here don't want to blow it. Yale is lots of striving young intellectuals who don't know why the hell they're striving. Now striving is cool—if you have a goal. Striving just to be striving is madness.

"Yes, I'm fond of Yale, I call it the nipple factor. Mother Yale . . . People say we were co-opted. So I was co-opted—so what? We got a black study program— before Harvard's—without any hassle. . . .

"Brewster—he's something else! The problem at Yale is that we have a good president. That's the problem! He does have a great sense of how to defuse things. . . . "

Not many students seem to know what they feel about Brewster now. A senior said, "In 1970, the university sanctioned civil disobedience. Brewster made it look as though he was *leading* the strike." Some still think Brewster very courageous. Others speak of him as "a slick operator," who is basically conservative and they expect him to make Yale more so in the future. "But it's all so damn subtle! The trouble is, nobody knows what's true around here. For example, they don't know what admissions are really based on. . . . There's no real *center* to the administration: you try to find it and you can't." "At Yale, 'the enemy' is such an elusive thing." At this point, one familiar paradox reels out of my mossiest cupboard: that Harvard, with its hard-line administration, still seems a far more liberated zone than Yale. In Cambridge people can unite their feelings against a bureaucracy. In New Haven, where many enjoy their apparent freedoms, "We have a progressive administration that's really conservative! And that's bewildering." (Another senior said, "You get some real screwball professors at Harvard. They just wouldn't be tolerated here.") But it's a lesson in the old uses of liberalism, and quite a lot of people seem happier at Yale than at Harvard.

And Brewster still kept them guessing. Some who graduated in 1971 were infuriated by the speech he made at their graduation—"I have not quite reached the great glad state of Hubert Humphrey's 'politics of joy,' but I do think things are looking up. There is a lot which is right about America and it is time for us to 'accentuate the positive' as the old song said." One graduate of 1971 said, "He was kowtowing to Nixon and alumni and parents, and I was just burning." In 1972 I was told that Brewster's baccalaureate address "really slapped Nixon and Agnew around."

~

A woman explained that the strike had made some more determined than ever not to be like their parents, and to resist traditional jobs and marriages: "To avoid the tremendous pull of our back-grounds, and the need for security. Fearing to wake up at thirty-five and to find that we were doing what they said we'd do. It *was* Either/Or: to avoid being *sucked* into your past. It's still difficult. . . . For example, I like flowers, and my mother likes flowers, and all the flower-arranging she does is part of the ritualistic life style that she's in. It terrorizes me that I like flowers too, it feels like Either/Or again: oh my God, I like flowers, I'll have a life just like hers. Even though I just pick wild ones."

~

In a sharp contrast to Harvard, I found that when I asked Yale students about the strike, some soon began to talk about their parents or their sex lives. Sometimes it was very free association: "I don't oppress women in my fantasies. Or do I? Once I dreamed about tying my girl friend up. But we'd been out looking for *string* that afternoon, for our kite, and we couldn't find any, it was Sunday, and string got to be an obsession, so I dreamed about *rope*. You see, I met her during the strike, and what I was going to tell you . . . " But since women are very new at Yale (the first ones arrived in the fall of 1969), the relations between men and women overlapped and mingled with questions raised by the strike, especially since some men kept saying that women's issues "weren't political." After feeling that they were unwelcome, or being sexually stampeded, or treated like Martians, many moved rapidly into the women's movement—perhaps even more swiftly than they might have done elsewhere.

One woman student said, "The men were schizzy about us. At first it was hard for women to get dates, yet the men were all horny as hell, and so were we. Dressed-up girls from other colleges were coming on weekends, wearing makeup. Should we dress up too—even if we weren't going out? I found a boyfriend quickly, as an anchor, to give me friends and an identity. He was a male chauvinist pig and I broke up with him. . . . After the strike I went through a phase of not being able to deal with single men—I dated married men, and blacks, and got interested in women. Because I just don't want a marriage like my mother's."

At Yale, as on other campuses, I heard much doubt about one-to-one relationships. But since sex is as available as Mars Bars, quite a few young men and women have started to mention love again—mainly wondering if it's possible, or possible to sustain, which many feel is unlikely. I met few who thought it realistic or desirable to spend a lifetime with one person. "But that doesn't mean that some of us aren't going to try. What's torturing is not believing that it's possible."

Another woman said, "The first year at Yale was just insane: all those guys who thought you'd been shipped in for their express pleasure. I even had a heavy pass from my favorite English teacher. I had several boy friends who were a pain in the ass. I thought all men were fucked up, and that all couples were fucked up. Some women turned lesbian, though I wasn't ready to. Though I did have a lesbian relationship during the strike. But I prefer heterosexuality.

"The whole gynecological scene at Yale is a drag. There's a Yale doctor who's all for the pill: like he thinks it's his job to see that Yale men have all the *intercourse* they want. Yale has a little sex book. They think it's so hip to give advice.

"When I went to Yale, I stopped feeling I could do *anything*. I had this feeling: oh, men are good at things, and I'm not. So I stopped doing things like writing."

$\sim$

After some three weeks' saturation in Harvard and Yale, I spent my last night in a commune of ten Yale dropouts, in the country well outside New Haven. It was a miniature farm, lavish with lettuce. There were chickens and a pig named Sabrina and goats (for "g-milk"), and stuffed zucchini for supper, before which almost everyone gave thanks: for a truck which had worked that day, for a small raise on a job, for the weather, for a newborn kid, for Sabrina. Later they played the *Missa Luba* during a sudden thunderstorm. I went to bed in an attic insulated with silvery paper which fell in great folds, like a deflating circus tent, with light from a glowing red lampshade flung against the silver.

This commune is about two years old; a few of the founders remained and quite a number passed through it. (One of the virtues of certain communes is that they suit transitional periods in people's lives; no one has to promise to have and to hold, or to stay forever.) Some may buy land together later on. For others, "This is a good halfway house. And a way to get out of Yale and into other things." Some potential members stay for a trial period, then the group decides if they live flexibly with the others. "That's a problem. We don't want it to be like a fraternity, to make people feel that they're being discussed. But it has to work. We had a difficult guy staying here last year, rather crazy, though every time he got mad, he'd take his temper out on fixing an engine or digging or putting up an electric fence! Which was helpful, but it was a relief when he split."

I've seen some distressed communes, but this one really seemed to be beating the economy. The house cost $250 a month, which was divided between ten; they produced much of their own food and traded their vegetables for oil and grains; most managed to earn approximately $35 a week: working in day care or a record store, a small offset press, a lumber mill, or a health food store. One had made money by folk-singing, and several men and women had been paid to do nude modeling for New Haven art classes. They clearly enjoyed living together; their festive supper, around a vast gleaming wooden table, had a relaxed gaiety many families might envy.

One woman, who had been on the Strike Steering Committee, had set up the first mass meeting, coordinated the marshals for May Day, and had made many speeches, pensively made buttonholes while we mulled over 1970. "We all believed every word we said—and I still do. I just don't believe it can all be changed as quickly. I still go to demonstrations, keep in with the movement. I went to Washington this spring—but it just felt useless. How silly we felt and how useless. . . .

"When I was first at Yale, I tried to be what I thought was a really good Yale student. Trying to conform. It's not that easy to be an ideal student. . . . Then I read a lot of political stuff. Everything seemed hopeless. . . . Some of the political dudes were doing smack—that was the *heavy* thing to do. Because that was what the lumpen proletariat was taking." She chuckled. "Acid was bourgeois. I did smack too, for about a week. It was despair. Oh, I enjoyed it. Though it made everything seem worse when I was off it. I didn't think I'd get addicted. I liked jazz—which I usually hated—when I was on it."

At this point, it should be mentioned that this person of twenty appears to be pushing sixteen. Her experiences, as she cheerfully—and often ironically—unwound them, seemed deeply felt but well in the past, and no stranger could have guessed what she had passed through.

"I used to be a heavy smoker too." She described joining a revolutionary group which was off campus in New Haven. "They were supposed to be lower-middle-class whites, so they didn't like intellectuals, so it was shut up. Take the word from your leader. There were a lot of fifteen-year-old girls, treated as subhumans, made to clean house, expected to sleep with any of the men, or with the New Haven Panthers. The Panther women weren't taking *that* anymore, so the Panthers moved in on these girls. This group was big on discipline, they called it 'mudholing,' which meant getting the shit beaten out of you by the others. Punishment for your own good. . . . When I joined, the leader pinched my ass and gave me a long lecture, mainly from Stalin. We were told to go out and panhandle. We weren't allowed to return until we had fifteen dollars. . . . No, they weren't very political: it was more of a glory trip. The leader told one guy to go steal him a green velvet shirt with ruffles from a boutique: and be sure to get the right size. Then they mudholed a guy who left the door open—that was against security. Then I split."

She rethreaded a needle and peered at a finished buttonhole. "I'd wanted alternatives. But that alternative was intolerable, unacceptable. So I worked a lot more on the strike, and with women's groups. Some women told me I shouldn't be working with men. Other people called me a fucking pig because I was a marshal. Some others were on huge power trips: they just couldn't resist having authority. And Yale's always looking for superstars: later, people began to treat me like that, and I began not to want to go out on the street.

"I was very tired and confused and I thought the revolution was right around the corner. . . . Each term I let my parents talk me into coming back. Yale was very nice about giving extensions. . . . Before the strike, I was having hallucinations—which demonstrated to me how alien society was. I was sitting in an anthropology class: I felt my whole seat rising up, until I was about twenty feet above the floor, holding onto the arms of the chair, I was scared. I willed myself down again, left the class, and left Yale. I thought it meant I was alienated."

More thread for the needle. "Right after the strike, I didn't know where my head was at. Then I saw the revolution wasn't coming. That's what happened to a friend of mine—she saw it wasn't coming, and she couldn't handle that, she had a breakdown.

"I was away for the summer, but I went back to New Haven, I still hoped and thought the revolution might be there. . . . I lived in a collective in town, and a guy with a knife came through the window at five-thirty A.M. when I was asleep, and I got raped. Yale did nothing for me, and the cops said I invited it—when I was asleep? My mother was so anxious to know if I was a virgin when I was raped. But *that* should have made it worse! For a virgin to be raped. The cops took my nice new bedsheet for 'evidence' and never returned it.

"All during the strike, I was so into being a free, independent woman, feeling physically free. So the rape—being physically overpowered, he was a big man, and I woke up with him on top of me, and he started strangling me—it was a shock.

"I dropped out. Oh yeah, the other thing that happened was I got pregnant. I don't know if it was from the rape or not. Maybe it was.

"At the Yale health department, they'd been giving me the morning-after pill. Then when I was pregnant, they told me that it gives you a 90 percent chance of having a deformed baby. Now, I wonder if that's true? But I believed it at the time. Maybe I could hack having an illegitimate baby. But not a deformed illegitimate baby. . . . I had a good abortion in New York."

She smoothed out her long skirt. "Well, that's where I was with the strike. . . . I still think the Panthers did a lot of good things, like their health clinic. It's very good, I've used it. And we did learn a lot from them, fast. But yes, this local chapter *was* fucked up. And we were naive: insisting that the others besides Bobby and Ericka had been framed."

Downstairs, someone was playing tunes that sounded Irish on a fife and we listened for a moment.

"I don't know what you do. Group living—being responsible for your own food supply, living in a way that doesn't rape the planet or other people— maybe these are steps in the right direction. It's such fun to live here. I'm working in day care now. But it's a partial answer—and not for everyone. Rural communes are lovely, but there's not enough land for everybody. . . . "

The sewing was finished, she stretched. "I love music, and I've worked as an electrician in a theater, lighting shows, but I don't want to get into that. Theater's hectic and stupid, licking asses and kicking asses. Too frenetic. . . . I still enjoy archeology, maybe I'll get into that some day. Now, I'm into mechanics and pigs." (She was in charge of Sabrina.) "Maybe I'll go back to Yale sometime: to become a veterinary."

~

What do you remember about Mayday now?

"I made tons of Familia. I had a lot left over afterward."

"I was a medic. I squirted water in people's eyes—even if they hadn't been gassed."

"People disappear. One politico I knew is keeping bees in Israel now."

"I was radical then."

Despite all the reasons for the fading of the movement—the sense of helplessness, the occasions where some radicals tyrannized others, fears of federal retaliation, fears of increased violence, cynicism, the draft lottery, and, as one black student said, "confronting the situation in America is hard to do *all* the time"—it's still not entirely clear why the commitment on some campuses has been muted. You wonder if there's such a thing as a temporary learning process: if some views, quite deeply held, can just evaporate.

A master said, "Some were permanently changed. For others, being nineteen means shifting your commitments. And then feeling guilty." A radical Harvard instructor said, "You have to remember that most people just aren't political!" He added, "The real failure of the left was not having a program. But kids can't provide that, they've no experience. Maybe it has to be an adult movement in the future."

Throughout the late Sixties, I think that many leftists expected too much of poor people and very young people, of blacks and students. Because there were so many of them, we hoped students might have power as a pressure group, as smaller generations—such as those born in the Thirties—did not. But they were overloaded with the expectations of those who were better off or more experienced than they. I also recall that many older people—including certain professors—asked the young to make sacrifices they weren't prepared to make themselves. These ranged from "being ready to put your life on the line" to demanding that students remain in their university towns all year round, to work on radical projects—as their seasoned mentors did not.

As for Either/Or: I imagine that black Americans would want to pose that alternative to all white liberals—in terms of their commitment to equality, to combating racism. Still, Either/Or was interpreted too loosely, in a way that made some feel they must abandon whatever they enjoyed or found worthwhile: music or raising vegetables or reading fiction. But although culture was sometimes called a middle-class luxury, I never met a revolutionary who hadn't listened to a song or two. Perhaps that was another error of the Sixties: the idea that politics must drive out every other experience. But of course none of these considerations would be valid in the the ghetto, in Vietnam.

Five Years After Kent State
September 1975

Among the parking lots and the bleak brick buildings of Kent State—which resemble each other so closely that it's easy to lose one's way again and again—where bulletin boards are aflutter with Beer Blasts and fraternity smokers, ads for tuxedo rentals and wholesale vitamins, or an impending lecture by David Frost on "Interviews I Shall Never Forget," where signs read "Welcome

Goodrich" (which leased some space in the library for its management development programs), where even young professors say "Pardon my language"
before a word like "crap," a visitor is forced to ponder the difference between
ghosts and scars.

The university doesn't seem haunted: eating meals with students or listening to the chatter of freshmen lining up to buy textbooks, you learn that
most know (or care) very little about the past. Lavish hair and jeans and body
suits and hiking boots make them look like the Aquarians of the late Sixties.
But there's no reek of history at Kent: for today's undergraduates the shooting of four students on May 4th, 1970 is as remote as Gettysburg. Initially it's
rather astounding to an outsider that an event which was once a nationwide
experience hardly reverberates in what one professor called "a politically
rinsed atmosphere."

But the scars emerge in conversations with teachers and graduate students
who were there at the time. The scope of perspective on the aftermath of the
killings is broad: few agree on anything except that the university has always
been conservative and has become much more so. Still, many (including
some who wouldn't label themselves liberal) emphasize that the National
Guardsmen weren't in danger—photographs taken just before the shootings
show this—and restate their indignation that live ammunition was brought
on campus. Moreover the campus was not under martial law, as was widely
reported; the crowd had a right to peaceful assembly.

A theme that steadily erupts is the hostility that burst upon the university
right after Allison Krause, Jeffrey Miller, Sandra Scheuer, and William
Schroeder were killed and nine were wounded. Although the hatred that the
murders unleashed has been widely documented, you have to go all the way
to northeast Ohio to fully discover its depth and its intensity—from those
who experienced it firsthand. A deluge of poisonous phone calls and waves
of hate mail descended upon the administrators. Much of the local and national reaction was that the dead students "only got" what they deserved, that
more should have been shot, that the victims were guilty. Parents repeated
this to their offspring and numerous individuals heard it from a hairdresser
or a florist or a teller at the bank. A *Newsweek* poll reported that 60 percent of
Americans thought the shootings were justified. It seems as though there has
been more public compassion for those convicted of the Watergate crimes
than for those who died at Kent State.

Soon after the killings townsmen were seen riding around with guns on
their front seats and there was much talk of vigilantes. And while some liberal
voices denounced Ohio Governor James Rhodes for his incendiary statements
before May 4th—which included the observations that American radicals were
"worse than the brownshirts or the Communist element" and that "No one is
safe in Portage County"—Major Sylvester del Corso of the Guard (who claimed
and later denied that the crowd contained a sniper), and Richard Nixon and

Spiro Agnew for the national climate, the university was reviled by many others, especially because it was assumed that "leftist" teachers had given students too much "liberty." Vietnam wives and mothers were particularly vocal.

~

Resentment of the university by the town had already accelerated during abundant campus expansion in the Sixties—just when beads and beards and dope and horoscopes began to bewilder an older generation that felt its values were being demolished. Many at Kent evoke the animosity aimed at teachers as well as students by storekeepers and landlords. But a townsman noted that citizens who were sixty in 1970 were old enough to remember the Russian Revolution, that many truly did associate beards with Bolsheviks. "The town's response was a reflection of our culture," he continued, "that there's no response to dissent but to shoot."

But it's also stressed that the town suffered in 1970, and the media is charged with not reporting that fact. On May 1st a downtown bar-lined street was trashed; forty-seven windows in fifteen buildings were shattered, and one financier has kept the piece of concrete that was hurled through his office window. A number of those arrested weren't students; some belonged to a motorcycle gang, the Chosen Few. On May 2nd the ROTC building on campus (a temporary wartime structure) was burned. Five years afterward there was still some uncertainty as to who was responsible.

Terror that the town would be bombed and burned was ignited by rumors that banks and schools had been selected as targets and that armed rioters would flock to Kent. Many feared for their homes near the campus. On May 4th parents frantically phoned the university to ask if their own children had been shot. At a time when it seemed almost impossible to untangle rational and irrational fear, quite a few actually thought "the revolution had begun." It's repeated that "there were no guidelines," that those weeks in May had no parallels in the lifetimes of anyone present.

In the midst of the frenzy, quite a few students asked to meet with "responsible" townspeople. A former chairman of the Portage County Republicans, who worked very hard on reconciliation between the town and the university, said that May 1970 was "the most depressing and the most harrowing of all the convulsions I've lived through—including thirty months overseas during World War II." He and some local ministers and church groups, businessmen and bank presidents, the League of Women Voters, and members of the Kent student government, brought students, townspeople, and teachers together in churches and private homes in an effort to build mutual understanding out of the rubble of fright and hatred. Centers for rumor control were set up. Trustees were invited to stay in dormitories and talk with students. Since 1970 Quaker groups have gone to Kent to offer seminars in nonviolent tactics for peace marshalls. Participants in the ongoing dialogues—which persisted

throughout two academic years—felt that some healing occurred. But those
who thought sensitivity was heightened in 1970 told me that communication
has dwindled and that there are now more guns in town than there were
then. The university has a winning football team which plays to a half-empty
stadium: few townspeople attend.

∾

Before May 4th, 1970, the name of Kent was often misheard as "Penn State."
But today the university seems like a paradigm of the nation at large: it appears to reflect and distil the anxieties and the dilemmas of this country more
than any institution I've encountered. Of course economic survival is the
groundnote of the Seventies. Most of the 15,090 undergraduates at Kent are
first generation students, raised in white or blue collar homes in steel towns
or small farming communities in or near the rubber plants of Firestone and
Goodrich. (Their parents in particular were appalled by the campus upheav-
als of the late Sixties. Some disowned their children after the shootings—as
though merely attending Kent meant contamination.) Many students have
fulltime jobs in order to earn their way through school. Naturally, delivering
pizzas or working at the Burg-a-Chef or at a tax appraisal company shrinks
the hours for study, and most are terribly worried about degrees and future
livelihood and whether they'll be employable at all.

The faculty members I met seemed sympathetic to their students' financial plight. Nonetheless many talked about the frustration of teaching a generation that doesn't easily catch fire. It's said that the most gifted students are
on a par with those anywhere. Yet one professor who spoke of the excitement
of his classes of a few years ago, concluded, "Now I teach sheep." Another—
who seemed especially attuned to students—thinks the word "despair" is far
more accurate than "apathy": "They feel that nothing anyone does can make
any difference." The late Sixties are constantly cited as a time when hopes for
change were high. Professors add that they hardly miss the fiercest confrontations or the glorification of the drug culture. However: "My students used
to challenge me, it was terrific. Now they just sit there. The zest is gone."
Another professor said, "The war continues, Nixon's pardoned, Model T is
in the White House. *What* changes? What good did it all do?"

Although May 1970 is still a milestone for many Americans—whether it
propelled them further to the right or to the left—it's discussed at Kent with
barely a reference to Cambodia or Vietnam. Not long ago students protested
the quality of food in the dorms; a graduate explained, "It's easier for kids to
get upset about the taste of food than about a war that's still going on in
Indochina."

Some felt that the path of those springtime bullets proved that no one can
be apolitical, that politics is inescapable. But it's also apparent that the four
deaths made many wish to shed their political instincts—because they began

to equate politics with violence, whether from the right or the left. While the violence condoned by the White House made many fear federal reprisals for even modest political efforts, certain small groups such as the Weathermen made some of the very young feel useless if they recoiled from violence. The feelings of futility about both nonviolence and violence ballooned even further after the blast that killed a physics researcher at the University of Wisconsin later in 1970.

A Kent professor paraphrased the hopelessness that he thinks most students feel about change—in relation to 1970: "If you try to change things, you can get killed." He also spoke about those who "had righted themselves with the McGovern campaign"—which was "another cruncher." Not that many Kent students felt cordial toward politicians. In the spring of 1970 Governor Rhodes had failed to win the Republican nomination for the Senate, despite the expectation that voters would appreciate his "show of force" on several Ohio campuses. It's said that he blamed Kent State for his loss.

～

Shortly after the killings, when the *New York Times* interviewed eleven Kent students, the reporters asked the group if they thought more students would be killed on campus. Most said yes. The transcript of that discussion was published on May 11th, 1970. On May 14th, 20-year-old Phillip Gibbs and 18-year-old Earl Green were shot dead at Jackson State in Mississippi; twelve others were wounded. The gunfire from policemen and Mississippi Highway Patrolmen was directed partly into a crowd of demonstrators and also into the windows of a women's dormitory—which was hit by "nearly four hundred bullets or pieces of buckshot," according to the report prepared by the President's Commission on Campus Unrest. There was immediate and copious media coverage of the slayings. But as many have noted, the deaths of black students did not involve the emotions of numerous white Americans: the national response to the killings at Jackson was never as impassioned as the reactions to Kent.

～

Musing back on 1970, several professors spoke of "the long range effect" on the Nixon administration in its pursuit of "subversives." Others referred to the FBI dossiers on Kent teachers. Twelve were investigated; their students were questioned about what those individuals discussed in and outside the classroom, and what organizations they belonged to. Plainly the investigators were looking for information that could be used to indict the professors for inciting to riot. Only one of them was charged and the charges were dropped.

~

Ever since 1970 there has been a May 4th memorial for the dead. From midnight until the noon service, people stand on the spots where the four bodies fell and there have been speakers ranging from the Harvard biologist George Wald to Julian Bond. Some of the faculty disagree about whether the occasion should be a political statement or simply an anniversary of mourning. Concerned students mentioned the rumors that can peak beforehand: in 1974 there were fantasies that the Symbionese Liberation Army was going to blow up the Ravenna Arsenal. That year some six thousand attended and a number found the commemoration extremely moving. Others called it "futile." A professor said, "Kent State is like Brigadoon. Every spring we come into public awareness, and then we disappear."

~

When some sift back to 1970 they appear to briefly relive the angry debates among the faculty. (A participant recalled remarks that "the students had no business to assemble, it wasn't murder but hooliganism, it was a question of maintaining order.") One professor, who felt the catastrophe was educational for some of his colleagues, said, "People here are talking about the demolition of their innocence . . . But no one can pose as innocent in this day and age, except maybe morons." He alluded to Alexander Herzen, the 19th-century Russian revolutionary theorist: " 'I met history on my way to work.' That's what happened to a lot of them: after thirty or forty years, they met history on their way to work." He paused. "Mention Herzen to most of the kids around here, they'll think he's a candy bar or an outfielder for the Mets."

Another reflected on some senior faculty members who seemed almost paralyzed after the shootings: "People who never realized that the world has changed, or turned. It's like poor Mrs. Hearst coming out on TV and saying 'Come home, Patty, come home, sweetheart'—to Tania. Doesn't know the world has changed." (Tania was the name Patty Hearst took after she joined the Symbionese Liberation Army.) There was also some derision of the "breastbeatings" and "personal purgings" among the faculty of 1970, including a reference to a woman who announced that she would die for her students and shortly thereafter asked, "When is summer vacation?" Some may have identified with a man who later called himself "an ineffective liberal: one who sympathized with students' aims and feared their methods."

~

When the veterans of 1970 are queried about the historical meaning of the shootings, most immediately refer to the dilating conservatism of the country at large. Then some zero in on a specific point. A professor who is also a minister said, "What really struck me was that my rights were taken away. Just like that." He recalled the days right after May 4th, when the town seethed with Guardsmen while helicopters churned overhead, when faculty and students were forbidden to enter the campus, when a memorial service wasn't allowed and the town churches were shut on the Mayor's orders. The National Guard ordered offices to close and the town was sealed off to outside transportation. Freedom of assembly did not extend to groups of more than four. "I saw how tenuous our rights really are, even in this so-called democratic country. If you can't have freedom of assembly, your freedom of speech is curtailed." He was halted on his bicycle by a Guardsman with a bayonet: "When I wasn't even headed toward the campus. Good thing I had good brakes."

A further evaluation of 1970 was: "It gave me a sense of the fragility of existence. Fragility in every sense of life . . . It meant that one has to take a stand on issues or be culpable." May 4th was compared to John Kennedy's assassination: "Nothing made sense, things were becoming more and more baroque. . . . It reminds me of Céline's *Journey to the End of the Night*: a guy who follows a military parade and ends up in World War I, and later, in the jungle. It meant that you can't escape the claim of history or politics."

One professor seemed more patient with today's students than some of her colleagues. "In 1970 we did have a crisis mentality, which meant that anything to do with ordinary living was suspect. There was a terrible time when if you asked a friend 'How are you?' he'd be disgusted"—because the question was too "normal" or cheerful. "But the later students taught us that we couldn't live with crisis all the time. I saw a couple kissing at the Pagoda [where the Guard fired] and my first thought was: My God, how can they do that here? My second thought was: Why not? We need to be reminded of life."

~

After Dallas one heard a number of individuals insisting that "we're all guilty" of the death of President Kennedy. During the earliest chapters of Watergate, Nixon talked as though the whole society was guilty of the break-in. In a culture which often revels in guilt, it seemed essential to explore that theme at Kent. But there it was firmly repeated that the faculty and students refused to feel guilty—even while they were blamed by vindictive outsiders for the atmosphere in which the four were murdered. Instead "many were quick to point the finger" at Rhodes, at Kent's then president Robert White (for his "absence of leadership"), at the government, at the officers of the Guard. It was also suggested that a number of the students who turned out on May 4th, 1970 were spurred largely by a proprietary interest: in reaction to the presence of the Guard on their turf. "Sure, they were tremendously angry," said a teacher. "But it was a spectacle to them. It was spring and kids were curious. How often had they seen battalions of soldiers before?"

A good many professors I talked with felt that a news blackout had been

imposed on the university and the town. There were substantial antiwar demonstrations there in 1971, 1972, and 1973, but the national media hardly
acknowledged any of them.

∾

Some at Kent are very disturbed by the romanticization of Allison Krause,
when Sandra Scheuer, William Schroeder, and Jeffery Miller aren't often
mentioned outside the community. Research by Peter Davies, author of *The
Truth About Kent State,* asserts that Allison Krause didn't put that legendary
flower in the barrel of a rifle, but merely spoke to a Guardsman who already
had a flower. (Apparently she did say, "Flowers are better than bullets" after
an officer had ordered him to remove it.) But it seems unjust to the memories of all four that so much mythology has been heaped upon them, both
from the right—there were tales that autopsies showed that their bodies were
ravaged by venereal diseases or hard drugs—and from the left, which sought
to canonize Allison Krause, probably because the others were not political.

Occasionally you hear about someone who's called "the fifth victim." Mary
Vecchio—the 14-year-old runaway whose agonized figure kneeling by Jeffrey
Miller's corpse became an image of the decade and the Vietnam War at
home—was inundated with abuse when she returned to her home in Opa-
Locka, Florida. For many people she personified the campus "bums" Nixon
had vilified just a few days before the killings. She and her parents—who
raised her strictly—received hundreds of savage letters calling her a whore
and a Communist; Claude Kirk, then the Governor of Florida, implied on
television that she was involved in a Communist plot; neighbors forbade their
children to see her and her high school principal publically praised the students who ostracized her. Without her parents' permission the famous photograph of her appeared on t-shirts and posters. Letters also regretted that
she wasn't shot dead and some recommended suicide.

Mary Vecchio became severely withdrawn, ran away once more to go to a
rock concert, and was committed to a juvenile home in 1971. Two years later
she was arrested for prostitution in Miami and fined $50. Her defense was
that it was hard to find anyone who would hire her. In 1974 she told Geraldo
Rivera on "Goodnight, America" that she had worked mainly in the street,
that it was "really rough," and that she'd left "the business." She characterized herself as "the hapless hooker." Her experiences seemed to chime with
the classical tradition of punishing the messenger who delivers the bad news.
(In 1980 she married and eventually became a cashier in a Las Vegas coffee
shop; in 1990 she told a reporter that the Kent State photograph had "destroyed my life.")

∽

"It's unfortunate what happened, but my sympathy is with the law": the word "unfortunate" recurs when you talk with some Kent townsmen about the shootings. They reiterate their relief that the Guardsmen were judged innocent in 1974. Some still cling to the concept that Kent was "picked" by outsiders intent on starting a revolution. Conversations about the killings can lead rapidly to indignant allusions to the national crime rate or not going to Cleveland for dinner or the movies "because it isn't safe." One businessman added, "Still, they've made a lot of strides in weapons since 1970. Ever fire an M-1? It'd kill a horse at two miles."

In an age of paradox, caution on the part of certain conservatives can take the form of sounding somewhat liberal. Perhaps they can afford to do so because this is such a conservative period; they may also want to disassociate themselves from Nixon and Watergate and therefore—briefly—from the G.O.P. The wariness about revealing associations is mirrored by the number of youngish persons who don't want it known that they were in the antiwar movement in the Sixties. Maybe the denial of experience is a national trait: in June 1974 a poll which questioned the voters of 1972 reported that McGovern had won the Presidency by a slight majority—that is, many who voted for Nixon could not bear to admit it.

At the same time traditional liberals now seem comfortable with sounding quite conservative: they can repudiate antiwar protests, their former students, or black activists with an ease that was rare five years ago. In contrast, a Kent conservative said he and most townsmen believed that young men "should serve their country" and then promptly volunteered, "But I don't necessarily support the Vietnam War." Yet lately I've heard some who call themselves liberals remarking that there was "no real alternative" to our Vietnam policy since 1965.

∽

It's rather startling to see a reference to "the golden Sixties" in an official brochure about Kent. But amid the pungent cynicism and the demoralization about change, I did find some teachers and students working in local poverty programs or on women's rights, or for the ACLU, which was involved in the wrongful death suits brought by the parents of the dead against Rhodes, White, del Corso, Brigadier General Robert Canterbury of the Guard, and the University's Board of Trustees. The charges were dismissed. Most of all, the families of the dead had wanted an official admission of wrongdoing and an apology, but they received neither. (In 1979 the families were awarded $15,000 apiece; the nine wounded students—one paralyzed for life—were given more substantial sums.)

A professor who declared that "Being political has changed its definition" cited Town Hall II—a counseling center and free medical clinic—a thriving food co-op, and "a fairly non-profit community store," plus a few environmental projects. Some others shrugged at such exertions. A professor who used to be politically active was contemptuous of former antiwarriors who now work with drug addicts or rubber packers or in the steel mills; he almost equated them with health enthusiasts who are "into nuts and stuff." As in many communities, people's perceptions of what is or isn't political—from sex to recycling—often clash. Perhaps the heritage of the Sixties, when political awareness fanned out in so many directions, has generated some confusions about the political weight of any simple act, like growing vegetables or challenging a landlord. Yet these distinctions seemed very clear a few years ago.

One direct response to the May murders was the formation of the Center for Peaceful Change, which was defined as "a living memorial" to the dead students. The department gives courses on nonviolent philosophies and strategies, including those of Gandhi and Martin Luther King. The workshops explore concrete techniques for change, such as organizing civic leaders to put pressure on Congress. The Center's newest branch is the Living/Learning Community, a co-ed dorm where some thirty-eight students "try to combine classroom experience with living experience." If the language there seems too abstract at times—what with the repetition of "impactful" and the ejaculations of "insight!"—one point that's forcefully made is that the students of 1970 knew far too little about tactics. (In the Sixties, when Nixon assured the peace movement he wasn't listening, it seemed inevitable that protest took more and more frantic forms—as many became more desperate to gain the government's attention.) A Kent graduate said, "We really wanted that war to end, we really wanted the Guard off campus. But the demonstrators were unskilled and they were acting out of their emotions. Now we're trying to learn the skills. In 1970 people only knew how to shout, and when that didn't work they switched from political activism to being geodesic dome-dwellers. And the dome-dwellers are no better prepared to deal with a war over oil than the old activists."

It appears that those who study Peaceful Change do encourage each other's hopes for a more rational society. But even there, amid a group relaxed on a red shag rug or over a vegetarian dinner, you hear echoes of the pessimism that seeps through the university—and this whole country. There was some enthusiastic talk about a community of older friends who "have made drastic changes in their lives." A young woman elaborated: "They're not wasteful. They know there's a world in trouble out there, and that what they eat and what they drive and what they cook affects it. And we'll all have to be willing to live with less if we're going to prevent a war over oil or keep people from starving.

"But I really fear that most Americans will refuse to make simple, gentle, daily changes in their lifestyles. The resistence will be so strong out there—from folks who'll be afraid that they'll lose everything they earned and worked for. And probably the concerned people won't do much but just wait for the worst to happen. And I think it will."

Firecrackers burst in the snowy night, sounding like gunshots; a sophomore shrugged in irritation: "Jocks." Conversation about "gentle change and democratic process" continued until one student ruefully suggested, "They should just give us all football helmets so we can bang our heads against the wall."

Another grinned. "Nonviolently, of course."

∽

A few members of the Revolutionary Student Brigade (once the Attica Brigade) kept appearing on the Kent campus in January 1975; in lobbys and lounges they unspooled a short documentary about the shootings, attempting to galvinize Kent students into demonstrating at Rhodes's inauguration. (He was re-elected in 1974.) Clusters of about twenty gathered to watch, but most fled at the end of the movie and many preferred a horror flick on a nearby tube. During the film the spectators guffawed whenever Nixon's face appeared, but they showed no response to his words about invading Cambodia.

The handful who stayed to argue accused the Brigade of naïveté and of "living back in the Sixties." (Beards confronted beards: the Brigadiers and those who scoffed at them were identically costumed.) Almost all were reluctant to demonstrate, and they seemed puzzled by the risks students took in 1970.

"You think people want to get shot at?"

"You can't change things—seventy-five percent of the folks in this country are too ignorant."

"Nothing will change: the government's too powerful."

The mistrust of ideology—any ideology—flared high and there were chuckles when a Brigadier said, "We're building a mass consciousness for when the revolution comes." Several students said they'd be willing to protest "the Kent State whitewash," but they refused to back the three other demands on the Brigade's leaflet: amnesty for all war resisters, no further aid to Thieu and Lon Nol, and "End All Attacks on Working Class and Other Oppressed People." One young man insisted that the issues were spread too thin: "I'm not gonna go to Columbus to yell 'Free Puerto Rico!' at Governor Rhodes. What will that do for Kent State?"

The Brigadiers were clumsy and defensive; when praising the demonstrations of the Sixties, they weren't able to make connections between the antiwar movement and Lyndon Johnson's resignation or the Nixonian paranoia that resulted in Watergate. A professor later told me that the Brigadiers were "neither students nor revolutionary."

~

After the shootings it was proposed that an old university building be called "Hyde Park" and used as a center for free speech. "You can go there and ask for a bullhorn and talk about anything. No one does."

~

During the Chicago convention of 1968, it was plain to many of us in the streets that droves of spectators were exhilarated to see others beaten for the length of their hair or for their press tags. Afterward, when a Harris poll reported that 71.4 percent of Americans thought the police violence was warranted, some wondered if a right-wing renascence was on the way. In the fall of 1970, former Attorney General John Mitchell told a journalist, "Listen, there is no such thing as the New Left. This country is going so far to the right you are not even going to recognize it."

Barbed wire barricades have not been erected to contain the inhabitants of black ghettos, and preventive detention camps aren't functioning today. But although the Chicago 7, the Berrigans, Bobby Seale and Ericka Huggins, the New York Panther 21, Angela Davis, the Soledad Brothers, Daniel Ellsberg, the Vietnam veterans of Gainesville, were either acquitted or had the charges against them dismissed, and though John Mitchell would spend nineteen months in jail after being convicted of conspiracy, obstruction of justice, and lying under oath, the radical movement can seem as remote as one's first pair of jeans.

Many expected that the Kent State killings would swell the forces of dissent, that the momentum of 1967 and 1968 and 1969 would be unquenchable. But most of the affinity groups were too far scattered to celebrate Nixon's resignation or to exult in the discovery that his fear of them had inspired a binge of lawbreaking. By 1975 many voices were saying that it seemed as though "the Sixties never happened." But as political events and policies (foreign or domestic) continued to govern our lives—as the war went on until the spring of 1975, while inflation and unemployment soared—many Americans appeared to want to shun them: a reflex that was perhaps first triggered by the killings at Kent State.

Part II

Utopia and Inferno

Here are two pieces of personal experience which haunted me for some years. One school and one job, each rooted in the realm of privilege: I kept celebrating my escape from both of them.

After I wrote an anti-utopian blast about my progressive school, I visited some communes and collectives I liked very much. (Well, they weren't utopian.) But I'm respectful of many communal efforts and also of experiments in education. What intrigues me here is liberal hypocrisy—or how an intensely conventional society pretends to be liberal. The unacknowledged stuffiness of my school demanded a degree of conformity I hadn't witnessed elsewhere. So I think it's useful to understand how whole communities can fool themselves. Still, after living through the Reagan-Bush years and the money culture, I became more tolerant of well-intentioned naiveté.

As for life on a women's magazine: the subject was unsettling for the women's movement. For feminists of the early Seventies, the question of how women treated women seemed as important as how women were treated by men or by society. Of course many women have been trained to be hostile toward other women, and the notion that women are natural enemies satisfies some men. But when I wrote about my stint in a women's office, I wanted to shame the employers who positively encouraged women to behave badly toward one another. And I thought plenty of men would recognize the habits of large corporations which approve of in-fighting among the staff in the name of healthy competition.

Boarding in Heaven
April 1968

> I'd rather keep bachelor's hall in hell than go to board in heaven if that
> place is heaven.
>
> —*Thoreau on Brook Farm*

As Palestrina's *Hosanna* poured through open windows, I reverently raised
my rack of test tubes gleaming with the urine of diabetic rats and carried
it between lilac bushes that were rocking in the sun. The experiment had
been successful, in that the urinalysis differed from that of normal rats and
predictably contained sugar. My latest sonnet had been completed the night
before; a new calf had been named for me; my little production of *Sweeney
Agonistes* had been applauded, and a teacher had told me that I was "incor-
ruptible" (because I didn't play bridge). Sliding my test tubes into a giant
kitchen freezer, I joined a Bach chorus rehearsal for Cantata 150: we sang
"And so my soul shall rest content." Perfection seeped from the walls and
from the blossoming trees outside; there was health and happiness and praise;
above all there was the promise of one's own superiority. Costumed for life
by accomplishments, lavished with credentials like "creative," "individual,"
"fulfilled," we would soon be bestowed on the fortunate world: by graduating from school in two weeks. I liked urinalysis and I loved Bach. It should
have been flattering to master art and science in a single day: in a setting that
merely asked one to unfold. Hence one felt a seedy ingratitude for failing to
believe in this Utopia, a viperish guilt for longing to escape Elysium.

Perhaps the utopian temptation is particularly American. After all this
country was at first supposed to be a Utopia in itself, and disappointment
drove various citizens to form their own Utopias as early as the 1690s—
although the nineteenth century was of course the uniquely utopian era.
Americans were rapidly repelled by what their own society produced or became. Our Utopias, whether religious or atheistic, utilitarian or aesthetic,
austere or epicurean, socialist or anarchist, whether based on the grittiest
economics or the wildest worship of Beauty, reconfirm Thomas More's pun:
Utopia can mean "no place" as well as the "good place." Their failures were

usually tinged with irony: as if high purpose was fated to parody itself, to bite off its own tail.

At Robert Owen's New Harmony, the principle of equal sharing dissolved after the communal cashbox was quickly emptied by greedy colonists, despite the anticapitalistic doctrines which initially drew them together. The unit also collapsed, as one member said, from "too much democracy—the community was talked to death," especially because votes were taken on every pinching detail. The transcendentalists' Brook Farm, which Hawthorne hated and even Emerson and Thoreau refused to join—Emerson decided that it wasn't necessary that "the writer should dig"—and Bronson Alcott's Fruitlands, where "spade culture" exhausted those who meant to "make a new heaven and a new earth" after only seven months, both sound like excuses for writers' blocks, although they were intended as shrines to the intellect.

The Oneida Colony, founded to nurture communism and polygamy, became thoroughly capitalistic, property-loving to the extent that it became "difficult to borrow a hammer"; soon it dominated the steel trap market throughout America. From an Eden where "amative intercourse" could become "a fine art," it lapsed into jealous monogamy. From Edward Bellamy to Upton Sinclair or Ayn Rand and B. F. Skinner, fictional Utopias show a ticklish similarity: in the assumption that everyone's needs and desires will be the same and that, as Robert Owen wrote, "man's character is not of his own formation." The last point may be mockable when applied to adults, but it can be queasily true for many adolescents. My coeducational boarding school appears as one of the few American Utopias that has survived.

The school was founded in New England in the Thirties. It was designed to offer freedom, art, nature, equality, and ideals to students who would receive a sublime education while learning to be peerless citizens. Actually it's a very old-fashioned place, engineered to grapple with the ogres of Victorian restraint. But it appeals to parents whose own education was repressive or frustrating. And the school is violently fashionable, especially because so many famous people have sent their children there. Teachers, parents, and students, all vibrate to resonant names.

The institution has had a colossal effect on other schools and it mirrors much that is occurring in our styles of education. But it can't be criticized. Those who love it and believe in it are more easily outraged by dissent than the devout of any faith—they're more dogmatic than Jesuits or the radical right. Perhaps Utopias must preclude criticism or humor or rage, or any jagged emotion, since the notion of perfection must be unyielding and cannot allow defiance or burlesque. Laughter or doubt sap the certitude that's essential to fuel an impossibility, to make a mirage concrete. The school is an impossibility, and yet it's resplendently successful. Only a few traitors feel that it fails—and that the treadmarks left on its nostalgic graduates are symptoms of weaknesses which dilute much of our education, our upbringing, and help to congeal some national neuroses.

Perhaps the most enfeebling doctrine ballooned out of the hallucination that everyone's an artist. The refrain was, "If it's in you, it's bound to come out." Although the intestinal imagery suggests elimination rather than production, almost any adolescent would thrill to the theme. Many of the convinced poets, painters, playwrights, and composers fell apart at college, where the fragility of their talents was revealed. Some wasted many adult years in trying and failing to flourish in the arts. Practicing an art was supposed to impart a condition of being—which was superior to any other state. During one commencement speech, the principal said that the school had produced many artists, scientists, and teachers, "and (distressful pause) . . . and lawyers . . . and (painful hesitation) . . . well, *bankers*." We knew that bankers, also most professional persons, were despicable creatures, wheezing away in the offices that made them miserable, clutching at filthy cash—they were quite justly gutted by the system they helped to perpetuate. Still, since we were meant to believe in equality, all of our own schoolmates had to be thought superior.

There was also the conviction that everyone can be good at everything, from calving to writing verse, the French horn or welding. I once took sculpture because I needed to fill an evening class. Being bootless with my hands, I wasn't surprised when my kneeling clay statue (called "The Outcast," subtitled "Cast Out") often caved in at the chest and constantly lost its enormous head, which rolled wetly across the floor after five minutes of wobbling on the thin neck of that doleful figure. I thought it was hilarious and felt it looked best holding the head on its depressed lap. But the teacher was demoralized. She kept insisting that I could "truly be" a sculptor. (I gleefully wrote this down at the time, along with the other quotes that appear here.) "You are tactile," she said. "Just as there is music in you, there is art." I disagreed eagerly, but tried to cheer her by carving a hideous wooden fish. She cried when my wild chisel shattered the tail into splinters. As a senior, fleeing from what was called "your literary bent," I resolved to be a biochemist—I'd been allowed to think that I was very good at it. (It would have been a disastrous attempt at college, where I certainly would have failed. I was lucky that false encouragement didn't propel me as far into science as it shoved others in the arts. Also, I was three years behind in preparation—in all subjects.) Ironically, the tyranny of thinking that everyone has talent perverted the possibility of developing happy amateurs: those who may sing or sketch for pleasure, without trying to be professional geniuses.

But artists couldn't be oddities. The school's most triumphant paradox was its extreme conservatism. (Due to peripatetic parents, I went to ten schools, and none was so oppressively conventional as this one.) There was infinite rhubarb about "individuality": the teachers twinkled, beamed, and breathed on us and urged originality. But students of that age are unnerved by hymns to freedom. Many teachers were so naive that the students recoiled from them and rebelled by constructing the most rigid social system I've ever seen. In fact the teachers' attempts at "permissiveness" resulted in conformity in the students.

Hence few had the courage of their eccentricities, since it was fatal to seem peculiar or even slightly inconsistent. Even absentmindedness was an ominous trait. In a midwinter fog I used to stand patiently knocking at the door of my own room: waiting for myself to let me in. This gave other students the horrors, despite my nice cousin's efforts to reassure them of my sanity. Loners were also disapproved. My faculty adviser told me to stop taking solitary walks and listening to music by myself because it was upsetting for others—that they concluded I didn't like them. Since we had no privacy, I said that I *did* often want to be alone, but would that prevent my making friends? She replied that it probably would—also "Man is a societal being"—and implied that solitude was unnatural.

Psychology was an earnest hobby for most teachers: they did adore problem children and sometimes sought symptoms where none existed. When I entered the school at fifteen, I had rarely made a bed and didn't plan to start. So I kept the window shade permanently lowered in my room—to hide the snarl of sheets and blankets. Years later I learned that several faculty conferences were held about my terrible emotional state. They thought I was curled in the dark in a foetal position—when I was out riding my horse over the hills. No one looked in the room for months; they consulted texts. Finally the unmade bed was discovered, and a teacher admitted that the truth was disappointing. However a couple of students with severe emotional troubles went unnoticed, and nothing was remarked until their parents carted them away for treatment.

From Plato to H. G. Wells, many theoretical Utopias have been guided by an elite, where power belonged to the most intelligent members. Some Utopias have even admitted to the presence of "the base and the dull"—which our school could not dare to do. The teachers wanted us to like them and as a graduate remembers, "They were in real trouble when we didn't." Their lack of influence clenched that reactionary social structure which resulted from student power. (We had the sovereignty then that many students demanded later.) While the faculty beseeched us to be unconventional, they didn't notice that a caricature of the public high school dating system was pleating our lives. It was crucial to be a couple: socially rather than romantically. There was a biannual dance for which we all submitted lists of preferred partners: it was an official popularity contest which meant far more agony for those rejected than it yielded pleasure for others. Girls cried and boys swore with disgust at the names they'd received: so many felt ashamed of one another. Couples were drearily faithful, although the one who severed the tandem was considered the more desirable. (Although the school's principal was a feminist, most girls muffled their minds in class, convinced that they would be more attractive if they made the boys feel brighter.) While these patterns are inherent to middle-class America, it's startling that they should reach their zenith in a Utopia which kept gargling about its freedom from the orthodox.

Certainly, being wildly in love at sixteen, amid baroque trumpets and in a beautifully tangled landscape, was an exhilaration that I'll never deny. The high pounce of those trumpets as one raced down a hill or embraced between the roots of a rustling elm, made daily life a pagan privilege—until one was interrupted. True, the sight of a flashlight still generates an adult phobia: the teachers were always hunting and finding couples under bushes, in haylofts, rolling about in fields and ditches, or clasped on the roof of the vegetable root cellar. Virginity was (sometimes barely) maintained, really because we had too little time to lose it—a bell rang, horses had to be groomed, or a meeting on World Federalism began, an arts conference opened, there was a rehearsal of Auden or Pirandello. Reeling and gasping out of one another's arms, we were kept exhaustingly busy.

One's role in the community was meant to be equally strengthening to the self and the school. It was supposed to be rewarding to make a contribution. This charming concept often collapses because few have multiple capacities. By my senior year, my deficiencies in leadership were noted. Hence I was made the head of a farm crew: to stimulate my executive talents. Mine was a dangerous little band which achieved some expensive damage. We planted a whole field of gladioli instead of the beans which were meant to feed the school, demolished stone walls which should have been repaired, and pulled apart electric fences which released cows into realms of disaster. Some of this pandemonium occurred because I misunderstood the toothless directions spat through a pungent Vermont accent. But the kind farmer and I despaired together about my being a leader. My crew grew flaccid through a communal sense of failure. To preserve the farm from further destruction, we were assigned weeks of cleaning the chicken house. Choking on ammonia and chicken turds, dodging cross hens, scraping the dripping roosts and breaking eggs, I recalled my family's observation that this school cost more than any university and they hoped I was damn well getting a lot out of it. A final spurt of leadership resulted in feeding the pigs something that made them amazingly sick—since pigs are supposed to have such good digestions. Still, I never quite shared Hawthorne's feelings (after he'd milked the "transcendental heifer") on Brook Farm's barn: "Of all the hateful places that is the worst. . . . It is my opinion that a man's soul may be buried and perish under a dungheap or in a furrow of the field, just as well as under a pile of money." Later he wrote, "Is it a praiseworthy thing that I have spent five golden months in providing food for cows and horses? It is not so."

Naturally farm work was preferable to the tyrannical athletic programs that traditional schools insist on. And it was splendid for city children to be unleashed in the countryside. There was a voluptuous mud season, preceding spring, when the ground cracked and shone, liquid earth ran down hills, and the melting snow made small temporary streams full of mysterious shrimp. Still, "embracing nature" was a piebald principle: we were supposed to respond sensuously to soil and clouds and leaves, but not to one another. Hugging a tree "didn't even satisfy my *spirit*," a classmate sadly said. The idea that physical work and merging with nature are sanctifying was belted about with a lack of sophistication that would have sickened Rousseau or Thoreau. (The Brook Farmers believed that educated people should do some manual labor in order to free the working class for some hours of cultural pursuit. But we had no such excuse.) Again our sensations were meant to make us superior: plunge your wrists into the potato field and it will magnify your soul. Far more credit was given for hard physical work than for any mental effort. We heard a lot about "honest sweat," which made me wonder what dishonest sweat might be— sexual or cerebral?

In recent years one graduate has personified the dilemmas of this heritage. An intensely urban man, he has occasional fits of feeling that he must move himself and his whole family to the country—as though a rural setting would make him a good person. Yet on mere suburban weekends he often finds the sun too hot, the water too wet, the breeze too breezey; pine needles prick his feet and sand infuriates him. When he finally said the ocean was too salty, I cautiously suggested that he didn't really like nature. He laughed and momentarily agreed. But for those of our education, a distaste for mud or wheat or birds can mean a sordid character defect. It's the knapsack mentality which haunts this kind of community: everyone simply has to revere the same things.

A maddened parent lately said, "They study only the snow up there." Many alumni agree that the teaching and the curriculum were phlegmatic—especially because each teacher was allowed to invent his own course. We were totally dependent on the personal skills or ineptitudes of each random instructor. In some courses, teachers deferred to the students and asked them what they wanted to study. Thus the already creaky tradition of making pupils responsible for what they learn: "sharing" in the educational process. So we played records of Edith Piaf and Charles Trenet in French class, learned a lot about using the metro, and were not pestered with grammar. There was some Maupassant and some Anouilh, the only apparent giants of French literature. Few teachers had much confidence in their subjects: they were afraid that we wouldn't like "old" things and feared to impose the past upon us. Contempt for the past meant that some subjects were superior to others—for example, Russian or Spanish was "better" than Latin. Historical sequence was usually disdained. We paddled along on the comparative approach, which is still nurtured in many colleges which bend the knee to general education. In a sphere of "creative thinking," as they called it, anything may be explained in terms of anything else: King Lear is like Christ who is like Socrates.

The most deplorable exercise was the teaching of English, where the students' choice of matter was the freest of all. In three years I was assigned exactly two Shakespeare plays (*Richard I* and *II,* for a paper on "subjectivity and objectivity"), yards of Katherine Mansfield and Archibald MacLeish, Upton Sinclair, *Patterns of Culture, John Brown's Body,* plus *A Passage to India* and *Darkness at Noon* (to learn how to hunt for symbols), and very little else— since no one wanted to rush us. I once asked why we weren't allowed more of the classics. I was told that we would have been bored by them, since the vocabulary was difficult and out of date. We were never supposed to be bored: another winsome preparation for adult life.

The English teachers were mainly capsized writers or would-be semanticists. They seemed so pleased with anything we wrote that there was no need to wrestle with the language. Stupendously bored in my first year, I ceased to work and failed three courses. My father said grimly that he could see how Latin and Algebra had gone awry, "But how in the name of Jesus could you fail English?" There was no honorable defense. We were supposed to work from inspiration, and I just hadn't felt inspired. For the last two years I did work quite hard, and learned nothing outside of polyphony and photosynthesis. The music and biology courses were excellent, due to the luck of having gifted teachers.

The superb music department was almost another irony, since the brilliant man who ran it was a scholar sure of his subject and unusually demanding: he gave difficult assignments and we loved them. His were almost the only courses which followed historical sequence. He also infused the whole school with a devotion to music—and to his shouting, irascible self. In his orchestra, chamber, and choral groups, students would strive for the precision that wasn't required elsewhere. The other teachers could have learned a lot from his example. But most of the academic experience was meant to be effortless: you lay back and allowed the text to stroke you. Acute mental exertion was considered a symptom of coldness or emotional limitation, despite all the benign nods to "the life of the mind."

But John Dewey needn't be blamed for the school's character. Although he emphasized learning by doing, he stressed that "the sort of material that instructs children or adults outside of school is fundamentally the same sort that has power to instruct within the school. . . . " He would probably have been appalled by the mental isolation that permitted us to float free from history, politics, and even daily events. One outraged visiting lecturer found the students innocent of the pope's death and the opening of the World Series, as well as the mere outlines of the international affairs he'd planned to discuss with them.

Competition and aggression ranked as vile qualities and the school's ethic breathed contempt on hustling. We had no marking system—which was also a wistful attempt to eliminate anxiety. Those who came to the school with headlong ambitions were whittled down. We rarely had to make decisions or to find our own directions. Many became rather passive, and subsequent years at college were miserable for them. It's been noted that the school had a far more lasting influence on boys than on girls. Many of the young men were especially vulnerable in later life: wavering, hurt, and bewildered. Those at Harvard used to revisit the school for constant weekends, telling us how dreadful it was outside. None I knew became cynics; some even wept as they talked, and it was the first time I'd ever seen male tears. Later, when I was at Radcliffe, most of the boys simply disappeared. Some left college quickly, others never found their feet in Cambridge—even though it was lavish with opportunities in the arts. Someone said that this school invented the dropout, long before the gesture became fashionable. Many of our teachers had been dropouts from city life or other jobs.

Perhaps an additional wound was gashed in the male side because students were deified for qualities which weren't much appreciated elsewhere: "ideals" (never quite defined), skill at chopping down trees or gaining a cordial response from farm animals. But being successful in that community often meant being unfit for any other. Confidence in what one learned there rapidly collapsed because the world had such different standards. Bronson Alcott had wanted to restore innocence: our school synthesized it as an artificial product.

Throughout there was the delusion that all problems have solutions. "Adjustment" was perhaps all the harder because of the hypocrisies that nestled in this Utopia. We were all supposed to be free: but it was a conformist society. Competition didn't exist: but socially, it was frantically competitive. The "community of equals" betrayed a fierce pecking order. All students were artists: but they weren't. Since capitalism was repulsive, the school was called "nonprofit," and no doubt it was; however it was and is one of the most expensive schools in the country. (I suspect that it must rely on admitting many of the children of the rich.) "Helping others" was often a disguise for helping yourself—for example, improving your French by being a counselor in a French camp, which was merely being polite in admitting Americans. (There was jubilant scorn for tourism; rather, you went abroad to help the poor, shiftless Europeans upgrade their farms. There were many shocks when the French or the English showed they were being patronized—or that we were simply a nuisance.) The school was said to be a democracy. It was really run as a benevolent dictatorship, in a fashion that enraged many teachers. As at Brook Farm, there was meant to be "no strife." In fact contentions crackled through the air and we even had a turbulent teachers' strike: a pre-Sixties school revolution. The faculty's own ideals perpetually came undone before us; they were embarrassed, as though their flies were open.

A minor delusion even hung on our wardrobes. Most Utopias censure attention to clothing—as though style or trappings were polluting. My school was antifashion and dirndls were encouraged. We all wore slacks to classes, jeans and boots for farm work; and the girls' dresses for dinner were meant to be plain. Despite policy, most of us dressed as gaily as we could. But it was yet another hypocrisy: our denims and flannel shirts were just as self-expressive as any cape or feather boa. While the teachers hoped that we would ignore our appearance, we grew defiantly proud of if and were delighted when our Levis disturbed outsiders or older people.

In any history of Utopias, you see an (often elaborate) conception of virtue, while many deny the existence of vice. For us, both were divinely simple: it was virtuous to be an artist and a "well-rounded," useful citizen. Vices were smoking, drinking, making money, or any sexual diversion beyond holding hands. But few agreed with these definitions of evil. Still, punishment bred severe quandaries. They couldn't punish anyone by assigning hours of shoveling coal or snow, since we already did both of those things and were supposed to love them. A boy caught smoking or drinking or staying out late was sent to live for a few days in an empty chicken house, where of course he smoked and drank all night.

There are naturally a few alumni who have done very well indeed. But the school's bulletin makes sad and fascinating reading. Many who graduated in the Fifties are selling insurance or trudging in their family's business; the names of Shell and IBM recur. Compared to the reports from my other schools, there's a stunning number of dull jobs, plus safe living in the suburbs, while desperate little notes assure others that "my interest in the arts" bas been maintained. Many disillusionments are described, as well as eternal Ph.D.'s or secretarial work, begun very late, after trying many alternate careers. There seem to have been years of "research" before compromise occurred. Those who seemed so conventional when very young sound rather infantile in maturity, especially those who were afraid to grow up for fear of losing their vision.

The early-Sixties' graduates had the Peace Corps and other varieties of official social service: the Kennedy years did provide a role for them. (The school's very fuzzy idealism probably blinded them to the arrogant and colonial nature of the Peace Corps, which was so well described by Paul Cowan in *The Making of an Unamerican*.) A number teach at other progressive schools, and some returned to work at the school itself. A few have started similar schools. It's carefully noted that siblings or children of alumni compose the enlarging torso of the student body. Also some students married one another; many others found husbands or wives who function like honorary graduates. Perhaps a whole race is being bred by a school which may primarily equip its students for coming back to teach there. There's one rondo theme throughout the alumni notes: that the years at the school were indeed the best in very many lives. Few American schools manufacture such recognizable products: asteroids without an orbit.

Surely the prescription of happiness in very early life is toxic, for two reasons. First, when nothing ever equals the bliss of someone's sixteenth year, it becomes the reference point for all that's later denied him. Second, the few who weren't contented felt mediocre and craven. It was rather like the spleen that erupts in Paris or committing suicide in San Francisco in the spring. The miscreant realizes a disgusting dearth within himself—for not living up to his surroundings. Ever since William Dean Howells said that "the smiling aspects of life are the more American," many have felt themselves in disgrace—in a form that can paralyze them. But not liking that school was also a salvation. For a few of us, college and the afterlife were infinitely preferable—and we didn't have to be grateful all the time. And I no longer regret my schooling: it was an education in contradictions which was oddly useful in living through the late Sixties.

The school was festooned with pleasures: from music to informal living. But the raveled ethos mainly created escape artists. It is all so native: the belief that happiness is the test of a character or a life—that good people are happy people, and that everyone deserves his slice of delight. The Declaration of Independence might have read "life, liberty, and the pursuit of property," if Jefferson hadn't corrected John Locke's phrase. The moral confusion can't quite yet be flushed as a cliché. Happiness as a standard still befuddles some of my old schoolmates, because—as a black militant said to me in Watts—"False promises make things worse." And it's merely a problem of honesty: being told how splendid you are, how happy you should be, or how inferior the world is, hardly prepares you for living in any kind of America—repressive or unbuttoned. Such an education produces the species of weak liberals who help to strengthen the right. Often the school's theories remind me of Bronson Alcott's policies on manure—which he refused to use because nature mustn't be forced.

Wages of Wrath
May 1970

There was often someone crying in the ladies' room. Sobs or gasps (and sometimes retches) came jerking out of those grim cabinets, while others swiftly swallowed pills, choked, sighed, and recombed their hair—to prolong that moment known as "away from your desk." Due to some spasm of corporate economy, there were no towels of any kind, so we had to dry our hands on thin, dissolving toilet paper. My sense-memory of working at one of New York's choicest women's magazines has always been peeling those wet wisps of paper from my palms and fingers as the notes of weeping receded down the hallway while I reluctantly walked back to my office, bracing myself for a fresh burst of violence—plus collective confusion, paranoia, and fatigue. Recently I admitted to a former colleague that the experience was the only one in my life which seems just as bad in retrospect as it did at the time. "Even worse," she said, in accents of awe.

My job was a good one. Veterans had warned me not to take it, but I'd shrugged off their sordid accounts as exaggerations. Being in the features department meant seeing plays and movies, reading some of the season's best books, interviewing luminaries, investigating the development of a new museum or Italian architecture or Scandinavian design, and . . . writing. But each day's ferocity was distilled from working for the kind of person who mistakes sadism for authority, or hysteria for energy. Male or female, these bone crunchers differ only in their compulsion to disembowel their own—or the opposite—sex. The identifying trait is to swell like a frog with rage; veins in the throat and forehead often stand out thickly. The nose looks as though it may burst. (As in some other firms, the company-founder believed that employees work best when they are extremely nervous: there should be one ogre in every department. But the hours and days lost in illness might have implied the waste in productivity. Quite a few on the staff spent their weekends in bed.) At any rate our employer zapped our vitals by being (quite triumphantly) unable to give directions: to merely convey what she wanted done. Some women still lack this ability: it's a deficiency of upbringing and education, which determine that women shouldn't be executives. But anger accelerates from not being understood: the flush of frenzy reveals the frustration of making almost no sense at all.

An average morning could begin with the furious question: "*What* are you *doing* here?"

"Why . . . I just came to work."

"You're not supposed to be here! You know perfectly well that you should be down . . . down . . . *down* there . . . Down there! Now!"

"Down?"

"Yes, you're interviewing what's his name, what's-his-name . . . *What's* his *name?*"

"I don't know." (Evidently an appointment has been made without one's knowledge. This happens constantly. Explanations are useless.) "Nobody told me."

"They *did*. I *did*. Why are you standing there? You think you're a guest in this department?"

"Where am I supposed to be?" (Patience and cunning.)

"You know! You know! You know *perfectly* well! Get on *down* there. . . . How can you??? And Danes are always so punctual. And Oliver's on the roof."

Oliver is an eminent photographer, but who's the Dane on the roof? Ten more minutes of detective work extract a reference to the Congo. So if Danish means Swedish—sometimes it means German around here—then the victim may be Dag Hammarskjöld, since the UN is downtown from this office. A photographic session on the roof? A heart-bursting race to the UN and into the building and up in the elevator reveals what tourists often learn: the guards don't want you to go on the roof. No trace of Oliver. Next a conference with the dignitary's secretary, who gently explains that no such appointment was ever made, "And besides, he's in Geneva at a conference/ dead/retired a year ago." A call to Oliver confirms some of these regrettable facts, but it's crucial to check the first assumption carefully.

"You mean you never heard a word about this?"

"*No.*"

"You're sure?"

"Very sure. And I'm actually on vacation—as they *ought to know.* I only came in town to look for a tie."

Back to the office, armored for the abuse which no rational defense can forestall. It will be one's own fault that the great man was croaked or absent, or that no one ever called him. Still, there's a hideous suspicion: should it have been the Stock Exchange? Maybe the Aquarium. One clings to a few securities in life: it can't be the Guggenheim, that's uptown.

⌒

Some experts believe that a spell in a woman's office is an inevitable chapter in most young women's lives: a bath of fire that many professionals must pass through. Until about 1980 there were more writing or editing jobs open to women in this area than in the news or feature magazines which implied that women can't write because their biological clocks are full of fudge or because "they can't think conceptually." But almost every young woman I've met who's served on an all-female staff has found it just as mangling as I did. From the initial astonishment of the application form, which inquired, "Have you ever tried to overthrow the American government?" to the first day's physical ("Have you ever had a miscarriage?"), to being savagely called *"Darling"* and *"Sweetie"* (and Pam and Jane and Doris) because one's name was punctually forgotten, dignity dissolved and the intestines howled.

There was no protection in refusing to fight. Once, as I waited silently for a bottomless tantrum to subside, my editor flung herself hard against her desk—not quite cracking a rib, as I'd hoped—and yelled, "Don't-just-stand-there-being-*polite!*" Colleagues wove a landing net of sympathy; when office morale is in rags, there are gusts of desperate jokes and nervous laughter as partners in suffering try to cheer each other. Since then I've measured the health of a department or an organization by the character of its humor: compulsive clowning or rapid, forlorn gags mean that the staff is reduced to childishness in secret defiance of a loathed parent figure. Usually, in offices where demoralization thrives, the employee is treated as a (good or bad) child.

Quite a few of my nicest colleagues had grim reasons for needing the money which shackled them to the magazine: expensive divorces, hospital bills, sick parents or children, drunk or unemployable husbands. So some felt trapped. As in the worst offices, many revealed too much about their personal problems, which made it awkward to deal with them professionally later: How can you ask me to check those proofs when you know I've just had an abortion/lost my lover/been kicked out by my shrink? Some have remarked that the office was destructive to their private lives: shredded nerves and humiliations made them testy and dyspeptic with their men or their families; the stark self-control used on the job meant overreaction to small irritations at home.

We all paid for the days when those above us were ripping one another apart. As they reveled in the mutual humbling process, we were lacerated by their brawls about the approach to Degas, vermeil, Sophia Loren, or Robbe-Grillet. (We'd keep rewriting our captions while each editor gleefully condemned the adjectives requested by the others. Among enemies, the loser could become a stretcher-case: "Read this for me, uh, sweetie, my mind's all gone today"—which was true.) Reshaping senior colleagues' work was sometimes part of the freshman hazing system: during my first week, I wrestled with an older editor's account of her trip to Moscow. My favorite sentence was: "If you care about thickness, take Nescafé and towels."

Reeling out of the office, detailing my horrendous days to friends, I was rewarded by cascades of laughter, especially from men. While I protested that my office mirrored many of the degrading experiences that we'd heard about from men in advertising and news magazines or from those who worked for LBJ, some of my male schoolmates startled me by repeating how much they approved of my job: more so than of the reporting and reviewing I'd previously done. They thought my position was glamorous, even though I told them it was tacky and brutalizing. Most asked eagerly if there were lots of lesbians on the staff. I said I didn't know, and anyway the dump was desexing for everyone. They seemed disappointed about the lesbians, but urged me to stick with the job: "It must be good discipline—mustn't it?"

∼

Over the decades the magazine has published many fine articles and stories, as anthologies can prove. But the staff-written text is adored by satirists, and pieces by the unfamous were often grotesquely restyled for "reader appeal."

(I once spent an hilarious two hours helping a writer—whose essay I'd commissioned—insert lots of clichés and repetitions, so that the dizzy editors would cut them without mutilating the rest of the piece. It worked beautifully.) As with many other publications, the stylistic level had to sink when fashion magazines ceased to be aimed at the consumers and were written to attract and satisfy the manufacturers and advertisers.

The attitude toward the readers mingled flattery with contempt. The technique was to tickle their vanity by suggesting that they were bright—through spurts of culture—plus the assumption that they were actually interested in Cocteau, Zen, the paintings of Emil Nolde, Milan's Piccolo Teatro, or the works of Marguerite Duras. But they were expected to be stupid. Every reference had to be explained: Nixon or Wilde could not be mentioned without a first name and an identification slip. Each idea had to be pitched down to basement level, even though the language was contorted. "Ideas" were frantically sought: the editors kept lists of titles in hopes that someone would invent a fitting topic. One author, offered the title "What to Use Instead of Money," finally wrote an essay on the joys of the five senses.

A brief snort of great works of art was sufficient for the beef-witted army of subscribers, who were usually addressed as "You" ("You and the Atom," "You and Picasso"), in order to plug them into a subject which was presumably baffling for them. Art was mainly advertised through personalities—by portraits and paragraphs that skimpily summarized the work and the life-style of the practitioner. "Find a phrase for it!": the habit of reductio ad absurdum meant trying to tease language into little headlines. Here I should hastily add that I like fashion magazines; looking at pictures of clothes is good for the soul and a wild text bestows a pleasurable jolt. But having to package poetry and sculpture and snips of history as though they were blouses or scarves or shoes felt like a binge of perversion—especially if the readers were such idiots as we were told. Moreover they had to be protected: I was once ordered to describe a movie about a black man and a white woman as "a sensitive account of an unhappy love affair."

The clanking irony was that our fat and fatuous paragraphs were regarded as *good writing*. At first, I'd (wrongly) imagined that parodying the magazine's style would produce what was required. But we were made to rewrite until the final word salad would have shamed an autistic child. The demand for "passionate" copy meant that we had to use words like "ebullient," "irrepressible," and "kicky" as often as possible. "Swerve," "veer," "sinewy," and "slithery" kept our pages effervescent—another favorite. "Implacable" also gained points. Ideally, personalities were "amusing," or failing that, "amusable"—which was even applied to Queen Sirikit of Thailand. Wit and wisdom often went together. Three adjectives were the norm for characterization: "bubbling, valiant, enduring" (an octogenarian actress), "tiny, mercurial, young" (Elizabeth Ashley), "austere, important, young" (Jasper Johns), "witty, beautiful, stubborn" (Mrs. Patrick Campbell). Marianne Moore was "gentle but not sloppy," Cornelius Ryan was "a gentle, bursting man," in contrast to "a bouncy, friendly, internationally famous astronomer." Only David Merrick won the space race: "a soft-spoken, good-looking, stage-struck, enterprising, single-minded, aggressive, rattrap-minded lawyer."

Sifting through old issues, I savor passages like this description of the first Mrs. Nelson Rockefeller: "a brisk, lapis-eyed woman of polite but unwavering decision, has a refreshing approach to public life that seems rooted in playing herself absolutely straight. . . . Like almost all near-sighted women, she lives in a slight, steady wind of curiosity that leads her into turning interviews inside out with such questions as 'What kind of camera is that?' or 'Have *you* been to the Museum of Primitive Art?' . . . When all this begins to seem too guileless, a small crash of asperity makes it ring true. . . . When she was asked what she thought of a statement in the William Manchester book, *A Rockefeller Family Portrait,* that 'Rockefeller women are bred to be wives,' she said instantly, 'Now will you tell me what that means?' "

I also enjoy reading more recent issues of the magazine, still grateful that I didn't have to write about "the feeling of relief at storing away the 'sixties and jouncing into the 'seventies," or refer to "the clangour of the Vietnam war," or describe a TV series as "marvelous, chatty, a window opened by a man whose mind is an orchard of plums."

Naturally the solution to a maiming job is to leave it, as many of us did. But several questions lunge out of the closet of past experience. First: what (the devil) were we giving women to read? The magazine showed them marvelous clothes and some magnificent photographs. But our features department betrayed a bale of potentially good material. The well-educated can ignore the kiss-off approach to culture, but it's repulsive to think of its effect on those who backgrounds are meager. Quite simply, the magazine insulted the readers' intelligence. Second: why are some women so horrible to women? In my office the old easy answers of envy and competition didn't apply: the already successful tyrants weren't imperiled by those they reduced to hamburger. Perhaps the mere guilt of being female—fighting the instincts of inferiority—makes certain women despise others and want to punish them, resulting in what Evelyn Waugh called "the ruthless, cut-throat, rough-and-tumble of the . . . Woman's Page." Perhaps the yelling and threatening was merely a tradition of behavior—the way certain women think they should treat one another. But neither the traditionalists who believed that women should devote themselves to nurturing their families nor the new feminists could persuade me that women were more compassionate then men.

Part III

New York for Natives

The fury of sound took the form of derision . . . and thus it *might* . . . have struck you as brazen that the horrible place should, in such confessed collapse, still be swaggering and shouting.

—Henry James on New York in 1904

Compounding poverty and privilege, horror and delight, from the ghetto to the penthouse, it has always been New York's nature to seem on the shore of collapse. Long before 1842, when Dickens was appalled by the wild pigs which roamed Manhattan's streets and the black slums—"where dogs would howl to lie, women and men, and boys, slink off to sleep, forcing the dislodged rats to move away in quest of better lodgings"—all but the richest natives have often declared the town impossible. Mugging, which is sometimes discussed as though it were a new invention, was probably even more lavish in the 1850s, when politically powerful gangs like the Bowery Boys, the Dead Rabbits, the Shirt Tails, the True Blue Americans, and the Plug Uglies (who wore stuffed plug hats to protect their skulls in battle) fought with guns, knives, axes, clubs, and spiked shoes in the streets. In the Draft Riots of 1863 the city was nearly conquered by the mobs, which burned and looted slabs of midtown New York; about twelve hundred were killed and many blacks were tortured, mutilated, and hanged.

Soon after the Civil War, residents deplored the city's "pace." When Henry James visited it in 1904 he was agonized by "impermanence," the "sense of dispossession," and the "alienism"—which showed most brutally in the treatment of immigrants. He feared that they would inherit only "the freedom to grow up to be blighted [which] . . . may be the only freedom in store for the smaller fry of future generations." He was shocked by "the perpetual passionate pecuniary purpose which plays with all forms, which derides and devours them. . . . " The voice of New York seemed to say: "I build you up but to tear you down," and James saw citizens reduced to human rubble as swiftly as the new buildings that were demolished.

Those of us who love New York cannot disagree with anything that visitors say about it. We simply want to live here—perhaps because this city rings a range of fascinations that seems unique. But many agree that daily life has become even fiercer than it was a few years ago—granted that it's never been celestial. It's a local joke that when there are certain strikes, it takes some neighborhoods a week to notice them, since the level of city services is so low.

Morale sinks into the sidewalk when our press and our politicians emphasize that New York may be "ungovernable." Natives feel an accelerating helplessness about this city, any city—especially since the "urbanists" are breathing doom. This coincides with the old Yankee notion that town is evil and that virtue resides in the country. We had an early hopelessness about cities; they weren't expected to be attractive or even decent.

In the Eighties I realized that I might be seeing the end of something: New York as I've known it all my life. I used to defend the city fiercely against all critics; later I had to agree with many of them. Yet I can hardly imagine committing myself to another town.

New York for Natives
August 1969

> My first day in New York has never quite ended. And eighty cents still
> seems too much to pay for orange juice.
> —*Sinclair Lewis, writing in 1937 about New York in 1903*

Once I thought I might hardly ever see New York again. Risking my plane at
Kennedy Airport, I caught a cab, hurtled to the bottom of East 86th Street
and raced across the headlong pavement below the East River, up the cres-
cent stone stairs of the Carl Schurz Park, to memorize the river in five minutes. The October currents blazed, the bridges swung, and I learned what
most travelers regret: no landscape is portable. Meanwhile scolding relatives
pursued me, waving baggage checks and little canvas satchels. Eluding them,
I wandered back into the street, swerving close to a bus, whose driver yelled
"Wake up! Get off the needle!" Leaving New York, losing the river, I looked
for substitutes and found none.

The John Finley Walk—built in 1941 and named for a dead editor of the
New York Times who often walked around the entire rim of Manhattan—can
still characterize much that addicted natives love about New York. Downriver
was my daily walk to school, staggering with sleep, banging my stumpy shoes
against the concrete, and hurling my unfavorite textbooks into the water at
the end of term. Even then I thought how lucky one was to be here, how dull
life must be for those marooned in Hollywood, Hyannis, Mexico City, Philadelphia—towns I already knew to be inferior to New York. The Finley Walk
runs for half a mile from East 90th to 81st Street. Entering the park you pass
huge glacial rocks where climbing is forbidden. Other signs warn, "No dogs,
skates, bicycles." The rocks are thick with children, who also surge along the
river on skates and bicycles, dragging their dogs. At eleven I used to haul a
lumpy spaniel to the park in order to tangle his leash with that of ex-Mayor
LaGuardia's small white bulldog. LaGuardia was old and unwell; he looked
cross. Each day he shouted "Don't!" as I launched the spaniel at him. It was
an honor to annoy the former mayor, who died soon after this abuse. A pleasing anarchy has always prevailed in Schurz Park, which is crammed with

rhododendrons, laurels, firs, forsythia, swings, playgrounds, and sandpits, even a hockey rink. Winter milks the river to so soft a gray that the falling snow seems white.

The park spreads over two small hills and mounts to a wide esplanade, which is the roof of the East River Drive. Cars pound beneath your feet as the river opens out before you. Several ventilators from the tunnel are hidden among the bushes; sometimes the shrubbery honks at rush hour, and once I heard the oaths of taxi drivers coming up through a bed of daffodils. "Bastard," said one flower. "I'll get yours," said the other. Exhilaration springs from elevation: the river churns at about fifty feet below while the tide runs in two directions. It feels like the top of the world. Here the river (really a tidal strait) is about eighty-five feet deep—it seems little for so much life. Tugs, yachts, steamers, cargo ships, aircraft carriers, small oil tankers, and garbage scows slide past the boat-shape of Roosevelt Island, where hospitals are isolated in the middle of the river. Much of the river traffic is freight: wool, tin, bulldozers and lipsticks, coffee, wheat and TV sets, cement and bananas, railroad cars, are sailing past you. Ships from Israel, Iceland, Sweden, anywhere, decked with brilliant flags, must use this river. Slow barges are weighted with gravel and jeered at by a speedboat. On certain days, clouds rest on columns of smoke from factories across the river. Mist makes the boats seem closer. On your right is the Queensboro Bridge; to the left, the looped arches of the Triborough and Hellgate Bridges, where cars glint jerkily in the sun. Standing there you dissolve into the background of one of the most breath-stopping views of Manhattan. *The Great Gatsby*'s narrator felt that "The city seen from the Queensboro Bridge is always the city seen for the first time, in its first wild promise. . . . 'Anything can happen now that we've slid over this bridge,' I thought, 'anything at all.' "

On the Walk, black ribs of an iron railing curve inward at elbow height: people lean against them while gulls flap before their faces. John Finley's small black silhouette is etched against the riverscape. No one is odd: on a bench at the brim of the river, two actors rehearse their lines—"You're sitting there knowing for certain that I'm going to give in—aren't you?—aren't you?" "Yes."—but get no attention. I once released twenty-five monarch butterflies— who must, in the fall, go south—standing on one of those benches. They made a quivering orange phalanx, beating out over the water toward Brooklyn. An Andover friend of mine, sixteen and drunk, raced a midnight tug from 90th to 81st Street, jumping over the benches. On top of the race and the champagne, he wrote a long, tightly metered poem in triolets, which he recited to the cops who finally led him from the park.

The river's brink attracts solitaries and couples; the friends and families stroll slowly past. At night there is quite a bit of kissing. A huge sign across the river—PEARLWICK HAMPERS—reminds me of teen-age necking. This is also a reflective spot for partings: there may be a couple hanging over the railing in some dialogue of distress, filling the river with cigarette butts, staring out over the water. . . . At your back is all of Manhattan: towers and turrets that gleam pink and green at dusk. This is a good point to examine many architects' perplexities in finishing off skyscrapers; the tops are often absurd: domes, spiky minarets, and a few vast 1920-ish zippers with the suggestion of sequins. Light lavishes along the river, strangely warm and gray in winter, cold with a shocking blue in the heat. The Walk's height feeds both fact and illusion, elaborates distance, until the sweep of clouds and bridges seems like one of New York's best designs. A range of motion, light, and water; car horns, boat cries, airplanes, shouts, barks, whistles, singing transistors, even the crack of hockey sticks. A pastoral prospect where the river is so urgent, intent on business. It is peaceful and tumultuous, the impossible mood of New York.

As any transient idiot knows, peace is scarce in what Henry James called the "vast hot pot." Since our calamities are notorious, since the daily awareness of so much suffering is now part of the pith of our lives, since decay is an accepted fact, many outsiders wonder why some of us still choose to live here—or how we can so desperately miss it: even when we're in San Francisco or Rome, or being pampered on a country weekend. Clinging to the grit, the ugliness, the shrieking expense, dwelling among many who simply hate their lives, spitting on the sidewalk when lungs heave against the filthy air, the native sanity is questioned by disgusted visitors, who often exit a day or a week early, pawing their adjectives and their luggage, afraid that either may be wrenched away from them. (Dickens wrote, "Debauchery has made the very houses prematurely old"; James, horrified by the snarl of traffic and the trolley tracks, felt that "the New York predicament leaves far behind the anguish represented by the Laocoön.") "Sorry about that" is an old New York phrase, as is the sarcastic "Thanks a *lot*." All of the bad news is true. Hence those who are unhappy here should depart if they can, leaving the town to those of us who think we own it, or feel that it owns us, that it's responsible for our characters. Relationships with certain cities can be as intense as those in private life. For some, New York is so emotionally demanding and rewarding that all the struggles seem worthwhile. At least for a while.

For over a century, New York's only enduring trait has been perpetual change—what William James called the "permanent earthquake conditions." But at least some of the mutations have been healthy.

As many have noted, this is where the agony is—where almost everything happens first—where the issues surge and shout and glare until they can't be fled. At times you might almost think that New Yorkers are defiantly proud that their city seems to have the worst afflictions in the U.S. It's typical of the past and present that few remedies are sought until a crisis bursts: in 1832, when the streets were deep in garbage, the city fathers finally had them cleaned when a plague of cholera struck. Among all the contradictions, our city belts us with its extremes. One resident, who settled here ten years ago, found his image of New York on his first night: during a fierce blizzard he met a street shoveler on 42nd Street, wretchedly dressed in thin rags, pausing in his work to inhale voluptuously on a fine Havana cigar.

Naturally change can be demoralizing. On a weekly level you can't be sure of your own neighborhood. After a short absence you may find that the delicatessen has been replaced by a discothèque, blunder into the new hairdresser's for a beer, go to the drugstore for your laundry, to the laundry for contraceptives. But change also means that the potentialities are staggering. Again *Gatsby*'s narrator felt it ticking over: " . . . the satisfaction that the constant flicker of men and women and machines gives to the restless eye. I liked to walk up Fifth Avenue and pick out romantic women from the crowd and imagine that in a few minutes I was going to enter their lives, and no one would ever know or disapprove." Most of the glamor that Fitzgerald loved is long gone; "the iridescence," as his contemporaries called it, has drained away even more swiftly in the last ten years. But New York is still romantic— even in his terms; it ignites the imagination more than any city I know.

Many find themselves adventure-prone. Here you are perpetually exposed to the inventions and the fantasies of others—which can penetrate and shape and fill your own life. (Of course there's the risk that they may damage it as well. Nonmasochists learn a lively kind of self-protection in this town.) And you can lead so many lives—among different people who will never meet each other. The same person, in his varying roles, can be a mentor for some, a clown for others; a grave, responsible employer may also be a maverick away from his desk. This personal variety is crucial for many of us, since the world of jobs and offices is horribly bracketing. Professionally we're unfree. For example, few editors are writers or vice versa; the two capacities are not expected to overlap.

Due to the range of its privacies, New York bestows the privilege of a mild schizophrenia: of having several characters at once. Paradoxically the luxury of self-escape is enchanting for egotists—and here a ripe ego is essential for survival. (In 1867 Mark Twain wrote, "Some day . . . may be, I shall acquire a New York fortitude, and be as shameless as any.") The egoless are soon lost: the city swallows them without leaving a foot or a handprint. Many who flourish in New York have had a spell of this; few of them ever forget it. Hence it's easier here than in most cities to identify with those who are wasted or ground into the pavement. Almost all but the rich know what it is to be fired, to dread the doctor's bill, to find no work when cash is needed for tomorrow, or to lose a home.

In 1941 Sartre wrote of New York: "Nowhere more than here can you feel the simultaneity of human lives." And as many say, it's a city where suffering is contagious—where intense poverty means the kind of misery which means heroin, which involves us all. As long as we allow so many to be so poor, we're going to pay for what hard drugs do to them, and they to us. Even the richest can't escape the city's punishments: they breathe the same bad air, slide—almost skate—in the same dogshit, hear the phone squeal and die in mid-sentence; penthouses and limos can't shelter them from the traffic jams and holdups. In Philadelphia the rich can still live in isolated neighborhoods, like Chestnut Hill. But there's no such sanctuary in New York—no defense against the entangling lives of strangers: you may sometimes get a bunch of flowers or a bullet that was meant for someone else.

New York has been called a devil's paradise: the great bazaar where everything is available. But many can't afford much of the cultural abundance; also the expense of operation has killed some artistic outlets: much of the theater, quite a few magazines, and new experimental art galleries; orchestras and chamber groups are hurting. Therefore many New Yorkers feel a cultural starvation. While no other form of nourishment can satisfy that hunger, some can draw sustenance from experiencing the city itself as a limitless dramatic stage.

No one is daft enough to claim that New York is a work of art. But it's a series of theaters which can reward a participating audience. The (often compulsive) involvement with neighborhood is probably increasing—along with the themes of decentralization and community control. When physical realms outside your own can seem inhuman, the emotional dependence on a few blocks answers an almost animal need. And certain New Yorkers seem almost helplessly committed to the crises on their own turf; a friend of mine who moved to New Haven felt lost in exile—and added, "I can't identify with the problems." *My* addicts, *my* muggers, *my* transit strike: these involve some of us more deeply than any national statistics.

So whether you live in Yorkville, amid the German goosegrease and beer halls, or among the Czechs, Hungarians, and Irish of the East Seventies, among the Jewish colonies of the Lower East Side, where Puerto Ricans, micro-boppers, and a few lingering street people can still meet the price of kosher food, in Chelsea, where vine-laced elegance collides with ethnic outrage, or in the spacious, fortress-mute apartments of the Upper West Side (so rich in resident psychiatrists that one stretch is called Spook's Row)—your gut-attachment is apt to be intense. Some I know are urban gypsies, who can't pay for what's called a home; instead they find pads or ledges in the neighborhoods that mean the most to them.

The New Yorker's irrational affection for his slice of the city spills through Claude Brown's delighted return to Harlem, after a childhood visit to the rural South: "This was a real Sunday morning—a lot of blood and vomit everywhere and people all dressed up and going to church. . . . I was so happy to . . . see it all. [Our] hallway looked . . . the way it was supposed to be looking on Sunday morning. Somebody had gotten cut the night before, and blood was still in the hall. And somebody had pissed on the stairs, and it was still there, just like it should have been." Certainly some residents of the Silk Stocking District can greet their own streets with the same elation.

Perhaps you have to be rather eccentric to like New York, or to bear it. It's no longer distinctly a town of winners and losers—that old seductive challenge for fledglings and new arrivals. Instead you meet a lot of well-paid compromisers who keep explaining, "My job isn't me." Some of those who seem to fare the best are adept at dodging the system, living in the present, spending amazingly little; their work can eventually thrive if they are stubborn about refusing to dilute it. But few can enjoy New York who try to plan for the future. The sanest New Yorkers may be those who cherish incongruities or ludicrous degrees of contrast.

Things loved (and shared by some): the stomach of Grand Central Station, with the zodiac on its blue ceiling and the mad visual spaghetti of winking ads; the impatient, greedy New York temperament, unable to wait for a green light, a bus, or a sandwich, which highlights the native conviction that life must be used—at once; dawn from any skyscraper; punctual derision of space programs in a local pizza shop; immense loyalty among friends, perhaps due to the fact that daily life in this city is so difficult that many offer mutual support; the New York logic, revealed when a member of the Sanitation Department—asked why so many public trash baskets were removed from Lexington Avenue —replied, "Because people were putting too much trash in them!"; eating artichokes on a roof on a summer night, hearing the Afro drums of the district throb from other roofs and fire escapes; infectious energy, which seems to leap from the pavements; a drugstore which serves as a communication center for its neighborhood: you can lean on the counter and learn *anything*, from politics to love and real estate; infinite leafy side streets; the drastic, provocative New York sense of comedy—overstated in tone but not in fact—as from a besieged friend who said, "If I weren't such a snob, I'd have a nervous breakdown"; the seals in Central Park, the archsensualists and exhibitionists of the whole city; a certain Italian butcher; the Unicorn tapestries at the Cloisters; the freedom to be furious: New York offers many valid reasons for anger, which is easy to express here; New York legends: for example, the Public Library lions roar whenever a virgin passes between them; concert rehearsals in nearby buildings: an open window means free Mozart; the statue of "Civic Virtue" in Queens, wherein a giant male nude strides over a prostrate woman, which was called degrading by early feminist groups and also defended as depicting the triumph of man "over graft and corruption"; the Olivetti typewriter (now gone) which was mounted on Fifth Avenue, where pedestrians typed poems, insults, and invitations; one or two good plays of the season; the Municipal Asphalt Plant; sun rippling down the avenues while one's pace springs faster and faster within a loose, swift crowd; slow walks where random lighting resculpts the city at night; the occasional sense that the whole town is an illusion, invented by some cosmic nut case, which allowed one to witness a myth—or maybe a movie.

Blackout
November 1965

Victims of time and geography who were not in Columbus, Ohio, on the Day the Dam Broke, hoped that James Thurber's ghost was in Manhattan for the blackout of November 9th. (It's a nearly perceptible spirit, since he was recently identified by an earnest graduate student taking an exam as "a muckraker in the age of Emily Dickinson.") Lacking Thurber, it was pleasing to know that Federico Fellini was visiting New York—it seemed like an ideal sequence for him. Since capes are now fashionable, it was stirring to see mantled figures carrying silver candlesticks flickering through the East Seventies under a full moon. Discreet invitations to join a gangbang circulated through P. J. Clarke's when the darkness was only half an hour old, while candles sold for a dollar apiece from sidewalk entrepreneurs on Third Avenue. In subways and elevators, heart attacks were promised, threatened, and maybe a few were had. Citizens draped in white sheets, directing traffic with rolled-up newspapers, made it look as though the Ku Klux Klan had captured the city. The Statue of Liberty's torch remained lit by a New Jersey plant, but shocked airplane passengers arriving from Washington heard the pilot say, "And now you will see the fabled lights of Manhattan—*Oh.*"

While national figures ponderously assured the public that it wasn't necessarily sabotage, numerous New Yorkers indulged their megalomania by claiming that they had personally caused the blackout. Police switchboards were clogged with calls (particularly from women) bewailing the electric egg beater, the hair dryer, or the waffle iron which must have fused the entire coast. The *Daily News* had the best headline—"NOBODY DIGS POWER FLOP"— but some residents still triumphantly insisted on their own responsibility. At my office, maintenance men apologized bitterly for the blackness until someone had the wit to look out the window. At home I sang loudly in the dark until matches were found, while the telephone rang with rumors that Governor Rockefeller was "satisfied" (presumably by the mobilization of the National Guard and Civil Defense). It was comforting to imagine the not-very-popular governor—perhaps surrounded with heirloom hurricane lamps and vats of whale oil—in his state of satisfaction. His later observation: "This may be a blessing in disguise" (since "steps will be taken") evokes the Riverside Drive statue of Samuel J. Tilden, the New York governor defeated for the presidency in 1876, inscribed with his most famous remark: "I trust the people."

One doubts the columnist who claimed that the eyes of polio victims in iron lungs dilated "in fear and wonder" as the machines ceased breathing, but the image serves nicely for the city fathers. Despite the next day's maudlin praise from sociologists, theologians, and politicians, New Yorkers were less noble than intoxicated.

The most unlikely people got drunk with determined speed, some on the 32nd and 50th floors of Wall Street offices. (Several men explained to their wives that walking downstairs is much more dangerous for the heart than ascending.) Five colleagues—one male editor and four secretaries—were approached by a courtly stranger wearing a private detective's badge, who asked if he could share the women. Leading them to a reserved table with six bottles of superb champagne, he alleged that he owned a fourth of Paramount, had married at seventeen but divorced his wife after she murdered their baby, but that he had managed to kill her lover first. Crawling up twelve flights of stairs on hands and knees at four A.M., the eldest and drunkest of the women realized that she couldn't locate her own apartment, and slept slumped across the stairs. She described her host as a nondescript liar, but she loved her evening.

Despite stimulating transistor reports of "pillage and rapine" in Rochester, Manhattan's crime rate remained minimal, although fires increased by 300 percent. While Massachusetts convicts rioted mildly, New York zoo keepers succeeded in keeping even the cobras warm. Vladimir Horowitz, in mid-concert, did not miss one note of Chopin and finished his complete program. Many heated their hands on the vigil candles at St. Patrick's, while others slept in the Lady Chapel; many complained because the cathedral has no toilets. While thousands were entombed in tunnels beneath the Hudson River, or walking across the Brooklyn Bridge, or having car accidents, women were still required to use the ladies' lobby at the Yale Club—although five women slept at the Harvard Club.

The city is said to have lost a hundred million dollars. Clay, New York ("a muddy hamlet," according to the *New York Times*), denied the guilt of its electrical substation, as announced by the Texas White House. The ultimate anti-climax came when the U.S. Department of Agriculture issued instructions for removing wax drippings. On November 10th many employees returned to their offices already nostalgic, looking hopeful whenever a small bulb dimmed. Aside from those who suffered physically, plus insomniacs whose candles burnt too swiftly, many who love New York had enjoyed themselves thoroughly. Those who dislike the city were exultant in their outrage. The native temperament is often charmed by violent surprises, such as meeting their own neighbors, rumors of imaginary meteors, or poets who actually read well. Perhaps the only creatures unaffected by the blackout were the legendary alligators (flushed away as childhood pets) who matured to inhabit the sewers; their eyes are said to shine red in the dark.

Hindsight: A rise in the New York birth rate was noted nine months after the blackout. Sociologists were quick to go on record with two explanations: some people couldn't find their contraceptives in the dark; others, because they were deprived of their usual TV programs, "interacted with each other" more than usual.

Years later I met an ex-biker from the Boston Hell's Angels who had been in a Massachusetts jail on that great night. He told me that the cells there had electronic locks; when the power failed, he and other prisoners were delighted to see their cell doors silently swing open. He and several cronies fought their way through a few guards and went over the wall, enjoying several months of freedom before they were arrested again.

The Cult of Ayn Rand
January 1966

Ayn Rand, the sixty-one-year-old abbess of the acute right, who sometimes wears a gold dollar sign on her lapel, leaves "any room" entered by William Buckley; the *New York Times* notes that he "presided over [her] excommunication." But he wasn't entirely successful. Her last two novels each sell between 100,000 to 200,000 copies a year; courses in her "philosophy," Objectivism, draw some five thousand students; her tape-recorded lectures are given in fifty-four cities and have been requested by American soldiers in Vietnam; Ayn Rand Clubs are formed at universities. Yet Rand, a former Hollywood screenwriter, born in St. Petersburg, an Aristotelian whose favorite modern novelist is Mickey Spillane, says the world isn't yet ready for an Objectivist political party.

Objectivism—as evoked in her two books, *For the New Intellectual* and *The Virtue of Selfishness*—grafts old-fashioned laissez-faire capitalism onto a fresh branch of paranoia: Rand's conviction that America is being destroyed by altruism and mysticism. Zen Buddhism is also part of the peril: the government is threatened by "doctrines created by and for barefoot savages who lived in mudholes." Plato and Saint Augustine are denounced as though they were modern liberals; "Plato was the transmission belt by which Oriental mysticism infiltrated into Western culture." Objectivism—the sole source of freedom and individuality—precludes "life as exaltation." (Rand finds men superior to beasts.) "Reality" is easily understood, mainly because "facts are facts." Rand has written that *"the achievement of his own happiness is man's high-est moral purpose,"* also that "the words 'to make money' hold the essence of human morality." Intellectuals ("frightened zombies") have failed the busi-nessman, who "looks at the universe with the fearless eagerness of a child, knowing it to be intelligible." Objectivists "will fight for Capitalism . . . as a *moral* issue." The choice between "Blood, whips, and guns—or dollars" is ur-gent now that the prevailing altruism is hastening "slavery, brute force, stag-nant terror, and sacrificial furnaces." In fact "the world is perishing from an orgy of self-sacrificing." Altruism includes any form of nonvoluntary taxa-tion, relinquishing a career to support a crippled parent, or allowing your wife to die of a curable illness by spending the money which could save her on preserving the lives of ten other women. (Saving a drowning stranger is perfectly moral if the rescue includes no risk, but it's immoral if it's danger-ous, and the would-be rescuer is accused of lacking "self-esteem.") Socialism is defined as "the grinning skull under bloody rags." America, a savagely lib-eral country, has enabled its throngs of mystics to weaken the citizens' self-confidence, which should inform them that they are heroic. Humor is sometimes used as a weapon of destruction: collectivists may "kill by laugh-ter." Europe is full of bad examples: due to England's welfare state, that country has become "a mawkish poorhouse," where people sell "their rights in ex-change for free dentures." But rational egotism may yet defeat the contem-porary lunge to sacrifice oneself.

Rand isn't shy of self-quotation, and the patience of a prawn peeler is necessary to read *The Fountainhead* (1943; 754 pages) and *Atlas Shrugged* (1957; 1,168 pages), the novels which attempt to bring her notions alive. Yet they are chronic best-sellers. Sales may also spring from the rumored sex scenes. These have the tang of severe sadomasochism, but the most graphic word is "blending." Still, there are occasionally daring sentences: "I want you like an animal, or a cat on a fence, or a whore." Nathaniel Branden, Rand's spokes-man, calls her "a Romantic Realist," since she writes about "what *ought* to happen." Her happy endings eschew the "man-degrading nature" of modern literature.

The Fountainhead details the lumbering progress of an architectural genius. Mystics and liberals conspire to ruin him, but he succeeds in rebuilding slabs of New York in his image. *Atlas Shrugged* is a fantasy of "the mind on strike." Because America is ruled by demented force, a brilliant inventor "stops the motor of the world," by persuading his fellow geniuses to disappear into a valley, where they continue to compose concertos, mine copper, sculpt, and build railroads; they use only gold coins. Without them the world literally disintegrates—into starvation, bloodshed, and a total electrical blackout. Civi-lization must await their construction of a rational society. *Atlas Shrugged* ends with the hero tracing a dollar sign in space.

Both the vast fictional samplers are embroidered in the women's magazine style of the late 1940s: "Nothing but your body, that mouth of yours, and the way your eyes would look at me if . . ." While Rand insists that everyone can master reason and that success is accessible to all, her own gigantic heroes are biologically superior. You can recognize her good or bad characters by their physical traits: her two heroes have "trembling copper" and "ripe orange rind" hair—elsewhere it's "liquid gold." One heroine, who runs a railroad, has "a sensual mouth held closed with inflexible precision." Both heroines embody intense fragility and discipline; one is so self-controlled as to marry two men she doesn't love, although her lover is an available bachelor. (Three men for each exceptional woman is the Realist's ratio.) Evil always has a lamentable physique: "Her skin was . . . dry, with enlarged pores showing on her nostrils"; "His posture had a limp, decentralized sloppiness"; "Her hips began at her ankles, bulging over the tight straps of her shoes." Clothes also reveal bad character: "She wore a filthy cotton dress and a crushed hat." Even names predestine moral quality: the heroes are Howard Roark and John Galt, while the villains or inferiors are Ellsworth Toohey, Wesley Mouch, Balph Eubank, and Lancelot Clokey.

Only those who have read and agreed with *Atlas Shrugged* are eligible for the Objectivist lectures. If a student attends only two lectures, he must explain why he has dropped the course. Nathaniel Branden recites the sermon, and Rand answers questions afterward. The audience is youthful, very well dressed, polite, and thrillingly quiet—when Branden asked if everyone could hear him, no one answered. The devout include some Young Americans for Freedom, many Goldwater fans—and a few I've met own a bit of not very valuable land which the wicked government presumes to tax. A few black listeners appear; Rand rebukes racists but she says that current black leaders have gone too far: "Instead of fighting for equal rights, they are demanding special race privileges."

The speakers' technique is making certain words interchangeable: communism, mysticism, Platonism, liberalism. The audience is clearly flattered by the repetition of "philosophy" and "reason," and the reassurance that everyone present must be intelligent. Also, understanding Objectivism guarantees happiness. And some seem comforted because the enemy is so easy to identify. The questions I heard were rather timid: "As the author of the world's greatest books, please define the difference between an author and a writer." "As an atheist, do you deny the existence of God?" "How far will Objectivism go in one's lifetime?" "Will there be a movie of *Atlas Shrugged?*" Later an MIT student told me that he used to flummox Objectivists by insisting that it was his inalienable right to uphold the freedom to relinquish his freedom.

Rand scolded some of her questioners for sounding "subjectivist." She emphasized that "In philosophy, one does not fail to reach an answer if one works hard enough," and repeated that everyone has the intelligence "to guide their actions rationally." Asked why disbelievers and non-Objectivists are unwelcome, Branden rasped, "I won't have a mystic or a communist in my living room, and I won't have one in my lecture hall." Rand explained that anyone who disagrees with Objectivism is contemptible and self-destructive: she then shouted, "Let him go to hell his own way!," and stressed the application of reason to particular contexts. Afterward a pleasant young man murmured to his companion in the elevator, "You do have to respect Hitler for his initial success in perceiving the reality around him. Of course he did wrong things. But he did comprehend his context."

Hindsight: Although Ayn Rand's books continued to be tremendous best-sellers during the Sixties, she was regarded as a somewhat comic figure during that era. But she was enormously influential in earlier and later decades. Rand left her country in 1926 after her family lost the property it had acquired in Czarist Russia. Settled in the United States, she eventually became the principal ideologue of the Hollywood right, holding seminars there and in New York to educate her adherents about the horrors of liberalism. In 1947 she was perhaps the fiercest of all the friendly witnesses before the House Committee on Un-American Activities. In the Seventies her disciple Alan Greenspan—who had done research for the steel industry scenes in *Atlas Shrugged*—was an economic advisor to Presidents Nixon and Ford; he became head of the Federal Reserve in 1987. He said his mentor had convinced him in the Fifties that "capitalism is not only efficient and practical, but also moral."

The Reagan administration was a honeycomb of Rand's admirers, among them Commerce Secretary C. William Verity, Jr., Representative Jack Kemp of New York, and Martin Anderson, Reagan's domestic policy advisor. Yet she had been passionately opposed to Reagan's candidacy in 1976; in a letter to the *New York Times* she stated, "Since he denies the right to abortion, he cannot be the defender of any rights." She also declared that he had "no program and no ideology." Rand had seen the New Deal as a giant step toward totalitarianism and had detected fascism in the New Frontier; her antigovernment rhetoric suited the spirit of the Eighties. Her abhorrence of all religions put her permanently at odds with such conservatives as William Buckley (whom she never forgave for publishing Whittaker Chambers's scathing review of *Atlas Shrugged* in *The National Review*.) Reagan officials seemed unruffled by her distaste for the president, and her beliefs—that taxation and welfare were despicable, that acquiring wealth was a mark of virtue—helped to shape government policies long after she died in 1982. At her funeral a six foot floral dollar sign stood next to her coffin, while Greenspan, leaders of the Libertarian Party (who called her work their inspiration), the editorial director and publisher of *Barron's* magazine, and professors of business and philosophy paid their respects. By the mid-Nineties, readers were still buying over 300,000 of her books each year. The first printing of an anthology of her writings, translated into Russian in 1993, sold out in Moscow after two days.

Seductive Banks
February 1966

An ocelot, a giant, a Santa Claus who seemed on the edge of upchuck, Salvador Dali embracing Huntington Hartford, silver space helmets, kilts, and a mystifying number of air hostesses filled the Trade Bank and Trust Company on Fifth Avenue. A woman in slashed gold lamé did deep knee-bends on a table to the laughter of bodyguards, while the musicians revived tunes from *My Fair Lady*. A woman in a coronet said, "I can't leave until I insult Hartford," and her escort answered, "Go ahead. He won't notice." Admittedly it was midnight: a publication party given by Bobbs-Merrill for Nicolas Darvas's *The Anatomy of Success*. Editors, dwarfs, and ghosts, seemed the only absentees among the crowd which pressed past the Pinkerton detectives.

While it wasn't quite the atmosphere in which you open a savings account, it seemed only an elaboration of what may be found on a lunch-hour visit to a bank: a pianist playing cocktail music, surrounded by bright rubber daffodils, or two ice-skaters on a small rink, an art exhibit, orange trees on piles of pebbles, a red and white sailboat tipped sickeningly on its side. (Muzak is traditional, but it's unnerving to write a $20 check to the tune of "Big Spender," which is playing in many banks these days.) Spanning all styles from schlock to a deluge of dignity, New York banks have followed the advice of J. Walter Thompson Company to the American Bankers Association, on how to make the public feel exhilarated, flattered, reverent, or flush.

Yet bankers must beware of a literal response to their invitations. One novelist, elated by receiving a sumptuous Ford grant, wandered into a branch of the Chase Manhattan and asked to exchange a Canadian quarter. Consternation and obstruction ensued. An official sternly inquired if he had an account there. No, he said, but he'd thought he had a friend. (The ads used to read, "You Have a Friend at Chase Manhattan.") Chase's altruistic advertising is imitated by the decor of many New York banks. A psychiatrist recently remarked on the fortress style of post-Depression banks, which stressed the security and safety of your savings. But the focus is now on friendship, availability, and the impression that there's nothing between you and the money.

The exposure theme—typified by the suburban drive-in banks—is best expressed at the small, transparent Manufacturer's Trust Company at 43rd Street and Fifth Avenue. It's one of Manhattan's handsomest buildings, topped by trees. The circular vault is in a ground-level window—the management boasts that a thief would need 380 years to find the combination—and the whole glass building remains alight until one A.M. Despite a menacing wire mobile resembling a huge handful of snarled hair, the aerial interior suggests a fantasy of enlightened finance.

Other banks have eliminated the tellers' cages and the brass rails which once surrounded officials, and another conspicuous motif is the (interfaith) cathedral. Some tellers stand behind marble altars which taper toward the floor, soaring lines proliferate, and the Personal Loan room sometimes appears as a small, discreet chapel. While it's almost impossible to deposit money without riding an escalator, the descent to basement level feels like a fall from grace.

Colonial banks are common; they evoke a reliable country bank in the city. The tone is gracious reserve rather than boisterous hospitality. A new branch of the Franklin National Bank calls itself "La Banque Continentale"; there are carriage lamps and urns at the entrance and a mural of Benjamin Franklin at Versailles. Amid the facsimile petit-point and the new Louis Seize paneling, thigh-slapping cash display would be embarrassing. Despite the gilt pineapples which are the symbol of hospitality, this bank seems fairly hostile to the public: a few of us who came in to inspect the decor were treated like small-time thugs.

The Chase's head office, near Wall Street, exhibits the dueling pistols of Aaron Burr and Alexander Hamilton. (In fact the same pair of pistols killed both Hamilton and his son.) The murder weapons are startling since the welcome is like a blast of ether, and exposure amounts to exhibitionism. Tours—prefaced by a movie about how Chase makes "American dollars available to friends abroad"—commence every half hour, to reveal Noguchi's beautiful Japanese water garden, around which the tellers' desks are wrapped in a vast circle; the atomic clock which announces the building's age in years, days, hours, and minutes; and an art collection including Larry Rivers' portrait of himself at the age of three and a West African water trough. There's also a fine Leonard Baskin owl, some 19th-century New England weathervanes, a Marin figure, and a Remington statue of "Rattlesnake on the Trail." As you plough across the caramel plush carpets, or hurtle thirty floors in an elevator at sixteen hundred feet per minute to the world's largest vault (behind bulletproof glass), awe wrestles with revulsion. The 60th-floor view is worth remembering forever—"The irony," said Henry Hope Reed, the architectural historian, "is that it shows all the great towers of the 1920s, to this building's detriment." The vast clattering temple does indeed feel like the center and circumference of the financial universe. It also feels like the iceberg that sank the Titanic. The chill of the long, low, lit ceilings is paralyzing, and humanity seems a shoddy standard here. Because after all, the visitor is made to feel rich. What other interior bestows the sensation of seething personal wealth? In Manhattan it's hard to reject such an ego massage.

Again in the elevator, while two young financiers discussed the jeweled cuff links and stereos they'd been given for Christmas, I read Chase's absorbing handout: "JUST FOR FUN. People are spending more for entertainment and amusement these days. . . . While some critics claim that our society has become too materialistic . . . " There followed some blurbs for power lawn mowers, bonded whiskeys, yachts, and pet foods, plus something about the "bottomless appetite for the good life." One of the young men said, "So I sold the cuff links, but the tie clip was just shit."

Throughout the friendliness competition, banks continue to force gifts such as bathroom scales on those who open savings accounts early in January, or aim caressing ads at "the Maturing Man of Means," or "the New York Woman"—including "the heroic coed holding her own in the halls of learning." It all intensifies the notion that good people must have good money (earned or owned), plus the impression that banks give it away just to be charming.

Hindsight: During the Seventies plastic shields rose between the tellers and the public, which became accustomed to the electronic errors of automatic teller machines. After the banks lost their choicest corporate clients to investment banks in the Eighties and their industry was badly bruised by faulty real estate loans, banks sought to rid themselves of small accounts; most required a minimum monthly balance of two to three thousand dollars for free checking, and many Americans began to pay more for fewer services. As major banks closed down countless branches—especially in the inner cities—their patrons could remember how banks had once offered free toasters or cutlery or spice racks to new customers, who were actually welcome in the Sixties.

Paperback Gothics
October 1966

Jane Austen needn't have apologized, in her "Advertisement" for *Northanger Abbey*, because "period, places, manners, books, and opinions" had changed thirteen years after the novel's publication. She was worried that her parody of the Gothic novel had dated. While the form has often been vaguely defined, it probably didn't improve until it was already dead—by about 1830. But it's reincarnated in almost every decade. New Gothic novels are the most violent paperback success, outdistancing the recently popular nurse books.

One hundred fifty Gothics sold over 1.5 million copies a month last spring. Published primarily by Pyramid, Lancer, Ace, Bantam, and Paperback Library, last year's flock did so well that a Gothic soap opera has commenced on TV: *Dark Shadows*. It's set in modern Maine, complete with Down East accents, a bemused governess, a small boy of bad heredity, a ne'er-do-well brother who has just returned from a mysterious voyage, and an old retainer of paranoid loyalties (combining Mrs. Danvers in *Rebecca* with Joseph of *Wuthering Heights*). There's a door which mustn't be opened for months (the cast suspects that the scriptwriters haven't yet chosen between a lost diary, a skeleton, a will, or a hidden passage), and a recurring line of dialogue: "Stay out of this basement." All the paperbacks' covers depict a running girl in a raincoat or nightgown shrinking from a vast castle or house which is just about to lunge at her. Jacket designs are so important that publishers have discovered that *one* lighted window in the mansion will increase sales.

The audience is "older women," who sometimes purchase six at once. These Gothics are so faithful to *Jane Eyre* and Daphne du Maurier that one editor simply buys outlines and clothes them himself. Many of the authors are pseudonymous, lurking behind such titles as *The Mistress of Mellyn*, *Thunder Heights*, *Durrell Towers*, and *Flowers of Evil*. They can be set in the last or present century, in New England or the Hudson River Valley or the moldering South. But whereas Mrs. Radcliffe and Mary Stewart have sent their heroines to the Alps or the Mediterranean, American Gothics depend on England: a crazed little kingdom largely occupied by the state of Cornwall, where cliffs rise in the middle of new highways and the weather is reliably vile. The peasants of Cornwall speak a foxy dialect: "Ee dun't know you, Miss." The English are given to spasmodic laughter, poisoning each other with herbal teas, stroking harps at midnight, and an occasional bruising kiss. Such Anglomania ("But how wonderful! Scones!") can furnish a villain with medieval ancestors, unobtainable in wildest Rhode Island.

Naturally the vocabulary has been purged for the drugstore trade; the rain has ceased its "incessant crepitations" on the pane. Most of the heroines are indeed orphaned governesses ("since the auto accident took Mother and Dad"); they're sensible, but "not wise," as they keep confessing. Brisk and priggish, they consider themselves plain—only a lover can reveal their hidden beauty. Just as Elizabeth Bowen stressed in her Introduction to Lefanu's *Uncle Silas* (1864), these Gothics are sexless and the women are triumphantly infantile. (At least there are two kinds of nurse novels: chaste and unchaste.) One New York Gothic editor says he allows "a kiss at the end if the heroine's been a very good girl." The contemporary governess is a classical teacher: "There's one thing to learn before you begin to ride, and that is to love your horse." And she's far too literal-minded to write a sonnet like Emily's in *The Mysteries of Udolpho:* "Go, pencil! faithful to thy master's sighs . . . "

Heroes (true or sham widowers), owners of the Gothic-Doric-Tudor homes, where "things have changed since the mistress died," always appear at first as villains; their unfaithful wives were murdered (usually by other women). They make disturbing first impressions—"I thought him somewhat dissipated, with brown eyes that twinkled ironically"—and their initial treatment of the governess ("Dammit, call me Caleb!") is brusque and "mocking." But none are ever so insulting as Mr. Rochester was when he called Jane Eyre cold, sick, and silly.

Plots haven't been so impudently prolonged since the search for the will in Wilkie Collins's *No Name*. After "the queer doings up at Greystones" have been established, there is normally only one murder in the past to be unraveled. The heroine stalks among cobwebs, crenelated towers, and headless gargoyles, wrestling with jammed drawers and self-extinguishing lamps. The wind is accused of pronouncing more names than all the witnesses called before the House Committee on Un-American Activities. The supernatural suggestions and the "nameless terrors" of the 19th-century models have been eliminated; the shadow on the blind is revealed as a mad in-law, not a ghost. For a period when sadism is fashionable, these Gothics are amazingly tame. (Also prosaic: "I have an upset stomach. I thought I'd better not exercise too much.") Hazlitt's condemnation of *The Castle of Otranto* as "dry, meagre, and without effect" is almost apt for these (largely architectural) productions. There are no extrasensory aids as in *The Moonstone*, and few such chilling lines as *Udolpho*'s: "You shall instantly be removed to the east turret." Corpses are rare: "the remains" may consist of an old brooch or a couple of very clean bones. Publishers have found that predictability certifies success, and since the covers are so similar, eager readers may buy the same Gothic twice. Gothics may appeal—as stated in the anonymous "prefatory memoir" to Mrs. Radcliffe's works—at moments "when the whole head is sore, and the whole heart sick." But no one quite knows why this should be an acutely Gothic year; the luxury may be fear made comfortable, long-skirted—and remote.

Hindsight: The spectacular sales of the paperback Gothics dipped in the spring of 1967. But they soon revived. The latest were somewhat more sophisticated: an editor said, "These girls now have feelings below the belt," and it was conceivable that the governess might go to bed with the master of the house, foreshadowing the bodice-rippers of the Seventies and beyond.

The wild success of *Dark Shadows* was intriguing because it appeared to have captivated both housewives and their teen-age children. In 1967 the show acquired a female Phoenix, an emissary of the Devil, and a vampire; later there were witches, warlocks, and so many apparitions and ghosts that someone observed, "You can no longer tell the living from the dead on this show." The vampire, who was deluged with fan mail, came from the stop-me-before-I-kill school. He hated to bite but had to do so for his own survival. Since so many people do things they don't want to, the public seemed to identify with him. According to a colleague, his sad soulful eyes established him as "a reluctant vampire." There was also a repentant werewolf; in his human form he used to chain himself to the radiator when the moon was full. His fiancée once gave him the last moon-poppy on earth to eat—to forestall his transformation. But it didn't work.

Dark Shadows people also switched identities—by inhabiting each other's bodies—and they made a humanoid of spare parts from the cemetery. When he needed a wife, they made him one. There were 18th- and 19th-century flashbacks (to discover how certain persons became vampires or werewolves) and earlier incarnations of some characters. There was also "parallel time," in which one person could lead several lives at once, as though he were on a series of astral flights. Seances and sometimes the *I Ching* were used to transport everyone back and forth in time; once they went up to 1995.

The time-traveling solved one of the oldest problems of the soap serial; normally, when a character gets repetitive or boring, he has to be killed off for good. But in *Dark Shadows* he was just moved back a century or two or else he was murdered, so that his spirit could roam. The cast was grateful for this steady employment; one actress said, "The only way we stayed on that show was to get killed off."

Dark Shadows died in 1971—some think because it had grown too complex. If you missed one installment, you couldn't possibly understand the next one. But it's fondly remembered by many, and was famous for rousing the passions. In 1969 a couple in Queens who had been married for thirty years fought bitterly because the wife demanded *Dark Shadows* while her husband was watching a very close baseball game: the Mets in the ninth inning against the Cubs, on Channel 9. When she flipped the switch, he killed her.

When the producer of *Dark Shadows* heard about the murder, he said he was grateful it hadn't been the other way around.

Requiem for the *World-Journal-Tribune*
May 1967

No grave could be deep enough to bury all the accusations for the death of the *World-Journal-Tribune*. Unions, labor disputes, insufficient circulation, diminished advertising, costs of all colors, plus stimulating (and unprintable) rumors of "internal" strife: all were blamed for transforming the starveling paper into a corpse after less than eight months.

Inappropriate to the sign of Virgo, the *WJT* emerged on September 12, 1966 as a species of desperation-sandwich. Visually it most resembled the *World Telegram & The Sun;* the atmosphere was still mainly Hearst's *Journal-American,* while the flaws of the recent *Herald Tribune* were preserved—pseudo-sophistication and the attempt to sound serious while frivolously reporting on serious topics. Between the columnists (ranging from Evans and Novak to Walter Winchell) and feature writers, the thin, gray fact pieces offered little which hadn't appeared elsewhere in the New York press. Three thousand lost their jobs when the papers merged. Of the seventeen hundred remaining, some were forced to switch their fields, which may have accounted for the notable bleakness in their writing.

In the paper's first three weeks, storms appeared as the most important world events: Hurricane Inez had the biggest headlines on October 1 and 2 (in smaller type: "Biggest Viet Clash Shaping Up"; also "Soviets Walk Out After Peking Blast"). Inez may have been an editorial favorite because her targets were Cuba and the Dominican Republic. Elsewhere "Typhoon Disaster in Japan" and other storm songs established the *WJT*'s concern for meteorology; it also carried New York's most garrulous weather report. Otherwise murders received the thickest page 1 headlines: SEEK JEALOUS SUITOR OF SLAIN GO-GO GIRL (smaller type for "Hanoi Charges U.S. Plotting Biggest War") on September 30, when the *New York Times* featured the war's worst week for casualties in Vietnam. Previously the Valerie Percy murder in Chicago had the *WJT*'s main headlines, even after the police had run short of clues. At that point the headings grew quite desperate: EVERYONE SUSPECT IN PERCY MYSTERY, and there were subheads like A LOVED, FAMILIAR FACE—AND TEARS. Also page 1: IT LOOKS LIKE THE REAL THING (Lynda Bird Johnson and George Hamilton). These days almost any woman called Candy gets a headline— thanks to the Candace Mossler trial as well as Terry Southern. Still, after the *WJT*'s first month, the headlines became slightly more international, per- haps because other papers carried some needling jokes on the subject.

Politically the paper ranged from "conservative to reactionary," as A. J. Liebling wrote of the whole New York press. William Randolph Hearst, Jr., denounced U Thant on Vietnam: "worst of all was his disclosed willingness to accept a peace at any price." Bob Considine announced that "China was enticed—rather than bludgeoned—into trying communism." On the edito- rial page only Art Buchwald, Joseph Alsop, and William Buckley continued to sound like themselves; the latter, on "LBJ and the intellectuals," mourned "the unfortunate coincidence between ultra-liberalism and ultra-articulate- ness. . . . If you can get, say, Richard Rovere, Arthur Schlesinger, Dwight Macdonald, James Reston, and Walter Lippmann to agree on something— and when can you not?—the reading public has just about had it. . . . " One editorial, "Love, the Miracle Drug, Will Lengthen Your Life," balanced nicely with a feature on "A Tasty Trick with Burgers" (olives, pickles, cheese). The *WJT* had no foreign news bureaus—only stringers' reports and wire services. On page 27 of the first issue, "Nuclear Power for Bonn a Delicate Subject in Europe" was a rare bulletin from outer space. As for the average level of Washington news: "Sad LBJ Yearns for Texas Hills": "the President is unhappy. The Vietnam war and its unwelcome handmaiden, inflation, overshadow all. . . . So, there is general restiveness."

The local New York reporting was frail; there was lots of space for "color," but little for fact. A characteristic shock headline, VIETNAM WAR COMES TO NEW YORK, disguised a story concerning Congressman Leonard Farb- stein's primary victory against Theodore Weiss—which some thought was due to Farbstein supporting the war, while Weiss opposed it (however the vote was very close). This was by Jimmy Breslin, distinguished for winsome bearishness and first sentences like this: "A bald man was playing the piano loud and the numbers guy sat at a table and drank Remy Martin." Breslin's writing was never better, but readers were disturbed by the lapses of other reporters who wrote well for the *Tribune,* but later seemed infected by the Hearst style. *Newsweek* noted that the average age of the sports writers was fifty-two.

Unheard stories were scarce, but a few appeared: "Communist Coed Romps At Berkeley" ("Hammer-and-sickle oriented Bettina Aptheker, 22, *is* far too busy being naughty to be nice"). There were occasional originals: "Why Tran- quilizers Aren't Used in Riots"—because the dart guns used on animals might kill humans. Otherwise "How Ginger Rogers Stays Young," or "Is Dreaming a

Waste of Time?" kept the pages limp. Factual errors were noted throughout, but the best was the first day's page 1 announcement that Mayor John Lindsay pushed the button to start the *WJT*'s presses—when he was actually barred from the pressroom by the Pressmen's Union's president: an unhappy glimpse of the mayor's relations with labor.

Space was largely reserved for a sloppy though enjoyable Women's Section; seven gossip columnists (whose bent was hardly salacious: "The Whitneys are remarkable for their complete unstuffiness"); Bishop Sheen ("When a man loves a woman, then it follows that the nobler the woman, the nobler will be the love of a man. . . . The English novelist, John Osborne, says that America is a 'sexual nuthouse' "); *Dear Abby* ("Will a home for unmarried mothers take in a married woman?"); comics, and dozens of shattering jokes, especially from Bennet Cerf: "Q. What city in Kansas is loaded with Peeping Toms? A. Topeka." The Sunday edition had *Book Week*, which had steadily improved under a series of good editors; it was the only valuable part of the *WJT*. There was also the Sunday *New York* magazine, which contained many excellent ideas for articles; the topics were admirably chosen. But the style of frantic with-itry made Manhattan sound like a psychedelic toy department. The Sunday gardening section had some of the *WJT*'s best headlines, such as "Time To Take Up Tender Bulbs."

In its first month the *WJT* reported: "AMA Journal Asks Limit On Uniting Severed Limbs": " . . . too many surgeons have been sewing on severed limbs that are better left off. . . . If a patient has one good leg, the AMA said, the other should not be replanted." At the time this sounded like wise advice for the three-legged paper. But the *Tribune's* best ligaments were not replanted and the *Journal-American* remained the stoutest limb of all.

Hindsight: Of course magazines are as manipulative of material as newspapers. In 1970 I attended a rebel meeting of *Life* staffers. The tie clips and well-ironed creases I associated with Time Inc. weren't there; amid the jeans and minis, a young man with yellow lace-up flies and Rapunzel hair told me, "Man, this fuckin' place is freakin' out!" A mutinous writer later referred to *Life* as "a paramilitary organization." He said that the magazine—which was doing badly—was currently shy of "negative news," and that editors were demanding "cheerful stories about America." Cheer meant "either what the United States was like thirty years ago, or an example of somebody pulling pearls out of the shit." He added, "They want stories about the triumph of the human spirit. But they really mean the submission of the spirit—not beating the system, but finding a way for *Life* to announce that 'the system made this possible.' " Like many others in the media, some I talked to at Time Inc. felt their own institution was responsible for acclimatizing millions to the continuation of the Vietnam war, to accepting disguised racism or sexism—all shaded under the umbrella of liberalism. After all you can add an upbeat ending to a massacre (how GIs gave food to those they'd orphaned), or make black militants appear as clowns. Still, a magazine that commissions a feature on a topless anthropologist wouldn't call itself conservative.

In April of 1972, *(MORE),* the New York journalism review, brought some three thousand reporters and press-minded persons together at their counter-convention, which was held while the American Newspaper Publishers Association was having their annual meeting. Aside from *(MORE),* there are about a dozen journalism reviews; the *Chicago Journalism Review* was founded after the Democratic Convention of 1968, when Chicago reporters saw how inaccurately some of their own papers covered the event.

Although there were many objections to the panels arranged by *(MORE)*— black and women reporters were sparsely represented, and the Vietnam Veterans Against the War were indignant that there was no panel to discuss the coverage of Vietnam—and despite some inevitable guff, the counter-convention was a heartening occasion. The towering concern was with the mass media's talent for twisting the news, plus the humble allegiance to the views of owners or advertisers. (General Motors is the biggest newspaper advertiser in the country.) Some suggested that journalists should demand editorial control of their publications, as some have done in France and West Germany and England. Newspapers were constantly referred to as corporations which simply protect their own interests. Many spoke of the widening news blackout—the subjects that aren't covered—and also about reporters being subpoenaed for their confidential sources: which will make many sources unavailable in future. Some kept quoting A. J. Liebling's reflection that "freedom of the press is guaranteed only to those who own one."

We all ripped our own publications apart as well as each other's, and the individual reporter's responsibility was underlined. At a panel on the new journalism, Tom Wolfe and Gail Sheehy took some wallops concerning inaccuracy and invention—which didn't seem to bother them. Calvin Trillin expressed some distress that it was no longer a serious criticism to say that a piece of journalism wasn't really true, and that errors which would embarrass a traditional reporter didn't seem to trouble some newer journalists.

Throughout "The Wayward Press Bus," those who follow campaigns were intensely critical of their own work. Martin Nolan of the *Boston Globe* stressed that political reporters spend far too much time trying to project into the future, rather than thoroughly covering the immediate past. Jeff Greenfield asked, "Who decides the character of a crowd?" He referred to the press reports that the New Hampshire crowds listening to Edmund Muskie were "attentively silent"—before it was acknowledged that they were stupendously bored. Dan Rather of CBS mentioned the reporters who have a vested interest in seeing a candidate win. "A good candidate," who's likely to be elected, "puts you on the air a lot." He said that TV "needs a mad dog for every candidate. A reporter who doesn't like him. But the trend's in the opposite direction—reporters who play cosy with the candidate, write a speech for him, give him advice."

Again and again journalists stated that their editors' pretense to neutrality was false: that altering a reporter's material to reflect editorial views was a more distortive act than allowing a reporter to express an opinion. Tom Wicker said, "What we have is the kind of journalism that accepts and projects the status quo and official policy," and he condemned "that spurious objectivity on which our editors insist." Of course rebels know they may get fired. In an informal meeting, some discussed the searing question: "How do you protest to your editor without getting on his shit list?" There were references to the punishment of being switched to trivial subjects, "or transferred from Paris to Queens." No one had an immediate solution.

The high point for many of us was the presentation of *(MORE)*'s A. J. Liebling Award to I. F. Stone. Among his remarks on reporting was a warning not to "over-personify the evils of our time"—not to hang them on a few public figures, but to trace them to the institutions which are responsible. Also: "I think a journalist should be committed—to the big issues of his time. . . . Yet you have to stand slightly aloof—so you can always tell the whole story." Stone also said, "Facts by themselves don't mean very much. . . . If people's concern for other people were greater, we'd have less of a job. What we're trying to do—part of our job—is to increase people's sympathy for each other."

"Far-*out!*": from an underground reporter behind me. And amid a crowd which included lots of cynics, sophisticates, infinite ambitions, punchdrunk frustrations, and many who detest each other's work, it was rather astounding that quite a few were there to talk about accountability in journalism.

League for Spiritual Discovery
December 1966

Hunched in white pyjamas on a low divan, caressing his bare feet to a background of plangent guitars, his hair tangled rather like a crown of thorns, Dr. Timothy Leary welcomed an audience of twenty-four hundred in a former Yiddish vaudeville theater in the East Village. "In the beginning, let us pray . . . " Then: "We know that you know that there is a hunger for more, for more . . . "

Pigeon notes have already been detected in his voice; indeed he sounds like a whole flock of something in St. Mark's Square. His six-week-old religion, sponsored by his League for Spiritual Discovery, is being advertised through a series of psychedelic celebrations, which he says re-create aspects of the LSD experience. Changing kaleidoscopic patterns from painted slides, film, collages, and mime on three layers of scrim accompany Leary's "gospel lectures." Ovarian shapes and visceral suggestions, fractured pinwheels, butterfly wings and ganglia, produce a very appealing brand of visual salad.

Leary's first service was "The Death of the Mind." Explaining that "you've got to die in order to live," he advised the overeducated person to "leave his mind behind," to stop being "caught in thought," and to enjoy the visions which "will come when the biochemistry of your body brings about a state of grace." The boy beside me wagged his head when Leary repeated, "The price of admission is your mind." An actor (who was also a doctor) behind the now scarlet screen mimed the sensation of traveling through his own arterial system—apparently a common LSD fantasy. At one point he felt he was drowning in his own blood, while Leary jovially remarked that doctors under acid are particularly prone to this "body trauma," and often think they're bleeding to death. Cooing praise for "the lattice work of cellular wisdom" and "the chemical bibles of the nervous system," while his disciple was "tumbling down the capillary networks," Leary promised that "protein memory banks are waiting with a million file cards." A successive stage recalls "all the couplings . . . the endless dance of male and female." Twitching chalk buttocks filled the screen: it was strictly a male fantasy. The subject next imagined that he had murdered a girl, and was reproached by Leary in his role as guide: "Didn't I teach you the chess game of life? And how to make a baby smile?" (Earlier he urged those over forty to look for their guides among their teen-aged offspring. He's also prescribed LSD for seven-year-olds, because "children are less entrapped in their minds.") Guaranteeing that he can remove "the delicious pleasure of guilt," Leary showed his subject happily reborn after "his heartbeat became the pulses of the universe."

Leary described his new League, which has four hundred and eleven initiates. They're trying to legalize acid—but only to be administered by spiritual guides like themselves, for whom "the temple is the body, while the shrine is the home." Admitting that "it's very easy to become a prophet," he explained turning on and tuning in and dropping out. Turning on means "contacting the energy within—turning off your mind—and you've *got* to do it biochemically." Tuning in: "You've got to become an active artist if you take LSD," and express your revelations. Dropping out: cultivate detachment, "get free of ambitions and jealousies." ("Yes, man, yes!" from some of the audience.) But: "These are not acts of rebellion—*please!*" My neighbor said, "Awww." Acid was recommended with almost no reservations, but in passing Leary did say that "For every ecstasy, there is terror and paranoia." Finally soothing mandalas appeared on the screen; Leary advised the audience to remain for meditation—as "a preparation for reentry after rebirth" into the vulgar, commercial world. He then adjourned to the lobby, to autograph copies of his book which were on sale.

Leary made $1,000 at the box office in his first week; he said his new religion will be tax-free. "The Reincarnation of Jesus Christ," an "LSD Mass," was the second celebration. Here the subject "drifted through his respiratory system," and also entered his own body through the center of his eye. Leary didn't actually say that he was Christ, but parallels were permitted. Acid was called a sacrament, which should only be taken by those in a state of grace; an act of confession before turning on was recommended: "Review all your sins—whatever *you* think you *shouldn't* do—because they will expand under LSD." He paraphrased the Gospels ("I am here to lead the brokenhearted"), and used cinematic litany (repeated shots of Christ), emphasizing images of the Consecration, including the Elevation. His main source appeared to be the Apocrypha. There was a sham police raid in the middle, because Christ (like Leary) was in trouble with the law. A former Catholic, whom I dragged along for my own education, said these parodies would probably not offend the church—except for the muddled thinking behind them.

Leary's audience had an air of silent, gleeful confidence: they appeared as more of a community than a gathering of reform Democrats. Leary welcomes "skeptics," and there are excellent seats for the press. He does seem like such a showman that it's hard to believe he's sincere. But he must be—to face the fines and jail sentences that are probably awaiting him.

Hindsight: I never tried acid because I've seen so much suffering among those who cracked up without drugs. And of course I thought that Leary was an ass. Yet I rather regretted my own fears of acid: I would have liked the rewards without the pain—which, as someone said, is rather like wanting to be Baudelaire without the syphilis. Still, I couldn't flow with the friend who said, "Oh, but the bad trips are the best ones"—meaning the most enlightening. All the agonies I heard about clenched my resistance against those who put so much pressure on the unconverted. In 1966 and 1967 I was also maddened by the "groovy revolution" talk which implied that a stoned America would automatically become a benevolent democracy—no more poverty or racism or war, not if we all stay high. As 1969 turned into 1970, Leary was optimistically announcing that the revolution had already occurred, even though Washington hadn't yet realized it. But even in 1967, some had already called Leary a bad prophet.

Yet I appreciated some of the changes that acid and other expanders wrought in our culture. And I enjoyed living in the psychedelic society of 1967, which affected many who dwelled far outside it. I learned quite a lot from individuals who'd taken acid—I can say that their experiences enriched mine. There's a nice speech from one character in Donald Newlove's novel, *The Painter Gabriel:* "The head culture is passing through the national body like waves of virus, shooting up everyone's imagination—even the imaginations of people who hate drugs. They can't stop its influence anymore than they can stop Coca-Cola ads . . . LSD and pot are . . . rippling over the continent, see, like the first effects of radio earlier in this century. Radio was a consciousness expander. Pretty awful, too!"

Eventually I saw enough casualties from acid and other drugs to loathe their history in this country. But I was amused by Leary's remarks about "revolutionary chauvinism" after he and his wife had been put under house arrest by Eldridge Cleaver in Algiers in January 1971. (Four months earlier Leary had sought the Algerian Panthers' protection, after he'd escaped from jail in California with the aid of the Weatherpersons.) As described by Michael Zwerin in the *Village Voice,* the Panthers' "revolutionary bust" occurred just before the Learys' first dinner party. Cleaver had decided that acid was destructive to revolution, that Leary's mind had been blown by drugs—"There seems to me to be something very wrong with Leary's brain"—and that both Learys were careless of security, in terms of the "uncool" people they saw and the guests they planned to entertain.

The Learys were guarded and held in custody for four days while Cleaver and Leary exchanged mutual accusations. Leary maintained his commitment to "internal revolution" as the precedent for any other revolution. "I've found there is revolutionary chauvinism. People say *my* revolution is the only one. You've got to give up your liberations until I get mine or you may never get yours because your liberation is really reactionary repression. . . . "

Subsequently Leary went back to Folsom prison, working as a gardener in charge of petunias, sweet peas, and marigolds. Cleaver was himself placed under house arrest by the Algerian government after he tried to force its members to meet the demands of two groups of black highjackers in 1972.

In 1994, when the seventy-three-year-old Leary was master of ceremonies at a psychedelic conference called "Gathering of the Minds" in Southern California, he boasted about getting stoned with his son at a Pink Floyd concert, announced that his newly born great-granddaughter was in the crowd, and told his audience he had discovered "the greatest drug of all . . . Senility!"

College for Policemen
March 1967

Academic discontent seems so prevalent that the landscape is teeming with furious or flatulent professors, pupils who say their courses mean little to them, tired blood, jargon, and disgust. So it's rather astonishing to discover an institution where a dedicated faculty repeats its praise for the students, while the students' eagerness and progress generates a contagion of cheer. The John Jay College of Criminal Justice perpetuates a level of morale which some academics could envy.

The college, a senior college of the City University of New York, started in 1965. This is the only college in America—perhaps in the world—devoted to the study and development of the criminal justice system in its entirety. However, the undergraduate program is about 80 percent liberal arts. Fewer police science courses are required than in any other police college in the country. There are about 1,475 undergraduates; the majority are policemen, plus some correction officers and "uncommitted" high school graduates.

Entrance is optional. The students are undoubtedly the most ambitious— and some of the most intelligent—in their profession. A degree doesn't mean promotion. Since all policemen must have high school degrees, any member of the force is eligible. The police are not given time off from their work to study, hence the four-year course takes approximately ten years to complete. (There are quite a few dropouts but few failures.) Most will graduate at about forty; the average age of the students is about thirty-five to forty. The professors have taught at Columbia, Princeton, Brooklyn College, City College, N.Y.U., Rutgers, and others. Most are now full-time at the college. They compare their students to the veterans of World War II: adults whose drive to learn makes them a delight to teach. Also these students are free from the wandering Socspeak or the garbled language heard at many other universities. A policeman will refer to "the whole fishbowl" when an Ivy Leaguer might speak of "a grouping of interrelationships." Speech at this college is notably graphic and lucid, and "dichotomy" or "charisma" are not there to wound the ear. Another scarce word is "cop," which was inspired by the copper shields which policemen used to wear, and by "constable on patrol." The term is still considered insulting when used by those outside the force. (Not until 1968 did other CUNY students refer to John Jay "Pig U.")

The college emphasizes education for its own sake, with a minimum of technical courses. President Leonard Reisman said that "the college stimulates the police to find a rationale behind their work." Dean Donald Riddle remarked that the police are a fairly isolated group, which needs to be related to the rest of the species. (Also policemen who've been to college are found to be less authoritarian than those who haven't.) The modern policeman is asked to be a lawyer, a clergyman, a psychologist, a linguist, and a neighborhood uncle—a quite impartial soldier who's supposed to be able to act more quickly than the brain itself. Yet their teachers constantly remind them that it's not their role to interpret the law, just to make arrests. The blend sounds like a recipe for schizophrenia.

While the New York force is still 50 to 60 percent Irish, Italians are plentiful. Hence Catholicism is still dominant. Before 1900 the department was primarily German. Jewish policemen increased right after the war, but there aren't many at present, and there's a general shortage of recruits, due to Vietnam. Though the height requirement was recently lowered for Puerto Ricans, few have joined. Black recruits are sparse, partly because those who are qualified prefer to work in less controversial departments of city service, and especially because black neighborhoods still don't trust the police. I asked all the John Jay students I met why they joined the police force, and the vast majority said they'd had relatives in the profession.

Professor Robert Pinckert's lecture on *Lycidus* included an analysis of the pastoral conventions, Dr. Johnson's abhorrence of the pastoral form, Milton's technique of delaying the verb, the devices of hyperbole, metonymy, and oxymorons, "the visualist fallacy," the controversies about the "two-handed engine," onomatopoeia, and the alternation of pagan and Christian settings. Water imagery was detailed throughout. The professor related certain themes and facts to his students' experience and background. After asking why Milton invoked "Laurels" at the start—"Yet once more, O ye Laurels"—he said, "How many of you have cooked spaghetti sauce?" Many hands were raised. "What do you put in it?" Chorus: "Bay leaf." On learning that bay is laurel, one policeman said, "It stays green. So that symbolizes immortality?" The professor agreed and remarked, "When you receive your baccalaureate, you too will be crowned with laurel." (Shy laughter.)

Stressing that everyone needs a fantasy life, such as the notion of the pastoral, Professor Pinckert added, "The American cowboy is to us what the shepherd was to Milton," and then compared Marie Antoinette to the U.S. cowboy—in light of her shepherdess games. When he explained that Memory (Mnemosyne) was the mother of the Muses, he referred to the "Mnemonics" (police code) which all his pupils had studied. One muttered "Bed pain that triggered first burglary"—a line of police code that sounds like Freudian poetry.

There was much discussion of the Muses as well as the concept of inspiration. During a discussion of river gods, the professor asked why rivers should be characterized as male. A policewoman laughed and said, "Because rivers are dirty!" (Groans from the class.) "And why should the sea be female?" First policeman: "Because it's just there." Second policeman: "Yep, and it's fickle. It keeps changing." The policewoman hissed mildly. Concerning "the mantle blue," the many Catholic students knew that blue is associated with purity and the Virgin. Professor Pinckert innocently added, "You men wear blue to signify your incorruptibility." There were a few smiles, but not many.

Literary judgments range from a strong identification with Coriolanus (who seems like a heroic figure who was "shot down," like General MacArthur or Goldwater) and admiration for Dostoevsky, to a complex reaction to James Baldwin's *The Fire Next Time:* most didn't like it, yet they voted to retain it in the course. Some said it had no literary merit. They were obviously suppressing their antagonism to the remarks about whites and about policemen. Freud was considered "too old hat"; aside from the familiarity of his sexual theories, his references to religion as an "infantile delusion" are offensive to the police. In examining Camus's *The Rebel*, they distinguished between crimes of passion (which they find more forgivable than others) and calculated or organized crime.

In the drama class there were lively disagreements about Hedda Gabler. One student said she was a sacrificial victim, while others felt she was the instrument of sacrifice. Another retorted, "Hedda Gabler is everybody's wife." The hair symbolism intrigued them: "Hedda thought she deserved a great bull-mop for herself." One student argued that the play is more of a farce than a tragedy, especially since Lovborg was shot in the bowels. Last year the drama class performed the Gide-Barrault dramatization of Kafka's *The Trial*, and has been rehearsing Aristophanes' *The Birds* with gusto. I saw one scene where a gigantic blond with a gun at his hip was declaiming: "Aha, you reckoned without the Muses! Fleet, fleet as twinkling horses' feet. . . . the airy, fairy rumor of the Muses sped to me . . . " In their written evaluations of the course, many policemen said that it helped them in the range of role-switching needed in their own jobs.

The music professor, Milton Schafer (who wrote the music for *Bravo, Giovanni!* and *Drat! the Cat!*), says policemen are responsive to musical categories because they've already been trained to think in an orderly fashion. Most prefer programmatic music, like Tchaikovsky's *Romeo and Juliet*, but are friendly to Mozart and Haydn. Quite a few students asked for a special course in contemporary music: "They hate it, but they want to know more about it." Still, one term paper compared the street noises of the 1966 New York subway strike to "a traffic symphony." The student wrote, "The Rhythm (Flow) of thousands and thousands of cars, bumper to bumper, hour after hour, across the bridges and through the tunnels. The car horns begging the vehicles ahead to move, possessed Tone, the medium of music. Each had its own distinct Pitch, Intensity, Quality and Duration.

"And how was this music listened to? Passively by those in the buildings who were not caught up in its ordered confusion. Emotionally by those suffering through hours of driving. Perceptively by police officers, who knew every sound had a meaning and guided their actions accordingly."

One of the most animated courses is a colloquium; the reading list extends from Shakespeare to Orwell and includes Bettelheim, Isherwood, and Hannah Arendt. A colloquium on *Catch-22* revealed the students' profound respect for authority. Many were indignant because the novel satirized a military organization. They felt that a similar burlesque on their department could be "corrupting" and very harmful: "Our uniform is covered with blood and guts and glory, and to mock it—that would be a sin." There was also an argument about the nature of satire—where "pure humor" was hotly defended against "the absurd."

"But a few of us could laugh at the military, or at a chaplain, couldn't we?"

"Not many of us."

"No."

Several were distressed by *Catch-22*'s distortion of fact—"Look, how many nuts do you meet in any organization?"—although the professor kept reminding them that it was fiction. Most of these men had fought in World War II, and gradually they began to agree that they'd known irresponsible officers. "I knew one who sent a man through enemy fire just to pick up a book he wanted to read."

"Well, what's wrong with that?"

"The book wasn't any good!"

Most policemen support the war in Vietnam. One said, "*Catch-22* is an antiwar polemic. It feeds the One-Worlders and the people who think that peace is the answer to everything." It bothered them that "the youth" would like such a "subversive" book—"when they're already bombarded by the liberal influence." One teacher told them that William Buckley had deduced that because fourteen professors at Yale had voted for Harry Truman, education was controlled by liberals.

"Well, it *is* controlled by liberals."

"Why can't we have a book of Buckley's in this course?"

"Aw, we read him anyway."

There was a reference to Norman Mailer:

"Listen, didn't he stab his wife?"

"So that puts a dent in everything he writes?"

"Yeah."

"Listen, he was probably a pacifist when he did it."

In a discussion of responsibility, there was a prickly dialogue:

"Anything that causes death should be eliminated? How about cars?"

"Look, guns don't kill people. People kill people."

"Bombs kill people."

"Yes, but somebody had to drop the bombs."

A professor asked if any of them felt that they'd been subverted by *Catch-22*.

"No. But we're not typical students. The youth of today have such pliable minds."

"The youth of today are just going into a corner and fornicating."

"Well, the youth who aren't well educated won't read it. Even the vocabulary was selected for the intellectual."

"Yeah, those four-letter words are tough."

Finally most did (reluctantly) agree that criticism of any organization is valid, although one man still held out: "This book undermines authority—it almost makes you feel that authority should be questioned!" In this class, as in others, the professors gently encouraged that idea. Other teachers said it's hard for most policemen to challenge their instructors, even when they violently disagree with them.

There are extensive courses in government and law, and everyone must take European history. After delivering a lecture on Louis XIV's centralization of the state and his suppression of the Huguenots, a history professor said his students are torn between their loyalty to the church and loyalty to the idea of religious toleration. While studying the Protestant Revolution, the police took serious issue with the idea of salvation through God's grace alone, without good works. (In the class I visited, most seemed ill at ease with the concepts of revolution.) The professor added that many policemen are now displaced because of the changes in the church, "and the discomfort shows in their faces when they discuss these subjects."

But the philosophy professor said that none of the reactions were extreme—or even particularly Catholic—in his Comparative Religions course. When the police study Judaism, Christianity, Islam, Hinduism, Buddhism, Zen, Confucius, and Taoism, "their ability to analyze is more conspicuous than any parochial training." Among philosophers they do prefer Aristotle to Plato, and many have said they approve of Aristotle's Golden Mean. The professor remarked that while his Princeton undergraduates are acquiring a frame of reference to apply to their future experiences, the police already have plenty of experience, but want the frame. Hence, he said, the exhilaration of teaching policemen: "They bring experience in search of interpretation."

A visitor to the college can momentarily forget that these students of polyphony or poetry work steadily among people who may kill them. While the police are ingesting liberal arts, they're studying their own craft. In a police science course called The Principles of Investigation, a lecture on the subtleties of "interviewing" showed how very skilled a practitioner must be. The lecturer warned against calling witnesses "friendly" or "hostile"; "cooperative" or "uncooperative" are preferable psychologically. (The printed outline for this topic includes "The Jekyll-Hyde technique," which recommends using a mild approach before a harsh one. The latter "may alienate the subject permanently," or he may feel that it's synthetic.) Later: "Emphasize the impression that you are not concerned with conviction or punishment. It is your duty only to learn what happened." "Giving him rope" is considered the best technique: "If a story is sufficiently involved, it's probably impossible for him to keep it straight." *Outline:* "(a) Consider that it will be impossible for him to lie consistently. (b) If he tells a phony story, let him talk. (c) Subtly have him repeat the key lies. . . . "

A "standard problem" is the "code against informing." It was repeated that the subject must never be threatened. People sometimes admit to something they didn't do, because it's easier—as in the case of traffic offenses. And there are numbers who are sufficiently disturbed to make false confessions. Another problem is the man who denies his guilt—when no one thought he was guilty. An irate citizen who makes "empty threats" at the police—"I'll have you transferred to Staten Island!"—may be showing symptoms of guilt rather than innocence.

In the "psychological battle" of confession, the detective may depend on a person's sense of guilt to make him feel uncomfortable: "A hardened criminal can have a keen sense of right and wrong." But he must be caught off guard. Moreover: "If we present ourselves as the forces of retribution, it won't work. You can't behave like Cotton Mather. Instead, present yourself as a bridge between him and society." Also: "You must have great self control not to express the revulsion that you feel towards certain criminals." And it's important to treat the wife and family well.

Timing is crucial: "When confronted with evidence, he'll often do the wrong thing. We want to capitalize on the fact that he'll be groping at straws." The "psychological stamina" of the professional criminal was acknowledged: he has been interviewed before, and he may feel quite confident of the detective's limitations. (The outline mentions "Friendly Forces Reduced," during the period when the suspect should be brought "to perceive confession as the path to freedom.") The danger of the whole process was admitted; throughout the imaginary confession scenes there was the possibility that the subject might pull a gun or attack. But the teacher renewed his warnings about the intricacies of assessing guilt. He stressed that innocence is often bewildered, rather than vociferous or righteously indignant.

The police are fiercely sensitive about their reputation. They feel quite persecuted and want to talk about it. Some kept asking me, "Are you going to write about police brutality?" In an advanced speech course, a brisk student panel examined the new Supreme Court decision on confessions. (Henceforth the police must inform a suspect that he has the right to legal counsel before making any statement.) The panel echoed with the words "hampered" and "hindered." There were many respectful references to the original Constitution and "the intentions of the Founding Fathers." Some were perturbed by the idea of amendments: "I don't think our forefathers meant to make the kind of laws we have today." Their intense moralism—"It would really shock me if a criminal went free"—appeared as strongly in this class as it did in others. It was clear that these particular policemen really want the public to obey the laws.

However, the delicate question of confessions was freely sifted.

"Do you think we actually railroad a guy?"

"Well, we all know what methods we've employed. We do sometimes elicit enforced confession. I know that I wouldn't want it done to me—what we do to some guys. The Supreme Court decision hinders me as an officer, but I approve of it as a citizen."

There was angry talk about the policemen whose malpractices blacken the reputation of the whole Department: "Maybe some of us are slow to learn. But we all pay the price for officers who make mistakes."

A panelist elaborated: "We've been taught how to make a person break down psychologically. I'm a very strong person psychologically myself. But some people aren't And we're trained to recognize mental defectives." He added, "The forced confession is the fruit of the poisoned tree."

Emphasizing that "our function is to detect crime and arrest it—*not* to prosecute," they concluded by approving the Supreme Court decision—with no enthusiasm whatsoever.

"Everyone loves a fireman—but they don't love us." Unpopularity was considered by another group. Some seemed unwilling to admit that racial hostilities are related to the reputation for brutality, but there were unhappy remarks about being disliked in Harlem. (There's a powerful reluctance to discuss anything to do with race. One professor said the police are controlling strong negative feelings—as they've been told to do.) Some thought the automobile was "the greatest single reason for being disliked": due to parking tickets and arrests for traffic violations. They explained that everyone associates the police with punishment: "We're not condemning people personally, we're condemning their *acts*. But they do take it personally!" And: "Sure, nobody likes to be arrested. We're a public animal—we're supposed to keep traffic moving, catch criminals, and stop noise. But people want these things applied to others, not themselves. You don't want your son jailed, just someone else's." Almost every man present had been bitten by a woman. Apparently female assaults on policemen are the highest for any group.

Asked to define a liberal, the class finally agreed on "obstructionist." "Someone who's more concerned with the rights of individuals. Whereas policemen are concerned with the rights of the group." "Yeah, a liberal tries to make your job harder, to erect roadblocks. He wants to make the laws more lenient." One said, "We *can't* be a semimilitary organization—that's like having a semi-leakproof pail." Yet self-criticism was constant. Several said they would like to work unarmed for certain assignments and that they regretted having to carry guns off duty.

~

A month after I wrote about the college, I saw some of the John Jay students patrolling the huge antiwar march of April 1967. Even a couple who'd made indignant remarks about "the youth" were beaming and nodding at the marchers, channeling them carefully through traffic and letting the crowd fan out where it wanted to. From seeing them in action, I felt that a lot had been learned and taught at the college—even if these particular men were just putting on an amiable act.

Since then, because many of us have acquired a bitter mistrust of the police, one's more concerned than ever with the training they're given. The intensely moralistic views I heard from so many seem to make them oddly vulnerable in a period of changing values. Since the Knapp Commission revealed gigantic proportions of graft, I wondered if cynicism came most easily to former authoritarians.

Small wonder that the police are confused, especially since some radicals, who claimed to revere the working class, forgot that policemen are workers too. In January 1971 there was a six-day wildcat strike of twenty thousand policemen demanding better salaries. When police union leader Edward Kiernan urged them to return to work at a Patrolmen's Benevolent Association meeting, some young cops yelled "more gutter language than is heard at protests that cops are usually called on to maintain order at," according to the *Daily News*. We also saw photographs of cops raising their fists and shouting slogans. To the strikers' demands for amnesty, the *News* replied, "Amnesty, nothing."

In *Revolutionary Notes*, Julius Lester remarked that some apparent enemies must also be regarded as "victims" of the system. "All too often . . . we confuse the doer with the deed and think that they are one and the same. It is the deed we must hate, not the doer of the deed. The policeman acts like a beast, but to call him a beast, a 'pig,' is only to negate the potential of man that is within him. . . . To yell 'Fascist!' at a Wallace supporter is only to guarantee that that individual will be a fascist."

Hindsight: In May of 1972 I went back to John Jay to ask Professor Robert Pinckert how the college had weathered the last five years. He spoke rather wistfully of 1967—"It was an academic paradise then"—and said that morale had held through 1969, despite bomb scares and threats of disrupted classes, which came mainly from other students in the City University. Since then morale had sagged.

In 1970 Open Admissions changed John Jay from a small criminal justice college to a senior college of CUNY—with a severe lack of space. Some felt that John Jay took on too many students. (From some 1,500 in 1967, it rose to about 5,500 students, then decreased to 4,900.) The cops, who were once a 90 percent majority of the students, dwindled to 40 percent. The new young students didn't have the same frame of reference as the police, and some teachers found it hard to devise lectures or courses that could be understood by both groups. Professor Pinckert said, "No, I couldn't give the same lecture on *Lycidus* now."

While race is rarely mentioned, the bathrooms have flowered with graffiti, ranging from "Fuck you, Whitey"/"Same to Niggers," also "Black/White Power" (both crossed out), and more elaborate retorts: "Nixon Masturbates with a Paper Towel"/"Thank the Lord For Such A Good President." "Right On, Spiro!" is frequent.

Professor Pinckert said the cops are no longer so moralistic in class. "They have their tails between their legs, but they still won't admit that cops can err. . . . But the moralism you heard five years ago was genuine, sincere. Now they're shakier, and resent it.

"Some cops are cynical after they've been on the force for a month. They're fed a lot of mickey mouse stuff in regular training—about how great it is to be a cop. The word corruption is *never* mentioned. Then they go to the precinct and find that everyone's on the take. That's where the cynicism enters— and all that basic training goes out the window. The few who are still idealistic put up defenses. Graft is just denied. And if a man has a guilty conscience, he'll become more vehement in the pursuit of criminals."

There's a big waiting list of those who want to become policemen. Applications have soared, especially from veterans returning from Vietnam. Many more blacks have applied, but Puerto Ricans are still very wary. White cops are complaining about the number of black ones and insisting that they're getting special treatment.

Professor Pinckert said the policemen he knows no longer believe in Hell, though they're still 80 to 90 percent Catholic. But there's still a vague belief in Heaven. During his class in *The Inferno*, the cops said they were sorry to see homosexuals in Hell. Then several added that they wouldn't want to see Hitler there either. He asked if they believed in universal redemption, and most said no. He pressed them harder and they expressed the hope that people "would somehow be cured"—and *then* "get to heaven." Guilt—apart from the guilt of dangerous criminals—was not a subject they were willing to discuss in class.

~

Photographs of arrested policemen doubled over, hands cuffed behind their backs, heads ducking away from the cameras as they were led off to their arraignments, became familiar to New Yorkers in 1994. The Mollen Commission's report on police corruption exposed more far-flung criminality than had been imagined in 1972, when the Knapp Commission divulged that many of our policemen shared bribes from bookies and prostitutes with their supervisors; although some were involved in the heroin trade, their numbers were limited. But too many New York cops of the Nineties were stealing drugs, money, and guns from dealers, selling cocaine, blackmailing dealers or even functioning as armed escorts for dealers transporting loads of drugs and cash.

Recalling the moralistic policemen of 1967, who had come of age before drugs were central to our culture, I suspected that those I met in the classroom would have been astounded by the mob of ten thousand off-duty officers who rampaged outside City Hall in 1992. Protesting Mayor David Dinkins's plans for an all-civilian police review board, they wore t-shirts reading "Dinkins Must Go," waved racist signs, and called the Mayor a nigger. Future Mayor Rudolph Giuliani harangued the crowd, denouncing Dinkins and the potential board, shouting obscenities. (After Giuliani took office he did support the civilian board, created in 1993.) About four thousand policemen suddenly burst through the wooden police barricades and surged up the steps of City Hall; the doors were rapidly bolted on the inside while the cops screamed, "Take the Hall! Take the Hall!" Many were drunk, scattering beer cans and broken bottles over the streets, leaping on top of parked cars and harassing pedestrians. Chanting, "Close the bridge!" part of the throng blocked traffic on the Brooklyn Bridge for an hour, defying uniformed officers who tried to disperse them.

Most of the riotous officers were very young; columnists reminded us that twenty-year-olds could become policemen and that they had had little or none of the sensitivity training given to previous generations. In 1995 at least fifty New York policemen who were in Washington for National Police Week indulged in a bacchanal: dancing naked through hotel lobbies, pouring liquor on escalator bannisters and sliding down them, singing and bellowing, groping women, spraying each other with fire extinguishers and setting off false alarms, harassing guests, they stimulated further demands for improved education as well as better training for the police.

The Mollen report of 1994 had described "police acting as criminals" and terrorizing black and Hispanic neighborhoods, planning robberies and raids on drug houses; "willfully blind" supervisors choosing to ignore the crimes because they "fear the consequences of a corruption scandal more than corruption itself," and the Patrolmen's Benevolent Association's efforts to impede investigations. "The principle of accountability" had "completely collapsed." Just when crime had become a campaign issue all over the country, when politicians who promised safer streets and capital punishment were likely to be elected, the cynicism of many New York policemen and most New Yorkers seemed almost perfectly balanced: neither expected a rebirth of law and order.

Go With The Flow

Diggers and Their Friends in New York
July–August 1967

Pinwheels erupt, mutate themselves, red blurts into blue: any galaxy of psychedelic lights is a valid image for the new consciousness, which can't be
captured by the panting media nor the earnest sociologist. Still, among the
oozing diversities of hippie phyla, pliant as plastic foam, the Diggers emerge
with some perceptible traits. Named for the 17th-century common-land culti-
vators, they evolved from the San Francisco Mime Troupe about two years
ago; there's now a New York chapter. Their philanthropies have caused comparisons to the Salvation Army—"But we don't make anyone sit through religious services!" Their Free Store, crammed with books, clothes, and furniture
that's collected by "going garbaging" at night, has only one rule: "You Can't
Steal." Free stew is dispensed every afternoon in Tompkins Square Park and a
Digger sweep-in cleaned up a startled neighborhood. Diggers collected and
distributed a truckload of food after Newark's riots—noting that canned food
was preferable, since it could also be used as a weapon and thrown at the
police. But the Diggers have quite amiable relations with their local East Village precinct officer, Captain Fink. When he heard someone say "Fuck the
cops," he asked if it meant loving the police.

Runaways in their early teens are now a national anxiety; the New York
Youth Board suspects that there are usually about four thousand under eighteen in the city, perhaps half a million in the whole country. While there are
rescue societies for lost dogs, there's no equivalent for humans. New York is
absorbing in a dual sense: aside from its fascinations, it absorbs strays to a
merciless vanishing point, rendering their afflictions and their very existence
unknown—as though they had fallen through the cracks in the pavements.
The youngest runaways are often sexually abused and exploited, made to
hustle or turn tricks as they grow more and more desperate for food and
shelter.

One Digger, who said he'd found some four hundred runaways sleeping
in Tompkins Square Park, formed the East Side Service Organization—motto:
ESSO—IT'S A GAS!—to take runaways off the streets and to find beds or jobs
for them. The Diggers also ran an ad in their newspaper: "Buddy, Can You
Spare a Bed?" There are rules—"No balling of chicks"—and selective screening to see who's capable of staying with strangers. Runaways spring from all

economic contexts, many from homes so brutal that it would be futile to advise them to return, although the Diggers suggest sending postcards.

The Diggers agree that the East Village attracts many ravaged waifs, who want drugs but aren't "conscious hippies." So the Diggers have kept an eye on certain "transits' communes"—such as one recently abandoned by a head called Galahad, which became so famous for amphetamines and syphilis that the Diggers asked the Health Department to close it. They also urge the organization of workshops to educate parents about drugs and are trying to establish a free medical clinic, plus free legal aid services, in their neighborhood. Free schools—bred of disgust with public education and the Digger practice of "pied pipering" (teaching children Digger values, telling them to reject straight jobs: "Don't do anything a machine can do")—are starting in other parts of the country.

Some thirty $1 bills floated down to the floor of the New York Stock Exchange, flung by Diggers who were miming "the death of money." Stockbrokers, clerks, and runners on the floor blew kisses and cheered, while others shouted angrily and shook their fists until the dollar-deriders were hustled out. The point was to give the dealers "some real money" instead of coupons and stock certificates, and to ridicule the entire Western economy. Often the Diggers hand out "free money" at their events. Well nourished in theatrical history, they've swiftly developed their concept of street theater. It's the recurrent tradition of dealing directly with the audience, with no division between actors and spectators, plus an opportunity for everyone to participate. Naturally spontaneity is cherished, but each performance has a purpose that happenings lack.

The Diggers' games sprinkle absurdity over whatever they protest. Con Edison, distinguished for pollution and constantly rebuked by City Hall, was recently deluged on Black Flower Day: the Diggers brandished a sign reading "Breathing Is Bad For Your Health," presented executives leaving their offices with begrimed daffodils and then threw soot on their white summer suits. The Diggers next set off smoke flares which stained the building responsible for soiling much of New York. Protesting the despotism of traffic, some of the same crowd blocked St. Mark's Place for about half an hour, chanted Hare Krishnas, and then polished the windows of the waiting cars. Later they planted a (quickly uprooted) tree, passed out five hundred free cups of strawberry yogurt, and had a street dance.

Admittedly our society hardly comprehends its clowns, especially those who marry protest to fantasy or burlesque. "Unpredictability is beautiful!" But parodies aren't always understood.

The Diggers and their friends live in what they call "intentional communes" (as opposed to crash pads), where they share the rent from their earnings from part-time jobs or making beads or painting posters. One "closed" commune, called The Family, was supported by a long-haired computer analyst.

Another is the Group Image, which has an acid rock band that has made $2,000 per week in uptown discothèques. It has thirty or forty members; referring to Christ's robe, one said, "The Group Image is a seamless garment!" (In California there's a legendary tribe of water sharers, inspired by Robert Heinlein's science fiction novel, *Stranger in a Strange Land.* Members share each other sexually; jealousy and possessions are forbidden.) In some communes, people choose the roles of mothers, fathers, or children. "Sure, there are some middle-class problems of authority—like who does the dishes. But you can't be rigid. People still need some privacy, need possessions—even like just a hairbrush." But of course the code is collectivism. "The idea of individuality is baloney. Collective energy is so much greater than any one person's, and even mediocre people can do more when they're together in a group." Solitary egos aren't admired; the goal is "collective ego." Since the waxing population forces everyone to live more closely together, the "Good Vibrations" that the Beach Boys sang about are considered more important than ever. (When someone's very upset by a bad trip, his tribe may start omming until he joins in, is forced to merge with the group, and is eventually made to feel better.) Diggers feel that people must take care of each other, particularly during spells of limbo, when someone "needs to be freaky." Predictably the styles in intimacy have titillated the press. However: "So many people think we're acting out their fantasies! But lots of us are shy, or lonely, just needed to come together. . . . Some kids feel desperate about all the lies in this country, the double standards. But dropping out is hard. You almost need a death wish to drop out."

In New York there was a tribal council where leaders from many tribes sat in an Indian circle, each addressing himself to the center, debating such problems as what kind of school to form, and—most urgently—"How do you protect yourself from being seduced by uptown?" A young man pondered the difficulties of maintaining an avant-garde—since the media makes everything public. "Now we're all acting out the myth created by the media." Many musicians and painters have been scooped up by the commercial world they thought they wanted to reject; they've already dropped out of the new society which some had hoped to build.

But despite the collective efforts, the Diggers insist that no one must impose his will on anyone else. The familiar dictum has been amended to: "Do your thing—until it encroaches on someone else's thing." "See, you can't *make* a cop take your flower—you can't *force* it on him." In the inscape of Things, everyone has a talent, from painting to driving trucks or having babies—or just being.

It's cheerfully admitted that most flower persons came from middle-class families. Voluntary poverty could hardly appeal to blacks, nor to anyone born too far outside the system to be able to reject it. Quite a few who live in the East Village are civil rights dropouts, especially those who were disillusioned about voter registration. You hear remarks like: "Marxism sounds like a groove, but Russia is just a drag." They dislike the Vietnam war but don't want to talk about it. "We don't know what to do about Vietnam or Harlem. But people must be turned on to themselves. Politically, a be-in is more meaningful than picketing." Still, they're amused that a statement like "Fuck it, I just want to be beautiful" can alarm a politician.

In the communes, those "clusters against meaninglessness," acid has been called "a binding substance." One young man added, "The whole process of growing up here is desensitizing. You have to peel off layers, and the easiest and quickest way is drugs. Drugs are more easily assimilated by someone of fifteen than somebody twenty-five. But you don't *have* to take them." Many feel that acid makes them patient and tolerant. "Oh, maybe you can call it a synthetic or artificial feeling of nonaggression. *After* acid, people can have that feeling naturally. Acid makes them *think* they have confidence. Acid can be the biggest copout *or* very helpful." At any rate the Diggers I encountered had such good manners that sulky waitresses in the restaurants where we met brightened up and gave us excellent service, even though one was freaked out by a Digger's complaint about the menu: "It's too linear."

I noticed that some who've dropped a lot of acid do speak very slowly indeed, and although they were perfectly willing to talk to me, it took them a long time to decide where and when to meet: those decisions seemed immense. One initiate explained that the chief problem that arises under acid is choice: "It appears as though perception is a ladder." So if a friend says, "It looks like a good day today," every factor must be considered before replying: is it *really* a good day? What's "good," anyway?

This world mistrusts words. "Once you define things, they're meaningless. Truth is just fact, and fact doesn't mean anything. Hey, you wrote that down! See what I mean?" Incoherence is almost a virtue; one very intelligent Digger even apologized for being too articulate. It's felt that how people speak reveals far more than what they say, that eventually (say in the year 2000) vibrations might replace speech—that people won't need to talk, but will converse through all their senses. Gibberish is very popular and there are fond references to Danny Kaye's old git-gat-gittle. Theater, movies, all visual experiences, and music are hugely preferred to books. But certain Eastern philosophers, Norman O. Brown, Alan Watts, and Buckminster Fuller, do have a small audience here, as does the *Wall Street Journal*, "the hippest paper in town." Fiction, the despair of publishers, is indeed ignored, with the rare exceptions of Thomas Pynchon, Joseph Heller, Ken Kesey, Richard Fariña, John Fowles, and Doris Lessing. These are enjoyed "because they don't preach, they're talking about personal experience." Otherwise "music is the literature of this generation."

Grass was long ago pronounced middle class. There's a slight new caution about acid, due to reports about chromosome damage, but many shrug that off. The San Francisco Diggers encouraged people to exchange free LSD, and liked "bad-assing the illegal drug trade." The slogan was: Don't Deal. Make It—Grow It—Give It—Share It. They had a group to bail acidheads out of jail, but they didn't aid those on speed, since they consider amphetamines dangerous. In the last year I've had the impression that many very ordinary people—especially those in jobs which bore them—were imbibing acid: insurance men and shoe salesmen as well as painters or students. One Digger said that *Time's* modish cover story "gave us thousands of overnight pseudo hippies." Moreover, "We got some who only know what they don't want—they're full of screaming, aggressive, hostile love—*pushing* flowers at people. Some love." Now he wonders if a "post-drug" period may lie ahead, mainly for those with substantial drug experience—although the newest hippies, who've made no "deliberate choice," are still clamoring for drugs. But he added that "the automatic record changer is even more important than psychedelics"—as a wellspring for electronic culture.

The Diggers say they do want to convert others, and they stress that the best way to destroy the middle class is to leave it. "Throughout history, Bohemia never created a subculture. Now we have the numbers to do it! But the country's making them into a criminal class." It's expected that America will become very ugly—as racism increases. Their answer is "not guerrilla warfare, but *monkey warfare* and *silly sabotage*," such as chanting mantras around the Pentagon to exorcise the evil spirits within. While depressed liberals contemplate the notion of national lunacy, these jesters are a cheering presence in the landscape: few humanists have their humor, and humorists are rarely so humane.

Memories of the East Village
April 1969

Read among the brisk spring sounds of clubs on skulls, the shouts of pain, the explosions of small bombs in schools and libraries, and the hoarse faculty voices in debate, while the sun glints off policemen's plastic face visors and riot helmets, Tom Wolfe's *Electric Kool-Aid Acid Test* seems almost as remote as a Bloomsbury memoir. And the Beats seem nearly Victorian. In 1959 Herbert Gold wrote, "The hipster doesn't want to feel; he keeps cool. He has checked up on experience and found it wanting; he doesn't dig overmuch. He carries books without reading them, drives cars without going anyplace, goes places without arriving anywhere. . . . He . . . is the delinquent with no zest, the gang follower with no love of the gang . . . the youngster with undescended passions, the organization man with sloanwilsonian gregory-peckerism in his cold, cold heart."

Who has lately seen such a creature? True, you meet a few querulous relics in New York, but their fatigue is no longer distinguished: being tired and numb is no longer a style in sensitivity. Most of those I've encountered have complained about the noise, the heat, the cold, the food, the young, and the air conditioning; they said everyone talks too quickly, and implied that anger and enthusiasm have "gone too far." Carping as creakily as suburban parents, few seem to have kept pace with Allen Ginsberg—a decade jumper who will probably bury us all.

As for what were called hippies: 1967 seems a long time ago. Lots of love beads got broken and rolled into cracks too deep to reach; horoscopes went awry; the moon betrayed Virgo; murders and diseases and threatening pushers drove them from the neighborhoods they hoped were theirs. The Diggers' Free Store in New York was raided by toughs who beat them up several times—even though they kept no cash and boasted that nothing could be stolen because everything was free. Finally they painted out "Love" on their window, painted in "Hate," and departed.

There are still urban hippies. But they are mainly the instant variety who arrived yesterday from Westchester, and who are concerned only with style— or the more militant brand, who wage revolution by undressing during political speeches or prevent speakers from finishing a sentence. Norman Mailer was stopped from describing his platform as a mayoral candidate by a few of the Crazies. (He'd come to a Panther dinner to ask the Panthers for their support, which he didn't get.) In passing he remarked that he wouldn't call cops pigs, "because they've got balls." A Crazy yelled, "No, they haven't, Norman." "Yes they have." "Stop bullshitting!" "I'm not bullshitting!" "Yes you are." "He is!" "I'm not!" "You are!" "Shut *up!*" "*You* shut up!" "You shut up *too!*" The Panthers rebuked the Crazies: "Stop this frivolous, silly shit." But we were never allowed to hear Mailer's fantasies about uniting the left and the right.

At any rate I miss the street gamesters of two summers past. The Beats were never funny—was that their tragedy?—but 1967 gave us some nimble comedians. Endearingly uncool, beguiled and beguiling, they seemed ready to be zonked by the gritty world; acid detonated feelings which the hipsters shunned. Those I knew were delightful company: gentle and generous, sweet if sometimes slow. Hence some of the *Acid Test* makes me rather nostalgic as for those brief, flowery fables about levitating the Pentagon. I was told that one of the levitators had visited a Pentagon official before the demonstration, who asked how high the building was going to be raised. "Oh, maybe ten feet." The official said it couldn't be levitated without his permission, and that he would allow it to go up to only three or four feet. One boy told me later that the levitation had gone splendidly, but the rest of us were too busy to notice it.

In 1964 the novelist Ken Kesey assembled his Merry Pranksters for a "group adventure. " They toured the country in their psychedelic bus, inviting others to "Go with the flow." In their California commune, even the woods were wired for sound, and the trees were striped with orange and green Day-Glo paint. Acid was legal until October 1966. Wolfe credits the Pranksters with the beginning of the whole Haight-Ashbury scene, the invention of mixed media, and even the style of psychedelic posters. But moments of horror tunnelled through the gaiety. Amid all the put-ons, the footloose clowning, and the snuggling atmosphere of group therapy (such excitement but so little apparent sex), there was the toppling paranoia that often accompanies LSD, plus the scenarios of madness for those who couldn't be reassembled. Wolfe makes no comments; he simply unleashes the Prankster "allegory of life" in all its defiance, naiveté, and freaking charm. Parts of the book are as repetitious and exhausting as some acid trips must be. But it does take you "into the pudding," as they say: by bestowing the experience of "the Group Mind," where even reading or smoking are selfish acts, since they gratify only one person and give nothing to the group. Those who can't read Wolfe's other books may well appreciate this one as the best account of tribal living that's yet appeared.

Throughout this celebration of technology, one irony nibbles at the unblown brain: the Pranksters and their heirs have been so dependent on *equipment*. Projectors, tapes, slides, cameras, loudspeakers, mikes, and amplifiers were essential to their spiritual or sensory liberation. Yet last month, when the Living Theatre disrupted a symposium at New York's Theatre for Ideas, the uproar included screams of "Fuck technology!" Perhaps machinery is tolerable only when you play with it; for some it may be a desperately necessary toy.

The *Acid Test* freezes and preserves the immediate past. And since history is hurtling, it's pleasing to remember that Emerson anticipated one maxim; in an 1841 essay he wrote, "But do your thing and I shall know you."

Hindsight: After I wrote the above, cool returned with a vengeance. But it seemed very dated and remote in 1967.

After Chicago 1968 some of us grew impatient with Yiphood, because it confused many people politically. The problem with put-ons was that the straight world sometimes took them seriously—just as the Chicago cops really believed that joke about putting acid in the city's reservoirs. But I still think 1967 was a rather innocent time, and part of the pleasure was parody.

A Riot Averted

October 1967

Rebellions, revolutions, altercations, and disorders: the vocabulary of "riots" is still scant on the words "incident" and "occasion." Many seem anxious to deny that diffuse anger and desperation need only a small event to build a revolt. The image of a fire hydrant extinguished on a hot day in the ghetto recedes in the search for nimble interstate inciters, employed by a crimson network which is keen to disgrace us abroad. But while national figures sift the ashes and the shattered glass for evidence of conspiracies, and eighty bills concerning punishment for rioters now wait before the House, the "antiriot" panelists might profit by learning how a particular explosion was prevented: in 1966 in Brooklyn's East New York section.

A "bloodbath" was expected; there was only "an eruption." One of the key peacemakers was Albert Gallo, a minor leader in the Brooklyn Mafia. Although a racial battle on the scale of Watts or Newark was potential—yet was averted—New York showed its gratitude by reviling the members of the Youth Board who enlisted Gallo, while the police complained that their "morale" had been "sapped."

It's true that Bobby Kennedy called Gallo and his two brothers—Larry and Crazy Joe—the "toughest witnesses" he had ever questioned; they were summoned to Washington in 1958 to testify on jukebox racketeering and extortion. Joe's first remark to Kennedy was: "Nice carpet you got here, kid. Be good for a crap game." Joe, who reportedly kept a lioness named Cleo in his basement to impress shakedown candidates, is in jail for extortion. His small gang has been reproached for the barbershop murder of Albert Anastasia in the Hotel Park Sheraton in 1957, principally because Joe said, "From now on . . . you can just call . . . us the barbershop quintet." But the killing was never solved. The other brothers have been accused of irregularities in the pinball and vending machine trades, trot-race fixing, loan sharking, and muscling into legitimate business. None of this has been proven, although they've been jailed for contempt.

The following account comes from my conversations with Frank Arricale, the Commissioner of Relocation, Rabbi Samuel Schrage, and others who were involved in the crisis in East New York.

The city has eleven other areas which share the characteristics of this slice of Brooklyn. It's not quite a ghetto; therefore poverty programs and other forms of organized aid are scarce. The community, molded by hostilities long before black people moved in, was dominated by "the three I's": Italy, Ireland, and Israel. The Italian group—according to an Italian expert—is anarchistic, mainly because the only group is the family; there's no civic organization and no corporate identification with the church. (Here the Irish identify with the parish, but Italians don't.) For these Italians the church means only the spiritual support of *la famiglia,* and provides no mechanism to cope with local problems. Gambling isn't considered illegal in this neighborhood. While Italians are the majority group in New York State, and the second largest group in New York City, they still feel like a minority and lack a political power base. Thus organizations like the Cosa Nostra—and others which aren't entirely illegal—do flourish. The tradition derives from the period when Italy itself lacked a robust central government and the vigilante groups emerged, outlived their function, and then became a threat when the government grew strong.

Coexisting but not cordial, the neighborhood Irish are very reactionary and highly political—children of the organized labor movement. Their church, still sympathetic to Joe McCarthy and William Buckley, is a corporation, but it doesn't heal their severe family problems, which are especially acute between fathers and sons. The very authoritarian families are eventually attacked and rejected in a way that the Italians can't understand, since Italians rarely turn on their own families. Among the Irish, drinking is lavish. The pub is the social center; there are two or three per block. (Drink is the puberty initiation for the Irish boys, whereas sex initiates the Italians.) Both groups used to be anti-Semitic. At the same time some of the neighborhood Jews mistrust the Orthodox and Hasidic Jews among them. Theirs was once a successful ghetto—unlike the troubled Irish and Italian clusters. But the Jews who prospered moved to the suburbs, leaving behind those who had not done well, whose sons did not make it to City College. Among these, bitterness at their own professional failures, plus the strain of aborted ambitions, has resulted in many nervous breakdowns. This particular Jewish group is known for its poor mental health.

Many of the blacks who joined the community had just won free of the ghetto: they were civil servants and others who had earned enough to escape bottomless slums. But this area is no tangible improvement. The pressures are as vicious as the ghetto's. City services such as sanitation and housing are bad. There are also some other absolutely depressed black people, who don't even have a welfare client league. For them this is worse than a slum. They're apt to be rejected by the advancing blacks, who feel they're being dragged down. When the blacks first arrived, trying to live the myth of integration, the Italian, Irish, and Jewish groups were united for the first time—in the tradition of racism. This became the dynamic of the neighborhood.

In July 1966 these factors fell into fury. The area has a street corner society which ranges up to the age of thirty and includes married men; adolescents join them. SPONGE (The Society for the Prevention of Negroes Getting Everything, a teen-age club) sent out pickets chanting "Two, Four, Six, Eight, We don't want to integrate." Groups of twenty-five to a hundred roamed the streets, while garbage cans, tire jacks, and bricks were flung about, and firebomb caches were found on roofs. At night priests of all churches paced the blocks in their "clericals," risking their lives by walking alone, trying to calm people; their role has been compared to Christian witness. The police were in full force, yet attempting restraint. There were even bullhorns, announcing that "Things are under control." But they weren't.

Frank Arricale, who was then the director of the Youth Board, had been working for months to forestall pandemonium. In February he'd predicted that "summer problems" were not going to be in the ghettos but in areas like this one. Social and poverty workers, civil rights volunteers, city officials, the local black nationalists (whom Arricale found very helpful), and many other groups—all had been called in, and still the danger accelerated. An eleven-year-old black was killed by a sniper and a black of seventeen was arrested (he was later released). The Youth Board learned that ample crowds (mainly Italian and black) were ready to bring their guns and rifles and join in from neighborhoods all over New York. (Many of the Irish were away, since their parochial schools give vacations that are different from the Italians'.) There might have been a traveling, city-wide siege which could have meant fiercer warfare than other cities have yet known. Whites began to invade East New York and blacks were threatening to come. Since organized gangs are rare these days, it's difficult to know who to deal with, or who might be a leader in an unstructured, roving mass, where the affiliations are formed on violence.

Fearing a shooting war, Arricale accepted the suggestion of Rabbi Samuel Schrage, a Youth Board official, that Albert Gallo should be asked for aid. Gallo could command allegiance from many neighborhood Italians and he was certain to know who the snipers were. (Neither the police nor the Youth Board could possibly identify the snipers.) Arricale and Rabbi Schrage visited a waterfront candy store, where Gallo and his friends often met to drink beer and talk baseball and politics. Gallo, who was stunningly dressed, sent his companions away and offered them soda and cigarettes. Both were impressed by his immediate concern; he too felt that many people might be killed. He introduced them to his father, who said, "You do it, Al." He said he was proud that his son should be consulted by the Youth Board. Admitting that he must first confer with his attorneys, Gallo agreed to help. One of his three lawyers was enthusiastic, but the others feared bad repercussions from much of the city administration and the press.

Gallo, who went only through sixth grade, "got on his own soapbox." He intently questioned Arricale and Rabbi Schrage about the Youth Board: "If you stop the fighting, it'll happen again next week. What are you going to do for an encore? What about education and jobs? They have no preparation. What are you do-gooders going to do about that?" He was insulted when Rabbi Schrage stressed that cooling the neighborhood must be done on "a social work basis," without threats or arm-twisting. Since his lawyers felt the police might assume that Gallo was making trouble, the officials gave him a letter stating that he was "a member of an ad hoc intergroup relations committee, working to ease community tensions." But Gallo was given no immunity, as the press implied.

Frank Arricale said, "The Gallo name will become like the Rockefellers': they weren't so hot to begin with." Gallo replied: "From your lips to the ear of God"—a Yiddish saying. The press wrongly reported that Larry Gallo worked with his brother; in fact Larry, an opera lover who was nearly garotted to death by the Profaci mob, a rival faction, and still wears the rope burns on his neck, "didn't want to get involved."

Albert Gallo began by phoning all the potential fighters he knew, instructing them to stay out of the neighborhood, and telling whites to leave blacks alone. The orders spread quickly: there was to be no more fighting in East New York. He held meetings in cafés, bars, candy stores, luncheonettes, and private homes, conferred with parents and with groups of older men, and collected embattled boys. The whites averaged about twenty-four years of age, while many of the blacks were in their late teens.

Sitting at the head of a long table, he began his interracial parliamentary conferences by asking everyone to introduce himself. He opened by announcing: "The purpose of this meeting is to avert bloodshed. I expect you to feel the way I do. Anyone who doesn't, say so right now, and I'll pay for his psychiatric fees. . . . " Then: "I'm not here to listen to your problems or your grievances, and I know they are many. Tell the rabbi about them later. But it's too dangerous to take the time now. How are we going to stop people from killing? Any suggestions?" Complaints would usually follow, with each racial group eagerly blaming the other. The line heard oftenest was "*We're* not looking for trouble—it's the others." Gallo would answer, "Then what are you doing in East New York? Shut up and sit down." He lost his temper only once: a white boy said, "We don't want anything to do with those niggers." Gallo, who has many black friends, slapped his face and said, "Don't you ever use that word again, you Goddamned wop!"

Usually he lectured slowly and quietly: "We're not animals, we're human beings trying to live with one another. We don't really want to kill anybody. Now I've no business being here—I've got more interesting things to do. I even broke a date for this crap over here. But I felt that we could prevent killing. And we're going to. . . . You have families, how would you like to see your sister killed?" Once he added, "If anyone has to be taken away from this world, let God do it." Eventually there was no further disagreement, and the young men asked what he wanted them to do. He replied that they were to keep everyone they knew out of East New York. Moreover, "I want you guys to stay home and watch a TV program, no matter how crummy it is. I want you to let the cops be—don't interfere."

In a few days the neighborhood was quiet. Gallo was not the sole engine of peace—he was one of dozens who tried to save lives. But as part of the whole mosaic, Arricale and Rabbi Schrage say that his role was unique: in personally reaching the key troublemakers. They themselves were swiftly summoned before a Brooklyn grand jury and numerous critics raised the rhubarb. Mayor John Lindsay defended Arricale, while phrases like "civic disgrace" and "deplorable abdication of official responsibility" exploded instead of the Molotov cocktails which might have been hurled in East New York. Some city officials complained that Gallo had been given "prestige" through the publicity. But it was they who made his efforts public, while larding the term "Mafioso" into every reference. A man in Gallo's position can hardly sue for libel. It would be foolish to endow him with a halo. But as he said to Rabbi Schrage, "I was never so clobbered for doing a bad thing as for doing a decent thing."

Last summer's emergency in Brooklyn yields an example of the unconventional methods which can be essential for coping with aspects of life in New York. Following standard procedures rarely works; citing the law is often as ineffective as flushing a broken toilet. Postponements, deadlocks, paralysis—and in this case, murders—can result from resting on traditional rungs. But New Yorkers, notorious for their collective impatience, hardly realized that they didn't have a riot to rival the most savage in the country.

Albert Gallo was arrested in October 1967 for activities (including extortion and coercion) related to an intricate ticket-cashing project at Roosevelt Raceway. He described himself as an "unemployed dress manufacturer." and was released on bail.

Hindsight: Joe Gallo was gunned down in Umberto's Clam House, on April 7, 1972, at 5:30 A.M. He was celebrating his forty-third birthday. At first the theory behind his execution was that some of Joe Colombo's men held Gallo responsible for the June 1971 shooting of rival mob boss Colombo. Since Gallo had made a number of black friends while he was in jail, and had announced on his release that more blacks must be hired in his own organization, he was suspected primarily because Colombo's assailant was black.

In May 1972 the New York police had a new idea about the murder of Gallo: it was thought that he had "masterminded" the $55,000 robbery of Ferrara's pastry shop in Little Italy, just south of Greenwich Village, which occurred just five days before his own death. Ferrara's, which opened in 1892, is one of the most sumptuous bakeries in New York and it specializes in wedding cakes. Since Little Italy is considered off-limits for organized crime (and is consequently one of the safest neighborhoods in Manhattan), the under-

world suspicion that Gallo had violated an unwritten rule may have shortened his life—even though he had claimed that he had retired from crime to
write his autobiography. (He kept announcing, "I'm a writer.") Finally it appeared that three of Columbo's men had done the shooting.

Larry Gallo died of cancer in 1968 and Albert Gallo succeeded him as the
head of the family business. But soon there were complaints that Albert was
an ineffectual leader. Some of his employees switched to working for Columbo,
and his nickname—"Kid Blast"—gave way to "Kid Blister."

However, a few months after Joe was shot, Albert was thought to be gaining in stature, according to the police officials who kept an eye on him. At
that point he claimed to support himself through investments in a furniture
company. They also said he had been marked for assassination, but he was
still on earth in the mid-Nineties, allegedly in control of a company which
distributed pornographic magazines.

New Yorkers and George Wallace
October 1968

A snowball: vanilla hairy with coconut shreds, overwhelmed with dark chocolate sauce. It wasn't an emblem of white purity drowning in Black Power,
but it was dessert for Wallace: at a dinner in the Hotel Americana at $25 a
head. Next to me, a sad middle-aged nurse said she'd been jobless since January and explained that thousands of Filipinos had infiltrated the New York
hospital system, depriving her of work. "Everyone knows that the Philippine
Islands have been communist for years, and our communist State Department is *hustling* them into our country." She said two Filipinos and two blacks
had mugged her recently—"They work together, you know"—and urged me
to join her local Birch Society: "You can't know until you've *studied,* and read,
and heard what's being planned against us now." She added that it had been
hard to choose a dress for this evening; she wanted to look her best, but had
so few things to wear.

She and the others at my table—carefully groomed family clusters—were
indeed "The Folks," as Wallace calls them: "the forgotten." Clenched in a tax
bracket which paralyzes them, their vulnerability is valid and so are some
of their fuzzy fears. Some observers think the terror of nuclear death has
gone underground: that the cries for law and order and the spasms about

communists and rioters are partial, indirect expressions of the fright instilled by the lavish H-bomb testing of the early Sixties. Shelters, air-raid drills, children taught to hide under their school desks, and the lunacies of "protection" accelerated—until civil defense became an acknowledged farce. But the fear stayed.

The treadmarks of fatigue and anxiety dent many pro-Wallace faces—which bloomed with delight when he appeared. (Earlier, Norman Mailer strolled in looking self-conscious, but in that crowd he wasn't recognized.) Wallace said very little; he just hurled a few unfinished slogans into the air. But his dexterity seemed confusing for this audience. They hardly knew when to hiss—though many booed when he mentioned "the newsboys" at the *New York Times*. Often he cleverly leaves sentences incomplete: "Now I'm not talking about race . . . "—which drew applause. They cheered at "I believe that God made all of us, regardless of race, creed, or color," were uneasily silent when he mentioned the number of black voters in Alabama, but clapped when he said his wife had received "a large Negro vote." Whoops rose when he shouted "Your family cannot go out on the streets at night!" heightened when he described how one of his followers had socked a heckler "for obscenity," and diminished when he chided, "I'm not recommending that you hit anyone . . . " Beside me a man said, "Safety's all we want." Wallace then challenged Nixon and Humphrey to a debate, inviting them to "Come down out of that antiseptic, touch-me-not bubble. . . . "

Later, penetrating the necklace of cops around Madison Square Garden, a friend of mine was given a free ticket by a benign officer—which seemed to confirm the rumor that some in the force were dispensing tickets. At the rally of sixteen thousand, many faces split with yells, and folding chairs crashed like cannonry. Wallace posters read: STAND UP FOR AMERICA, suggesting an erection policy that increases virility—as when he told a Texan crowd that a vote for him means that "You've asserted your manhood." Other banners proclaimed: IT TAKES COURAGE! WALLACE HAS IT! DO YOU? (The anti-Wallace signs also showed sexual inspiration: "GEORGIE IS THE ILLEGITIMATE SISTER OF LBJ" and "WALLACE WAS BREAST-FED BY AUNT JEMIMA.") Some Wallace supporters joyfully waved a picture of a pregnant black holding her belly with a cryptic, downward glance, wearing a button that announces "Nixon's The One." This is a favorite poster of the left, sold in hip shops. But it enchants the far right, yielding another (recurrent) example of how the trappings of dissent can be tools for the dissenters' opponents. There's an innocence on both sides: the Wallaceites kept giving the peace sign and the raised fist. Clearly they think these gestures mean victory—without realizing that both belong to radicals.

Wallace's running mate, retired General Curtis LeMay, was cheered when he unleashed one of his best lines: "I've never been a politician and I don't profess to be one now." As fights flared across the floor, he said that Wallace will "restore our reason," while several blacks, who were accompanying a pastor from Harlem, were attacked and thrashed, and hundreds of men shrieked "Niggers, niggers!" "Throw them out!" "Kill them!" "Get him!" The police quenched the fights quickly and rushed the warriors out. Although many policemen support Wallace, they were very restrained within the hall, although some blew their cool on the streets.

During the twenty-minute ovation for Wallace, the screaming crowd bounced up and down under red, pink, and yellow balloons—surely a guileless choice of colors. Many literally leaped with glee when he mentioned communism. His speech was the familiar one he has recited before: in favor of states' rights; against "kowtowing to anarchists," "the domestic mess," open housing, "the sick Supreme Court," "pseudo-intellectuals," "students who collect money and blood for the enemy"—"and there are two four-letter words they don't know: W-O-R-K and S-O-A-P," and "professors calling for communist victory." On foreign policy: "We must always be superior. When you are superior, you can always go to the conference table. . . . We should never have gone to Vietnam by ourselves"—instead we should have appealed to the Allies and told them to join us or to repay all foreign aid.

Wallace is said to welcome hecklers; he offered to "autograph their sandals." Certainly their presence intensified the crowd's frenzied response to him. As a turmoil of toughs howled for Law 'n' Order, noise seemed like an overkill weapon. Yet despite Wallace's lack of programs, one of his main strengths may be enabling people to express themselves. After an evening among the faces gashed with fury, you realize how thoroughly anger has changed to hate. There's a crackling nervous contagion that rebounds from walls and buildings and hurtles into open windows: into anybody's home. You can feel it even at the deli and the drugstore. People are frightened of so many things that it distills a mutual fear of one another. It's beginning to seem almost impossible for various groups in this country to continue to live with each other. Squatting in the mud in a Harlem park last week at a Panther rally, hearing a speaker say, "We should give the man a deadline for stopping that war, or we start a second front here," and then eating with the Wallaceites, who shout for their own protection, makes it hard to imagine how these passions can coexist for many years. A weary ironist said, "If Wallace is elected, we can get the revolution over by Christmas."

Hindsight: Things seemed simpler in 1968, when Wallace ran a mainly racist campaign. In 1972 Dan Rather of CBS referred to a poll which asked voters whether Wallace was moderate, liberal, or conservative. He came out equally in each category, but some said that he was all three. It's the old reminder that a politician is defined more by what people think he represents than by what he actually says or does. But by early 1972 Wallace had become harder to classify. He had already built new state medical schools, junior colleges, and trade schools in Alabama; he had substantially raised the rate of unemployment and workmens' compensation benefits. And he even took to finishing his sentences. At the Democratic convention in Miami Beach, when he said, "I believe in *quality education*" (a phrase he repeated), he completed his statement against "the senseless, asinine busin' of school children." The ambiguities had dwindled. So despite all the confusions about "real" or "phony" populism—despite the bullet in his spine and the pain in his face—his long-term supporters heard more from him about specific issues than they had in 1968.

It took the professional pols and the press until about the end of September 1969 to discover Wallace's constituency. Aside from the Nixon-Agnew silent majority speeches, the mayoral candidacy of Mario Procaccino in New York had a lot to do with that enlightenment—mainly because working-class voters had so greatly preferred Procaccino to his rivals in the primaries, including former Mayor Robert Wagner. Suddenly there was a rush of cover stories about the working/forgotten/average man. There was a huge, crude astonishment on finding that working people couldn't afford more than a sparse existence—and that they didn't want to lose what they had. John Lindsay's campaign for his second term as mayor reflected the same last-minute discovery, when his staff realized that Lindsay had been neglectful of the Bronx, Queens, and Brooklyn. And the response to Wallace did educate us about those who are taxed for a larger percentage of their income than the very richest persons in this country.

Whenever I saw a Wallace button in New York, I recalled the botched attempts on the left to reach these people. A group of young radicals who were trying to organize the impoverished whites of my neighborhood in Yorkville had concentrated on housing. It was a good idea, since many tenements were being demolished to make way for luxury apartment buildings. When they called a meeting to oppose some local landlords, a large number of worried tenants—many of them elderly—showed up But when a speaker lectured them about "fucking bourgeois pigs," they didn't linger.

Of course anyone can stop a bullet in this country. But Wallace's mere presence did seem to bring out violence in others. I'm accustomed to wild audiences and fierce speeches, but the crowd which screamed for Wallace in Madison Square Garden in 1968 was the only one I've found frightening. There was no surprise when he was shot.

On the first day of his trial, Arthur Bremer had three times as many guards as Wallace did on the day of the Maryland shooting. Bremer's diary informed us that he had switched his assassin's focus from Nixon to Wallace while he was seeing *A Clockwork Orange*. But Bremer wasn't sure that killing Wallace would really make him famous. "I would have done better for myself to kill the old G-man Hoover," he wrote. "In death, he lays with Presidents."

~

The racist rally I witnessed in the Garden and the Wallace gubernatorial campaign of 1982 seemed almost a century apart. In Martin Luther King's last years, he had hoped that indigent blacks and poor whites would band together—and for George Wallace, they did. The man who had promised, "Segregation now! Segregation tomorrow! Segregation forever!" in 1963, who had sent state troopers to beat and jail people who were marching for the right to vote, and whose name triggered memories of police dogs and cattle prods, won ninety percent of the black vote when he was re-elected for his fourth term as governor.

Admittedly he also received the white liberal vote not only because he had begun to repeat, "I believe that segregation was wrong," but because his Republican opponent was an extreme right-winger. (Some wondered if Wallace had actually changed his views or if he was simply pursuing votes.) Impoverished whites heard him shouting from flatbed trucks, "The rich are getting richer and the poor are getting poorer!" During the 1982 campaign he displayed photographs of gaunt sharecroppers from James Agee and Walker Evans's *Let Us Now Praise Famous Men,* warning that "when the Republicans were in power before, we had people like this all over the state of Alabama," and that if the G.O.P. continued to run the country, "there'll be people like this all over Alabama again." (In fact Evans took those pictures while Franklin Roosevelt was president, but Wallace saw similarities between Ronald Reagan's economics and Herbert Hoover's.) No longer an inciter whose words fuelled the fury of racists, Wallace recommended "soaking the rich" and aiding the poor.

By the mid-Nineties the enfeebled former governor was remarking that both Democrats and Republicans had seized on his themes—welfare reform, lower taxes for the middle class, the iniquities of "big government"—and that he was the first of his political contemporaries to speak to and for blue collar voters (who would later be identified as Reagan Democrats). As he continued to apologize for his past embrace of segregation, skeptics thought that as a born-again Christian, he was seeking redemption while his life expectancy was dwindling.

In 1995, when he was seventy-five, he asked for forgiveness as he sat in his wheelchair surrounded by African-Americans who had just retraced the path of the great 1965 civil rights march from Selma to Montgomery. They applauded when his aide read his message to them: "Welcome to Montgomery . . . May your lessons never be forgotten. May our history be always remembered." Some of his listeners recalled the terrors of "Bloody Sunday" on the Edmund Pettus Bridge in Selma, when Wallace refused them the right to march and troopers on horseback charged into the throng, breaking heads wide open with their billy clubs and knocking marchers off the bridge, while policemen with automatic rifles, whips, and shotguns, hurled others off their feet and assaulted children as freely as adults. Thirty years afterward Wallace held the hand of the Reverend Joseph Lowery, president of the Southern Christian Leadership Conference, who had been one of the organizers of that march, while the crowd around them sang "We Shall Overcome."

Harlem on Many Minds
February 1969

> White Man's
> DREAM!
> of
> White Being
> Supreme!
> Has Turned to
> Sour Cream

Thus a sign in Harlem, 1964, next to a poster urging "Buy Where Black Santa Claus Is"—reminding Christmas shoppers to patronize black stores. Caught in one of the many superb photographs in the Metropolitan Museum's well-intended show, "Harlem on My Mind," which has been used as a racial spittoon, this little rhyme recalls Malcolm X's remark about enjoying cream: "Coffee is the only thing I like integrated." Cream gone wrong is an ironic emblem for this show, which offers a wealth of magnificent lore and yet fails as a whole. The failure hurts some, enrages others, and it has probably made history. The exhibition has had the largest attendance of any in the museum's existence and more black viewers have come than ever before. The exhibition has also been lambasted by several powerful art critics because it places black culture on a level with European culture.

Many single pictures make it worth seeing the entire display: two black grandmothers of 1900, arm in arm, their faces puckered with pain as they simply gaze into space; Ethel Waters in 1919, a slim, pensive waif; two very young bridesmaids of 1926, with flat chests and celestial smiles, their excitement radiating from beneath enormous hats; a 1931 line of unemployment registration, where men's bodies are squeezed together behind a prohibitive rope; the 1943 riot, where chests burst with blood, while three teen-age boys pose in looted tail-coats and silk hats far too big for them and are later trapped by cops who are also too big for them; Helen Levitt's 1945 *Graffiti*, where someone has chalked a small circle on a crumbling stone wall and written "Button to Secret Passage—Press"—a fantasy of escape from the ghetto? There's a 1948 billboard on which a pretty Wasp boy weeps "I am *so* an American!", followed by YOU BET, Sonny... No Matter What Your Race or Religion! FIGHT Racial and Religious HATE; in front of the board, a couple of hunched black figures stroll—the cherubic boy etches an insult in claiming to speak for them. In 1954 fatigued young men sit on garbage cans; obviously there are few alternatives before them. In a 1968 street demonstration, hundreds of sober faces fill a wide block with the suspense of waiting.

Adam Clayton Powell praised the exhibit, but many other black people have denounced it; some because it includes no painting or sculpture by contemporary black artists; others because they feel it distorts their history. Pickets outside the museum passed out leaflets: "Soul's Been Sold Again!" Unfortunately these critics are right. Though much of the staff was black, it was assembled by Allon Schoener, a white, and his show is naively patronizing. There are far too many happy laughing faces—even in the sections on the Depression and the Sixties—and there's an excess of pictures of show business figures, athletes, dressy Twenties' weddings, beauty parlors, and nightclubs. The old phrase *"clever as monkeys"* seems to caper through these rooms. A quote from the 1930 *Herald Tribune* characterizes much of the show: "The attitude of the average white New Yorker to Harlem is one of tolerant amusement. He thinks of ... prosperous nightclubs; of happy-go-lucky Negroes dancing all night to jazz music...." In the same article it's noted that "90% of the nightclubs in Harlem are owned by" whites.

The total effect of the show is rather like going slumming for pleasure, as many whites did in the Twenties. Poverty isn't carried up to the present; there's almost an implication that the poor belong to the past, and one set of Sixties slides flashes color shots of corn on the cob, clothing stores, and Afro-American groceries—as though plenty were the just reward for lots of dazzling grins. Many of the Twenties' and other period pictures stress black prosperity, which is exaggerated by this show. Throughout the past, the nonfamous black faces turned to the camera look timid or defiant. Many who posed seemed to be asking for tolerance; surely an all-black staff would have chosen a fuller variety of expressions. Yet the seeds of protest and militancy lie much farther back in history than many whites realize, although few of the circumstances are explained. Of course the show couldn't (and shouldn't) have been merely a record of suffering. But it's amazingly jolly—in terms of what anyone's heard about the black experience.

Gurgling tapes, buzzing sound domes, slides, lights and voices which collide only to negate each other: the use of mixed media deprives the show of dignity and makes it seem all the more merry—and terribly difficult to un-ravel. In his foreword to the catalogue, Schoener states: "We don't respond, as we once did, to an orderly progression of facts thrust at us in a fixed or-der." Thus: "No attempt has been made to describe the sixty-eight-year his-tory of Harlem as a continuing sequence of events." Hence most ideas and many facts are omitted. What can a photograph of Marcus Garvey tell us about his views? Flashing slides that give figures of black unemployment pass too rapidly to make any point. And how does a record label of "Paradise Wobble—Stomp" instruct the spectator? The trouble is that mixed media can't think, and the sum of racial culture and racial agony is just too serious for a twinkling discothèque style. Sensitivity slid out of sight when this choice was made. It's regrettable when experimentation is a mistake. But a tradi-tional show could have taught us much that's still unknown about Harlem.

The museum withdrew its catalogue because Mayor John Lindsay franti-cally proclaimed that its introduction (written by a black student as a term paper when she was sixteen) was "racist"—during a week when anti-Lindsay feeling was most acute among some of New York's Jewish groups. When the "anti-Semitic" sentences are read in context, they don't sound racist; they merely reflect the strains which the U.S. has long stimulated among the poor of many races. Allon Schoener, who is Jewish, revealed that the particular "offensive" remarks were actually paraphrases of *Beyond the Melting Pot* by Daniel Patrick Moynihan and Nathan Glazer (the latter is also Jewish). Schoener unwisely told the adolescent author to drop her quotes and foot-notes, which cited the book, and to translate all source material into her own words. Therefore Moynihan and Glazer's observation that "subconsciously" blacks may find that "a bit of anti-Jewish feeling helps them feel more com-pletely American, a part of the majority group," became " . . . psychologically, blacks may find that anti-Jewish sentiments place them, for once, within a majority. Thus, our contempt for the Jew makes us feel more completely American in sharing a national prejudice." Editing has always been a peril-ous trade, awash with unsound advice. In this case, where the editor is forty-three and the author is now seventeen, one wishes that she'd been old enough to ignore him. The *Times* thoughtfully noted that *Beyond the Melting Pot* "was not attacked as being anti-Semitic when it was published in 1963."

The show and the teachers' strike in Ocean Hill-Brownsville, aided by hys-teria from the press and the mayor, have congealed many natives' notions about hatred between blacks and Jews. The only valid sources now are one's black and Jewish friends—who are pleading for sanity. Certainly some mu-tual dislike has existed—depending on the nature of particular ghettos. And some black militants' remarks about "kosher nationalism" haven't helped. (In 1967 James Baldwin wrote that the Jew "is singled out by Negroes not because he acts differently from other white men, but because he doesn't.") But anti-Semitism was hardly invented by blacks—as some pundits seem to imply—and many Jews have fought for blacks' rights. Five years ago a Jewish writer most unhappily told me, "Don't forget that the Negro is the Jew's Jew"— and proceeded to deplore his lifelong feelings, his admitted preference for segregated schools. A black writer said recently, "Of course I don't blame my Jewish editor for what our landlord did in Harlem. But I was very wary of him at first." Currently one has the bleak suspicion that the theme of black anti-Semitism is being magnified as an excuse for whites to put down blacks. By inflating the idea that blacks and Jews are steeped in enmity, the media is nourishing conflicts which could later be used as ammunition against both groups.

Hindsight: "Harlem on My Mind" foreshadowed the battles about multiculturalism that would erupt in the Nineties. And before the opening of the exhibition, the relations between African-Americans and Jews had received a painful amount of publicity during the city-wide teachers' strike in the fall of 1968, when more than a million children were kept out of nine hundred public schools for forty-nine days. The teachers' union was striking in support of nineteen teachers who had been scheduled for transfer from Brooklyn's Ocean Hill-Brownsville schools, where an experimental decentralization project—partly funded by the Ford Foundation and grudgingly permitted by the central school board—had developed into a crisis of community control. Even neutral sources said that those individual teachers had harassed the local governing board while opposing community control.

The neighborhood was mainly black; at that time the majority of New York's teachers were Jews. While the mayor had initially backed decentralization, he dithered as the issues congealed; severe anti-Lindsay sentiments ripened among Jewish groups, which also accused the Ocean Hill blacks of anti-Semitism. The press intensified this theme and concentrated on confrontations. What was lost in the uproar was the central issue: the low reading level of the pupils themselves—in fact the failures of public education. The concerned black parents were alarmed by the Board of Education's inability to improve their childrens' range of learning. They thought that through community control they could hire better teachers than the ones they already had—whom they felt were neglecting black students. Teachers were often transferred in New York public schools. But Albert Shanker, the union's president, apparently relied on the general ignorance of this fact when he reviled the Ocean Hill governing board for "arbitrary firings," which he claimed had forced him to put all the city's schools on strike.

It seemed clear that union provocation, especially through charges of "black racism," even "black Nazism," was responsible for the pandemonium—which increased whites' fears of blacks and highlighted the subject of black anti-Semitism. It was impossible to measure the latter's proportions. But the mayor panicked. Having given so much verbal (though not practical) support to blacks, he then tried desperately to recoup the Jewish vote. He assailed two black teachers from Junior High School 271, one for reading a poem by a fifteen-year-old student on the radio, and the other for criticizing the mayor's investigation of the poetry incident—adding that Lindsay was "in [a] hurry to appease the powerful Jewish financiers of the city." Lindsay said that neither man had "any place teaching" in New York. The poem, put "under study" by the Superintendent of Schools, was dedicated to Albert Shanker. The first lines were:

> Hey, Jew boy, with that yarmulka on your head
> You pale-faced Jew boy—I wish you were dead.

Later it continues:

> When the UN made Israel a free independent state
> Little four- and five-year-old boys threw hand grenades;
> They hated the black Arabs with all their might
> And you, Jew boy, said it was all right.
> Then you came to America, land of the free,
> And took over the school system to perpetuate white
> supremacy.

Passionate anti-Semitism (at all levels) had flourished in New York for years, as some liberals could hardly bear to admit. But that a teen-ager's verse could result in the probable dismissal of two teachers showed what a frenzy City Hall was in: about its own image. No one should have been surprised to hear blacks make anti-white statements—about any kind of whites. The mayor was rebuked by various voices for fueling the tensions between blacks and Jews—because he seemed to hurl his total support back and forth between the two. (Having said he loved "Harlem on My Mind," he then attacked the catalogue.) Naturally he castigated racism of every stripe. But his awkward and hasty pledges made both groups mistrust him—and each other—even more.

～

White New York liberals began to examine what Murray Kempton called "the specter of black anti-Semitism" in the mid-Sixties. Those who thought it a fleeting phenomenon were unaware of its history. While there had not been many Jews in the slave trade—in the eighteenth and nineteenth centuries, less than half of one per cent of the total American population was Jewish—some black historians of the Seventies and later were angered because many Jews seemed reluctant to face the evidence of that participation. And as black slaves converted to Christianity, they may have harbored a special hatred for Jewish slave-owners. Inadvertently the black Baptist church—perhaps especially in the South—taught that the Jews had killed Christ: those feelings were deeply rooted among black Baptist children, instilled in their Sunday school classes. A Louisiana minister's wife, raised in a devout Baptist family, remembered a childhood rhyme, maybe for skipping rope:

> Abraham Lincoln was the king of the Jews
> He shit in his stockings and pissed in his shoes.

Black Christians (like many white ones) tended to feel that Jews couldn't be trusted, and that belief was enforced when some Jewish slumlords and ghetto merchants overcharged and exploited the poor in the Deep South as well as in Harlem.

In 1967, when whites were expelled from SNCC, most of them were Northern Jews—as were most of the civil rights activists from the Thirties to the Sixties. Many were wounded by that ejection—and the sense that Jews were no longer welcome in civil rights organizations. Young African-Americans had grown very impatient when they heard that the movement "owed" a great deal to Jews. Many thought Jews were paternalistic. By the Eighties there was abundant skepticism about a black-Jewish alliance: some blacks doubted that it had ever existed, others thought it had been exaggerated. The idea that the two groups were united by their experiences of oppression was rejected by numerous blacks, who probably agreed with James Baldwin: "One does not wish, in short, to be told by an American Jew that his suffering is as great as the American Negro's suffering. It isn't, and one knows that it isn't from the very tone in which he assures you that it is." And although many secular Jews had no particular attachment to Israel, they were expected to regard the Palestinians as enemies who could destroy the Jewish state, just when some blacks had begun to feel a connection with the expanding Palestinian movement.

Some older Jews who had seen themselves as liberals in the Fifties emerged as neoconservatives in the Seventies, and they became effective opponents of affirmative action and federal spending on social programs as they became advisors to the Reagan administration. In New York one heard them saying that African-Americans had "had their turn"—as though equal opportunity had been achieved in the Sixties, even though the educational and economic opportunities open to large numbers of Jews were never available to most blacks. Though the rapid professional success of many Jews was not possible for parallel numbers of black Americans, conservatives kept asserting that lack of effort, even indolence, was the cause of deprivation, that much of black poverty stemmed from irresponsibility.

Each time a black public figure—from Lionel Jeffries of City College to Minister Lewis Farrakhan of the Nation of Islam and his assistant Khalid Abdul Muhammed—made ferociously anti-Semitic statements, black leaders and commentators were called on to denounce them. But as many noted, no one asked powerful whites to excoriate white leaders (such as Richard Nixon) for anti-Semitic remarks. Sometimes it seemed as though almost all African-Americans were blamed for the extremists' utterances, as if those men represented everyone of their skin color. Yet when radio host Bob Grant spoke of black people as washroom attendants and told black callers he didn't need his toilet cleaned, that did not deter New York's Governor George Pataki and Mayor Rudolph Giuliani from being on his program.

When I wrote about blacks and Jews in the late Sixties, the impact of the media seemed to outweigh the influence of history. That may have been an illusion. But I didn't foresee what the *New York Times* called "the official racism" of the Reagan-Bush years or the uprooting of civil rights legislation that occurred in the Eighties and Nineties. Regarding the uses of racism and anti-Semitism by such political figures as Pat Buchanan and David Duke, Richard Goldstein wrote, "the omnipotent Jew and the rapacious black male are twin specters in the Western psyche." Jewish liberals were still distressed when black intellectuals appeared to disdain their support. But to see the two as adversaries could only satisfy groups like the Christian Coalition.

Racial cyclones tore through Crown Heights in August 1991, when Gavin Cato, a black child, was accidentally killed by a car in the motorcade of the Lubavicher Grand Rebbe, and Yankel Rosenbaum, a young Australian Hasid visiting Brooklyn to study the Holocaust, was stabbed to death in a crowd of black teen-agers seeking vengeance and shouting, "Kill the Jews!" The neighborhood was about eighty percent African-American and ten percent Hasidic Jews (whom the blacks thought received preferential treatment from city government). While youthful blacks were smashing windows and burning cars, the Hasidim—whose forebears remembered the pogroms of Europe—publicly urged blacks to go back to Africa and young black males, mostly Caribbean immigrants, chanted "Heil Hitler!" in the streets. The chanters were surely unaware that Hitler despised blacks even more than Jews, and they knew little about the Nazis, but they realized that the Fuhrer's name was a magic weapon against all Jews. For the Hasidim, those days of terror in Brooklyn seemed like a flaming sequel to the Holocaust; it appeared very likely that much more Jewish blood could be shed. And it was plain that when throngs of young blacks and Jews threw rocks at one another, the white establishment—deploring the events, calling for "healing" and "dialogue"—could continue to overlook the full weight of their past experiences and their separate tragedies.

Christmas Crises in Manhattan
Children's Toys December 1965

Detoxified alcoholics in Santa Claus suits collect money in their wooden chimneys outside New York's department stores; their intake aids the Volunteers of America, which operates a men's shelter in the Bowery as well as helping prisoners' wives and children. The Santas are instructed to keep their breath pure and not to promise to deliver the presents that children demand. Within the toy departments, it's crucial to remember that children are far more resilient and less morbid than adults. Amid the debris there are cloth-bodied Van Gogh dolls with one ear apiece next to some martyred-looking Einsteins, also "Marybel—the Doll Who Gets Well," whose kit provides crutches, arm splints, and pastable spots for chicken pox and measles. Games include "The Big Funeral"—the winner gets the most expensive rites, and the losers become zombies who aren't buried at all; "Live A Little," in which you murder the other players in order to collect their insurance; and "Administration," which is won by contriving to pay the government the smallest amount of taxes. Nearby is the "Witch Doctor's Head Shrinkers' Kit," which "actually shrinks your favorite monster before your eyes," with two captivating incantations: "Powdered Flesh Feels Like Skin Mysterious," and "Turns Bonelike As It Shrinks Unbelievable."

All these seem far less sinister than a well-intended educational toy: two three-dimensional mannequins, "The Visible Man and Woman," complete with "all vital organs." In childhood I inherited two thoroughly honest Victorian cardboard mannequins, which revealed every property of the inner man. But the modern equivalent is unnecessarily ugly. The pink plastic pancreas is so unattractive that it makes you dislike your own. By disfiguring the body, the toy seems like a stimulus for future hypochondriacs.

The famous polygamous dolls (Barbie, Ken, and Midge), who are packaged three in a box, have been joined by "Ken's buddy, Allan." Allan deceives no one, despite the claim that he escorts Midge "when Ken and Barbie double-date"; he has the face of a surburban wife trader. Midge's expression has grown slyer since she was a bridesmaid at Ken and Barbie's wedding; she seems more in character when she's sold as a detachable head for wigs and hair dyes. Subscribing to the quartet's wardrobe can cost about $150, a sum probably emulated by GI Joe, the first doll for boys to succeed in many years.

He has over a hundred accessories, including costumes for jungle warfare and the ski troops. Although his face (with one small scar) is a compilation of twenty winners of the Congressional Medal of Honor, GI Joe is considered morally odious by the many pacifist groups who would like to end his existence. All in all the toy stores offer little to ignite Christmas morning's usual exhibition of lust, greed, and envy, except for a charming set of finger puppets: five realistic fur mice ranging through brown, white, and gray, which can move delightfully on one hand. Still, it was unsettling to hear someone call them "very sexual."

Hindsight: The *New York Times* reported that GI Joe was "the most popular toy in America" throughout the Christmas season of 1982. Made in Hong Kong, the updated doll was equipped with a Mobile Missile System. Concerned citizens, who wrote to the manufacturer to protest, received a letter from the senior vice president for marketing, explaining that GI Joe was "dedicated to preserving the American way of life and protecting your right to your own opinions," and that the missile system didn't have nuclear warheads. Moreover the toy "didn't teach boys to love war." In fact the first generation "who played with the original GI Joe later went on to protest and eventually stop a war in Southeast Asia."

Adult Games
December 1968

Although the chairman of Tiffany's observed that "diamonds remain an important staple for the holiday," games for adults are lavish among the trembling tiers of gifts in elegant stores. Dr. Eric Berne noted that games are an escape from the boredom of pastimes as well as from the "dangers of intimacy." Hence, perhaps, the waxing popularity of adult games, bought hip-to-hip, elbow-to-rib, and jaw-to-shoulder by throngs of shoppers, all too intimate in elevators and crowds. Christmas *cafard* has two conspicuous sources: the neuroses imposed on most large cities, where traffic and fleshpacks swell until communal claustrophobia incites a passionate crossness, plus the dread of spending the day with lots of relatives one rarely sees. Decades of unforgivable Christmas scenes will be recalled. The horrors of family intimacy bristle in anticipatory nerves—they befrenzy our already electric air. (Affectionate families like mine sometimes agree to pass the day apart; we have it with friends. This helps us to sustain our liking for presents, food, songs, wrappings, and each other.) No one has quite explained why children cry so much on Christmas day—disappointment in their gifts? Or too many presents? At any rate adults can sympathize. Many, yearning to yell or weep themselves, may flee to games.

This year many adult games flatteringly insist on the intelligence of the players; these promise to "stimulate," "challenge," and even "ignite" the intellect. "Sophistication" is underlined, while "Games for Thinkers" are often "scientific." Stock market games, like Acquire and High Bid, abound, along with Student Survival. Some have frightening names, like Agitation or Jeopardy—where the players are given the answers and asked to supply the questions.

Many are hooked on Diplomacy, which was invented by an MIT professor in 1959; it's been played with passion for years in Cambridge. The board is a map of Europe, circa 1901; there are seven countries for seven players, who try to capture each other's countries. Each has two armies and a navy; every time you seize a city, you acquire an extra army. Moves are made at fifteen-minute intervals; in between you confer with others and make alliances. (Some favor conferences in the bathroom, with all the taps turned on.) But there's no obligation to make any move you've promised. France may be in league with Germany against Italy, but Italy may at the same time ally with Germany against France. "The essential beauty," said an addict, "is that you're supposed to lie *all the time*. It combines the tactical skills of chess with all the arts of cajolery, deceit and intimidation. Threats are vital." "It turns people into monsters," said a detractor. Apparently alliances can lead to adultery, while those who've betrayed each other often explode with every other hostility that plagues their private lives. Diplomacy can be played for days, and has been called "the game that breaks up more families than Monopoly."

Others are less cerebral. There's the "Executive Mental Block: The *Infuriating* Three-dimensional Jigsaw Puzzle—How to Drive Him Out of His Mind in ALL Three Dimensions." There's also a rash of new ESP games; the instructions and equipment are so complex that they would surely fuse anyone's psychic flow. Plastic phosphorescent ouija boards are everywhere. As a devout ouijaphile since childhood, I've discovered that it should be used mainly with strangers and is perilous among partners: JACK LOVES LINDA is ominous news when Linda is after all married to Tim—and the board says that Tim hates Jack. YOUR ROOF NEEDS REPAIRING can tempt a marital homicide as easily as JOANNE WISHES AAGGHH THAT RODNEY WERE DEADXHMPH.

For more amicable evenings, Bar-Spreezy requires that you sip a drink for every point won; you skip sips by drawing "Intoxicards" or landing "On the Bowery." The literature encourages you to "Take Your Friends 'On the Town'

in Your Own Living Room!" where "All Sorts of Crazy Things Can Happen to
You!" Surely the sequel is "Mate-Match," the "Computerized Compatibility
Fun Game for 2 to 50 People," which will determine if "Your Mate Is a Real
Swinger." There are also lots of "body contact games" devised for teen-agers,
but flourishing in the adults' departments. These involve getting looped together, scooping or dropping plastic cubes from or into a bucket tied to your
opponent's waist, or, as in "The Game of Love," smacking down your hands,
knees, and other extremities all over the playing board. There are also many
solitary games: for those who detest the party? Or for those alone with a
broken TV set.

One of the best games I've seen is "50 Easy Steps to the White House,"
created by Godfrey Cambridge. While the board's addressed to blacks, it's
offered for "discriminating people of all races." You start at Watts, Harlem,
Mississippi, and Newark; at thirteen you become a moderate or a militant. A
moderate "seen lunching with Stokely" goes to jail; a militant loses two turns
for "pasting black power posters in the White House john," also if his son
"intermarries, goes to Africa in search of roots." For straightening your hair,
you go back to Gary, Indiana. Later "You run for mayor and win assuring
people that you will not be a 'Negro' mayor. Roll again." It's selling very well,
although many stores were wary of carrying it. The manufacturers were questioned by the Secret Service, which feared that the game promises to "over-
take" the White House, and that it showed a map of that citadel.

Scrabble repels those who find pushing little squares of cardboard around
a depressing substitute for talking. If "interpersonal relationships" are too
intolerable at social gatherings, charades still seem the best escape. At least
people must leave the room to dress up, rehearse, find props, and no one is
a victim. An adolescent favorite of mine was extension: eggs—stench—shun,
which gave an opportunity for hen-like misbehavior, a wonderful passage of
gagging and retching, and the necessity of snubbing everyone on hand. Hopefully charades are not yet marketed: unlike Christmas, they come free.

Reels of California:
A New Yorker's View
1969-1972

The extreme East (Manhattan) and the acute West (all California) each maintain the same myth about the other: that the opposite coast is where everything happens first. Both New Yorkers and Californians suspect that their politics and clothes and horoscopes and language are being predetermined across the country by slap-happy or formidable strangers who sculpt the future with all the carelessness of media freaks. I've had seven Californian trips in the last three years; as a New Yorker I feel that the left and the right are farthest along in California, though the natives tell me that New York is the capital of radicalism. Landing in Santa Barbara or Berkeley, I lunge toward locals with urgent questions which they interrupt to demand tidings of New York. We each think the other's drug culture is more lavish than our own, along with the span between magic and mantras, self-destruction, revelation, revolution, celebration, or beads. (Still, some Californians have said their head scene may be more frenzied than ours.) So I can only record what delights or alarms a New Yorker in a state which seems more foreign than any European country I've known. California ignores Europe and most of the globe—a fact which sets an easterner adrift.

The sheerly physical exhilaration—simply expanding into space—seems to triple the energy that can be curtailed by canyons. Bombing down those great silky highways in a souped-up Mustang, with electronic rock ribboning out of the radio, made three adults feel about twelve years old. We were impatient when the music broke for bulletins on the first moon walk. (As the spacemen were put in quarantine, the back seat asked, "If the astronauts are contaminated, do we send them back?" The perils of exposure to moon dust make the old songs about stardust sound quite sinister now.) The excitement of California driving overwhelmed our normally vast appetites for news, although we were desperate for newspapers that reported more than an outbreak of mumps in Santa Ana or San Luis Obispo as soon as we climbed out of the car. California makes you feel your contradictions. We complained about the provincialism but sometimes found it infectious: when you feel extravagantly healthy, your own body seems more important than many world events. (I could never feel that elsewhere. But one's ethics back up the spout in California.) The surfers on the beaches we passed seemed justified in their isolation, their ignorance of everything but the next wave.

Yet other forms of ignorance were infuriating. Political misinformation spat through the air like birdshot. Denials were shrugged away. The car also taught us that many San Franciscans don't know where they live. We gave lifts to white radicals after some evenings at a Panther conference: most weren't able to guide us to their own addresses, and we drove in giant ovals until two or three A.M. while they explained that they'd moved to California forever—six days ago. (The frontier mentality lingers: the West still seems to promise to enlighten or enrich you.) One boy nearly lost us for a lifetime with his street directions: "Right on" meant straight ahead (*not* right); "Ray-Gun (argot for Ronald Reagan) meant turn to the right; for making a left, he murmured, "Socialism, man." Wondering if we'd still be on the streets at dawn, I remembered driving in Santa Monica on Labor Day some years ago: the radio was regularly announcing state-to-state car crashes as though they were football scores: "Massachusetts, 12; New York, 17; and *California* is *still leading* with 24 road deaths!"

The car makes it easy to see life as a movie: watching your own footage, which draws in others or is rewritten by them. It's the state of mind that was developed by the acid converts of the early Sixties and the sensation seems especially Californian. John Barth nailed it nicely in *End of the Road* in 1958: "We are all casting directors a great deal of the time." Later in the novel a character remarks that "a man's integrity consists in being faithful to the script he's written for himself." Quite a few in California seem to have lost or betrayed their own scripts, while others hunt for them.

∿

People often argue that New York gives you too much reality, while California yields an overdose of fantasy. It sounds too simple, but I can't reject it. Riding the New York subway or just trying to phone the Health Department because you've had no heat for a week seem to have no parallels to being stoned in the sun, staying warm, getting tanned. Watts was full of red flowers beneath a blue sky: someone kept repeating that it didn't look as harsh as Harlem.

∿

Walking down a Santa Barbara street at dusk: some feet ahead of me, a young man draped in quivering buckskin fringes strolls and punctually yells, "I'm going to die!" Not frantic: he's just telling the world. He's probably descending from acid, or just rising, as the sunset ebbs and chills. House owners emerge and stand on their porches, each gripping a huge flashlight as though it were a gun. Beefy men in bright shirts watch silently until he shouts himself out of sight: the street is lined with grizzled householders protecting their own steps, their electric weapons ready. Self-defense takes on a new tang: they do look ready to attack. "I'm going to die!" And they probably wish he would—it's a collision of cultures that just can't live together. The paranoia that often springs from acid or speed seems contagious for them. So they're afraid of losing what they have; he fears he's already lost it. His drugs, their homes and flashlights, his noise, their ominous quiet: the threat is mutual, as unforgivable as death.

~

In the windows of shops on Telegraph Avenue in Berkeley, groups of people lie jiggling on waterbeds covered with patterned rugs; they read and chat and exchange the day's news, heaped casually together. Here I'm pleased to learn that "fucking your Ma" means nothing Oedipal—just living free at home if you're a student.

~

Some California deaths are hard to miss. The *Los Angeles Times* reported that a young man in Hollywood was found frozen stiff inside his own refrigerator. His hands clutched a rope which kept the door closed.

His neighbors said he lived on a diet of Cutty Sark and Hostess Twinkies, and that he was obsessed with fighting crime. He had a homemade life-size robot to "sniff out illicit drugs," and he alternated between wearing his police costume and a Superman suit, in which he used to jump on roofs at night. The cops heard complaints that someone dressed as Superman had startled pedestrians by springing at them from phone booths. But no action was taken against him because he had no record. His landlord said the young man had tried very hard to make adult friends, but few people responded, since most of his conversation was about comic books.

~

Legendary Hollywood is scarce; since most of the big studios are sagging and more than half of the usual number of studio staffers are out of work, the industry and its survivors are on the defensive. Still, those I saw were friendly because my father wrote the movie of *Gunga Din*. But they and the younger scriptwriters I met clearly suffered from the same affliction that was famous in the Thirties: so much commissioned work unused, so many scripts and projects scrapped, all that rewriting and polishing for nothing. Paid for, of course, but it still feels rotten. And some of the abandoned movies sounded as though they might have been good.

Looking for lore, I was rewarded by a seasoned publicist who described working for a producer of costume serials, B-Westerns, and jungle pictures of the Forties. He explained the problem of dealing with chimpanzees: "After seven years, you can't work with any chimp: their brains get bigger and start pressing against their craniums, and they get very mean. When that happened with Tomba—she was our best chimp, we'd used her for years—my boss thought he'd simply get rid of her. I told him, 'Sam, you just can't drop a chimp like that.' I insisted that she be retired. I made up a lovely little story: that Tomba had been having dizzy spells, and one day she finally passed out during a scene with Johnny Weissmuller. I said she got knocked up by a chimp named Hooligan, who went off with a traveling circus. So we showed pictures of her knitting booties, there were pieces in *Variety* and everywhere about her long career. So when it comes to Sayonara, there's no need to be a schmuck— you don't have to break a broom handle off in anybody's fanny."

Someone said that Tomba's retirement could yield a lesson in humanity for all of Hollywood: "Mostly you just get the foot. Then blam. You're over."

~

"No lice in my wigs!"

Sitting in a motel lobby, famished for world news—forgetting how the car had made me indifferent—the only factual report I could find on TV was an interview with a pet-shop owner in Long Beach, whose piranha fish had been stomped to death by the local police. There was some question about the legality of breeding such deadly fish in California. But the distraught fish-loser exhibited his empty aquariums hung with little black drapes and signs reading "Police Brutality"; he was vowing to sue the state.

Meanwhile I was aware of shouting near me: "My wigs are pure!" a salesman wailed into a public phone, his voice trembling with the threat of tears. I gathered that he was talking to an assistant DA. He said $10,000 worth of his merchandise had been seized without a warrant—here his voice broke— because a female competitor had bought a wig and then claimed that it was crawling with lice. "She did that because my wigs are *cheaper* than hers. And now they're sitting in that bastard's office—collecting dust and crap and for all I know people are *walking* on them—and my sale's supposed to start tomorrow!"

The desk clerk looked miserable; his gaze cringed around the lobby in fear that the motel would be accused of sheltering parasites. "And you know," the salesman screamed, "lice couldn't live in wigs. They need *warm-blooded* animals. They depend on a bloodstream. . . . "

On TV, photos were shown of the dead piranhas while their owner elaborated on their wholesale and retail prices. Momentarily all California seemed insecure: so easy to lose your fish or your wigs to ruthless servants of the law—to be stripped of your marketable property. "How's a man to make a living!" the salesman howled. Writers of junked scripts would have understood him.

Indeed despite all of California's coastal splendors, you're less aware of the rich there than of the many who haven't made it. You meet the rich in their own homes, which are often tastefully remote from town centers or main streets, lapped in shielding shrubbery. The very poor are usually in isolated ghettos—you don't see them daily, as you do in New York. But the strugglers swarm through motels and drive-ins and Pizzaburgers, clanking with failure: the boom state withholds its promise from them, and the Gold Rush seems like the remains of a real estate flack's lies. So it's eerie to remember that I got my name from the Gold Rush: my grandmother's uncle was a Forty-Niner, searching for nuggets in Sonora, California. She was named for the town in hopes that it would reward him, but he struck no gold at all. I regret that the name was shortened by the time it came to me—I'd like to feel a closer kinship to all that elation and certainty, when the West spelled a guarantee.

~

Charles Manson told *Rolling Stone* that "Death is psychosomatic."

Musing on Manson as part of an American ballad or as one of our handiest myths, I can see why he has something for everyone. Not young himself, yet he gives some people the excuse they've been waiting for to hate the young. After Manson's conviction, one of the jurors said: "I hope this verdict will be a lesson to the young people of this country—that you can't just go into a person's house and butcher them up. . . . " And Manson was as satisfactory for Weatherman as he was for their conservative elders; the Liberation News Service reported this slogan: MANSON POWER—THE YEAR OF THE FORK!

Manson did understand that he was a symbol. "Anything you see in me is you. If you want to see me as a vicious killer, that's who you'll see, do you understand that? If you see me as your brother, that's what I'll be . . . I am you, and when you can admit that, you will be free. I am just a mirror."

One of the women in his tribe explained, "Charlie taught us that instead of dying slowly and treacherously—aging—you can speed up the process and do it in your mind. Because you're right at the point of life and death all the time. Every time you're totally willing to die, it brings you right back into living. The point of death is rebirth."

Dear old death and rebirth: these days it almost sounds like grilled cheese and bacon. But while people are on death trips all over the country—nowhere do I feel it so strongly as in California. It's said to have the highest suicide rate of any state.

In 1972 the director of the Los Angeles Suicide Prevention Center told a convention on "Suicidology" that more young people were killing themselves than in the past. He said, "I've never known a generation as interested in death as an experience, something you can pass through."

~

From L.A. to San Francisco, you meet the beached remnants of 1967: the searchers who haven't yet fled to rural communes—gentle freaks and strung-out waifs who may still learn self-protection. California seems to display even more casualties than New York, perhaps because the brilliant skyscapes and delectable styles of living make the battered or vulnerable faces more conspicuous. There you're more conscious than ever that many have lost the courage or the mere enjoyment of language, that words have yielded to vibes. At the Esalen Institute I sat reading in a parked car for several hours while a friend had interviews inside (fairly enough, the directors didn't want a writer wandering about and collecting haphazard impressions). Still, the inmates were hospitable: a few fed me chocolate bars through the car window and one said, "If you want to . . . you know, um, you know . . . if you want to . . . you know . . . it's over there." I thanked him, hoping that the very expensive Esalen treatment would eventually strengthen his confidence in being able to name the bathroom.

~

After all the enchantments of driving down the Pacific coast, envying the lushness of anybody's garden (a New Yorker hardly sees a weed these days), reveling in the spaces and breezes, astonished by the cordiality of strangers and the sweetness of abalone steaks, still riveted by the crusts of Hollywood and the density of the occult, I returned each time to the East convinced that New York is the most peaceful and rational of communities, soothing in its stability after all the conflicts of California. Snuggling into the Manhattan ooze, savoring a reflection from Donald Barthelme—"This muck heaves and palpitates. It is multi-directional and has a mayor"—a native yields to New York chauvinism: California is stunning, but . . . all that freedom seems illusory when Ronald Reagan blows his nose.

Part IV

Theater and a Couple of Movies

In earlier and later times, many Broadway and Off-Broadway productions were non-topical, disconnected from contemporary experiences. Starting in about 1966 the theater began to echo the political and social themes of the period as well as the sexual malaise. So many plays were nagging at America, reflecting or rejecting what we lived with.

Off-Off Broadway
June 1967

Intolerably white lights glare off tinfoil walls while two voiceless giant dolls with vacant faces tear up books, sheets, and curtains, smash pictures, write and draw obscenities on the walls, dance, and goose one another. Throughout the defilement, the vast gray motelkeeper obliviously drones her praise of the room: "All modern here, but . . . with a tang of home. . . . The toilet flushes of its own accord. . . . Oh, it's quite a room." Her monologue is an advertisement—a style that's currently exploited onstage. A siren howls while the dolls rip the walls apart and then wreck the motelkeeper's body; they then strut proudly down the aisles. *Motel,* one of Jean-Claude van Itallie's three plays in *America Hurrah,* superbly directed by Jacques Levy, distills the most crucial ingredients of the new theater which resides in lofts, cafés, and churches, drawn from a wellspring of workshops.

Triumphantly visual, unverbal, concerned with images rather than characterization, the movement is wary of content. (Naturally no one from Off-Off-Broadway quotes Henry James, but if they did, he'd come in handy: "The subject doesn't matter; it's the treatment, the treatment!") Consequently some of the plays' problems are rarified, such as how to build a bookcase, or persuading a dead cat to drink milk, or living with varicose veins. Still, certain themes are discernible: destruction (as in *Motel*); hoaxes (from government to art, especially as expressed in the style of the TV commercial); quandaries of sexual identity; the panics instilled by forms to fill out, hating one's job, trying to learn the time, or even obtaining street directions; growing old; Vietnam. Simultaneous effects—noises, lights, dialogues in unison, yells, gunshots—collide to make the audience feel that everything is happening at once—as it does in a war, or during the familiar (and total) confusion that can assail you while watching TV. (Jacques Levy stresses that TV provides a state of consciousness wherein the attention is free-floating and unfocused.) When this style is at its peak, as in *America Hurrah,* the spectator can feel he's having a private hallucination.

On the savage ending of *Motel,* Levy wants the audience to ponder two different kinds of killing—or ruin. He said, "How do you feel about someone who takes an axe and kills his wife's lover in a fit of jealousy? Now compare him to a doctor in a concentration camp who experiments coldly with the threshold of pain. You're *not* sorry for that doctor. He must be from another planet—but he looks more like you, like us, than some wild nut." Levy explains his concept of the doll-monsters by contrasting the old film personifications of Frankenstein (pitiable, even sympathetic, with no control of his emotions) and Dracula (motiveless malignity, "unshakable cool"). The *Motel* monsters are Dracula's descendants: uninvolved by reason or emotions; Levy says "they're just doing their thing." Part of the calculated shock is their human appearance; their masks are chill but cheerful Pop cartoon faces: clean-cut, not grotesque. Neither an orgy nor a purge, *Motel* succeeds as an image of senseless destruction where many naive antiwar plays have failed.

Off-Off-Broadway is more than an incubator; not only has it hatched some of New York's best productions, but its virtue is that it can afford to fail—financially as well as artistically. A few years ago, as Broadway and Off-Broadway died from expense like mastodons sheeted in ice, New Yorkers who love live acting despaired of having any kind of theater. (At present there are fewer commercial plays running than there were during the Depression.) While it's true that most of the professional offerings are feeble, dim overnight critics who can close a play after one performance have empowered economics to kill the existing theater. Usually only a eulogy in the *New York Times* can preserve a "serious" play. But in a loft a production can cost under $200; a three-week run—with or without critics—can often be guaranteed. Many groups hope for subsidies or grants, and almost everyone involved must earn his living elsewhere. The movement cheats two near-impossibilities in modern Manhattan; first, the product isn't controlled by money or publicity, and second—in a period when the newest and the latest are hourly proclaimed, and then followed by some ancient familiarity—something we haven't seen before is actually occurring.

Definitions would cause most of the new playmakers to choke. Still, since so many have worked together at the Café La Mama, the Judson Memorial Church, the Caffe Cino, The Open Theatre, and many others, they share certain stylistic preoccupations. The workshops sometimes enlarge the actors' conceptual role to the extent that when the plays develop out of classes, the dramatist becomes more of an editor than a writer. Occasionally the actors may have so much power that they can refuse to deliver lines they don't believe in. Many actors and directors say they must agree with a play's statement if they're to perform it—or at least believe in its "antidote." As a result of the workshop evolution, most of the new plays are so "visible" as to be unreadable; it's difficult to judge them outside production. So far, most of the experiments have produced more fine actors than playwrights, opportunities for brilliant acting rather than durable plays.

Denial of language is sometimes an obsession. (But since the movement is intentionally antiliterary, readable drama is no criterion.) Improvisation, which is sometimes related to the spontaneity of happenings, and to the notion that all of life is art, can yield some toxifying boredoms which make you wish the author had had more control. But the opportunity for production—which was previously so rare—is far more important than the frequency of stillbirths. In particular, Ellen Stewart, the founder of La Mama, has managed to stage plays against odds which would have capsized the most resilient producers.

It seems unlikely that most of the productions could be transferred to larger theaters or to film. Physical proximity is essential to the style. When an actress two feet away screams directly into your face while gazing into your eyes, it's hard to feel detached from her pain or ecstasy. *Futz*, a recent award-winner by Rochelle Owens, which concerns an amiable man who humps his pig so enthusiastically that his enraged neighbors kill him, depended almost completely on the smallness—hence the intimacy—of La Mama. The play (which proves that nonconformists tend to suffer) is negligible, despite a few appealing lines, such as "Hell has no fury like a woman scorned by a man— for a pig." But if you accept the dictum that content isn't important, experiencing the excitement of the production is tremendously rewarding. Baked in brick walls, in body heat, the tiny café throbs to zither notes while a young man makes rhythmic farting sounds into the neck of a jug; a girl blows the recorder while hanging from her knees around his neck. The chorus orchestrates a murder confession with gasps and wheezes, grunts magnificently while the invisible pig enjoys her human lover, and springs head over heels in exuberant body celebrations which only a born paralytic could reject. Delight of the limbs is made contagious—especially since the actors are nearly in your lap.

Here an already mossy conflict must be acknowledged. Most of the directors shun naturalism. The voices of Off-Off-Broadway insist that the audience must remember that it's in the theater, must be constantly reminded that the stage action isn't life, and should never be lulled into "taking anything for real." (For this reason, Lanford Wilson's *Balm in Gilead* rapidly repeats a murder scene.) In light of keeping realism at bay, Jacques Levy said, "Pop has more balls than Camp. Pop has a cool that I love—it has a way of discussing subjects at a distance." There is also the physical assault by actors: you get touched, stroked, and patted while performers run through the audience, shouting accusations or endearments. The aisle is full of noises. You're hugged while bombs explode. (Before some audience-participation shows, the spectators eye each other nervously—as though wondering what they'll have to do to each other later.) John Lahr, the drama critic for *Manhattan East*, has objected to "the tyranny of the actor" on the grounds that no artifice is attempted—that the directors are really resorting to the naturalism which they claim to have eliminated. Again the suggestion that there's no distinction between art and life. Currently there's a happening in the Village where you can pay 50 cents to watch a family that simply lives on stage.

In this same context, there have been objections to the extremely convincing sacrifice of two chickens in Sam Shepard's *La Turista* (also directed by Levy). This furious yet impersonal play shows two young American tourists stricken with savage diarrhea in Mexico; they're serviced by witch doctors who fail to cure them. (The travelers' disease is locally called *la turista*.) The Americans, both named for cigarette brands, seem to personify the collapse of "the Greatest Society"; their sterility is itself a disease which can't survive the dirt of poverty. The production aimed at making the audience feel uncomfortable and out of place—like tourists. The famous chickens were condemned by some as a naturalistic device—especially since Levy originally wanted to use live fowls. (He has retorted that there's no difference between eating a real or sham apple on stage, and refers the debate to the end of *Motel:* when the dolls demolish the motelkeeper's body, it's a valid shock to learn it's an empty figure with a recorded voice—that "nobody's there.") The arguments will of course continue, and some spectators may follow John Lahr's rebellious advice by leaping onstage, or flinging the actress who fondles them to the floor in a passionate embrace.

The influence of movies—from parodies of old Westerns to reincarnations of Laurel and Hardy—is conspicuous, as is the employment of film techniques. The use of sudden stills recurs, as in van Itallie's *Interview,* directed by Joseph Chaikin, where the actors' faces are frozen in silent screams while a governor says that he can't give a statement on Vietnam. (In classes Levy also works on "mesmerization"—suddenly going dead—as television watchers sometimes do.) Sharp transitions—or often the absence of transitions—can resemble fast film cutting; sometimes montage is used. The spectators are asked to make the connections for themselves. Using filmic devices is another antinaturalistic effort—to make what's seen "less real." While using the theater for "live movies," Levy took one straight three-act play, cut and changed the sequence, and produced three plays all occurring at the same time—as a way of combining past and present.

Swift transformations of character are common: an actor may spring into a new role or abruptly demonstrate a contradictory force within the persona. Motives are considered far less important than the way people affect one another; their styles of behavior and mutual response take precedence over their conscious intentions. Much of the new theater shows how everyone plays games, detailing the degree of seriousness or viciousness through actions rather than words. Van Itallie's *TV* is shot with the game of humiliation: a man gagging on a sandwich crawls choking on his hands and knees while his colleagues quarrel about whether to give him bread or water. Motives are related to perpetual game playing.

Games of course rouse the question of Camp—we can't yet abandon this tiresome discussion and many of the new plays keep it plodding. A recent success, *Gorilla Queen* by Ronald Tavel, directed by Lawrence Kornfield, dredges the jungle flicks of the 1940s to deify a winsome Queen Kong: God is a homosexual gorilla, complete with sequinned nipples. Mens' crotches are caressed beneath grass skirts, male spectators' ears are licked by a chuckling, redbearded "Brute," a transvestite's false breasts are squeezed, removed, and restored, while a huge lesbian named Paulet Coldbare is nearly burnt as a sacrifice until it's realized that she will increase "smut pollution." It might be amusing if it were truly outrageous. But most of the jokes are desperate—"I now pronounce you man and wife, or man and man"—as are the lyrics: "Dip your tricky dicky/In the sticky soft spot."

It's been said that the intended dreadfulness makes *Gorilla Queen* and other products of the Theatre of the Ridiculous impossible to criticize. But it still seems worth protesting the boredom of these romps—even if Andy Warhol has said that he loves to be bored. A good recent essay by Jacob Brackman in the *New Yorker* described the put-on as "a basically hostile means of expression," enabling an artist to be "hostile to his materials, his audience, and his own talent." Many who've seen *Gorilla Queen* are timid of admitting that such hostility leaks all over the stage. Camp theater may continue to thrive simply because the terrors of squaredom can keep most audiences humble.

Infantilism, willful obscurity, ghetto club-forming, the conviction that anyone's an artist if he says he is—none of these irritations invalidate the finest 5 percent of Off-Off-Broadway. Initially some saw it as a halfway house to the professional theater. Now many call it a distinct alternative, since failure and dullness compound the sludge of Broadway and Lincoln Center. Producing plays on minimal money has been a stimulus for certain imaginations. But it's ridiculous to deduce that the theater flourishes on austerity. Still, there's a pleasing irony: at a moment when culture is furiously fashionable, some gifted practitioners have made a mockery of publicity and economics.

Further Off Broadway
March 1968

Lately the Off-Off-Broadway actors' involvement with the spectators has so intensified that you fully expect to get laid during the next evening at the theater. The performers are sometimes so close that you smell their sweat before it's shaken onto you. Actors sprinkled throughout the audience heckle those on stage, yell advice or derision, correct their lines, throw sugar at them. Hisses, grunts, and squeals accelerate to replace language; gibberish is refined; respiratory noises have been perfected as exclamations of horror. Some directors insist that "content isn't important," that style's far more significant than any subject. But between an expert grope-in at the Open Theatre (where a church meeting flowered into a vast bisexual feel-up), the wistful put-ons of certain hopeless hippie musicals, and some inept, despairing charades about Vietnam, racial themes recur with the relentlessness of the unfashionable. Although racism isn't the central subject of these plays, they're directed to force the audience to think about it: the topic that so many would love to shelve or shun, since it's more tangible than "peace."

Perpetual game playing is still an obsessive style. Games of hostility and destruction stress the helplessness of mutual aggressors, as well as their ignorance of their own motives, their unconscious need to assault. A fury of whiteness focuses the ferocity of Sam Shepard's *Melodrama Play* at the Café La Mama, where the whole cast wears white military suits against a glaring white vinyl setting. When it's time for killing, there is even a white pistol. A menacing guard tyrannizes a flighty songwriter. Threatening his victim with immediate death, the guard alternates his murderous impulses with childish insecurity: "What do you think of me as a person?" The murderer is desperate to be liked, while the thrashed suppliant writhes with the terror of being killed at any moment. At the end, although his life is finally preserved, he continues to crawl on hands and knees in a slow, small circle, wheezing out his agony, moaning, howling, retching. Reduced to a crying animal, he can't yet—if ever—recover his human posture. Finally all the actors bow while blood trickles from their mouths onto their white jackets.

The tyrant's role was written without racial specification; in Europe it was played by a white—in New York by a black man. The character can personify police brutality and/or sudden black aggression; his personal fear of being disliked embodies both the very American neurosis of yearning to be loved by everyone and the black's natural anguish at being scorned. Literally bringing a person to his knees is what whites do to blacks; it's also a black's fantasy of what he might do to whites. It yields a searing image for the current atmosphere of the country; beating your random opponent into submission, battering him into mindlessness. Meanwhile the phrase "psychological victory" comes dribbling out of Washington to describe recent events in Vietnam.

Aside from the excruciating finale, Shepard's play is a dispassionate metaphor. Earlier, three people are killed onstage, and—despite the dramatic shock—one doesn't care, because they haven't been characterized. As allegorical figures they impart no sense of loss when they fall dead. But during Israel Horovitz's *The Indian Wants the Bronx,* the intimacies of torture are so intolerable that some spectators have admitted that they wanted to jump on the stage and stop the action. The torment springs from magnificent characterization. Two street boys—high-strung, humorous sadists who are not dislikable—attack a meek East Indian on an isolated bus stop. He has just arrived in New York, needs directions to find a relative in the Bronx, but knows too little English to learn his way. The polite, turbaned foreigner is at first merely puzzled by the twitching boys. He smiles hopefully as they dance on the edge of hysteria, drum their heels against ashcans, and mock their social worker, "Pussy-face," a woman who gave them knives as presents and has urged them to "play games" to release their energies. The Indian becomes their game—just because he's there. The sport evolves as their moods flicker, change, and flare. They pantomime burning him at the stake, suddenly knock him to the ground—apologize frantically to him: "Everyone gets crazy sometimes, don't they?"—and finally pummel him into such a frenzy that he wails to an empty telephone booth for rescue. They cut the wires. The play ends with the dead phone ringing while the terrorized Indian screams into a severed receiver: "Please! . . . Thank you! . . . *Thank . . .* you": the only English words he has.

Since nursery school we've been told that we're a violent people. Early in life the notion of native savagery becomes a cliché, almost as hackneyed as a radio commercial. But it has a new meaning now. Since Jack Kennedy's assassination, the climb of crime, and the nationwide riots, the possibility of being suddenly maimed by a stranger is unsurprising. (Murder—as opposed to mutilation—still occurs oftener among friends and relatives than strangers.) Stray madness or "things that just happen" or being in the wrong place at the wrong time are chances that we all have to live with, without indulging in irrational fear. There's a sense of haphazard execution in our gritty air: a barber has been killed by a customer who didn't like his haircut; recently four were shot in a luncheonette because the waiter was slow in serving the soup; a woman stabbed a cab-driver in the face and shoulder when he said that he was off duty and on his way to breakfast. Also we have a new term: "involuntary manslaughter," an act which was committed by parents who told their daughter to kill her dog; instead she killed herself. In the pressure chamber that we now inhabit, Israel Horovitz has expressed what everyone knows and few writers have achieved.

Of course no subject should be shielded from humor; no one has been funnier about racism than the black militants I met in Watts. But Bruce Jay Friedman's *Scuba Duba* is repellent in its effort to squeeze a merry evening's entertainment out of racial hatred. It's particularly depressing from this author, whose splendid novel, *Stern*, was a comedy of humiliation about a Jew who fed his own fears of anti-Semitism until he gave himself a nervous breakdown. The distinctions between racism and personal neurosis, sympathy and ridicule, were flawless. In his new play, the hero is meant to personify the dishonesty of the white liberal—who is really encancered with prejudice. An amiable, infantile man, who once thought himself enlightened, loses his wife to two black lovers. He spews forth the loathing that's supposed to lurk in us all: "coon," "shine," "goddam spade," "chocolate shit-head," "fucking Mau-Mau"—until the blacks politely tell him, "You're far from a credit to your race." As a "one-handed" lover, his sexual jealousy peaks at paranoia, which he tries to dilute by clowning: his own game. After abusing one of the black men, he says, "Just overlook the racial stuff." The play is clearly intended as a shower of honesty about bigotry, but—since the humor is so heavy and naive—the result is a deluge of hate. The two blacks are insulting caricatures: a sleek, impudent monster of bullying sexuality and an overeducated Uncle Tom.

The well-dressed audience laughs cozily at the very simple oneline jokes about *Ebony* and Freedom Marches, which clank like spare parts from the old-fashioned Broadway situation comedies that have benumbed the commercial theater. Ticket buyers can go home feeling comfortable after a pseudo-contemporary snigger. But what passes for probity is a very native flight to an easy psychological excuse: if a black maid punished you as a child, you have a reason for the racism that embarrasses you as an adult. *Scuba Duba* is a feverish success. Soon there may be a new folk-rock refrain: "Black is black and what is white?" Self-laceration is becoming another white luxury: a way of petting and forgiving oneself.

Hindsight: I wrote this piece at the beginning of March 1968, but by chance it happened to be published on the day that Martin Luther King was murdered. In that early winter, just a few weeks before My Lai, we saw some of the most devastating photographs yet released of the dying Vietnamese. At home we were still getting used to our own atmosphere of random death, which became the groundnote of 1968.

Howling for Help

July 1968

Encounter groups have been rewarding for some I know and maddening for others. Certain rebels report that they resent learning what all small children know: that a group can make one person cry. But you're constantly reminded that an outsider can't presume to judge an experience that enriches others.

Still, despite the threat of losing the empathy race, it's painfully easy to judge *The Concept*—as theater. This bath of actuality has been improvised and acted by former drug addicts from Daytop, the rehabilitation center which is run by ex-addicts. (As the playwright's role dwindles on Off-Broadway, while the actors' and the directors' power swells, *The Concept* is the last possible refinement: it eliminates the author altogether.) Hailed for its humanity, the play has been nuzzled by some of the most loving reviews in New York. Punctuated by yells, screams, mutual accusations, enough hostility to win a war and sufficient tenderness to sink a whale, *The Concept* congeals the process of a marathon T-group which can last from thirty to forty hours. A "new brother" is made to plead for admission to Daytop, until he gags, "Huhhhh . . . lllp!"; then, *"Help?"* After he's carried out shrieking, it's explained that "Your investment for getting in . . . is howling for help."

Inhibition appears as the fiercest problem of 1968. An actor said in an interview that it's essential "to relate from your feelings instead of from your image. You have to blow your image"—as though it were your nose. Onstage the group keeps bullying a member because his "image gets in the way." Yielding the self to a group becomes a higher morality: "You're part of something bigger than yourself, which everyone is building." Privacy or loneliness or independence are made to seem equally destructive—a theme of the tribal Sixties. "I saw something last night that really flipped my guts—a new brother, sitting alone." Groans and moans reply, as though the notion were the worst one in the world. Amorphous guilt seeps through those who are too uptight to unzip fully in public. In this symbiosis, no experience seems to exist until it's shared, while the fractions seek their identities from one another. Some T-groups have been rebuked for developing such meshed dependence that members seem lost without each other. Sometimes neurosis seems to bind these relationships as egg-yolk binds a sauce, while confessional horror can range from the revelation of a cigarette left burning in a linen closet—"I did it! I did it!"—to lying.

The evening improves when each person admits his most "embarrassing moment," from being caught "cattle-rustling in New York" (stealing steaks from a supermarket) to: "I'm really making love to this chick, and her teeth come out"—also she turns out to be a man. The rather muted humor is welcome, as when a boy describes being discovered while swiping a TV set, by a huge man who hisses, "What's the matter, sweetie, don't you want to watch TV with me?" The boy adds that he stayed and earned fifty dollars.

Education through suffering—that cherished American tradition—is hymned as pain is propelled; perhaps pain is needed as a proof of feeling anything at all in this cool age. At the end, the performers demand of each other: "Will you love me?" A girl cries when she's made to beg for love; finally a man onstage hugs her. The actors then dispense free hugs to the audience. (I remained unembraced only by scowling furiously into space. Due to the intimacy of the small theater, I wrote some of my notes on a surface which suddenly turned out to be a stranger's thigh.) The ending recalls a line which bedecked many Broadway plays of ten years ago: "Why don't we touch any more?" This favorite seems ripe for a revival.

One can't deride the success of a program that aids addicts—nor mock their belief in it. But the grizzling tedium of a T-group is dulled by the demon of "honesty": verbally this is a true group-grope, since rambling incoherence and repetition are preserved for probity. Some insist that boredom is justified because therapy itself is boring. Since the acting's indifferent, you're urged to remember that these are *real* addicts—like the real blind children who were used in *The Miracle Worker* some years ago. Yet reality on stage seems a pathetic argument for fine theater: it's like praising a company for hiring real black actors instead of smearing on the shoe-polish.

Watching a T-group seems about as rewarding as taking someone else's pill prescription. Yet numerous observers respond as though the therapy includes them. Some in the front row even swing their legs in rhythm with the discussion. Actors have been plunging into the audience for several years; now—as in some recent productions—the spectators have started to surge onto the stage.

Black Theater
July 1968

Gleaming like a vast, unwinking mirror, the black experience reflects our white society; "Negro art" not only helps black Americans to define themselves, but it also forces the white audience to face its own world. While it's not news that much of the system is splintering, liberal whites may wring their withers over the prickling doomsday sensation, but few blacks seem surprised. The ardent white self-flagellation that Leroi Jones's work encourages isn't needed to nail the point. Every clear black voice echoes our condition as well as theirs; as James Baldwin remarked, *"Whoever debases others is debasing himself."*

The current productions are not furious. The superb Negro Ensemble Company chooses plays which express suppression of any stripe. (They've said they might include Sean O'Casey on the Easter Rebellion.) Peter Weiss's *Song of the Lusitanian Bogey* details Portugal's savage domination of Angola. The theme is liberal hypocrisy: "the exploitation of the people for their own good." Whites say that they have tried to "raise" the blacks, but the blacks have "failed." Members of the all-black cast—ranging from jet to some who look mildly tanned—alternate in playing cruel whites with gusto, with the authority of those who know cruelty from the receiving end. A black actor shoves out his chin in a succinct imitation of an Irish cop, actresses purr like benevolent liberal ladies or lift a pearly nostril in disdain. The bogey is a junk deity: its metal jaws clang open to disgorge a series of raging authoritarians. Straining and stamping in a circle with outstretched arms, trotting helplessly in unison, the players sing and dance out their anguish. A man stands on two kneeling bodies, which crawl to support him—later they form a human chair; a ballet of brutality rounds up beaten workers; enslaved women's slippers soundlessly paw the floor. Families are torn apart and shattered, and a pregnant girl gets kicked by a cop in the stomach—until she isn't pregnant anymore. The final wild wrecking and looting of the bogey leaves the stage full of debris and gasps of exhaustion. Ironic, snowy-toothed smiles stab the audience during a song that guarantees that "The white visitor meets only friendly and grateful faces." The play is muddled because there's so much factual and economic information to be dispensed, which is clotted by the neo-Brechtian form. But the stunning performance compels a witness to writhe with black oppression throughout the world. What we learn from our own ghettos becomes international fact.

The NEC has also revived *Daddy Goodness,* which was written in 1958 by

Richard Wright and Louis Sapin. A nearly buried corpse rolls out of a wheelbarrow, yelling "God *damn!*" Although he wasn't dead—merely dead drunk—
his friends believe that Daddy Goodness (nicknamed for his foul character)
has been resurrected as "the Lord." They promptly build a new cash-happy
religion around him. (The play was inspired by Father Divine.) Coincidental
"miracles" propel a feverish adoration of the randy old whiskey-head. At first
he protests his apotheosis; then he comes to believe it. Promising joy and
instant paradise on earth, he also asks people to "forgive themselves," rather
than to ask for forgiveness, and emphasizes that sin does not exist. He opens
workshops and soup kitchens for the poor and entreats society to do away
with money. But the hysterical religion becomes a corrupt business corporation, and soon "the New Faith" is as fraudulent as the Great Society. A con-
manager shouts, "This Heaven's lousy with Revolution!" Someone tries to
shoot the wretched Daddy Goodness, who finally drinks himself to death.
The play is flawed with rambling repetitions, but it was extremely worth producing for its contemporary themes: guru-making and the search for magic,
lying institutions, a hippyish love cult, poverty, "violent demonstrations" by
the unemployed, and assassination. "The Lord's" final bewilderment is agonizing to watch: the bemused, hesitant, tormented face of an old bruiser,
contorted with the pain of being rejected by those who also demand his help.

   Much of the performance maintains the NEC's impeccable standards. But
slabs of it slide into a style that's amazingly recurrent in black companies: the
same shuffling, head-scratching, Stepin Fetchit routines for which black groups
have rebuked Hollywood and the commercial theater. (Lawrence Olivier's
strutting Aunt Jemina act in *Othello,* in which he seemed perpetually eager to
serve flapjacks, was almost a parody of the old-fashioned movie Negro.) Since
black troupes are formed to stamp out these very clichés, a white spectator
gapes at the deep knee-bends, rolling eyes and pouting lips, the ultra-drawling
accents, the sniggering exaggeration of black women's sexuality, and the overstatement of black "simplicity": "Mmmmmm *huh.*" The black audience—which
is often at least two-thirds of the house—laughs freely. At first you wonder if
it's all a defiant put-on. But it seems too broad—and too familiar—to be a
subtle form of black camping. Many whites share a puzzled reaction and cannot guess why pioneering black companies should dish up a hominy-grits
style. Again James Baldwin offers a clue: "People are not . . . terribly anxious
to be equal . . . but they love the idea of being superior." Naturally he was
writing about whites. But perhaps middle-class black laughter at foolish black
behavior betrays a whiff of superiority.

   An identical perplexity is triggered by *The Believers:* a dazzling review of
"the black experience in song," performed by The Voices, who can sing
screams without feathering a crescendo, or fall to a whisper on the same
note. In 1965 Ronald Bryden asked in the *New Statesman,* "Is it still permis-
sible to say they dance brilliantly?" It is, and The Voices do. Shyness about

praising black rhythms could date from the 1850s, when Frederick Douglass, the escaped slave who became the foremost black leader of the 19th century, grimly observed that "slaves are generally expected to sing as well as to work." But black culture now celebrates the pulse that was once patronized. As *The Believers'* program notes, the American black "has expressed his lot in song," from 17th-century slavery to the Sixties civil rights marches. (At times, music must have been the only safe release.) The show opens with leaping, drumming African incantations, kidnaping blacks for slavery, and proceeds to the plantations, the freeing of slaves, a Gospel meeting which jumps into jazz, and a blues scene among the jobless in Harlem. Between the voluptuous dances and songs, black actors once more caricature themselves with a fish-fry winsomeness—as though they couldn't speak without squealing or cackling. As in *Daddy Goodness,* the black male is often a baggy figure sloshing whiskey into a tipped-back head or a naughty twinkling child. The players finally achieve the dignity they've been denied in a joyful militant finale, where the dancers flash glistening posters of Malcolm X and Martin Luther King, while the African drum throbs.

At a symposium afterward, The Voices asked the mainly black audience for its opinions. Since no one could fail to respond to that music or those bodies, all were enthusiastic. One young Afro said, "Millions of black people didn't accept the term 'Black Power' until lots of whites did—very recently." He stressed that the same applied to black music, from spirituals to jazz and soul: "We are just starting to accept what we ourselves produce." So a white leaves the theater humbled by realizing (all over again) how triumphant suppression has been—and confident that the sound of shuffling won't last long.

Blacker Theater
January 1969

Love-baths in the theater are subsiding. Now, instead of shouting "How I love you!" or—like the Living Theatre—stroking spectators while murmuring "Holy skin, holy hair, holy sleeve, holy wool," the actors are beginning to declare their hostility. While the grope-ins were mainly farcical, the new form of audience involvement is not: because the actors are black. At last there's a searing validity in participation—since we're all in the racial situation. (Malcolm X said "the Negro problem" should be renamed "the white man's problem.") But many—especially the critics—seem astonished that blacks are angry at whites, and chide them for rebellion.

There's a curious contrast with England in the Fifties: when *Look Back in Anger* and kindred works lashed the issue of class in Britain, much of the public was acutely interested; as the denunciations of the system grew more furious, the audience seemed increasingly fascinated and concerned. But here, where black revolt and even indignation have been slow to surge, a racist society is startled by reproach. The playwrights have been accused of "going too far," "losing perspective," "expressing their own point of view." The sound of shuffling has dissolved—completely. Black theater has developed so swiftly in the last few months that members of many cultures can be envious: at the potent evolution of a style that swells and celebrates and stings.

In the Wine Time by Ed Bullins, author of *The Electronic Nigger,* unskins the exhaustion and hopelessness of the ghetto without any references to whites or to white racism—which are unnecessary. A simmering August night: on a worn wooden porch, a family marinates in cheap port, while a strolling cop swats his club against a wire fence, neighborhood voices yell down the block, their words entangling many lives, and people mutter through screen doors. A husband bickers with his pregnant wife. She berates him for being jobless while she goes out to work: again and again she says that he's not a man. At first he parries her nagging with mocking affection, calling her his "Hottentot queen." She asks if he couldn't call her "something more northern . . . Ethiopian?" He teases her about a Ubangi great-grandfather and the Irishman who seduced her grandmother. Finally she cries, "I'm the one who made a man out of you—when your mother and the whole United States Navy failed!" After he slugs her, he adds ruefully, "Ahhhh honey, I'll forget about it if you do." Their teen-age nephew watches queasily, later to be rebuked for a small independent gesture by his aunt: "You gettin' kind of *mannish* around here." It's the recurrent theme of poverty: that women have the authority (which they also resent) because more jobs are open to them and because whites have crippled the black male. At the same time more and more black women are rebelling against this role casting—and against the accusations made against them by black men.

As the gentle, uncertain boy tries harder to seem like a man, he appears even more childlike. After some bawdy chat with his uncle, he admits that he's never slept with his girl: "We just look at each other and smile." The uncle is horrified—and the Harlem audience whoops. Neighbors join the querulous porch life. People swear at each other for swearing, fight without meaning to, remark grimly on the numbing repetitions in their lives. Ed Bullins has distilled the language and the experience of the ghetto so magnificently that we learn more from this one mood play than from scores of sociological studies about growing up in the black slums, where the fatigue that oozes out of suppression seems even stronger than despair. While the play has a limp, sudden ending—the drunken boy kills a man who stole his girl, and the uncle pretends to be the murderer—the last ironic crunch is almost unbearable. The man says to his violently trembling nephew, "It's your world, go down there and claim it, boy." Shaking from foot to skull, he stands there peering at a world which will discard him.

Harlem's New Lafayette Theatre, where Bullins is resident playwright, belongs devoutly to its neighborhood. There are very few whites in the audience, which often joins in the play as you would in the life of your own street. They may shout encouragement—"Give it to her!"—or applaud what's most familiar: like the community drunk, whom everybody knows. Fingers snap in the darkness as cool, prickling jazz precedes an act. But (unlike many Broadway audiences) they were not taken in by a forced conclusion: they laughed at the contrivance. It's a theatrical education to see a play among those who respond only to its most honest moments—which were abundant in this production.

KNOW WHO'S BLACK: a sign on the stage of *Big Time Buck White* brandishes the quest for selfhood like the clenched-fist power salute. This gritty satire, by the white writer Joseph Dolan Tuotti, ripened out of the Watts Writers Workshop, and had a three-year success in California. In the office of BAD (Beautiful Alleluiah Days), a "poverty gig," black men battle over funds and the power they'd like to wrench from one another. Feverish insults fuse their collaboration: *"Superspook,"* "Who you callin' nigger, nigger?" "You mahogany Eskimo!" punctuated by the slow, mutinous hiss of "Shhhhhhiitt." They repeat, "Why do we have to fight all the time?" (At a black rally in Harlem, last October, a militant said, "Blacks are the most *un*together people. . . . We spend more time fighting ourselves than fighting the enemy—which suits him. We've got to get our shit *together.*") Later an Afro-style leader takes over, and the blacks batter whites instead of one another. The mainly white audience is invited to ask questions, most of which spur savage or scornful replies, such as: "Yes, the white man's got a conscience. Enslaving a human being is against his feelings—so he has to think of blacks as animals." A white inquires if white help can still be accepted? "Yes, you can help after you've cleaned up your own neighborhood. Go home and clean up your mother's mind." (Malcolm X: "Let sincere whites go and teach nonviolence to white people!")

Buck White has been criticized as an indulgence for white masochists, which is a silly complaint. In fact it's a partial T-group, spliced with wry put-ons, which succeeds as an experiment. It's flawed by clichés of black characterization—a glossy, threatening street hood, thumbs hooked in his back pockets, and a strutting, huffy bantam—and by the fact that some of the questions are asked by actors who are planted throughout the audience. But whites can only profit by hearing directly how blacks feel: for once the moldy term "dialogue" is valid. The director says that on some nights, "people forget it's a play. Birchers and Panthers get up and start shouting at each other across the room. For blacks, it's a celebration of the black spirit, and for whites it's an opportunity to become involved in the black experience." *Buck White* helps to destroy the silence which has become dangerous for us all.

The linguistic brilliance of Ed Bullins and the free-fall exchanges of *Buck White* are complemented by the nonverbal *Riot*—a slice of the new gut-theater, which involves the audience physically so that shocked senses may later ventilate the mind. *Riot*, from Boston's OM Theatre Workshop, was conceived and directed by Julie Portman during the summer of 1967 in "response to what was happening in the street." In a church basement a panel of liberal and conservative whites, and moderate and militant blacks, churn helplessly in a racial debate—until they yell with fury at each other. The discussion alternates with bursts of revolt: real bayonets are thrust within one inch of the spectators' chests in the front row and karate teams drill: "Kill!" Under frantically flickering lights, the actors' faces freeze in tableaus of agony—which were culled from the news coverage of the Newark riots, when many were photographed at the very moment of being shot, screaming, shooting, fleeing, dodging or dying. There's a terrifying silent pause in the dark, when you don't know what will happen—and dread what will. The players drag chairs across the floor until that metallic whine becomes a shriek that's more sickening than a siren or a human howl. Then amidst the peppery stink of burning, the space erupts: beer cans and bodies hurtle through the air, people fall dead at your feet, shots and explosions heighten the gasps of anguish, groans wrench the ribs of writhing figures which can't get up.

You keep telling yourself that you're in the theater, that you must be safe, while knowing that accidents can happen—as in any riot. Or theater. (One critic's hand was nicked by a bayonet, and another's ankle was bruised by a beer can. As a coward I cringed in the third row.) Finally the basement is still: every single body lies crumpled on the floor. The stunned audience rises slowly. No one claps. And no one gibbers about "artifice": *Riot* has all the reality that anyone can bear. The play embodies what James Baldwin wrote in 1962: "The Negroes of this country may never be able to rise to power, but they are very well placed indeed to precipitate chaos and ring down the curtain on the American dream." One can hardly ask more of the theater than words made flesh.

Rapture Unwrapped
August 1969

Ritual and ecstasy are becoming rather like ham on rye: available at any drugstore, unreliable in quality, sometimes fuzzy on the tongue, a quick bite in a hurry. (There's a Harvard cafeteria where, if you order poached eggs, the waitress howls *"Drop* two on *toast!"* to the kitchen, and couples often flinch. It's the problem of the new theater: should you take it personally?) But although some producers of the theater of liberation do resemble short-order cooks, certain moments at the steam table are still worthwhile. *Dionysus in 69,* a hashed-up serving of *The Bacchae,* validates the use of nudity—as some other fleshpacks have not.

The Performance Group, directed by Richard Schechner, plays all over a room tiered with wooden jungle-gyms. Oozing throughout the audience, the actors climb in and out of their shorts and T-shirts, proclaiming their mythic characters in some lines, rejecting them in others—announcing their own names or the fact that they come from New Jersey. (Perhaps falling in and out of roles is even more popular than falling in and out of bed.) One slumps when they talk about "making this room a community," and starts to attention at the percussive splat of people slapping their own bare flanks in relentless rhythm. There's the pleasure of watching good acrobats: a slow headroll or a backward rotation shows the flutter and ripple of muscles beneath tight skin, the exhilaration of elasticity in control. Three passages (quite amazingly) succeed: the birth of Dionysus, who writhes through the spread legs of several young women who straddle him (inspired by an Asmat Indian birth ritual); the pursuit of Pentheus by the Bacchae—his panting nakedness is intensely vulnerable as he runs and leaps to escape the thud of their brutes' heels; and the triumphant bloodbath at the end, in which red paint unspills a shock when it's smeared over jerking bare bodies. Then the ceremony sags as Dionysus hoarsely begins to parody a modern radio announcer: "There's only one ritual in the country now—it's killing." Thanks, but we understood. It's the familiar flaw in the best nonverbal theater: as soon as the words return, they're apt to be mediocre. When the bodies are so articulate, the fudging of language betrays the fine use of arms and legs as well.

The performance changes constantly. When I saw *Dionysus,* the experience was abstract though intriguing; one reviewer called it "the funniest Greek tragedy I ever saw"; another remarked that "it's impossible to really dislike or be disturbed by it"; several of the most critical minds I know said they were painfully involved and moved. On certain nights, the impulse to rescue Pentheus has driven some spectators to hide him or hold onto him. Naturally the seduction of "participatory games" rides on the strength of the production: while an actor whispered deep in my ear that "Dionysus cannot bear a mocker or a scoffer," I managed to keep a straight face, but he didn't—an unwilling snort burst out of him. I decided that was his problem and not mine.

Schechner uses group therapy (known to a friend of mine as weepstakes) in his actors' workshop and has declared that "life style and performing style are not separable. You simply cannot be a great performer and a lousy human being." Lousiness means failing to understand yourself and the world, not being "whole." But despite all the cheese in *that* conviction, and the chunks of clumsiness and naiveté in *Dionysus,* this particular group-groping toward a fresh style is riveting—when it isn't hilarious. Relevant to the textual revolution that's current in the theater, Schechner has one robust point: that the "traditional" theater in America treats the playwright with as much contempt as the new experimenters do.

If only *Oh! Calcutta!* had indeed delivered "elegant erotica," celebration, "fun." There's a rather lovely dance in the buff for two, with the women bicycling slowly in the air on the man's back, and some lyric capering, plus a few engagingly caustic lines, mainly between a querulous couple in bed: " 'Move this way—that way'—you're like a goddamn *traffic* cop," and "Come on, it's role-reversal time!" Otherwise one suspects that virgins who see the show may cling to their condition. (At the performance I saw, many of the people in the audience were terribly and pathetically unattractive, ranging from obese to crippled. So I couldn't help wondering if *Oh! Calcutta!* was being used as an alternative to sex—by some who were deprived of it.) Since the authors were asked to contribute their sexual fantasies, or "observations," it's startling that almost all of them stress the difficulties or the miseries of trying to score.

The nimblest skit (*Dick and Jane* by Jules Feiffer) details exhaustion and raging tension between two people who can hardly stand each other; the coital cries are all out of sync. Finally the man introduces a wheelbarrow, a basketball, spray paint, and so much other paraphernalia, that—after shouting how good it was (for once)—he discovers that the woman herself wasn't even there. So he's upset when his speech to his wife turns out to be a soliloquy: "Don't you feel good, Jane? I feel good. Don't you feel loose, like your limbs are floating in air? Don't you, Jane? The best I ever had it . . . Janie, honey, come lie in my arms for a minute. (*He lights a match.*) Jane. Where are you? . . . (*Dick rummages through the debris, calling out for his wife.*) Jane! Hey, Jane. Hey, weren't you here? Don't tell me you missed it. Jane! Jane!"

Sexual substitutes occur in other charades: "fucking an aardvark in a parking lot," desperate wife-swapping in hopes of juicing up a flabby marriage, references to girls who "like a finger" as much as the act itself, plus a frantically grim sketch about men who masturbate before a "telepathic thought-transmitter"—their visions of vast breasts appear on a screen, rekindling one another, until they're all switched off by one man's appetite for the Lone Ranger. Throughout, frenzied crotch-grabbing and gagging orgasmic groans remain unsensual. In a heavy spoof of sex research, a man plugged full of wires finds it dreadfully hard to perform. An atrociously winsome house-playing scene, where the man and woman are dressed as children and drooling with babytalk, ends in botched rape. As in so many contemporary movies and novels, bad sex gets all the publicity (it's funny how pleasure tends to be private). *Oh! Calcutta!* actually denies the delights of bawdy, and as many have agreed, the total effect is desexing. It also reminds you that various forces seem to be unsexing many urban societies: fatigue, office strain, money grubbing, fear of failure between the sheets.

Some clammy considerations about nudity. . . . If you're fond of the human body, parts of *Dionysus* and *Oh! Calcutta!* are beguiling. There's a special charm in seeing some variety: such very different shapes are handsomely sculpted—there's no longer a classical norm. But all the bodies have to be very good ones. When buttocks (the main feature of *Oh! Calcutta!*) clench and unclench, some sag and others grow mottled; the haunches pleat unbeautifully at certain moments; sharp ribs don't enhance a pot belly. It's hard to forgive the imperfections in a body you don't know personally. Self-dislike promptly follows: how unfair to be critical of a body. Soon the spectacle makes you clinical—and that's not likable either. To see so many random genitals at once, when none of them bears any relation to your own body, is disturbing simply because it isn't exciting.

But if one were impassioned by slabs of nakedness, one would have to cope with the codes of cool that are now imposed upon us. So many experiences are "not supposed to matter": "freedom" demands the discipline of not allowing oneself to feel very much. The new puritanism is emotional, not physical, and it certainly has a repressive effect on comedy. Jokes wither in this chilly air. It's odd that the word "screwing" is still so frequent, at least in New York—surely the term is derogatory. After all, if you say that you were screwed at the laundry, you mean that they mangled half of your drygoods, lost the others, and overcharged you. Unfortunately the image serves for *Oh! Calcutta!*

Knocking the Nation

October 1969

History as a hanger, a coat hook, a contemporary hang-up: the theater can (and often does) do worse. Arthur Kopit's *Indians* is the most robust play on Broadway, granted a fragile competition. Buffalo Bill is characterized as the wrongheaded modern liberal who helps to destroy what he claims to save, patronizes those he pretends to champion, sells out the constituents who have been derailed by his false promises. His self-delusions are so lavish that he doesn't perceive that he's lying, while—drunk on public relations—he reels away from facts He unfurls the currently fashionable political excuse: lack of information at the time. Hence he kills thousands of buffalo without realizing that he's depriving the Indians of their food; he later says he didn't know that buffalo reproduced so slowly. The savaging of the Indians naturally suggests the persecution of blacks and the killing of the Vietnamese. But the parallel isn't slammed into our skulls—it doesn't need to be. A few cold-water radicals have complained because Stacy Keach, the rousing young actor who had the lead in *MacBird!*, resists the wheezy temptation to mime LBJ again. But that benevolent drawl grinds loud enough in anyone's short memory, and Buffalo Bill's lines sound very much like Washington in the late Sixties: "There's always someone who'll call an overwhelming victory a massacre."

Virility: rawhide: old Westerns: power notched by the number of scalps swinging from the belt. It was an excellent idea, and we do need some red studies. But *Indians* is no mere text: there are flashes of fine theater. Bill lollops up to the footlights on a wonderfully nervous wooden horse; as the jouncing, rearing, sidling animal fights against its rider, it's impossible to believe that the actor's own body bestows all life to this prop. Under flickering silent-movie lights, drums throb and threaten, flutes squeal, and there's an actual stink of sulphur from the effects. In a delightful scene in which Bill presents a self-justifying skit at the White House, Italian, and German actors take the Indian parts, snorting through their accents to play primitive: "Ze white man izz grrreat, ze Indian—nothink!" Later the ghost of Sitting Bull details the humiliation of "imitating our own glory" when the conquered Indians perform in Bill's Wild West shows. During a massacre, when the dying Indians drop to a stylized white sheet of snow, some frozen arms stick rigidly upright; the tableau recalls many news photos we've seen from Vietnam. The strongest line is narrated, not shown: when Sitting Bull was shot, his horse began to dance—because a gunshot was its cue to perform in the rodeo.

Bill isn't presented as a slavering villain: the treatment is sympathetic when he learns that his promises to the Indians are being betrayed by the government. Like a Sixties politician, he protests, "Things are just getting beyond me." At the end he still clings to the shafts of self-defense: "Anybody here who thinks that we have done something wrong, is wrong." He pathetically entreats the audience to buy some feathered headdresses, postcards, and Navaho dolls. He says the sale of these trinkets will help the Indians "to know themselves, and raise their spirits." It sounds quite like the rhetoric about self-determination which used to spurt out of the poverty program.

The themes are what we live with now: property and ownership, treating people like objects or animals, genocide. The play hurts when you think about it later—more so than when you watch it. It's stronger as a metaphor than as a full dramatic experience, partly because the lines have a definitive flatness which makes them awkward for spoken delivery. And there are swatches of boredom, when the Indians talk slowly, proclaiming their own nobility. *Indians* has been called "sick at heart" and "a guilt glut." Those who think it exaggerates a native ruthlessness must have very snug lives indeed, bereft of even audiovisual aids. Or perhaps conscience has become a sagging trampoline: numb flab that's been jumped on too often.

Jumping all over the U.S. now means deploring or condemning policies and history; in the Fifties it merely meant mocking social behavior and the clichés of pop psychology. (Perhaps only Jules Feiffer has managed to do both.) Elaine May's play *Adaptation* is a gentle skit which seems at least ten years old, safe in its references to all the hang-ups that we know and love. A few fingers are waved at the new left and the CIA, but the context is pre-pot, pre-revolution. The jokes of the Silent Generation weren't deadly or daring; there was thumb-sucking (as in this play) but no clenched fists. Deriding the sorrows of suburbia predated black satire from the ghetto. The comedy of love gone wrong was hung on alienation rather than sexual discord; many plays unveiled characters who "just couldn't get through to each other."

Still, May's mild play does bristle with her marvelous deadpan use of platitudes, recalling the devastatingly straight lines she and Mike Nichols used to fling at one another, often tinged with the triumph of discovery. A young woman explains: "I have this problem. I can give but I can't take"; a psychiatrist reveals that "We can't change the world until we change ourselves." Another woman says, "I believe that we've got to try to be good instead of bad. I suppose you think I'm crazy for having ideas like this?" (She has just given her boy friend a copy of Kahlil Gibran's *The Prophet*: "This book is an outcry, Phil.") The child of Wasp liberal parents asks his mother what sex is; she replies, "Sex is a term." But when he asks what a Negro is, she evokes birds and bees, light and dark flowers, adding sweetly, "You must think of the Negro as something very, very beautiful that God gave white people to enjoy."

As the poet of cliché, Elaine May has directed her cast to uphold a bright, brisk, nose-to-nose delivery: they are meant to be unconscious of their own acute self-consciousness. And the audience laughs faithfully, on cue. But most of the cozy, fur-clad spectators personify the very American failings that Kopit and May have decried. The happy banalities she parodies fill the lobby after her play; a man said, "Oh God, it's all so *true*"—and referred to his suburban neighbors. Women near me at *Indians* kept saying what fun it was, with all the horses and the costumes. . . . Perhaps merely sitting in the theater bestows a sense of safety, laughing at or censuring those who aren't there, or at the amusing-awful creatures on the stage. Last year, after a preview of *The Great White Hope*, the elegant audience gave the sweating James Earl Jones a standing ovation. He deserved it. But self-congratulation sparkled in the air: they seemed to be applauding their own liberalism.

Head Pics
February 1970

New York film critics—envisioned in Hollywood as eyeless parasites besotted with power—haven't deterred vast audiences from crowding into Antonioni's *Zabriskie Point*, just as bad reviews failed to dent the voluptuous success of Kubrick's *2001*. The now audience doesn't lie down with the *New York Times* or wake up with *Newsweek* or *Time*—a fact which ought to soothe Spiro Agnew about the influence of the media. While the critics were accurate about the absurdity of Antonioni's America, the Department of Justice betrayed an unnecessary panic when it summoned eleven people from the film's staff before a California grand jury to testify about the movie's anti-Americanism. Actually the film won't pollute any patriots; instead the U.S. seems to have corrupted Antonioni. Although he has leaned heavily on the trappings of capitalism—evil billboards, the wicked slogans of ads—he himself appears to have been seduced by a brand of commercialism: the souped-up Hollywood love formula which has sold infallibly for fifty years. The boy on the run from a crime he didn't commit and the girl who's seeking "a fantastic place for meditation" unite to synthesize one of our most marketable products.

Even the industry's creakiest dialogue has been trotted out: "Would you like to go with me?"

"Where?"

"Wherever I'm going."

The conversation between these two switched-off waifs recalls the remark of an old film publicist about sugary movies: "If you had diabetes, you'd die in the front row." (MGM cut the line which made preview audiences howl: "I always knew it would be like this"—an afterglow reflection in Death Valley.) Between the speaking glances and glancing speeches which are routine in Antonioni's movies, there's only one exchange we've never heard before: after the first kiss, the girl jerks her head toward the desert, saying, "That gypsum?"

"Well, it ain't table salt."

When the Open Theatre does its familiar grope-in—embodying the girl's fantasies after smoking a single joint—you can recognize the ancient Hollywood tradition of lovers merging with the whole creation, when all of nature tends to sing along with them. Children of the elements, they also mingle with the earth to the extent that it's hard to imagine them ever making it again without lots of dust or talcum powder. The sex isn't exciting; the girl does most of the work, while the boy is passive, becalmed. The two amateur actors (Daria Halprin and Mark Frechette) seem stunned by their own lack of skill. She alternates between a brow-puckering stare and ticklish laughter; he, who looks quite like Hedy Lamarr, relies on parted-lip reaction shots. Antonioni has also succumbed to another native fallacy: that society's victims need only return to childhood, that lost innocence can be recaptured by playing games outdoors.

Still, the movie would be inoffensive if Antonioni hadn't messed up several crucial themes, such as violence, death, and revolution. His early campus revolution sequence can only inflate the public's confusion on this subject, since he presents no tangible issues behind the confrontation. He has muddled Fifties' alienation with the politics of the Sixties. By making the youngest generation seem stupid, he will unwittingly satisfy those who condemn them and their freedoms. When the boy is killed by the police after returning a stolen plane, Antonioni's image of radicalization is a long shot of the girl swaying within a cactus grove, conveniently dressed in cactus green. Just as his critique of materialism is weakened by banality, he has even made death dull.

But none of the nonsense prevents long young lines from forming at the box office. Much of the movie is so visually delightful that you can enjoy it by ignoring Antonioni's ideas as much as he ignores ours. As the girl's car bowls between the squatting haunches of bleached hills, or a red sweatshirt flung from a plane floats down through blue air, there's an immense privilege in sharing the director's eyesight. And of course the optic experience is the main interest of many audiences now. There's also the question of whether *Zabriskie Point* qualifies as what *Variety* calls a head pic: a movie for those who are already turned on. Actually the style is far from psychedelic, although some might be able to trip to the mass feel-in scene or through the final recurrent shots of an exploding house, where tables, TV sets, cloths and clothing, books and fluttering papers, drift quite beautifully in space.

People have been expanding with grass and pills at movies for some years now. During pictures like *Yellow Submarine* and *Monterey Pop*, the smoking sections of many theaters almost bestow a free high and usually smell like the back of a Morocco bus. Acid converts have told me they "always" go to *2001* at intermission so that their trips will last throughout the psychedelic passages. On a recent visit to Hollywood, I found that quite a few youngish actors assumed that anyone who liked their favorite movies must also drop acid. For them taste is predetermined by the acid plunge.

During one California conversation about science fiction films, a man referred to his own plane. Someone eagerly asked, "Do you fly high?"

"Yes, always. It's the only way."

"Wow! What's it like?"

A five-minute misunderstanding unleashed some lovely dialogue, until the flyer mentioned the advantages of altitude. He cautioned that flying on acid is bad for landings, "because you just wouldn't care."

At any rate we can soon expect some movies which advertise the drug experience, since Hollywood is able to exploit it more quickly than the cigarette companies which may be considering the styles of ads for rival brands of grass—in the event of its legalization. Movies do, of course, cleave to some compulsory suffering, such as Peter Fonda's in *The Trip*, or the random sobs of hallucinators in *Easy Rider*. But it's easy to foresee drug imagery being used as a pacifier as well as a celebration—as well as a commercial enterprise. Also one can't help suspecting that some officials in this country would rather see the young absorbed by soft drugs and drug culture than by radical politics. Some of the "tolerant" responses to Woodstock showed a wistful desire to believe that the Chicago demonstrators of 1968 were tranquilized by pot and pills and music in 1969. But I doubt that more than a few of those at Woodstock were in Chicago—the individuals in those two crowds had very little in common. Besides, many radicals are against drugs; on the left, the movement against them is widening.

The ultimate trip movie of early 1970 is *Fantasia*, which lost Disney so much money in 1940. Currently its New York revival is jammed with heads and hippies: the ticket queue previews all the underground fashions for the year. It's astonishing to see how contemporary *Fantasia* is now. It's also far less sadistic than Disney's other pictures. Kitsch and Camp collide with spurts of Op and some exhilarating graphics; his most abstract work was always his best. It's all curves: there's hardly a straight line throughout. During Bach's

Toccata and Fugue (hideously hoked up by Leopold Stokowski), suggestions of violin bows chase each other like comets amid all the blinks and blurts of light, and great striped waves of magenta and purple devour one another. Stravinsky's *Rite of Spring* holds up well as the dinosaurs march like a dying army, or the pounce of a predatory creature leaves a few floating feathers behind. Moussorgsky's *Night on Bald Mountain* casts some hallucinatory spells: Satan's colossal hands trickle down a mountainside, their shadows blackening a town, while ghosts drift upwards from their graves. *Ave Maria* is sung to an almost black screen: what seems to be a church spire finally penetrates it and then turns out to be a chink in a glimpse through a forest. Disney's gift for making you feel you're in motion surpasses the effects that Timothy Leary used in his League for Spiritual Discovery celebrations of 1967. Disney causes you to swim in space, glide, and definitely fly, while shapes and objects dissolve and merge into each other, sensually satisfying in their mutations. While you don't quite "tumble through the capillary networks"—as Leary used to say—parts of *Fantasia* yield a heightened sensitivity, plus the pleasure of basking in yourself.

But other sections of the movie underline the hypocrisy of censorship in this country, from the Forties to the present. Those who worry about obscenity on the screen could treat themselves to a fit at *Fantasia*. Here sex is prettified and distorted for children—transferred to animals, which makes it safe. As some have noted, the Disney creatures have a bewildering sexuality and they switch roles with all the deftness of a mod bisexual. (*The Realist* published a cartoon of the Disney animals "doing all the things they couldn't do while Disney was alive, like balling each other," and those familiar faces look very natural in flagrante delicto.) In *Fantasia* you can't miss the genital obsessions: even a shot of a hippo's uvula manages to be phallic. In *The Nutcracker Suite* a dance of some macho mushrooms is followed by flowers opening and turning inside out in a cleverly vaginal passage. Buttocks are stressed, whether huge and baggy (on elephants), heartshaped (cupids), or coyly exaggerated (on elongated fairies). Bosoms are eliminated—although the female centaurs in Beethoven's *Pastoral Symphony* wear ghastly flower bras—but the animals keep posturing in the pinup poses or the Forties. Their enormous eyes and mouths are especially provocative, as when a frilly fish with languid lids and mammoth bee-stung lips trails her see-through fins like a stripper's veils.

Even evolution is sexy: orgasmic volcanos yield to microscopic organisms teasing one another, and fission is perhaps the most erotic act of all: there's a happy little shudder when a round shape elongates and divides. The castration sequences provoked roars of adult laughter, especially when a big female hippo flattened a sword-shaped male alligator, who later almost deprived a unisex elephant of its trunk and tail. I couldn't fight off a strong spasm of awe: Disney must have known exactly what he was doing, and *Fantasia* is the only pornographic movie I've seen. It might have startled the old animator had he known that his inventions would one day be absorbed by the drug culture, and that his own fantasies would be reshaped by uppers and downers, grass, and the insight of acid.

Death On and Off Broadway*
May 1970

> How nice—to feel nothing, and still get full credit for being alive.
> —*Vonnegut*, Slaughterhouse-Five

Now they say that you can get cancer from swilling low-cal drinks in front of your color TV set. Are artificial sweeteners going to croak you? Much of New York's recent theater has been stiff with artificial sweeteners and spiritual cyclamates, and some critics talk about dying of boredom. Hence it's an appropriate irony for 1970 that the Open Theatre is one of the few groups which gives our theater life; its theme is death.

It's probably hard for foreigners or visitors to realize the degree of death-in that we're feeling here: from the ghetto and Cambodia to the campus, across the hall or upstairs or after lunch or on the way home. Nothing new, of course. It's just that we feel it more than ever. The Open Theatre has mimed the anguish as it mounts each year. Their "ceremonies" are intentionally fragmented—like most native emotions now. In 1968 their nonverbal war games ranged two lines of actors toe-to-toe, making friendly and hostile sounds—squealing and then retching at each other, building to swamp-at-night noises. Then hatred hissed. Moans and mutual comforting followed, plus some happy howling which diminished to whispering and suspicious shrinking apart. Enmity was senseless, but it couldn't be turned off.

In 1969 they uncoiled Jean-Claude van Itallie's *The Serpent*, in which assassinations were played back at us, repeated (as they are on TV and with old random film clips), and then reversed—as by a movie camera run backwards. The actors functioned as parts of computers, chanting "I-am-not-involved . . . I stay alive." In a charade of Eve's temptation, they played with apples and writhed like a whole treeful of snakes with flickering tongues. Soon the apples splashed and split against the floor and Cain killed Abel while the chorus

---

*I wrote this a few weeks after Kent State and Jackson State.

stressed that Cain *wanted* to kill his brother, but had failed to realize that killing Abel would actually cause his death. (Chop-logic is daily food: one of the FBI's motives for investigating the Kent State killings was to determine "whether the civil rights of the students who were shot had been violated.") During the murder, some actors became perfect sheep, baaing on all fours, quietly nibbling grass as Abel died. "Did you know that you could go into eternity screaming with pain?" Haphazard voices punctuated the action: "A field of dead men is very loud! Teeth clack! Bones snap! . . . the last sound is the trumpet of escaping wind." But it all ended blithely with the old song, "We Were Sailing Along on Moonlight Bay": the artificial sweetener once again.

The whole company compiled its newest work—*Terminal*—which begins with the blank-faced incantation, "We come among the living to call upon the dead." With their "Dance on the Graves of the Dead," introduced by listless harmonies on wavery mouth organs, they remind us that there are bones beneath the floor of the church they act in, that everyone living is dying gradually now. They evoke an institute where the not-quite-dead are made up for their appearance after death, while they're cheerfully instructed about embalming: "We stitch the lips together for a more attractive expression. . . . Of course we prefer to work on faces which are already well-preserved." A tall man becomes a jerking, dancing puppet, grinning while he gibbers about the sufferings of his people; his dance grows more frenzied as he assumes a monkey-see-monkey-do accent, parodying a funny dusky native or one of the Vietnamese. The voices of futility build: "Pa, why don't you do something?" "Oh, but I do . . . I train people and they train people. I have children and they have children." There are ghastly bulge-eyed imperson-ations of death; an embalmed corpse wails on a table; bodies hang by their knees and elbows from a coat rack, wasted and unimportant among old clothes. "I was walking down the street—buildings topple—what have I done? I saw a woman chewing at the pavement, she had no teeth—forty-one dead— what have I done?" "What was given me was impossible to work with." Then some are bound and gagged (at that image from the Chicago courtroom, the audience murmured "Bobby Seale"). The dying crawl, arms clutching each other's thighs. At the end they gaze sardonically at the audience while it claps. The Open Theatre has distilled the numbness that seeps through a society which also worships guilt.

Living deadness is also the motif of *Company*, the Broadway hit musical with excellent lyrics and bittersweet music by Stephen Sondheim. *Company* crumbles the tradition of musicals about New York. Unlike *On the Town, Won-derful Town*, and *West Side Story*, it's triumphantly unromantic, undramatic— urban fatigue has replaced excitement and even pain. It's also the first musical I've seen that's focused on the love life of a man: a wan bachelor of thirty-five who recoils from his rich friends' compulsion to marry him off. Their dinner invitations aren't hospitable, but are demands for diversion from couples who don't want to be alone with one another. They sing naggingly at him from terraces and platforms and fire-escapes on an elegant abstract set laced with elevator shafts, in which he rises and sinks in isolation from all the couples who drive each other bananas. Thus a marital chorus: "It's the little things you do together . . . Children you destroy together . . . Becoming a cliché together, / Growing old and gray together / Withering away together / That make marriage a joy." Spouses plant their fantasy lives on him ("Have I Got A Girl For You") and itch to hear what the chicks are like in bed; "Marriage may be where it's been / But it's not where it's at." A couple announces their divorce with bashful dimplings—as though it were an engagement—in keeping with what my parents' generation called "divorced in name only." On a wedding day a bride sings of her terror, while the groom—hunting for his pants—punctuates her horrified aria with "Today Is Forever."

Company drops home truths that any native can savor: "You know what the pulse of this city is?" "A busy signal?" The friends who scare the hero off marriage croon to him, "Poor baby, all alone / Throw a dog a bone and it is still a bone." But he finally climaxes with a dead finale about "Being Alive," entreating "someone" to be a burden, to simply make him feel something: "Someone to hold you too close / Someone to hurt you too deep / Someone to need you too much / Someone to know you too well." While the rational fear of marriage—inspired by the experiences of others—is expertly detailed, it's noticeable that all the women in the show are dumb or drunk or threatening or frantic: "too busy to know that they're fools." The men are just tired or brittle.

As a New York operetta, *Company* is fascinating and irritating; the calculated aridity is valid, but it's hard to bleed over the problems and the weaknesses of the rich. After all, chic is neither our prime crime nor the main source of city suffering. Society may be empty but the subway isn't. And Sondheim's dancing pantsuits and tunics who flavor the coffee with cinnamon and complain about soot on their terraces and envy those who don't diet are not the ultimate New Yorkers. Yet this hymn to unfeeling has a harsh, sour strength that underlines the Seventies' sense of helplessness and the dread of (half-desired) change. As in *Terminal*, the characters protest against being stuck with their lives, against accountability, and the cast of *Company* looks almost as dead as *Terminal's* at the final curtain. It's not an accident.

Nostalging on Broadway
December 1971

Fleeing the present: nuzzling at what you've never known. While teen-agers are reviving the pop culture of the Fifties—pony tails and Howdy Doody, old Elvis ducktails and slow, wailing songs about loving forever and ever, really and truly—some of us who were students in the Fifties have to remember that we ourselves shunned the period. As apolitical aesthetes we escaped into history and English literature, snugging into earlier centuries while turning off the tube. We blocked out most of McCarthy and Eisenhower, feeling that the past was superior to the present—just as Europe was superior to America, or art to politics

Hence it's rum for the Silent Generation to get a dose of the Fifties now. While the cultural landscape is smeared with revivals, plus reincarnations of old material, it's astounding to realize that the new nostalgia is only about fourteen months old. It expanded soon after the emotional exhaustion following Kent State, the bomb that killed a researcher at the University of Wisconsin, the sense of futility about nonviolence *and* violence, the final inability to respect professional politicians or to expect much of the immediate future. So—we've been blanketed by the immediate past. But the presentation isn't joyfully escapist: instead there's a theme of self-flagellation, which is even reflected in two tremendous hits on Broadway.

Under murky mauve lights, beneath a tattered, spleen-colored map of the U.S., *Lenny* spills out images and facts from the life of the satirist Lenny Bruce, who died of drugs in 1966. The show starts in 1951. The play's based on Bruce's own routines and Cliff Gorman is brilliantly hysterical as a comic falling apart during his own act. The message is that Bruce was "a*hedoviz* time," as my neighbors kept remarking loudly. Bruce's trials for obscenity and narcotics, his marriage to a druggy stripper, his sputtering, frenzied gags about rebellious prisoners whom the warden orders shot, North Korea, contraceptives as blown-up balloons, his wife as "the heroine of his nocturnal emissions," homosexuals, the 1958 recession, the Lone Ranger, lesbians ("It's hard to spot dykes, because sometimes we're married to them"), nice Jewish boys from Brooklyn, exhibitionists, Orphan Annie, niggers, spics, and grease-balls, how President Kennedy "jacked off during the Cuban missile crisis," sex with a chicken, "Grandma Moses' tits and Norman Rockwell's ass," and a song about "coming too quickly or not at all"—all evoke the man who loathed racial and sexual hypocrisy, especially the self-deceptions of the "liberal-schmiberal." In the Fifties and early Sixties the style was ponderously ana-lyzed as sick humor. Now, since four-letter words have so little impact and fuck practically means hello, Bruce's personal desperation emerges much more strongly than his social rage—which isn't the dead man's fault.

There's a nice moment with Nixon as a drunken dummy sitting on Ike's knee, discussing the 1958 headline "Nixon Stoned in Caracas", and a lively scene where Christ and Moses return nakedly to earth while the pope and a cardinal panic over the reception committee and call each other schmucks, and lepers play trombones. I like dirty jokes and also very bad ones. But here many of the old boffolas shriek with the strain of trying to be startling: the boy killed by Leopold and Loeb "was a snotty kid anyway;" or, "Ya can't stop masturbating gradually, ya gotta do it cold jerky." For those of us who never saw Bruce, it seems unfair that he should be allowed to appear forlornly unfunny—although I'm willing to take his comic genius on faith and de-lighted to agree that the Fifties were hideously stuffy.

Hair's director, Tom O'Horgan, and the author, Julian Barry, have cel-ebrated Bruce's private anguish but confused it with his fierce protests against society. Backed by vast Mount Rushmore-like heads of Nixon, LBJ, and Kennedy, Bruce's final bankrupt misery—as he thrashes on the floor with his own tapes, unleashing great animal retches and then cackling like a tape recorder run backward—is as devastating as it should be. But then the direc-tor can't resist showbiz: Nixon's huge pâpier-maché face opens to reveal Bruce nude and dead over a toilet bowl. Lights blink inside Nixon's skull as Bruce's corpse is photographed, flutes peep sadly, and it's easy to imagine that Bruce would have sneered at such a chic image for any death, including his own. Yet the audience adored it. So the old device of turning a hearse into a band-wagon still seems foolproof. The play certainly insisted that Bruce took all our sins upon him—and that reminds me how our quality lit. courses of the Fifties taught us to look for scapegoats (as well as waning moons), and that redemption through suffering was a favorite literary theme.

Follies, in which aging stars reunite at a last party for a Ziegfeldish theater that's about to be demolished, is an impressive piece of musical history. Stephen Sondheim has written songs of the Twenties, Thirties, and Forties, which define the styles of each period; Alexis Smith, Dorothy Collins, Yvonne DeCarlo, and Fifi D'Orsay leap about as living memories. The middle-aged hoof their old routines while the ghosts of their young selves, sheathed in fantastic blacks and whites, mimic their movements behind them. Old troop-ers reassure each other that they haven't changed—"You look as cute as ever"—as they glide down steps with hands on hips or arms extended in pinup gestures of the Forties. A fat woman does high kicks; a bald man turns a somersault; as shapeless bodies dance with grace and gusto, you chide yourself for being depressed by their looks. *Follies* uses elderly people well, yet it also uses them

cruelly: by making them act winsome or downright pert. It rather recalls the
occasion when the writer Anthony West, who was researching old age homes,
saw one institution where a great iron grill divided the two sexes. The director said, "Well, you wouldn't want them *breeding*, would you?"

Amid the rhymes of "eerie" and "dreary," two former showgirls and their
jaded husbands reveal that their marriages are lousy and rather frantically
try to relive their youth. A raucously romantic little woman grabs uselessly at
an old boy friend, even though she has clung to her husband: "On his shoulder / I won't get older," while he sings, "The girls I'll never know I'm too
tired for." The need for illusion fights with the sense of self-disgust—"I just
wanted her. Until I had her;" "I thought you needed me." "For *what?*"—and
no one gets what he wants, including rejection. A man yawns while he tells
his wife how terrific she used to be in bed. There's some deliberately tired
wisecracking: "I love the way you hate it when I'm happy and you're not." At
the end the spouses plod off together, resolving to start afresh, which is impossible.

The prize-winning *Follies* has a weary fascination, especially when the vital-
ity of old numbers is pitched against the characters' own numbness. And the
theme of show folk trying and failing to live out the fantasies of stage life is a
rich one. But the virtuosity of its range is weakened by the fidelity to period
styles—despite the top hats and feathers and bugle beads and marvelous tap
dancing, many of the songs are soupy or boring. We've had bitter musicals
for over ten years now; *Follies* merely carries self-dislike further than
Sondheim's own *Company*. Countless graffiti have announced that nostalgia
isn't what it used to be.

Part V

Contradicting the Conventions

The Democrats
July 1972

The Laocoön: outside the Eden Roc Hotel, statues of the Winged Victory, the Apollo Belvedere, and an unidentified goddess were momentarily looped together in a snarl of TV cables. Well before the convention began, they were released. But the brief alliance of those snowy stone figures stays with me as an image for some of the coalitions formed around McGovern's nomination: a simultaneous struggling that might not last. To some of us, much that happened in Miami Beach appeared to be very fragile and many collaborations seemed temporary.

Infinite commentators told you that those who fought in the Chicago streets of 1968 were inside the Convention Hall in 1972, that this was the youngest, blackest, most female etcetera. On the floor it seemed much less so; one most powerfully felt the presence of the old pols, the hacks, and the establishment. Yet it was hard to find the edge of some people's cynicism; for many—except for the youngest McGovern delegates—cynicism overlapped with hope: some cautious hope. While those who've campaigned for months usually end by believing all the puff they've been putting out, some of McGovern's supporters seemed to believe less of it than they had in the spring. But when McGovern was nominated, others behaved as though they'd already won the November election. The evidence of both mentalities swelled the doubts of yet other participants.

Amid all the frenzy, after some eighteen months of uphill work, what seemed to be lacking was almost any sense of consequence—the idea that we might really have to live with what happened within that Hall for the next four years. Here were thousands of people jellied in the aspic of fatigue: a stiff but transparent wall had thickened between them and the issues. Some seemed dulled to what McGovern was supposed to represent, such as the rights of blacks or women or the poor; they could think only of gaining delegates. And in some cases, certain McGovern aides seemed immune to anything but scoring small points for their own power.

From the first night, at that moment when the backs of our hands were stamped with invisible ink while the band played, "What The World Needs

Now Is Love, Sweet Love"—I kept peering at my paw to see if some stigmata would surface—to each evening's battle for a floor pass, and then diving into that sea of bodies with the credentials slung around one's neck like a life-preserver, or watching others emerge from the floor looking half-drowned, one saw the waves of collective numbness spreading. After three days some of us felt that we lived at the Hall, that we would return each night for years to come. But no wonder that security was tight—since it was quite easy to break. On the last night I saw dozens from Flamingo Park, draped with passes, also someone who'd been rumored to have been blown up in the Eleventh Street townhouse occupied by Weatherpeople in 1970. (I managed to gasp, "I thought you were . . . in Europe.")

You don't have to be dead to be a ghost, I realized. Until Ted Kennedy appeared on the final night, igniting the kind of excitement which might be provoked by the Resurrection, he seemed almost as ghostly as his brothers. Even news photos of his portly figure racing his small son on a Squaw Island beach seemed to recall Chappaquiddick.

Despite one low-keyed rendition of "Hello, Lyndon"—which nearly gave me a hallucination of that jovial face swimming up on the huge projection screen—LBJ was hardly mentioned. Kennedy did say " . . . and Lyndon B. Johnson promised us that we shall overcome, and with George McGovern we shall." There were cheers—but not so loud as those for the lettuce boycott. Johnson is like the living dead and almost no one wanted to raise him.

In Miami Beach, where the average age is 65.2, I was told that a number of vehicles which collect the dead or the dying are made to look as though they belong to the Fire Department; no one wants to see so many ambulances. Bunched and pleated brown flesh, withered feet in sandals: somehow the elderly look much older when they're deeply tanned and wearing orange or purple playclothes. Hence the irony of many skin-flick marquees, which are labeled "Adults Only."

Nowhere else but Miami have I seen such a number of whitehaired couples holding hands. At a large rally for Senior Citizens, where the White House was accused of neglecting the old, I even saw a few freckled fists raised. A speaker announced that four years of Nixon was enough; "*Dig* it!" said the bald head beside me. When McGovern promised to improve the lot of those over sixty, a skeptical grandmother kept repeating, "Beautiful *words*." Some young people held up signs: "Long Hairs and White Hairs/Struggle—Unite" and "We Are The Senior Citizens Of Tomorrow." The elderly made a rather unruly audience: they pushed and shoved more than many crowds I've known and wouldn't stop talking during the speeches, not even when their juniors tried to shush them. *The Miami Herald* had a nervous headline: "Heart-Pill Culture Feels Strange Surge of Youth."

One of the more political events during the convention was the Wedding of the Generations. Allen Ginsberg and others had decided that it was time

to end "youth chauvinism." At Lummus Park, close to lots of retirement hotels, Ginsberg and his friends decorated a lamppost like a maypole, backed
an altar with vast bunches of flowers, and handed out chrysanthemums. First
a rabbi performed a symbolic wedding between two old people. The rabbi
told the spectators to sit down "on Mother Earth," and then compared marriage to wine: "The older it is, the better it gets." Ginsberg in a yarmulka led
the crowd in a slow, winding circle, while he played on his harmonium and
sang: "The younger generation is living in a Marx Brothers movie . . . / Do
you remember the Marx Brothers movies when you were young / And everyone was happy and Harpo Marx did not have a tongue?" He sang to the ring
of seated white heads: "The younger generation—because it felt all alone /
Married the entire world / So that it would not turn to stone . . . / If everyone over seventy would take us by the hand"—which they did—"Everybody
in Miami Beach is married to you and to me." Revy Wikler, the author of *Sex
and the Senior Citizen*, gave out copies of her book, which were flourished aloft
while Ginsberg intoned: "The generation war is at an end."

Abbie Hoffman, in a shirt sprinkled with pineapples, climbed onto a stepladder and read a statement in Yiddish. Some clucked when they heard his
accent: "It's not good, but he tries, he tries."

Ed Sanders, former Fug and Manson biographer, read a salute to his grandmother, who made it with her future husband in 1888.

> We are here on a tropical
> beach to tell you that we love
> you. . . .
> And we have changed
> the mode of love
> > & we have
> > changed the mode of our will
> > & we have changed
> > into true-tempered humans of peace. . . .

Everyone took a glass of orange juice and Ginsberg sang "Shalom" again
and again, accompanied by Peter Orlovsky in a patchwork vest and pigtails,
while flowers were thrown over the delighted crowd. A photographer exclaimed, "This beats all the Bar Mitzvahs I've ever shot!" and the TV camera-
men looked ready to faint in a body. Then the young and the old seized
hands and danced the hora and sang "Sholom Aleichem" and "Hava Nagilah."
One young woman said, "Let's do Mayim;" an old woman shouted, "You good
Jewish girl!" and embraced her. Ginsberg jumped off the ladder to join the
dancing and several grandmothers cried in protest, "You'll break your foot!"
He sang an impromptu hymn, and everyone repeated his lines:

> McGovern will win this year
> The war will be over this year

> The old will have peace this year
> The young will find the old dear.
> To the Vietcong I give a big cheer.
> The old in Vietnam need a cheer...
> The old folks in Vietnam are here ...
> The old in Miami don't fear...
> The young and the old are all here
> The young grow older each year
> The old and the young are more near.

An old woman in a wheelchair kept time with a chrysanthemum. Then she hollered, "The hell with Nixon!" and the crowd whooped. Commanding, "Harmonize, Allen!" she and Ginsberg sang "An Old-Fashioned Girl," "I Wonder Who's Kissing Her Now," and "Once I Met A Blue-Eyed Sailor." He began "Last Night the Nightingale Woke Me," but was interrupted by old women crowding up to hug him. One said, "Allen, I've been reading about your trials and tribulations and your miseries." He answered that he wasn't miserable now. She replied that she could see that, and went on to praise his poem, "Kaddish," which details the mental illness of his dead mother. She added, "Your mother was one of us gals, Allen."

Several old people told me how much they'd feared the kids before they arrived—had dreaded muggings and purse-snatchings by dopefiends. An old man added, "Now I've got three sleeping in my house."

At sunset, we were back singing around Ginsberg on his stepladder by the sea: "We've had a mystic marriage here." As the TV crew packed up: "And now the eye of the world departs from us /We hope the cameraman will give us his blessing."

> Finally:
> Behold the common family
> Extends from here to Saigon over the sea.
> We hope the elders of Hanoi
> Participate in Miami Beach's joy.
> We hope the people far and near
> Are able to dispel the words of fear.
> We hope the myth that we're at war
> Is ended here for evermore.

The next morning I heard Kirk Douglas and Dinah Shore soberly discussing the generations on TV. They decided that there should be "more reaching out."

When some Yips came to Miami Beach weeks before the convention, they stayed in cheap hotels where they encountered the elderly. They began to focus on what the old and the young have in common in a society which mistrusts both. They visited Senior Citizens' groups, shared meals, and tried to diminish the community's alarms about invasion. They also gave out balloons reading, "We're your friends." For some evening meetings, the young brought guitars and their seniors had mandolins; they taught each other their instruments and exchanged songs.

A very young girl told me, "We've got to revive respect. So many of them have a history of picket lines—they kept fighting, the way their middle-aged children never did." Meanwhile the elders of Miami Beach have their own divisions. Some are left of center, with a lot of early union experience; others are far to the right. Those I met said they had been for Humphrey, because of his initial efforts on civil rights and Medicare, but that they would vote for McGovern.

Among the 87,000 year-round residents of Miami Beach, some 55,000 receive some form of Social Security. There were many complaints that the old were under-represented at the Democratic Convention. With the Yips, some picketed the La Gorce country club for discrimination against Jews. One old woman said that perhaps her contemporaries in Miami Beach were some of the most independent in their generation—because they lived there on their own, rather than with their younger relatives. Almost every Miami Beach native I talked with came from New York or New Jersey.

I heard many elderly people praising the young visitors. It was repeated that grandparents and grandchildren often get on better than parents and children. A woman of seventy-eight said, "The forgotten people are the young and the old. Lots of us are broke, and they can't get decent jobs." She added that she came from a very strict family, which "didn't approve of" her: "That comes back to me when I see the kids now." While she and her friends were dubious about grass and also about mothers holding jobs—"You cook, you bake, you sew, you bring your children up. *Then* you go out to work. Not before"—they were also very tolerant about new ways of life they would never share.

Some took food to the young campers in Flamingo Park. One woman, horrified to see them eating peanut butter, asked how it could give them strength for demonstrations. She returned with knishes and matzohs; others brought lots of bagels and cream cheese, and gallons of turkey soup. One leaflet suggested:

A LITTLE CHICKEN SOUP NEVER HURT ANYONE
SO MAKE A MITZVAH IN THE PARK

There is a pipeline between the Senior Citizens and the kids
    Which you can fill with Love
    and a little chicken soup
    or a kugel or a kigel
    or a few cookies
    or whatever
What could be bad . . . ? ? ?

What to do?   COOK AND BRING
Where?   Flamingo Park, of course
Who do we give to?   Anybody and everyone
(Who wouldn't like your cooking?)
What do I get?   **Naches
   **Love
   **Lots of smiles and thanks and whatever
else they have to share with you
   **And a little more understanding on the
chicken soup pipeline
What could it hurt???

In Flamingo Park I felt rather as though I was back in the Sixties; especially since so much was going on at once, it seemed like the old mixed media. Frisbees sailed past my nose while about forty marchers took off under SDS banners for the Playboy Club—"We-don't-want-your-fucking-war" was hastily changed to "racist war" after two old people said *"Oh"*—while a few Jews for Jesus sang about rocking in Abraham's bosom, others in sweatshirts stenciled SCIENCE NOT POLITICS preached "cybercultural revolution power"; an evangelist yelled, "De*struc*tion is coming *soooon!*" and some wistful young Bible readers crooned about Jacob and Esau to indifferent ears, while the bodies of those on a smoke-in dangled from the branches of a giant banyan tree or lay coiled among its roots. There I heard a heated argument about whether coffee is really a drug: "Not if you don't *abuse* it." I've never seen so much grass in public, and the police didn't interfere. But I saw none on bad trips or heavily stoned. There was some worried discussion about catching "the mad shitter" who had been fouling the pool where some swam naked at night. A twilight feast was designed to dishonor Nixon, whose face was outlined in pieces of watermelon lying on the ground; a sign said, "Nixon Is A *Seedy* Character—Eat Nixon Tonight." Many did, while a stern young black with a bullhorn warned them to *"deal* with your rinds " and not leave them lying about. At night the park became a world of split screens: a movie of the bombing of a Vietnamese hospital was projected on a white wall, while about thirty feet away an outdoor color TV set showed cops chasing robbers to those who lay upon the ground.

The mood was mainly mellow, but some of the Jesus people produced tensions. Their attitudes towards dope and women angered some, and although one old woman urged tolerance over a bullhorn—"It's just their trip"— which brought applause and shouts of "Grandma Power!" some began to bait a grizzled hysteric who screamed, "You've *got* to come to Jesus!" They circled round him laughing while he ordered them to "throw away crutches like sex," and denounced marijuana because it wasn't "a seed-bearing plant." (He got a lot of corrections on that one.) He also outraged a group of gay men by insisting that they were dirty sinners. While some feminists sang, "We no longer will be prisoners in the same old gilded cage, / That's why we're marching on," another religioso shouted that they were "sexual devils." A young man in overalls growled at him, "Quiet, *garbage-mouth.*"

Stew Albert of YIP addressed the crowd as the irritations accelerated. He said, "We're not against Christianity," but that many of the Jesus persons were using their religion to build a right-wing movement. (Of course some also claim that Jesus was a radical. But few of that viewpoint were present.) Albert said that it troubled him to hear the Jesus people "using our language and our culture:" calling themselves freaks or speaking of liberation. However: "We have no right to put them down—because parts of our own movement have been really fucked up, really ugly. So some of our people went into bad drugs—and then off them into the Jesus movement. It's *our* fault . . . We have to be self-critical now . . . Why has our movement become a tourist attraction nightmare?" He urged his contemporaries to rebuild their programs—"We need to be so that McGovern will listen to us"—and to recognize the Jesus people as a by-product of the drug culture. He got some sturdy applause. And I thought of his speech that night when I passed the old man in the neck-and-chest brace outside the Convention Hall, where he sat in a buggy drawn by a small burro labelled, I'M PULLING FOR WALLACE, with a tiny burro reading, ME TOO. The owner said that his burros were descended from the one Jesus rode into Jerusalem.

On the first night of the convention, as Ralph Abernathy and a black saxophonist led a march of the National Welfare Rights Organization and others, I again flashed on the Sixties when Abernathy included the verse about "black and white together" in "We Shall Overcome." I hadn't heard that line for several years. Old people smiled and waved from their balconies, but I doubt if they heard a few Zippies shouting, "Free Arthur Bremer! Give him a second chance!" Outside the Convention Hall's $75,000 hibiscus-covered chain-link fence, where you could see guards with legs akimbo through the flowers, there was a rally which stressed that the Democrats—"who are *supposed* to be the party of the poor"—had turned their backs on poor people's issues. Speakers repeated their demands for a $6,500 yearly income for a family of four. (This is the minimum needed according to surveys by the U.S. Department of Labor, Bureau of Labor Statistics.) After the rally, Abernathy's group and some Vietnam vets pleaded with the crowd to disperse. (The theme throughout the convention was "Don't mess it up for McGovern.") But some of those who remained stormed the hibiscus fence and brought a part of it down. Injuries were slight, clubs and gas weren't used, but there was a little Mace.

The small SDS meetings I attended seemed like parodies of the Sixties. As was evident on campuses in the spring of 1972, they have a gift for picking the wrong issues or for confusing the public about their main concerns. I suspected that the extremely young SDSers I saw had joined very recently, probably well after the organization had divided into warring factions in 1969.

They seemed to know nothing about the best years of SDS, and appeared to be trying to catch up with the experiences of their elder siblings. So they sounded like an anachronism—even on the issues which still absorb us all.

Outside Flamingo Park, an ice cream vendor aroused their wrath because he had raised the price of banana splits from 50 cents to 90 cents. The filthy capitalist was denounced with all the passion once reserved for LBJ; a young man urged others to link arms around the ice cream truck to prevent people from buying. A Vietnam vet rather wearily said the guy wasn't a capitalist, that he probably just broke even. But few even wanted to boycott him. By the time that SDS and others confronted McGovern in the lobby of the Doral Hotel, many of his delegates were just as disturbed as they by his statement about keeping residual troops in Thailand. (Later he said that any such troops would be withdrawn after he'd had ninety days in office.) But SDS and some Zippies made it seem as though the legalization of marijuana was just as important as the war. Again they lost the support they might have had.

One of SDS's major targets was a fashion show sponsored by Mrs. Reuben Askew in honor of the candidates' wives. About twenty-five demonstrators marched around the circular marble lobby of the Americana Hotel—the circles made me think of Ginsberg's ceremony, and the spheroid nature of this convention—shouting, "The rich get fat! The poor are starving! A thousand dollars a dress!" And: "More jobs, higher welfare, no-more-fashion-shows!" They jigged off, yelling in a crescendo, "Attica means! Fight back! Welfare mothers! Fight back! The Vietnamese! Fight back! SDS! Fights back—fights back—fights back!"

Inside, where a large gathering of middle-aged women—many wearing little plastic oranges in their hair—clapped timidly when told, "Today we want you to meet the women behind the men behind the wheels of Florida," three young women from SDS began to stage a "poor women's fashion show," showing the jeans and T-shirts that could be bought on welfare. "Notice the worn-out heels—" They were very roughly ejected. A grey-haired woman in a long printed gown came up to tell them, "A lot of us are with you," but they shrieked, "Wait till the revolution!" The display of clothes from Saks that followed almost made me feel that the fashion copy had been written by or for SDS. As the models pranced in to wavering organ music, we heard "It's cotton canvas that's *in* this year," and "The American closet is red, white and blue, and it's *you!*" Silk moiré pajamas by Mollie Parnis appeared to the tune of "The Caissons Go Rolling Along," and a white jersey caftan flowed by to "The Stars and Stripes Forever." Different regions were symbolized by colors—"For the East, it's soft gray interpretations" (flannel)—but my favorite was Chicago: "A city of contrasting power: vibrant in coral or restrained in beige and camel." Chicago means baby-blue for policemen's helmets to me.

Throughout the convention, YIP (which now wants to be called the Youth International Party, not Yippies) was assailed by the Zippies. There aren't many of the latter; they're led by garbage-analyst A. J. Weberman and Tom Forcade, director of the Underground Press Syndicate, who had claimed that Abbie Hoffman had ripped him off for editorial work on *Steal This Book*. (Hoffman said that Forcade didn't contribute. The facts are uncertain.) The Zippies also said that Rubin and Hoffman were elitists who had sold out the revolution—mainly by urging people to vote for McGovern. The Zips threw pies and water in hotels—frightening the old people there—and then said YIP had done it. The Zippies also announced that they would have a Che Guevara Appreciation Day, which would have infuriated the large conservative population of Cuban refugees in Miami. Fortunately it was called off.

Several old people told me they thought Forcade was a cop and that the Zips were paid provocateurs. One elderly woman said, "*Plants.* I think I'm seeing plants. To discredit the youth movement." Meanwhile the Yips, who were trying to establish themselves as a community organization, also had some fond words for Martha Mitchell: "She's really one of us. And she's being treated like one of those Russian writers who gets called crazy." A few discussed the notion of forming Martha Mitchell Brigades for the Republican Convention.

I spent the last afternoon of the convention with Tom Michaud, a deserter from the Marines who planned to give himself up on the floor of the Hall that night. He was a very quiet Connecticut Yankee from a French Catholic family, who had spent some eleven years in an orphanage in Lowell, Massachusetts—"Hell's Angels territory, you know." He had enlisted at seventeen "for general patriotic reasons," and the need of a job. He'd volunteered for six months' service in Vietnam, where he served in the 3rd Marine Division, 3rd Reconnaissance Battalion, at Quang Tri. There he'd turned against the war and the military after a few months. "When you're in the bush, and you get fired on, you just turn around and pull the trigger. You don't even know who you're firing at." After three years' service, he split from Camp Lejeune, North Carolina. He then spent three years underground, mainly in New England, where he'd worked as a maintenance man in big hotels in Boston, in a hunter's camp in Vermont, on a compost project in New Hampshire. He described life on the run: "For the first six months, I was looking over my shoulder, looking in post offices to see if they had my picture on the wall . . . Then I got used to it. But I couldn't use my own name, or make any long-range plans—I'd like to buy land and build my own house—and I couldn't be open with people: that felt bad. I was tired of having to hide something." At moments his manner was withdrawn—as he had trained himself to be; at others he talked rapidly with the relief of one who has been silent for too long. He'd decided to surrender himself to the Democratic Party because amnesty—which McGovern had mentioned so often in his campaign—had become a muted issue at the convention. Michaud felt that he represented another 100,000 deserters, some of whom might be likelier to surface after a test-case like his own.

On turning himself in, he might get a dishonorable discharge—or a maximum sentence of five years' hard labor. "I'm not nervous about it now. But when I hear the helicopters here all night—it sounds like being back in the Nam." We stared out the window: high up in a Miami Beach hotel, with blue skies reflected in the pool, it hardly felt like being underground. But he was a country-dweller to whom simple freedoms meant a great deal, and I didn't like the thought of him in jail.

That night Michaud revealed himself by talking to TV interviewers on the floor, near the California delegation. Meanwhile dozens of flags massed and paraded down the aisles to a military march tune; we were fenced in by flags while the audience pledged allegiance and stood through the national anthem. Michaud and his lawyer, Tod Ensign of the Safe Return Committee, which works with "self-retired veterans," spoke quietly about the war, while TV reporters grew cynical: "How do we *know* you're a deserter, or that you were ever in the Marines?" The crowd thickened around them, while (by coincidence) a Gold Star Mother gave a strong antiwar speech from the platform, and then a Vietnam vet from Alabama praised the war and attacked amnesty. At this point frantically upset security men rushed Michaud off the floor, enraged to find a visitor without credentials. Soon the FBI hustled him away in an avocado green car. He was later delivered to the Marines, who removed him to his original point of departure: Camp Lejeune.*

I'd never thought it would be possible to feel sorry for Hubert Humphrey. The memories of his pro-war speeches are still so powerful—well before that stunner of 1967, when he referred to Vietnam as "our greatest adventure, and a wonderful one it is." Sitting in the Convention Hall in '72 there was the ashiness of reading his booklet—headed, "Tomorrow is the first day of the rest of our lives," a line borrowed from the rock musical, *Salvation*—after he had withdrawn. His positions on tax reform ("Our tax system is rigged against the working family") and Vietnam ("Our prisoners home, our involvement ended within ninety days") had the tired desperation of someone who knew that he was already defeated. Many of us felt a new surge of anger when he tried to stop McGovern by such tactics as making him appear like an abortion-freak, as he had in the Catholic neighborhoods of Omaha. But as many noted, Humphrey's earlier liberal history was permanently cancelled before Chicago, and he probably knew now that he had been beaten for '72 in '68.

Quite a few of McGovern's supporters left Miami Beach feeling they knew less about what their candidate represented than they had before the convention. I heard some repeating Jane Fonda's sentence, which was quoted in

* On September 20th, Michaud, who had pleaded guilty to "unauthorized absence," was sentenced to a year's hard labor, foreiture of all pay and allowances and a dishonorable discharge. His military counsel, protesting the harshness of the sentence, argued that he felt that the court was influenced by President Nixon's acceptance speech at the Republican convention, in which Nixon had opposed amnesty.

the *Washington Post:* "I think he would wage wars with a heavy heart." They'd been warned by many—even by Abbie Hoffman—that McGovern would move to the middle as he drew closer to the nomination. People kept saying "But we want to elect him" to those who were demoralized by seeing so many of the minority planks voted down, including those on tax reform, frozen rents for the poor, civil rights for homosexuals, and government-subsidized housing.

Perhaps one of the most crucial (and often neglected) aspects of political campaigns is not so much what a candidate represents but what voters *think* he represents. Some of McGovern's young troops—as well as some of the opposition—*thought* he would be friendly to abortion or to a more substantial guaranteed income for the poor. Yet McGovern's own radical following was asked to vote against the very issues which mattered most to them. The fact that these planks were defeated may not be clear to some who deplore McGovern: I'm willing to wager that some still believe that he upholds abortion on demand and "free money." (*The Miami Herald* continued to trot out nice headlines: "Antiwar Issue Plagues McGovern On Eve Of Success"; " . . . And An Unkooky Platform.") But some of the young went home uncertain whether they would continue to work for him. Angered on learning that "the open convention" was slickly and thoroughly controlled by a new machine, they were also chewing on the old discovery that you can change the person but not the system. Some older radicals considered the disillusionment to be educational: "There's nothing like a toe in your ass to raise your consciousness." But McGovern had acquired one of the mustiest of politicians' problems: risking some of his earlier constituents in the efforts to gain others.

Staring at the screaming crowd on the floor on the final night, a 21-year-old delegate said to me, "I guess the grown-ups need a freak-out now and then."

The women's feelings were among the most diverse. Some were immensely heartened by the number of women delegates (38 percent as opposed to 13 percent in 1968), and by the solid women's rights plank which was rammed through. (There wasn't a word about women's rights in the 1968 platform.) After Mayor Daley and 58 of his delegates were thrown out and replaced by more women and more blacks under the party's new rules, I heard a few young black women shouting happily, "Shaft the Shamrock!" But it was steadily repeated that too few women were included in policy-making, although feminists of all ages and backgrounds kept meeting in hotel bathrooms and lobbies to organize support for the women's movement.

Many were extremely bitter about the defeat of the abortion plank—while others insisted that its passage would have sealed McGovern's defeat in November. Some considered abortion "the one non-negotiable demand." An audience of women who had hugely cheered McGovern became suddenly indignant when he dodged a question about abortion by cutting his speech short and promptly leaving; the chant of "We want McGovern" was almost drowned out by those who changed to "We want abortions!" Many were disgusted when he said on another occasion that "the abortion question . . . must be resolved at the state level." Some McGovern aides later admitted that the plank—which also included sterilization and birth control—would have passed had they not worked against it. The actual wording read: "In matters relating to human reproduction, each person's right to privacy, freedom of choice and individual conscience should be fully respected, consistent with relevant Supreme Court decisions." To those who said abortions would be legal throughout the country "some day," many replied that it's hard to ask anyone to wait for an abortion.

Some women were also very disturbed by the manipulations of the McGovern team concerning the South Carolina delegation, which had only 28 percent women—when the state contains 51 percent. The National Women's Political Caucus tried to replace nine men with nine women. McGovern had promised his full support on this challenge. However, fearing that winning the credentials on South Carolina would risk losing the credentials on California (due to some parliamentary fudge), the McGovern aides arranged some nimble vote-switching, so the challenge was defeated. Some felt that McGovern's staff had overridden his wishes on this matter; others thought he simply hadn't understood it. For certain women South Carolina was very important as a symbol; for others it wasn't crucial when the California delegates might be at stake. But throughout this convention, symbols were considered a test of McGovern's sincerity.

Moreover, many were appalled by the TV coverage of women's issues or representatives. Cissy Farenthold finished second behind Eagleton in the balloting, but her actual nomination by Fanny Lou Hamer hadn't been shown—it was time for everyone's commercial. Walter Cronkite joked about "a lady named Farenthold," but failed to realize that her nomination was serious, or that it also signified a rebellion by the women who had been promised backing on abortions and on South Carolina. There were also many grim remarks about the "white-out" of Shirley Chisholm: "As far as the media is concerned, Shirley's name is 'others.' They just talked about the big candidates 'and others.' " And the ridicule of women—and the habit of judging them by their faces—was a familiar groundnote throughout the convention. I heard a cameraman grumbling that there weren't "enough pretty ones." When Chisholm arose to speak, the man behind me laughed and said, "If only she could fix her buckteeth!"

But Florynce Kennedy, the black lawyer and founder of the Feminist Party, said she felt that women hadn't yet worked hard enough, and that some were still relying on men's efforts. She urged women to elect local pro-abortion candidates, and to "put the foetus-fetishists out of office." She added, "But it's a sad sack scene: how little people work. We still want the husband to provide; we say: come on *George*, bring home the *bacon*, bring us an abortion plank. As though we expected him to bring it to us from the store on the way home. We're too busy saying he's backsliding, asking: Georrrge, did you bring the *wine?*"

As Ms. Kennedy packed her bags in her hotel while talking with a few friends, those who spoke of their disappointment in the media were chided for their expectations: "Look, telling people that Muskie was a front-runner is like telling you that Arrid Extra-Dry will get you a husband." She was also eloquent on the subject of "loserism," especially among black people and women. "It's neurotic to want something and then to talk in a way that's likely to prevent it happening. Liberals stand in the way of what they want—maybe because they didn't get what they wanted in childhood. It's pathological to put McGovern down when you want Nixon out . . . When you were a child, in the family car, you misbehaved and your parents said: *Wait till I get you home.* I feel the same: we should put McGovern in the White House and *then* make fire under his ass." She slammed the lid of a bulging suitcase. "But people who've been oppressed don't trust their leaders or themselves: they nearly elect someone and then they kick over the milkpail. . . . It's part of fear. Success imposes a tremendous burden on you. Failure leaves you free—to whine and wail. Agonizing instead of organizing is typical of all oppressed people."

At this point someone looked out the window and reported that the hotel staff was trying to clean a large swimming pool with one small can of Ajax. Laughter exploded when it was called a metaphor for the women's movement.

Flo Kennedy gave us some cold fried chicken and we gnawed away as she continued: "Once McGovern had a clear path to the nomination, everyone pounced on him and did a piranha bit. They tore off his flesh. The bones were just about to go when he lost the California delegates—then they could tolerate him again. But only just . . . I'm telling students to work for McGovern; they've got nothing else to do between jerking off and going to the laundromat. Not that he's great. But we gotta get rid of Nixon. You see, we never really recovered from the victory of getting Johnson out. So we weren't angry enough at Nixon. And we get a function-lock on our ass when we get what you call success. Then we go into a catatonic seizure for three or four years."

The analysts and the delegates and the press and the very young drifted away from Miami Beach, still arguing that *something* had happened, or that little had, that the "difference from Chicago" was highly significant or unimportant. He's not a radical: older liberals told each other happily, while some of the young shared that revelation—glumly. There were those who said that they'd "give the system one last chance," others who talked of regrouping for 1976, some who felt wiped out and said they might not vote, and a few optimists. Most agreed that the disregard for working people was probably disastrous. But there were almost some flights to magic: did merely criticizing McGovern cast a bad spell, ensuring Nixon's re-election? Many seemed quite superstitious, but few seemed really sure of their own feelings.

Hindsight: The local astrologers had been pessimistic all along: well before Miami Beach, they'd warned that the eclipse of the sun on the first night of the Democratic Convention was going to be destructive to McGovern. After the Eagleton uproar was underway, people kept speaking of "accidents" that would influence the presidential election: Wallace's paralysis, Chappaquiddick, Muskie's televised tears in New Hampshire, or Eagleton's reticence about his three sojourns in hospital for clinical depression. Soon his mental health seemed less of an issue than his reluctance to tell the truth. And when McGovern delayed on dumping his running-mate, some of his former fans began to mention Adlai Stevenson's vacillations. As Mary McGrory wrote, McGovern's keenest supporters did "not applaud his loyalty to a man who had duped him." And as McGovern himself admitted, the whole crisis obscured the issues of the war and the economy.

Others were disturbed afresh that McGovern still wanted that pinnacle of stability, Ted Kennedy. Indeed Eagleton's suppression of facts reminded some of Kennedy's first responses to Chappaquiddick. We bleakly remembered that the Democrats' vice presidential candidate was supposed to show up the irrationalities of Agnew. Rep. Ronald Dellums of California said, "Senator Eagleton on the couch is a thousand times better for this country in these times than Vice President Agnew standing up." But Eagleton's murky record gave Nixon the opportunity to speak of Agnew as "a man of poise, calm, and judgment." When Barry Goldwater praised Eagleton and said that his medical history was not important, it showed what a gift he was to those opposing McGovern.

As many agreed, 1972 was not a year for charisma. Some voters seemed almost relieved by their own lack of interest in the personalities of Nixon or McGovern. But for a couple of weeks, Eagleton's was the dominant personality in the election year, and he seemed to revel in promoting himself.

Toward the end of Eagleton's eighteen-day candidacy, there was a grim fascination in studying the man who almost seemed to personify a Democratic death-wish. That desperate presence on TV, the head pitched slightly forward, the eyes sunk deeper and deeper into a forlorn and defiant face, his speech speeding up while he pantomimed phone calls with McGovern, holding an imaginary phone while gesturing with the other hand or tapping his temple with a rigid finger—all this did rouse some sympathy for his past depressions, along with a distrust of whatever he might say now or in the future. I was intrigued by his habit of referring to himself in the third person: "What's a skeleton to Eagleton?"; " . . . you have to put yourself in Tom Eagleton's shoes. Imagine that you're Tom Eagleton . . . "; "This is definitely not my last press conference and Tom Eagleton is going to be around for a long, long time." Some of us will remember him signing his letter of resignation with several pens—as presidents do when they sign certain bills. He gave the pens to his staff as souvenirs of his candidacy.

Perhaps the most absorbing detail was his response to Frank Mankiewicz's question: "Tom, do you have any old skeletons rattling around in your closet?" Eagleton's answer of "No" rested on his concept of a skeleton—which almost became a Rorshach test among some New York Democrats. ("What's a skeleton? Cheating in school?" "No, making it with your dog in front of your children." "Christ, that's much worse than a *skeleton*." "Maybe a sticky divorce?") To some the image is a weak one, suggesting a cardboard figure for Hallowe'en or a joke in a horror picture; medical drawings and cartoons have purged it of troubling associations. The closeted skeleton is even less concrete and it sounds Victorian, like a "youthful indiscretion." But to Eagleton, "A skeleton is something that's dirty, filthy, corrupt, illegal, sinister. There's nothing about having been fatigued and exhausted that I found sinister, dirty, or ugly." Few would disagree with the last sentence. But Eagleton's dishonesty showed that he truly feared to reveal his past. Also: "Skeletons are things where you have committed a crime or violated legal ethics or something sinister like that." As he continued to discuss skeletons—"I was not concealing anything. I was consciously hiding nothing—" it began to appear that McGovern's staff should have asked him about an albatross.

By the time Sargent Shriver was secured as McGovern's seventh choice for the candidacy, many Democrats were even more bewildered by McGovern than they had been in Miami Beach. Selecting a Kennedy stand-in with some cold war taint upon him, a man known as a clumsy administrator, married to an impassioned enemy of abortion, hardly smacked of the new politics. While the press referred to "Camelot"—an evocation that's been scarce of late— the pundits forgot that the Peace Corps was discredited among many of the young, who had come to see it as a form of imperialism, and that much of the OEO had been a mishmash which had increased the mistrust of black communities. McGovern's messy tactics for getting rid of Eagleton—such as instructing Jean Westwood, the party chairperson, to say on TV that Eagleton should resign, or making ambiguous remarks to the press in hopes that Eagleton would get the message—decreased the confidence that McGovern could be straightforward. The "1000 percent" support of Eagleton made some Democrats very dubious about McGovern's pledges of support for other issues in the future.

The Republicans
August 1972

The handwriting on the wall may be a forgery.
—*Ralph Hodgson*

Magnificent coleslaw: perhaps the best I've ever had. It's crisp, the vinegar rests lightly on the sour cream, the shreds of carrot are firm and fresh. At most conventions there's no time for meals: you live on stand-up hot dogs and pockets full of chocolate, and—if you're in Miami Beach—quarts of Kool-Aid mixed in a garbage can in Flamingo Park. But during the early sessions of the Republican convention, there were opportunities to sit down at Wolfie's 24-hour delicatessen restaurant for platters of fine tunafish and salmon. But the convention wasn't boring, as some observers claimed. In fact it was an education for anyone who wasn't voting for Nixon. And there were many lessons for students of recent history—especially about the pliability of history.

I heard more references to John Kennedy at this convention than I had among the Democrats. Apparently JFK (who had been brotherless—no one mentioned Bobby or Ted) was a Republican, and had embodied the traditions of the GOP. His "spirit" was cordially evoked, and it was evident that Nixon's molders hoped that some voters' nostalgia for Kennedy might turn into affection for Nixon. One of the films of Nixon showed the President walking by the waves on a beach in a shot which almost parodied those of JFK ten years ago. However Nixon was dressed for the office and had his shoes on—black Oxfords that shone in the sand.

It was also startling to hear Goldwater quoting "Ask not what your country can do for you, ask what you can do for your country" on the first night. I remembered that a middle-class black community organizer had said to me a few years ago, "Did you realize, that was a totalitarian statement!" The sentence has since been called "Stalinoid" by some young radicals: "Man, that's the *old* party line. Strictly *old* Moscow." So it was intriguing to hear it springing from the lips of Goldwater, the demon conservative of the early Sixties (who now seems rather moderate), who was featured to reassure the Republicans who think that Nixon is too liberal. (Later, at two different caucuses, I heard the "Ask not" line directly attributed to Nixon; soon it may appear embroidered on GOP samplers.) Naturally much of the Kennedy-clutching was intended to make bruised Democrats feels welcome. A feast of sympathy was offered to those whose party had been "seized" by McGovern. And some reporters felt rather wistful when the Republicans made McGovern sound like the radical he wasn't.

In an effort to make the President appear warm and accessible as well as commanding, the convention movies showed Nixon being funny about Duke Ellington's birthday, strolling through a tomato field, "bringing order to the chaos he inherited," being bussed by his wife, trying to lower the property tax—"He's always working, he thrives on work"—pronounced shy and sensitive by his daughters. All in all "a man of vision born out of his own trials." He looked rigid throughout. A rather frightening zoom-shot of his mother suggested that the tension might be hereditary. But the film-maker (David Wolper) was determined to make him seem lovable—a project which had earlier been abandoned by some of his staff.

During the convention it was especially instructive to study the treatment of particular groups which were thought to be partial to the Democrats. One black caucus, sponsored by the Committee to Re-Elect the President, was visited by Julie Nixon Eisenhower, who was introduced as "our friend." She began, "I am one of a small band—but a growing band—who believe that the government will do more for black folks." She explained that the White House had done its best for "the black man in this country," but that busing "would never include all the children we needed to reach." But "the Nixon administration really cares about your children," and will "put more money in schools." A man behind me said, "Why, she's gonna give us two million peanuts! Like feedin' the monkeys." Later a young alternate delegate wrote in the Miami *Herald* that she had made the very same speech to a Spanish delegate caucus.

I heard scant enthusiasm for Nixon or the Republican party at this gathering, where most were middle-aged but many called each other "brother." A Miami delegate announced that the Republicans in Dade County had spent "lots of dollars" on attracting Cuban votes, but none on black voters. While it was repeated that Nixon had done little for black Americans, there was lavish disgust with the Democrats, who were mainly evoked as Wallaceites or the false-promisers of Lyndon Johnson's administration, especially those in OEO. It was stressed that "We are tired of federal money going through Democrats"—specifically white mayors. There was a great deal of bitterness against the Democrats in Congress, who were considered reluctant to pass appropriations bills which would aid black people. While tensions rose within the caucus—seemingly, less from disagreement than from a general nervousness about the future—Floyd McKissick was the only one I heard use the word "racist." (He said they must watch for "racist flaws" in the wording of official documents.) McKissick, once of CORE, had received a pledge of fourteen million dollars for his Soul City in North Carolina, but he said his support of Nixon had no connection with that grant. Another man said, "The

Republicans don't care. But I don't want to knock the brothers who are part
of the administration—I think they've done a helluva job considering the
circumstances."

An elderly man sprang to his feet: "*Why are we here?* I'm *sick* of white reporters calling me Uncle Tom because I'm here. Things are still bad for blacks
despite all the work. We're *here* to get some power for black people . . . " Someone else replied, "We're not being candid. We can't get much from the administration until we deliver the votes to them." Throughout, "Representation
in *both* parties" was a recurrent phrase. The only reference to black militants
that I heard came later, from a black woman from Michigan: "*They* don't
represent the poor. Look at Bobby Seale's $650-a-month penthouse." (It
seemed irrelevant to say that the penthouse was Huey Newton's.) Among the
black Republicans I met, one quiet groundnote did emerge: that at least Nixon
didn't *promise* anything; hence some respect him more than those Democrats
who had guaranteed wall-to-wall advancement for many black people.

Later I heard one (very light-skinned) black for George Wallace expound-
ing for a radio station. He was asked, "What message do you have for do-
gooder whites?" He replied, "The only ones who want to integrate are teachers
and sociologists and preachers. *They* ain't got a nickel. The ones I want to
integrate with is DuPont."

Some five hundred Vietnam veterans for Nixon were promised, but only
about fifty showed up. They denounced amnesty as though McGovern had
already granted it to every deserter, suggested that the antiwar vets had never
been in the military at all, and referred to those who had "died" in Vietnam—
as though they hadn't been killed.

Women were told that they were going to "come of age through the Republican party"—which did sound rather like aging. At the "Women of
Achievement Brunch," featuring a low cholesterol lunch with margarine and
yeast by Fleischmann, and a slide-show plus living models of such achievers as
Dolly Madison, Amelia Bloomer, Mamie Eisenhower and Clare Booth Luce,
we heard that "Martha Washington was no Women's Libber." The narration,
by Altovise Davis (wife of Sammy), Pat Boone ("who represents the qualities
we admire most in this country"), and Sammy Davis, Jr., included "all men
and women were created equal." Boone racily replied, "But that was before
Raquel Welch."

It was said that "the sewing machine and the typewriter gave women their
freedom." Soon the earliest feminists "were dabbling in civil disobedience"
(refusing to pay taxes because they had no vote). Sammy Davis said that women
"like the political kitchen as well as the real one." He also confessed that "the
first thing about being a Republican is stepping in when you're needed."
(Davis was later extolled by Nixon, who said, "We both came from rather
poor families, we both have done rather well." Davis spent much of the convention denying that he had insisted that the Republicans provide him with a

$4000 privately chartered jet-ride to Miami, as some Nixon staffers had complained.) At the end of the brunch, cochairperson Anne Armstrong told Davis, "We're awfully glad that your ancestors decided to leave that old country"— meaning that she was grateful that blacks had chosen to come from Africa so that their descendants could enrich our culture.

While many women at the Democratic convention had left depressed, feeling that they had been put down by their party, the most serious of the Republican women seemed very pleased to have been allowed to participate in their own convention. They had pushed through a strong child-care program for the party's platform, although there was a "loophole" sentence which worried a few: "We oppose ill-considered proposals, incapable of being administered effectively, which would heavily engage the federal government in this area." (In December 1971 Nixon had vetoed the child-care development bill on the grounds that it was too expensive, administratively impractical, and threatening to the family unit.)

At a woman's caucus I realized that environment and consumerism were considered the safest subjects for women. We learned that there was a controversy about a Senate bill on "zero discharge of pollutants." A male speaker said, "We're opposing that. Some say that the administration's bill is weaker. But it's impossible to have *no* pollutants. Why set that kind of standard when everyone knows it can't be achieved? This is a problem in America today: the *other* party has made impossible promises. Republicans must tell people not only what the government will do—but what it *can't* do." Again I appreciated the intelligence of a tactic which had drawn some to the GOP and helped to define their anger against the Democrats.

Details on clean water, fossil fuel, the removal of sulphur oxide, and the urgency of buying low lead gasoline (which sounded like an ad for Lead-Free Amoco), made many droop with boredom. Afterwards one woman murmured, "Why should our issues be so dull?" Then we swung into packaging: "We *must* buy returnable bottles." Also it's time for citizens to rebel: a woman launched into a saga about Philadelphia Cream Cheese, which used to be simply wrapped in silver foil. Now it has a box around it. "But we can protest! Against that box." Everyone was urged to start a recycling center in her community. A discreet discussion of child-care was interrupted by Betty Friedan, who spoke for abortion. Flurries of alarm rippled through the room. Natalie Moorman, a black physicist, gestured at Friedan: "This lady and I are both *past the point* where this is a pressing issue for us!" The questions of reproduction were hastily shelved and many applauded when Friedan was made to stop speaking. A small group joined her in the hall to discuss abortion, and soon drugs were denounced, mainly in terms of how much they cost the country. It was said that drug addiction has decreased under the Republicans. But no form of drugs should be legalized, and "heroin is different from Methadone."

For the women's lunches and meetings, I wore a linen office dress from

1966; it shields the knees. Most of the women I met were both shy and friendly; few seemed accustomed to talking to groups of strangers of their own sex, and the conversations tended to range from diets to sunburn. A number asked me the same question: did I get my credentials due to being a delegate's wife? It was another lesson: I've rarely been in those realms where a woman would not be expected to function on her own. "Womanpower" (a recurrent phrase) clearly meant influencing your husband.

The Republicans' efforts to manipulate the young betrayed a certain contempt. It was assumed that fledglings are always guided by their elders; Goldwater said that even the young who have "a distorted view of America" have been steered wrong by adults—they would never come to such ideas on their own. Later the demonstrators who hassled delegates were repeatedly called, "those McGovern protesters outside." It was reasoned that they were *for* McGovern, rather than against Nixon or the war.

Some of the young Republican delegates I talked to firmly supported abortion and the legalization of marijuana. But the Young Voters for the President with their "ELEPHANTS LIKE LETTUCE" buttons were something else. Like their seniors they assumed that everyone in Flamingo Park was part of one vast network: they saw no distinctions between the Vietnam vets, the Jesus people, SDS, the visiting American Nazis, YIP, the feminists, the gay activists, or the Zippies. Of the antiwar demonstrators, a YVP said, "Oooo, I could just kill them. Just let me punch their face." She and her friends then excitedly discussed the question of whether Pat Boone had *really* said that if the Communists took over America, he would shoot all five of his daughters. (He did make that statement at a Goldwater rally in the Hollywood Bowl.)

Nixon's buttery tributes to the young—"you have inspired us with your enthusiasm, with your intelligence, with your dedication"—were all the funnier because we knew that the YVPs' "spontaneous demonstration" had been programmed and directed with a paramilitary precision. Their supervisors had insisted for days that their frenzied outbursts were fired only by their passion for Nixon and his views. Many spectators were amused when the Nixon staff unintentionally distributed some copies of the extremely detailed YVP script to several news outlets, including the BBC; CBS promptly put it on the screen.

I was on the floor when Nixon was renominated. A screeching conga-line of YVPs, bearing long olive green garbage bags filled with inflated balloons—air within air—thundered down the aisles. The balloons burst like gunshots, sticks from wildly thrashing flags imperiled one's eyes, people jumped on your feet, you couldn't budge, the elbows jammed against your ribs weren't yours. "*Four* more *years!* Four MORE years!" In that suffocation, the crushed crowd began to run in place, jerking their knees up and down. It was my idea of an urban riot: people trapped and screaming, frantic to breathe or move. Older delegates smiled indulgently at the ecstasies of the young. As the howls subsided, a YVP laid his hand on the floor-pass over my wishbone: "It says 'Press.' Can I press now?"

Reeling off the floor, I remembered that these teen-agers weren't born until after the Checkers speech, that they were seven or six or less in 1960, that they knew only the newest of Nixons. They shrieked, "Hey, hey, whaddaya say, Nixon, Nixon, all the way!", having probably been too young or too sheltered in '67 or '68 to have heard the identical rhythm and phrasing of "Hey, hey, LBJ, How many kids did you kill today?"

None of the Republican blacks or women I met acknowledged that perhaps they were showcase tokens for the Nixon administration. But that did occur to some of the very young. Later some YVPs said they had been excluded from most of the functions they'd expected to attend, had been kept in isolation, were "herded around like cattle," pressured to buy souvenirs, such as expensive gold cuff links engraved with Nixon's face, and merely used as stage props. "It was a . . . bummer," said a YVP from Ohio, rather as though the word was new to her. "When I get home, I'm not working for Nixon, and neither is my friend Debbie." Would she still vote? "Ummmm—probably."

~

"You don't want to use those ice cubes—they're old," the bellboy told me. I thought of haunted ice cubes, or old ones—whose had they been? Frozen for what purpose . . . I thanked him, but used them anyway. He was fairly old himself.

In Miami Beach I stayed in cheap hotels with cigarette burns on bedspreads, purple TV (the color so stricken that all politicians looked very ill), faucets that screamed thinly when you touched them, a few sluggish roaches. In this neighborhood you could have your blood pressure taken for $1 at Woolworth's. "Pullmanettes" are advertised outside some retirement homes—they sound even smaller than the efficiencies. Is a Pullmanette a shelf for the body to lie on? Tired electric fans hardly cut the sweat in these realms. Hence the shock of the frosty plunge into the huge, chandeliered uptown hotels, where the bands played rumbas and a few couples did the Lindy Hop. Some lined up to buy ballpoint pens in the shape of Nixon. The rich weren't much in evidence—I felt that they had been shooed away to their yachts or parties in villas, since this was meant to be the year for mid-America.

Within that setting, certain phrases and concepts reappeared rather punctually: "Better Americans," who were often evoked but never defined—except that they were better than those who burned their draft cards; "bricks and mortar" (what we need more of); and—to my mild surprise—"self-defense." I heard one alternate delegate argue that "If you had gun control laws, then only the criminals would have guns." (The platform did agree to "safeguard the right of responsible citizens to collect, own, and use firearms for legitimate purposes, including hunting, target shooting, and self-defense." Citing the national murder rate, the *New York Times* called the statement "shameful.") It was steadily said that "other countries" want Nixon reelected, also that the Democrats have become isolationists. I heard that McGovern is "very unstable" and that he has "a terrible temper." Those who had favored abortion were sometimes rather innocently called "abortionists"—as though they performed the operation itself. There were a lot of awkward jokes—"A good speech is like a bikini: brief, provocative, and revealing"—but the mood was certainly confident and expansive: people agreed that the last four years were "something to be proud of," a fine time for us all. So it was odd to recall that Nixon had been called a possible "one-term President" in 1970, when some even thought that he might not choose to run again.

After a certain amount of folk wisdom, it was a relief to head for Flamingo Park. But much of what occurred there during this convention was rather sad. Some different groups got on very badly, while brain-frying heat and fatigue heightened the mutual hostilities. Quite a few had to be restrained from throwing punches at the Jesus people. (The latter made a stunned audience for the Hare Krishna dancers: they gaped at the orange whirlers as though they'd never seen them before.) The gay men and the feminists were needled and sometimes attacked by visiting local thugs. Tom Forcade and a larger band of Zippies than had been at the Democratic convention drowned out other speakers with their rock band. Forcade seemed loathed by almost every group, and some—including the Vietnam vets—said he had physically threatened them. He earned quite a few comparisons to Charles Manson.

Medics told me that there were a lot of bad downers and speed on hand, also some heroin; they were constantly called to cope with sufferers. (They said they'd had no similar cases during the last convention.) Rocky Pomerance, the benign Police Chief of Miami Beach, had told the campers that they must police themselves. And so they tried: everyone dealing "death drugs" or "harassing" others was meant to be ejected from the park. The approved technique was to surround the culprit and walk—so that he was simply walked out of the park. I saw that well-done several times, especially by the vets. But as they themselves said, they hadn't come to Miami Beach to be cops and they didn't relish the role. They had to fight hard to expel some twenty "Nazis" who invaded the park, made anti-Semitic remarks, and seized the platform. The vets also turned a man over to the police and destroyed the wrist-rockets and two fused Molotov cocktails they said they had found on him. As far as the general public was concerned, the vets' silent marches— led by three crippled men in wheelchairs—and their sober speeches, were obscured by the street games of the Zippies.

There were meetings every morning so that different groups could work out some means of coexistence on "the land," as the park was called, or create their own laws. But these debates often became battles about the use of the communal sound system. (Eventually rock music was vetoed.) Dealers kept returning and the women were pawed so often that they put up a fence around their tent. That just seemed to provoke more attacks—it was tempting to those outside it, rather like the rope around the Pentagon in 1967. But I also heard some rather touching male consciousness raising going on just outside the women's fence: "Would you like to get up on a stage in just a jockstrap?" "Christ, no."

Tripping over tent pegs in the darkness of early night, exploring the picture exhibits of maimed Vietnamese children and charred flesh, or xeroxes of "Ripped Off FBI Files," listening to wistful voices: "We must show Richard Nixon that the movement is stronger than ever," watching an incredibly thin boy dancing alone, fluid despite a bandaged rib cage, reading the hand-outs— a Jesus paper which praised Governor Reuben Askew as "a heavy brother on the Lord," but regretted that Julian Bond had said that he wasn't "very big on Christ or Christianity personally," or a recipe for steamed placenta, to be sauteed with onion and served with crackers, or warning information on ingredients used in some ice creams, such as pipernal, a chemical used to kill lice—declining to buy a sweatshirt stencilled, "Bernardine Is Hiding In Our Hearts," hearing a speaker say, "We're ready now! All we need is the projector and the slides and some electricity," glancing at placards for PIMP (People's Independent Military Party) while angry voices rose when a gay man was accused of grabbing a woman's breasts, and a singer taught others a new uplift song to the tune of the Coke ads: "I'd like to see / The vic-tor-ee / Of every people's war . . . It's the re-heel thing, re-vo-lu-hu-shon," and others spoke kindly of "Crazy Tom" (Eagleton), and the tiny communist cadre from Tampa closed their tent to a couple of squealing Zippies, I watched recurring lightning flashes without thunder. It suited this atmosphere of dry heaves.

All the tension that mounts before a major demonstration . . . Some discussed conspiracies: the CIA had John Kennedy assassinated because he was definitely going to pull out of Vietnam; the CIA was distributing the pills (especially Quaaludes) which had flooded the park, so that the protesters would be "all tranked up" and wouldn't want to march. Peering up at the night sky, someone said: "Stars that move—they must be helicopters." They were. And the dry heaves rolled through the park again: was Nixon plotting a violent final night, would he want to show his strength by the numbers of cracked heads? In contrast to 1968 and 1969, I heard no one saying that Nixon's presidency was a fine thing; he's no longer considered a tool for revolution, as he was a few years ago.

A young woman said to me, "There are lots of people here who aren't political, and it's troubling." Quite a few Miami teen-agers had simply come to the park in search of dope. But most of the others I met were also under twenty-one. For many this was the very first form of protest; perhaps it would be their only one. Movement people from the Sixties and the early Seventies were conspicuously absent. Public figures like Rennie Davis and Bobby Seale made scheduled speeches at rallies, but you didn't see them mingling with the very young. (At the Democratic convention, a speaker had asked for Davis and David Dellinger to come to the platform and identify themselves. Few of these new troops knew the movement veterans by sight.) But without a number of the steady dissenters from the past, the beginners could have no sense of continuity, no indication that opposing the policies of the government was a long-term project. There were old FREE ANGELA posters—but Angela was already free. One 17-year-old told me, "I have no history to bounce this off of." He added, "I don't know anything about '68." He was against the war, he thought racism was expanding. But he felt the park was fairly isolated from these issues—he doubted that he was "doing anything" by being there. Since the movement has always insisted that it's leaderless, the field was left to Tom Forcade.

Almost no political education took place in Flamingo Park during the Republican convention. Some fine speeches given by three Vietnamese students—who referred in detail to Vietnamese politics, the Thieu regime, and also American strategy—puzzled much of this crowd. The listeners seemed especially bewildered when one speaker suggested that demonstrators should cease to display the NLF flag, which "belongs to the Vietnamese and shouldn't be used here by those who make it an object of hate to the American people." The audience chanted "Ho-ho-ho" at certain moments and raised their fists, but some clapped when Forcade complained over the mike that these talks by the Vietnamese had delayed the performance of a rock opera.

~

"Did you hear? That bastard has ended the ground war": thus I first learned from a friend on August 12th that the combat troops were departing from Vietnam. But it seemed to have little impact as an election strategy. The *Daily News'* big headline that night was "CLERK CHARGED IN 1M-PLUS GYP/Banker, Clergy Are Pigeons"; below, there was a much smaller heading: "The Field Is Theirs—Not Ours." The next morning the *Times's* lead editorial was "Vietnam Mirage," and it emphasized that "aerial firepower" would continue.

Meanwhile memories came in little gusts: Walter Lippmann recommending "A Vote For Nixon" in his column in 1968, hoping that Nixon would end the war in his first term. (Lippmann's main reason for backing this candidate was that "the country may demand and necessity may dictate the repression of uncontrollable violence." Humphrey would hate to face this. Therefore "It is better that Nixon should have the full authority if the repression should become necessary in order to restore peace and tranquility in the land.") Since Nixon's visits to China and Russia, I've been asked to admire his foreign policy "if you'll just overlook Vietnam." If you mentioned backing Pakistan's dictatorship against India, you were told, "That was a *mistake*," also that "people here don't care about those countries."

In 1972 when we read about the methodical destruction of Quang Tri, it seemed a long time since we'd heard about "winning back the hearts and minds of the Vietnamese people." The President had sought to end the anti-war movement more systematically than he had tried to end the war. (Yet if he had achieved peace in 1972, some would have credited McGovern's candidacy for pressuring him into it.) But in Miami Beach in August, the war was hardly allowed into the Convention Hall. Senator Edward Brooke of Massachusetts, a keynote speaker who had written the last antiwar resolution to pass the Senate, skidded over it all rather tastefully: "Vietnam—well, we all have our differences . . . "

During the convention there was a variety of interesting reversals, such as Agnew condemning those who "fasten group labels on people, and in the process . . . turn American against American . . . " He deplored "the practice of pitting the most publicized minorities against the least publicized minorities," a tactic which "will most assuredly push America backwards . . . " And the platform mourned that "the isolation of the People's Republic of China . . . went endlessly on" until Nixon's trip—as though he and his party had not upheld that isolation, had not even opposed negotiation with China.

As we skated around between the decades, I realized that an old Fifties phenomenon was surfacing: speakers were strumming on the idea of individuality in the midst of conformity. (Those two words used to go together.) Every five or ten years we're reminded that individualism is the property of conservatives, as was revealed when Goldwater tried to swing—when he said that the young wanted "to do their thing," and praised them for their sense of personal freedom—and later at a Jewish seminar, when an ex-Democrat said, "Nixon stands for achievement. So do we . . . And the highest form of Mitzvah is to help a man to become independent and self-sufficient, to be an individual. That's why very orthodox people are drawn to the Republicans." Throughout liberty was fiercely protected by the GOP—especially against the tyrannous socialism of McGovern.

∾

The demonstrators' "Street Without Joy" (named for Highway One in Vietnam) brought Nixon's coffin, a baby elephant, coolie hats, hands and faces dripping with red paint, and many white-masked women dressed like peasants with dead-baby bundles in their arms, to the Convention Hall. A few spectators gasped at the starkness of that silent throng. But when the guerrilla theater began—as about a hundred acted out the death of Vietnamese peasants, screaming and falling down while pâpier-maché bombers were rushed over their heads and smoke bombs exploded—much of the audience began to chuckle, as did the large Cuban family who invited me to watch from their porch. Few of the delegates saw the show, since the marchers had been given the street and those entering the Hall were rerouted. As the Cubans laughed and the kids playing peasants wailed, I realized that guerrilla theater moves only those who already agree with what it states—unless it's very, very good. (Or funny: like the Diggers throwing money on the floor of the New York Stock Exchange in 1967. Perhaps comedy is mainly what succeeds.) My Cuban hosts nudged me as a mock B-52 bomber and the coffin were set on fire and flung over the fence surrounding the Hall, where they sizzled quietly in a light rain.

On that night and on the one that followed—when my local horoscope read, "Pay attention to the young today. They will surprise you!"—the tactical script drawn up by the Miami Conventions Coalition was abruptly abandoned. The script—which had been shared weeks in advance with the police—called for "militant non-violence," pledged "non-disruption of the senior citizens' community," and warned against "attacking or provoking" police, the National Guard, or GIs. In a speech on the night before, Rennie Davis revived the righteous style of the late Sixties: "We will seal off this convention with a people's quarantine . . . We'll resist, they'll have to drag us into the paddy wagons tomorrow . . . " Also "we won't trash small businessmen, but the Lincoln Mall shops can be regarded as symbols of this convention or the administration." But "We won't be violent with individual delegates."

SDS and the Zippies had refused all along to cooperate with the MCC (which had served as an umbrella group for most of the organizations that were there). SDS said it was all right to "trash imperialists." No scenario could have worked on the final night, especially since so many in the park had already clashed with one another, and also because a number of unaffiliated outsiders were on hand. No movement spokesman had any authority to tell others what to do—or not to do. The Hall was finally barricaded with derelict buses, which prevented the mass sit-ins leading to arrests which so many had planned on. So some freaked out in the streets, while a small group of vets picked up the benches which others had overturned, and the Miami Beach police—who had been very restrained, on Rocky Pomerance's orders—grew rougher.

Until the last day and a half, the cops had frustrated some by their reluctance to make arrests—in fact the police were practicing peaceful resistance. A few had even wheeled the crippled vets up the steps of the Fontainebleau Hotel for an antiwar protest. I saw one arrest (for "impeding traffic") of five young men which might have been choreographed by Balanchine. One pair of handcuffs called out, "Our enemies are not the police, the enemy is Nixon," and pronounced his arrest "orderly." As I talked with those in the paddy wagon, a state trooper shoved me back: "Look out, they'll spit on you!" "No, they won't." "They *will.*" He glowered at the spitless young men. Shouts of farewell from the wagon: "Goodbye, take it easy!" Elsewhere I saw some state highway patrolmen throttling demonstrators with sticks held across their throats; Pomerance's instructions were forgotten by some as the night deepened.

Later we heard that three marchers had been run down by vehicles on separate occasions. Some random cars and buses were damaged, and there were brisk bouts of tire-slashing and trashing.

As gas billowed down the avenue and cries rose from blocks away, two Nixonettes reproached a black press photographer for dropping his popsicle wrapper on the ground: "Ooo, you just littered." "Murderers! *Murderers!*" the crowd yelled at delegates, who shouted back, "Nixon *now!*" I went into the Hall to hear the "Salute to Working Youth." A young man was saying that "youth" would be misrepresented if "people like us weren't heard from." A young woman spoke after him: "President Nixon has listened and understood the speech of the people . . . we young people." Outside once more, I was in time to see a sun-shelter burst into flames on the nearby golf course. The shelter had a thatched roof and some exultant photographers exclaimed that it looked like Vietnam: "A beautiful shot!" Huge vans crammed with those who'd been arrested emitted muffled cries: "Power to the people!" The police then set off more gas than might be needed to subdue half of Cuba and I dashed inside to hear Agnew. He seemed to be talking about "justice in the raw"—did gas effect one's ears? (It was actually "justice under law," unlike the lawless justice that we're used to.) A delegate jabbered, "My eyes are burning, those kids are crazy, the gas is their fault, they threw potatoes with razor blades in them, they threw decayed meat with soup-bones in it!" I doubted the deadly potatoes; a young woman reporter laughed. He said indignantly, "Listen, soup-bones hurt."

This time, the whole world wasn't watching—little news from the street was shown on TV. The actions, which had been intended to delay this session of the convention and to knock Nixon off prime time, had postponed the whole program by exactly seven minutes. The protests merely involved the participants—not the delegates who observed them, whose minds were hardly changed by what they saw. It was all too far removed from the war and no political point was made. In Chicago many had been outraged by Mayor Daley and his troops, but the mayor of Miami Beach and his police chief had tried to save heads. So the delegates recoiled in horror from the demonstrators—just as we had responded in 1968 to the Chicago police. (A young man said rather wistfully to me, "LBJ was such a good enemy. But Nixon doesn't *personify* his own policies, the way Johnson did. Somehow, it's harder to hold Nixon responsible for what he does.") And in 1968 the issues had been out front. But in Miami Beach many were too inexperienced to know how to make a statement about the country or the war.

Those days among the Republicans taught some of us more about the mood of 1972 than infinite skirmishes in the streets. Throughout that whole shower of joy—the celebration of a happy and healthy America—one marvelled at the ability of many people to screen out the facts that litter the sidewalk or hang from the walls of anybody's home. Most of those present truly seemed to believe what Nixon and the Republicans told them: "your dollar buys more," crime is dwindling, peace is nearly sewed up in Vietnam, women are more equal than ever. The platform stated, "We have brought about a rapid rise in both employment and in real income." (But the unemployment rate, which was 3.2 percent in 1969, had risen steadily; it was just under 6 percent before the Convention of 1972.) Inflation—which wasn't really a part of the last few years—is also receding into history. (The next morning, the layout of the *New York Times*'s front page made a deadpan reply: right beneath NIXON IS RENOMINATED . . . the headline read,

"Prices Rise 0.4%
Increase Biggest
In Last 5 Months.")

Goldwater announced that we have "come closer to solving the problem of poverty than any nation in the history of the world." (There were cheers for that.) He also said that "we have a free press"—while some of us fingered our credentials, which read LIMITED ACCESS, perhaps the surliest welcome we've had in years. (For the Democrats, our tags simply said MEDIA.)

We're all accustomed to politicians' guff and to audiences of any faith which enjoy being deceived. But coming from a realm of skeptics, I was rather staggered to learn that those I met at lunches and caucuses really accepted what they'd heard. It was clear that the Republicans had persuaded many to ignore or mistrust their own experiences. You can look in your wallet, or check out the price of spinach, or discover that the muggings have accelerated on your block—and then you're asked to erase the evidence of daily life: as though it came from outer space or belonged to science fiction. Coming on the heels of the Johnson administration, these tactics are bold ones— when you remember a theme from the late Sixties: that the public could no longer stand being lied to, that "credibility" was dead, that few seemed able to trust politicians of either party.

Another device conspicuous in this campaign was giving people false alternatives, such as insisting that there has to be a choice between good education and busing. Some of the other distortions rely on non-sequiturs. A letter sent to voters from the Finance Committee to Re-Elect the President, signed by Maurice Stans, asked, "Do you agree with the Democrats that inflation (caused by uncontrolled government spending) is a good thing . . . or do you favor President Nixon's drive for a return to law and order?" (The dots are his. There you can see the hook-up between inflation and crime.) Other mistruths depend on subtle implications: for example, some "special Americans" (read blacks) have been rather pampered; now their privileges must be extended to "all Americans."

Nixon has deeply flummoxed his followers by mingling liberal and right-wing policies until people no longer know what he really represents. (At other moments he masks reactionary ideas in progressive language.) Lowering the voting age of course pleased liberals of both parties; promising to make the Supreme Court even more conservative satisfied their opponents. But what of the rather moderate Republicans I met in Miami Beach—who seemed fairly dazed as well as seduced by what they were told? Peter Schrag, who wrote *The Decline of the Wasp,* remarked that Nixon had "liberated them from their principles." And one certainly felt that in the air. In the past, many had been hardline anti-Communists, like Nixon himself; their ideas of right and wrong were as sharply defined as the President's when he praised Westerns like John Wayne's in 1970 because "the good guys come out ahead in the Westerns, and the bad ones lose." Since his visits to China and Russia—which were applauded rather cautiously when convention speakers mentioned them—many long-time Republicans no longer seem to know what they believe, or what to believe. Hence, I think, the malleability, the uncertainty about what is actually going on around them.

After hearing the negotiations with Peking and Moscow repeatedly hailed, many swallowed their lifelong convictions. They may also have been confused when Nixon evoked Roosevelt, Truman, Kennedy and Johnson as beacons of foreign policy. And they had good reason to be perplexed about some of his other positions. In 1969 it appeared that the President sanctioned some form of guaranteed annual income for the poor—an idea that was hard for many Republicans to accept. Later this was translated into the Family Assistance Plan, which turned out to be far from liberal. In 1972 the platform gave some muted support to Nixon's "welfare reform" plan, but stated, "We flatly oppose programs or policies which embrace the principle of a government-guaranteed income"—which was still supposed to be the aim of Nixon's plan. So his most loyal constituents continued to struggle with the switches he had pulled on them—all couched in extremely moral terms. Many of us who were grateful for the beginnings of diplomatic contact with China and Russia still thought it premature to regard these prefaces as complete chapters. But loyal Republicans might later be told that the communists had regained their evil or that they were not worthy of our trust.

CS gas combined with Mace makes some people vomit. And as the delegates came hawking and retching into the Hall, many had been frightened by the demonstrators, demoralized by the pain in their own throats. Yet during the final session, what was happening in the streets was hardly acknowledged. Nixon and Agnew had campaigned on domestic "chaos" during the Congressional elections of 1970. That fall—when campuses were quiet—Agnew had talked as though a nationwide bloodbath were underway. But at the Miami Beach convention, it was implied that the antiwar protests were part of the past, like the war itself, and both belonged to the Democrats who had ignited them. Inside the Hall, there were the realities of the Seventies, which culminated in a warmth-binge: Nixon shaking hands with a rapturous line-up while the lights gleamed on Agnew's forehead. What went on outside was back in the Sixties: a suppressed memory of bad days that were over.

Afterword:
Sports and the Weather Next

The President kept assuring us that he would not resign. Still, as the waves of Watergate broke afresh each day, the press embarked on a gloat-glut: many reporters were congratulating themselves as though they had personally cracked the story. Quite a few felt that the media had regained its credibility only because Nixon had lost his.

But earlier, shortly before the 1972 election, some of us were feeling that the power of the pen was no greater than the power of the penny. Many billions of words had been written opposing the Vietnam war; our policies were unchanged. On October 26 Henry Kissinger vowed that peace was "at hand." Most commentators remained skeptical, and after he made that statement, the lead story on the New York airwaves was that five hundred Long Island trainmen had just decided not to strike.

Political astuteness amounted to keeping the voters perplexed: peace now but not yet. Therefore publishing pieces about politics seemed as effective as hurling our typescripts into the nearest trash basket. So we mused on "the climate of opinion"—unable to escape that ugly phrase, since "climate" was a Presidential favorite. Patrick Buchanan, the most conservative of Nixon's speechwriters (and a future Presidential candidate), was once asked if he thought it was easy to alter public opinion. He answered, "Yes. Drip by drip by drip. It wears them down." Indeed it did.

And yet after the election it was still too easy to say that the American people didn't care, which was the refrain in my local delicatessen (buying a sandwich after the election was like attending a suicide's funeral; my drugstore was the crematorium), or that infinite voters thought that if they themselves had enough money, then nothing could be wrong in the United States—although the latter was certainly one of Nixon's most successful strategies.

But we had to keep acknowledging the Republicans' continuing cleverness in keeping contradictions on the boil: as when the White House proposed a guaranteed annual income, then later de-balled the program, then finally killed it. Each step was designed to reassure white voters: we'll pay off those black people who frighten you, / well, we'll trim their privileges, / no, we won't actually use your earnings to enrich them for being lazy. . . . Hence what was daintily called "the hidden vote"; those who analyzed the *New York Times*/Yankelovich polls deduced that race was a key issue in the election. Many voters questioned felt that blacks and Puerto Ricans were "receiving too much attention"; somehow they'd forgotten benign neglect.

Just before the election, Edmund Muskie urged Americans not to be swayed by the Republicans' "politics of fear." However crime—the Seventies' substitute for Communism—housing, education and welfare had all become racial issues, and the government had given the impression that it was going to protect white people from black ones.

In Nixon's America, words and actions were growing farther and farther apart: as in the Carnasie section of East Brooklyn, where some of those protesting school busing chanted "Nigger, nigger, nigger" and others threw rocks at black children, while white parents insisted to reporters that the uproar had nothing to do with race—it was simply a matter of "decentralization". Concerned journalists spoke of the need to re-connect words and facts. But no one had the exact recipe on hand.

~

Sifting our memories, we rediscovered what many had forgotten: that Muskie was ahead of Nixon in the Harris polls from November 1970 to May 1971; that Nixon's landslide was achieved through an unusually sparse turn-out of voters: the lowest in twenty-four years; that McGovern's decency was drowned in the public mind because he had not made his views or commitments clear.

As Watergate unfurled, the plotters and plumbers helped to harm McGovern, as when CREEP sent thousands of telegrams to Nixon and put ads in the newspapers to give the illusion that many citizens were supporting the President on the bombings and the mining of Haiphong Harbor. And of course Buchanan's drips had already created the atmosphere for McGovern's demise: the Republicans had persuaded much of the populace that the young who followed McGovern were the anarchists, dopers, sex fiends, and "hippies" who endangered our country to a degree that justified the war. But McGovern and his staff were also responsible for the bewilderment they engendered, and the dithering over Eagleton was only one strand in the tangle of mismanagement. The $1000 a year income-grant program that turned out to be just muddled economics—and which McGovern later retracted; the remarks in favor of and against a "quota system" to increase the representation of blacks, women, and other groups; the support for and the recoil from legal abortion; the endorsement of right-wing Democrats, including Louise Day Hicks of Boston—all served to thicken the soup of confusion. And within a snarl of good intentions and poor planning, the candidate whom many still greatly respected had contradicted himself too often, and no one could chide the Republicans for that.

~

So we learned that peace was not upon our plates in October or November of 1972; we then saw the heaviest bombardments of the war, while Kissinger spoke of "good will," and the *New York Times* questioned the difference between "deception" and "naiveté." We'd long known that "peace-keeping" meant war-making. But the threat of a bloodbath, which had also been very useful to Lyndon Johnson, had miraculously evaporated by January 28 of 1973, when the *Times'* headline read: AMERICA'S LONGEST WAR HALTS—not "stops" or "ends", but "halts". The next day we achieved more than a hundred bombing raids over Cambodia and Laos.

Nixon had used up four years—the length of the American Civil War—to extricate Americans from the fighting. So there was no cheering; the shame of the war had gone too deep. When had we last seen any celebrations? Only on March 31, 1968, when LBJ pulled out. Immediately after that announcement, people eagerly phoned each other to share the news. I saw a few jigging and skipping on Central Park West late that night, and a friend of mine said she was so happy that she nearly raped the postman the next day. Some really dared to hope that getting rid of Johnson at that moment would mean peace. Later others were hopeful when the Paris peace talks began in May of 1968. Naturally that little spurt of optimism curdled into cynicism soon. Since then, distrust of the government made it hard for many to believe that even good news could be true.

~

The radical movement of the Sixties began to fade rapidly in the fall of 1970. Many of us picked over the wreath of reasons for that massive retreat: acute fatigue; the loss of confidence about being able to restructure American society; the lack of any solid political program for the future; fears of more Kent and Jackson States; fears of the government; the flight from politics to intensely private lives—as though the two had to be mutually exclusive; the media's insistence that the movement was declining—which made some feel that their own efforts were useless; the waning of the draft; the crunch of recession and the urgency of hustling for jobs and livelihoods; dropping out into dope—plus the confusion between drugs and "revolution" (some actually thought a stoned America would mean equality and liberty for all); further confusions between politics and the occult (in New York, Brentano's bookstore cleverly displayed Che Guevara's diaries and the *I Ching* on either side of the cash register); infinite fights among those who were on the same side—as when Weatherman trashed SDS in 1969; and the triumphant destructiveness of those who contended that violence was the only proof of moral principle, that possessing a moral sense meant being violent. I listened to turgid arguments from individuals who cherished the slogan "Shoot to live" while promising that their store-front instant hot soup collective was going to save "the people's" children, concluding with lines like, "But most Americans would rather burn babies than give them vitamins." The reasoning almost equalled that of Weatherman Mark Rudd when he urged white middle-class revolutionaries to model themselves on Captain Ahab in *Moby Dick*—"with one thought: to bring down the white whale." Apparently he'd forgotten that the whale was the winner.

It has to be stressed once more that those who embraced violence were a minority. And some of them were bursting with hot air: they didn't act on what they said. But their voices carried a long way. And so they passed ammunition to an administration which needed symbolic enemies—in fact almost welcomed them.

In 1973 Arthur Miller wrote, "the nation has both rejected and digested" the ideas and events of the late Sixties. Many came to hate war as they (and previous generations) hadn't in the past. Yet many also appeared to be rather indifferent to the continued bombings of 1972 and 1973. Questions of racial and social injustice began to be ignored in a way that would have seemed inconceivable in 1968 and 1969, and yet more Americans seemed aware of those issues. And some ex-radicals travelled into realms where few of their former colleagues could follow them. Rennie Davis—once one of the most committed of the antiwar activists—began seeing with his third eye and worshipping the Guru Maharaj Ji. According to Davis, that fifteen-year-old "perfect master" was going to eliminate wars and racism, and a glorious time lay ahead for the United States in about 1975. Questioned about his views on the tenant of the White House, Davis replied: "Richard Nixon is equally blessed, as blessed as any of us, because he has a body and a soul." When I asked Davis if the future held any imperfections, he echoed the Maharaj Ji's prediction that New York would be totally destroyed by an earthquake in 1973.

~

Although the radicals of the Sixties failed to establish an enduring American Left, we have to remember that the earliest tides of opposition to the war didn't spring from Congress or the media—both of which missed the transition from a cold war to a real one, and at first criticized only the strategy of the war without challenging its existence—but from the campuses. That generation of the Sixties forced their teachers and the press—and eventually many politicians—to re-examine foreign policy. Peace became respectable, as Jerry Rubin once complained, when moderates of all sorts rebelled against the killing.

Having fuelled the momentum that shoved out LBJ, radicals hardly seemed to make a dent on the Nixon administration. Yet Watergate had the effect that no amount of protest or criticism or rebellion ever had. And when we first learned that some of the lower level Waterburglars—such as Bernard

Barker and James McCord—really seemed to believe that they were acting patriotically by trying for forestall the forces of dissent, it was evident that the tattered, scattered movement had left an imprint after all. Later the testimony of John Dean, John Erlichman, and H. R. Haldeman showed how deeply Nixon had feared the movement—even at the very time when he'd told us he wasn't listening: in November 1969, when he watched a football game during the country's largest antiwar march. In 1971 even a solitary picket holding an antiwar sign in Lafayette Park upset him.

Nixon, Mitchell, and others had so exaggerated the danger of dissidents that many Americans could believe that McGovern volunteers or students or Mothers For Peace or Vietnam Veterans Against the War were a profound threat to the country. Soon after Nixon took office, a treasonous label was pasted on almost everyone who could not support the White House on Vietnam. But although the President detested demonstrations, some of his aides thought they highlighted his own purity: in 1971 Haldeman wrote "Good" and "Great!" in the margins of memos which warned that "violent" protestors with "obscene" signs would be present when Nixon appeared with Billy Graham in Charlotte, North Carolina.

In 1969 Kissinger and Nixon told the FBI to tap the phones of seventeen persons who were suspected of having leaked to the *Times* the fact that we were secretly bombing North Vietnamese base areas in Cambodia with the "acquiescence" of Prince Sihanouk. (Sihanouk denied that he approved those raids. He said he had steadily protested the bombings in messages to the U.S. Embassy in Phnom Penh, and he declared that Nixon was lying about his alleged cooperation.) More than a year later, when William P. Rogers (then the Secretary of State) was questioned about U.S.-Cambodian relations, he said: "Cambodia is one country where we can say with complete assurance that our hands are clean and our hearts are pure." He had participated in the decision which led to the fourteen months of secret bombing.

Also in 1969 Nixon instructed the CIA to investigate the possibility that unfriendly foreign governments were giving financial aid to groups of black and white American radicals. The CIA delivered two long reports which stated that there was no evidence of any such activities.* The President's response was to order FBI offices to be set up in twenty countries. Their research repeated that of the CIA but still produced no evidence. Nixon remained unable to believe that ordinary Americans could genuinely oppose the war or rebel against racism on their own. And the White House was never able to distinguish between the professional politicians and editorial writers who

---

* A CIA official who worked on this project said: "We tried to show that the radical movements were home-grown, indigenous responses to perceived grievances and problems which had been growing for years. We said the radicals were clean and that we couldn't find anything."—*New York Times*, May 25, 1973.

criticized Nixon and the street-fighting militants or even the Yippies. Many of us were amused by the mildness of the "enemies" list, which contained almost no real radicals. Once again we realized that Nixon didn't know much about his fellow Americans.

Then there was the "partly illegal" 1970 security plan, which J. Edgar Hoover rejected; Nixon approved it, but claimed in 1973 that the plan was killed five days after it went into operation. Senator Sam Ervin said the documents of the plan revealed an effort "to spy on the American people in general, or at least on those who didn't agree with the administration." Soon many moderates were making references to the possibility of "a police state"—a term which the old New Left had often been rebuked for using. Of course putting the squeeze on radicals or liberals was also tied in with selling Nixon's foreign policy to his conservative supporters; as Garry Wills wrote in 1972, Nixon "can hug communists at high level meetings, so long as he cracks down on the kids and blacks at home."

Never had we dwelled in such a realm of bad memories as were exposed by some of the witnesses at the Watergate hearings: "Not to the best of my recollection," "Not to my knowledge," and "I don't exactly recall" became the equivalent of taking the Fifth Amendment. Among the most educational moments were Mitchell's unregretful insistence that he'd protected Nixon from the truth about the Watergate plumbers because the President would have "lowered the boom"—that is, unleashed an investigation which would have begrimed his own campaign; the discovery that ex-cop Anthony Ulasewicz was involved in a proposed plan—on instructions from the White House—to rent a New York apartment where attractive men would be hired to seduce some women friends of Mary Jo Kopechne (who drowned in Edward Kennedy's car at Chappaquiddick), photograph them in the act, and then blackmail them into yielding information about the dead girl and the party preceding her death; and Erlichman stating that the burglary of Daniel Ellsberg's psychiatrist's office was justified. Also, after being asked if the President would have the right to commission a murder for the sake of national security, Erlichman said he wouldn't want to draw the line.

As James Baldwin later observed, "The American people wanted law and order, and they voted it in, and they *got* it." Dick Gregory reminded us that Nixon "said he was going to take crime out of the *streets*—he sure centralized crime."

The tired senators were jolted anew on hearing Haldeman's February 1972 memo to Dean—three months after the President's reelection: "We need to get our people to put out the story on foreign or Communist money that was used in support of demonstrations against the President in 1972. We should tie all 1972 demonstrations to McGovern and thus to the Democrats as part of the peace movement. . . . This is a good counter-offensive to be developed. . . . " The counter-attack, Haldeman admitted, was directed against the Democrats' probe of Watergate. Questioned angrily by Republican Senator Lowell Weicker of Connecticut about the allegations of communist affiliations—"What are the *facts?*"—Haldeman confessed quietly, "I don't know."

~

Since the conspiracy cases against numerous radicals did fail—from the Chicago 7 to the Berrigans—and when Watergate taught us even more about the use of illegal wiretaps, authorized break-ins and burglaries, intercepted mail, succulent payments for undercover activities, bribery, blackmail, spying on the press, the forging and burning of official documents, calculated harassments, sabotage, perjury, and provocateurs, some felt rather refreshed to realize that the "paranoia" of the Sixties wasn't irrational after all—or that it was far healthier than the President's.

Inefficiency, as well as insecurity, began to appear as a federal trademark. (Dick Gregory remarked about Nixon's White House tapes: "Imagine feelin' so lonely and insignificant that you'd bug your own phone!"). Some liberal or radical telephones sounded as though dozens were eating toast and celery along the lines, and one man I knew picked up his receiver and heard—instead of a dial tone—a recording of his own voice ordering a cheese Danish and a double cocoa from his drugstore. Still, there was a shred of comfort later when an expert wiretapping specialist said the Watergate equipment was "sloppy" and "amateurish".

Meanwhile some reporters acquired the habit of watching particularly provocative persons in crowds, and wondering if they'd been planted for certain occasions. Twice in 1969 I was intrigued by a couple of black men who exorted their hearers to "bring it all down" and yet seemed very ignorant of the themes of black militancy. They didn't even get the language right. And I'll long remember a rather elegant young redheaded man in a beige maxicoat, who hung around the steps and corridors of the Manhattan Criminal Court when the New York Panthers had their first hearings on the reduction of bail. Two fourteen-year-olds told me that he had urged them to rush at the police and attack them, also to phone in from outside and say there was a bomb in the building. They'd refused. But they grew very suspicious later when we saw him jabbing his forefinger at a row of unblinking policemen's chests and shouting "Pig! pig! Straighten your swastika!"—and afterwards chatting cordially with the cops inside the lobby.

But no one spotted George Demmerle, the thirty-nine-year-old former John Bircher and (lowly paid) FBI informer whom one frequently encountered as "Prince Crazy." Demmerle's feathered Day-Glo helmet was a familiar sight at antiwar rallies, and he enjoyed a mild fame from suggesting that the Brooklyn Bridge be blown up with a garden hose. He was made the Defense Captain for the Young Patriots, a chaotic white group which had its headquarters near my home in Yorkville. I also used to see him at the Panthers' occasional Sunday night suppers, where his revolutionary gargle was blithe indeed. In 1969, after Demmerle was arrested with three dedicated bombers (including Sam Melville, later killed in the siege of Attica), the charges against him were dropped and his informer's status was revealed. He explained that it had been very easy for him to infiltrate a variety of militant groups: he had simply imitated the style of Abbie Hoffman and Jerry Rubin. Those who were astounded to learn his real identity recalled that he used to talk eagerly about constructing submachine guns at a low price.

≈

During the Watergate hearings some of us remembered Nixon's pre-election remarks of November 5, 1972, when he promised to end "the whole era of permissiveness", while managing to equate criminals, addicts, welfare clients, and liberals who backed domestic programs for the poor. Thus the passage that few will want to forget: "The average American is just like the child in the family. You give him some responsibility and he is going to do something. If, on the other hand, you make him completely dependent and pamper him and cater to him too much, you are going to make him soft, spoiled, and eventually a very weak individual."

Those sentences served as a dry run for his 1973 Inaugural speech: "In our own lives, let each of us ask not just what will Government do for me, but what can I do for myself?" The men behind Watergate appeared to have heeded that point. And soon the President was knocked for his permissiveness toward them. Hence the inevitable lameness of his counterattack on Watergate at his dinner for the cheering prisoners of war on May 24. (They called him "Richard the Lion-Hearted".) He told them that secrecy had been crucial to negotiating with the North Vietnamese, and also with the Russian and Chinese leaders. Defending secrecy, Nixon neglected to defend honesty or respect for the law. Instead he entangled the lies of Watergate with the concept of a successful foreign policy, and made "secrecy" a substitute for national security. The *Times'* subsequent editorial was even brisker than usual: "Total security is the fantasy of a child."

≈

The first phase of the Watergate hearings gave us some imagery and language which may nestle in the national consciousness for years. Senator Sam Ervin as a beachmaster: the term for the old sea lions who rule the sands around them with such ease that they get little competition from younger males. Tapes: not merely the ones that Nixon made of his phone calls, but those bits of masking tape the burglars put on the Watergate door latch—if they hadn't, we might still know nothing about the hidden corruptions of our Government. Haldeman (on being told that John Dean had gotten together with the prosecutors): "When the toothpaste is out of the tube, it's hard to get it back again." The poetry of code: when Anthony Ulasewicz told Herbert Kalmbach that "Our laundry is in the icebox," he meant that the money for the Watergate defendants was in a vault in New York. Shredding: not only the incriminating documents which vanished, such as the Gemstone file, but G. Gordon Liddy shredding $100 bills—which were traceable to CREEP—and a number of hotel soap wrappers which could have revealed his travels as a spy. Assassination: not just the memories of Malcolm X, two Kennedys, Martin Luther King, but Liddy's offer to stand on a street corner and be "assassinated" if that were thought necessary to preserve his silence on Watergate. (Although he felt badly about having "goofed", Liddy was "morally opposed to suicide.") The hoax: when someone pretending to be Treasury Secretary George Schultz called Sam Ervin in July to say that the President would release the tapes, that incident seemed appropriate for the period: an imposter standing in for a member of an administration which had been hoaxing us since 1969.

In 1972 many pundits seemed certain that eight years of Nixon would be followed by eight years of Spiro Agnew. On October 11th 1973 he was forced to resign, admitting to income-tax evasion in 1967, but still denying that he'd been taking bribes for a decade from engineers who wanted government business. But he had to agree to let the Department of Justice publish forty pages of evidence on his guilt. In return it was arranged that he would not be sent to jail, and he was fined only $10,000. His lapses were explained in terms of the pressures on high-ranking politicians to live lavishly, in a way that would impress their wealthiest supporters. But Agnew wasn't a rich man. In addition to the thousands of dollars he had received in pay-offs, he had even accepted free groceries from a supermarket executive. And when he bought a new $190,000 house in 1973, he had to take out a $160,000 mortgage—and still could not afford new draperies.

As a convicted felon he claimed in his farewell speech that he had resigned for patriotic reasons, since "a dangerous war" was "raging in the Middle East," and because the country was "still torn by the wrenching experience" of Watergate. He ended by quoting a tribute to Abraham Lincoln from James Garfield, delivered right after Lincoln's assassination: "Fellow citizens, God reigns, and the Government in Washington still lives." A few days later, bumper stickers announced, "One down, one to go."

While we were still brushing Agnew's words from our ears, October 20 brought "the Saturday Night Massacre": Nixon's sudden firings of special Watergate prosecutor Archibald Cox and Deputy Attorney General William Ruckelshaus (who was dumped because he refused to fire Cox), and the resignation in protest of Attorney General Elliot Richardson. These three had been considered the most (and almost the only) respected and trustworthy members of the Nixon administration.

In theory Cox was ousted for being overly aggressive in demanding the presidential tapes "at a time of serious world crisis". But many suspected that Cox's relentless investigation of other White House scandals—such as the government's relationship with the International Telephone and Telegraph Corporation, the "possible abuses" of the use of the Internal Revenue Service, and further evidence on illegal Republican fund-raising, including the $100,000 donation to Nixon from billionaire Howard Hughes—was Nixon's real reason for purging him. Not long after, Richard Kleindienst. the former Attorney General, retracted his earlier statement that the President had not been involved in the ITT case.

The public outcry was greater than any roused by the earlier chapters of Watergate. The calls for impeachment or resignation became deeply serious— among Republican politicians as well as Democrats. We were told that the President was so absorbed by the war in the Middle East that he had no time to spare for national dust-ups. It was also reported that he spent much of October 21 watching his favourite football team, the Washington Redskins, on television. Prominent figures, such as George Meany, the president of the American Federation of Labor and Congress of Industrial Organizations, loudly questioned the "emotional stability" of the President. On October 23, apparently overwhelmed by the huge coast-to-coast reaction he hadn't expected, Nixon agreed to release the tapes he'd refused to yield for three months. Many assumed that the tapes would be well-doctored by the White House. Then the White House said that two of them had never existed at all.

On October 24, Nixon vetoed a bill in Congress which was designed to reduce the war power of the President. On October 25 U.S. armed forces all over the world went on alert for the Middle East. We were assured by Henry Kissinger (who had just been awarded the Nobel Peace Prize) that this piece of brinkmanship was in no way designed to distract attention from Watergate. No one then knew what the Russians' plans had been. The White House was responding to what were called "ambiguous" movements of Russian troops, plus some stern notes from Russian leaders. Brezhnev said the U.S. was fanning tensions with "fantastic rumors."

Many continued to suspect that the prime reason for the global alert—the first to have occurred since the Korean war—was Nixon's compulsion to show that he had not been disabled by the domestic crisis, which had been precipitated by his own behavior. But the alert itself had seemed dangerously provocative. Much of the American press called it an "overreaction," and our European allies were very disturbed that they had not been consulted by the White House. By the end of that incredible week, Washington echoed with the line, "A crisis a day keeps impeachment away."

On October 27, during a press conference, the President said the alert had prevented a major confrontation in the Middle East, and that "the outlook for a permanent peace is the best that it has been for twenty years."

Then he lashed out wildly against the television networks. Denouncing the "outrageous, distorted" coverage of recent years, he added that "people are pounded night after night by frantic, hysterical reporting," and implied that all the problems of the administration were the fault of the media.

~

Almost any death—whether it's someone you knew well or that of a public figure—makes you relive your experiences with that individual. Many felt they knew Lyndon Johnson more personally than any other American leader, since his emotions exploded so freely: we usually knew exactly what he was feeling. Learning that he was dead on January 22, 1973, some of us at first remembered our huge anger at him about Vietnam, and his wrath at us in return. Yet since his botched but urgent efforts to build domestic programs were being erased at the time of his death, it was rather amazing to recall that a recent American President had acknowledged the existence of the poor.

Sometimes you suspect that a person has unconsciously chosen the moment of departure. On the day of Nixon's Inauguration (January 20), I imagined LBJ in a towering rage. His widow later told us that he did know of the cease-fire agreement: that Nixon himself had phoned "to report the final breakthrough." But Johnson died a bit more than twenty-four hours before the President announced the truce. After all that the war had done to America, and after Johnson's own foreign policy had discredited him, it seemed unlikely that the former President would have wished to hear his successor hailed as a prince of peace. Despite some editorial protestations that LBJ would have been "pleased," it seemed possible that his heart had responded violently to an event he couldn't stand—and his conscious self didn't linger.

~

What some commentators called "the tragedy of Watergate" was simultaneously hailed as a triumph of justice: after Nixon's resignation, pious editorials kept repeating that "the system worked," that Congress, the Supreme Court, the House Judiciary Committee, and "the structure of American democracy" had functioned superbly in the removal of the President. Only a few voices retorted that "the system" had little to do with his departure: Nixon would not have had to abdicate if he had not taped himself. Had he destroyed the tapes that made him impeachable, he could have retained his throne.

Although some on the left regretted that he was not impeached—and were well aware that deposing a president would not change the nature of our government—there was an exhilaration in watching his helicopter rise from the White House lawn. We didn't then know that FBI director Clarence Kelley had put the bureau's fifty-nine offices on a nationwide alert in case "dissident groups" attempted a coup, but he added that "there wasn't a ripple" of insurrection.

Next day we learned that late on the night of the resignation, a crowd stood outside Gerald Ford's house, where there was nothing to see. Asked by a reporter why she was there, a young woman replied, "Because I want to be a part of history." And it was true that the late Sixties and early Seventies made quite a few Americans feel that witnesses were participants, that their lives were linked to events they had partially helped to shape, even though they couldn't control them.

∽

As we reeled further into the Seventies, the headlines continued to be beguiling: "Nestlé Is Lifting Cloak of Multinational Secrecy"; "Pope Regrets Peace Snag"; "Cry Of the Vanishing Whale Heeded"; "Youth Found Cool To Career in FBI"; "Mood of Negroes Is Found Uneasy"; "Mafia Badly Bruised"; "Men Cautioned On The Efficacy of Frozen Sperm"; and " 'I Have Never Seen So Much Dirt And Dust in My Whole Life' ": an Apollo astronaut's response to the surface of the moon. And even the radio bulletins seemed more eerie. Right after a spate of horrendous news—more dead in the Middle East, three old women murdered in Queens, new testimony about perjury and Watergate—there was the lilt of the cheerful conclusion: "Sports and the weather next."

∽

The final voices of this book must be those of some Vietnam veterans. Those I met in 1973 emphasized that the return to civilian life was just as devastating as having participated in the war. (Most of these were enlistees whose politics had altered gradually. But they felt that other veterans who still defended the war—or were apolitical—shared the same problems). Greeted by incomprehension and indifference at home, as well as by a sparsity of jobs, they found themselves "the most invisible soldiers in history," since they served as unwelcome reminders of Vietnam. They felt their war experience was unique, that it could not be compared with having fought in World War II.

Many citizens have been hostile to the veterans: "Even liberals treat us like we belong in a cage. As though we went off as mercenaries and came back as something less than human." In the late Sixties their fellow students on campuses sometimes called them pigs. Others seem startled that veterans have emotional problems, even though, as one said, "Being involved in the deaths and sufferings of millions of people: that's no adolescent growing pain." Another explained: "The war within ourselves is nowhere finished."

The veterans' relatives and old friends tell them to forget the war: don't be so serious—where's your sense of humor; you're no fun any more. In light of the apprehension about returning to the U.S., several compared memories of the huge hush on the planes that brought them back from Vietnam: "Everyone's thinking about getting on that freedom-bird and going home, you think there'll be parties on the plane. But it's very quiet—just silent people looking out the windows. Nobody talks much."

Some have worked to free themselves from the emotional paralysis that the war bestowed by re-examining and expressing their feelings with other veterans: they meet regularly in rap groups. Above all the military told them that men must not have emotions of any sort; also "Don't be afraid, you're a man." This is known as "the John Wayne thing." An ex-Marine murmured, "In my case, it was Errol Flynn." One referred to Simon and Garfunkel's song, "I Am A Rock," and its last lines: "And a rock feels no pain / And an island never cries." Another said, "The whole image of a man in America today is: you can't feel. I say, goddamit, let me *feel*."

They were also informed that "orientals set a very low value on life." Hence "it's okay to go over there and kill even the wrong ones. We were told that civilians could be our enemies because they supported the VC. And we believed this. . . . Once I went to a Vietnamese funeral. The amount of crying and grief was just incredible. And I realized that the Vietnamese set a *high* value on life. . . . People here don't know. They just think the Vietnamese leave their dead lying around."

Many comment on the unreality of being in Vietnam itself: "I might as well have been in the New Jersey swamps." Afterwards some find it hard to remember Vietnam at all. One enlistee, who served for five years and returned in 1971, said: "What the public doesn't know is the things that guys have committed in Vietnam, and what that's done to them. About six years ago, we would go into the Mekong Delta—a free fire zone—simply burning down villages with no one in them but civilians. I remember leaving some old women just laying there in the burned down village—just laying there. They had nothing: the village was their life. And what that means to me—that I took part in that—I'll have to remember that for the rest of my life." The confusion about civilians and enemies never ceased: "We rarely questioned ourselves about who we were killing."

He continued: "I *saw* the body of someone I killed—with a grenade. Maybe he was just some old farmer. I saw the bodies of two others I killed—with a machine gun. They were supposed to be carrying weapons. I didn't see the weapons. But I saw the bodies."

Some arriving in Vietnam were repelled by the poverty: "I just couldn't believe that these were the people I was coming to defend. I kept thinking: there must be somebody else—some other people to defend. My mistrust of the Vietnamese started from that day. Little beady-eyed people who were going to shoot at me. I treated the Vietnamese with utter contempt while I was there. Absolutely hated them.

"Americans just can't accept the simple existence that most orientals live. They feel it's threatening—it's somehow *cunning* that people can exist and even prosper with so little. So you feel that they could be very harmful if they tried. . . . When I was first in Saigon, I was shocked that the Vietnamese could be doctors or lawyers, that they weren't just little slant-eyed gooks running around. And I was shocked at the intelligence of the people in the villages. Even bargaining for a banana they made very complex."

Most of the veterans I saw said they'd had severe problems with women since leaving the military. They spoke of numbness and the difficulty of feeling anything at all. Also mistrust: "I threw everyone away when I came back—my girlfriend, my family, my friends. I felt that they couldn't understand. At the time, I thought they'd deserted me. But I was really pushing them away."

A veteran who worked closely with many others described the dilemma of the homecomer: "He may wonder if he should deal with women as a tough guy—maybe the uniform will get them? Then he finds out that if he comes on macho, they may think he's homosexual! Some guys come back very horny; it's true that they think of women only as sex objects. And they think that women's liberation just means laying everybody: they heard on the radio in Vietnam that it's free love time back here. The recently released veteran thinks if he can just get sex out of the way, then he can get the rest of his life together. So the priority is to score—even though that's no more satisfying than a bar of soap."

Most veterans naturally resent being regarded as "time bombs, skyjackers, dope fiends, and baby burners." And they've found that employers almost automatically expect a veteran to be crazed or on drugs: "Some raving sickie who shoots up women and kids in the streets." But for many, the impact of the war is delayed until about eighteen months or two years later: then the rate of breakdowns is higher than during combat.

Once more I asked a veteran to tell me why post-Vietnam life was as painful as being in the war. He answered carefully and rather slowly, pausing for emphasis, perhaps reviewing it for himself: "Coming back from a situation where life and death for thousands is decided every day—to a place where that fact is ignored, or is of little concern—is just . . . mind-boggling. . . . From time to time I say we're scarred for life. Not just from war scenes. But scarred in another way. I don't think that any of us will be able to justify—in our own minds—what we were part of." Some of the veterans could educate a whole society—if millions could bear to listen. So the last words on this page belong to one of the survivors: "We went to Vietnam because we did not know then what we know now."

Index

King's Courage

By Stacia Deutsch and
Rhody Cohon
Illustrated by David Wenzel

SCHOLASTIC INC.
New York Toronto London Auckland Sydney
Mexico City New Delhi Hong Kong Buenos Aires

To Darrell, Jeff, and Rick Steinberg—

All working to better our world. And to their parents,

Bud and Arlene, who taught them to pursue justice.

With special thanks to Jeff, who has dedicated his

life to educating students about the Civil Rights Movement.

With deepest respect,

Stacia and Rhody

ISBN-13: 978-0-545-07176-5
ISBN-10: 0-545-07176-3

Text copyright © 2006 by Stacia Deutsch and Rhody Cohon.
Illustrations copyright © 2006 by David Wenzel.
All rights reserved. Published by Scholastic Inc., 557 Broadway, New York, NY 10012,
by arrangement with Aladdin Paperbacks, an imprint of Simon & Schuster
Children's Publishing Division. BLAST TO THE PAST is a registered trademark of
Stacia Deutsch and Rhody Cohon. SCHOLASTIC and associated logos are trademarks
and/or registered trademarks of Scholastic Inc.

12 11 10 9 8 7 6 5 4 3 2   8 9 10 11 12 13/0

Printed in the U.S.A.   40

First Scholastic printing, January 2008

Designed by Lisa Vega
The text of this book was set in Minion.
The illustrations are rendered in Winsor Newton watercolor.

Contents

1

Monday

We were about to slip the cartridge into the back of the time-travel computer. Suddenly the classroom door swung open.

Jacob shoved the computer behind his back at sonic speed. I swear I heard a popping noise when his elbow broke the sound barrier. That's how fast he moved.

"Jacob and Zack, are you in here?" Mrs. Osborne asked as she walked into the room. She was carrying their sleeping brother, Gabe, in her arms.

"Oh, good," Mrs. Osborne said to her twin sons. "I found you. I need you to watch—" She paused when she saw me standing there. "Hi, Abigail," she said.

I've always liked Mrs. Osborne. Jacob and Zack live

next door to me. We've known one another forever. I hang out at their house almost as often as at my own.

"Hey, Mrs. Osborne," I greeted her, with a casual nod of my head. I'm good at looking like nothing's up, when something really is.

Mrs. Osborne smiled at me and turned to look at Bo. "I don't know you," she said to him. "What's your name?"

Bo's real name is Roberto Rodriguez. He's the new kid at school. I like Bo. He's supersmart. He reads a lot and remembers everything. But Bo is also really shy, especially around adults. I figured I'd better help him out.

"This is our friend Bo," I told Mrs. Osborne.

"Hullo," Bo mumbled, staring down at his shoelaces.

She tried asking Bo a few questions about his family and how he liked our school, but his answers were all one word. "Fine" or "Good." Stuff like that.

"You do it, Abigail," Bo leaned over and whispered. "Tell her about me."

"Bo's an only child who lives with his mom," I

informed her. "Once he gets to know you, he talks more."

Mrs. Osborne thanked me for the information. Then she took a long, careful look around the classroom.

There we were: four third graders all alone in social studies room 305. No teacher. Backpacks neatly stacked in the corner. And Jacob, standing like a statue, with his hands held tightly behind his back.

If I were Mrs. Osborne, I'd be looking at us carefully too.

"I thought you had History Club with Mr. Caruthers after school on Mondays. Where is he?" Mrs. Osborne asked us, squinting her eyes slightly with curiosity. "What are you kids up to?"

"Nothing," Jacob answered a little too quickly.

"This is our History Club meeting," Zack explained. Zack wasn't lying. Bo, Jacob, Zack, and I liked to call our time-travel adventures "History Club." During History Club our social studies teacher, Mr. Caruthers, sends us on missions to visit famous people in American history.

Mr. C had invented a time-travel computer. The computer looked like a handheld video game with four red buttons and a large screen. Slipping a cartridge into the back took us to the past. Pulling out the cartridge brought us home again.

Our teacher had told us that American history was in danger. He'd showed us a little black book full of names. For some mysterious reason all the famous Americans in Mr. C's book were quitting. They weren't inventing, or speaking out, or fighting for what was right. They were giving up on their dreams!

Mr. C wanted more time to focus on his newest invention, so he asked the four of us to time-travel for him.

It was our job to prevent history from changing forever!

So far we'd been very successful on all our adventures. We'd managed to keep history on track—no small thing since the computer gave us only two hours to get the job done.

Seriously, if Mrs. Osborne had walked into the classroom two seconds later, there would have been a green glowing hole in the middle of the floor. All she would have seen were the tops of our heads as we jumped down through time.

"Who's going to tell me what's going on here?" Mrs. Osborne asked as she looked at each of us in turn.

First, she stared long and hard at her two sons.

The twins might have looked alike but they were very different. It was easy to tell them apart. Today Jacob was wearing slacks, a white collared shirt, and a belt.

Zack was the opposite. Shorts, T-shirt with a big food stain on the front, and tennis shoes so dirty they looked like they'd been run over by a garbage truck.

Their clothes were different and their personalities were different too. Zack worried a lot and quit everything he tried. And yet, he was also totally goofy and very funny. Jacob was more easygoing and adventurous. He never quit since he did only one thing—computers.

Their mom pinned her gaze on Jacob, who still

had his hands locked around the computer, safely hidden behind his back. Afterward, she studied Zack. Zack's lips were pressed so tightly together, they didn't even look like lips. They looked like two flat pink worms. The twins weren't talking.

Next, she looked at Bo, but saying "Hullo" had been hard enough for him. It was obvious he wasn't telling her anything more.

So she turned to me. "Abigail?" Mrs. Osborne was looking for the truth.

I felt a teeny-weeny bit guilty that we were hiding something from her. "It's—It's just History Club," I stammered. "Really."

I think she believed me.

"Mom," Zack asked as he moved to the side, away from Jacob and the computer, "what are you doing here?"

I guess I really had convinced her nothing unusual was going on, because Mrs. Osborne stopped surveying us suspiciously and answered, "Well, tomorrow is Election Day."

Election Day is a special Tuesday in early

November when people can vote for government officials and new laws. I knew that our school was a polling place—a place to vote. Last year my own parents voted in our gym during their lunchtime.

"I'm in charge of organizing the volunteers this year. We have a lot of volunteers coming to help out." As Mrs. Osborne spoke, she shifted Baby Gabe up and rested him against her shoulder.

Even though Gabe was almost two years old, I still called him "Baby Gabe."

Honestly, Baby Gabe was a destructive mini-monster. Nothing was safe if Gabe was around. But he was also superadorable. Today he was wearing the sweetest little outfit: blue pants and a bright red T-shirt.

"I'm sure I told you boys I'd be here after school to help get everything ready," Mrs. Osborne said. "Don't you remember? I asked you to watch Gabe for me while I set up."

What! I nearly yelled the word, but held my tongue. It was a good thing because Jacob and Zack said it for me.

"What!" they cried at the same time.

Zack bit the inside of his lip. "I don't remember you telling us!" He was so surprised his eyes were bulging out of his head like a cartoon character. "I'd have remembered a thing like that!"

"I'd have remembered too," Jacob added. I could see the panic on his face.

The twins couldn't babysit today! Mr. C was counting on us. According to his little black book, Martin Luther King Jr. was the next to give up and quit. We had to convince him to follow his dream.

"I—," I began, thinking of a hundred reasons Jacob and Zack couldn't watch their brother. But I didn't get a chance to tell Mrs. Osborne even one good reason.

She checked her watch and said, "Oh, my goodness, I'm late." And before I could get another word out of my mouth, Mrs. Osborne spread a blanket out on the classroom floor and gently lay Gabe on top of it.

"I'll be back when club time is over," she told us. "That's exactly two hours from now. I'll be in the gym if you need me." She handed Gabe's diaper bag to Zack. Like me, he wanted to argue, but couldn't get the words out. Zack just stood there sputtering, "I—We—You—Me—"

"Gabe should sleep the whole time I'm gone. He won't bother your club meeting. If for some reason he wakes up," Mrs. Osborne continued, "give him the crackers and sippy cup of water from his bag. I'm counting on you kids to keep him out of trouble."

With that, she left the room.

2

Baby Gabe

I looked down at the sleeping Baby Gabe. "What are we going to do?"

"I don't know," Bo said.

"Us either," Jacob and Zack answered together.

After a few stressful moments of silence, I asked, "If Mr. C were here, what advice would he give us?"

Bo answered. "He'd probably ask us one of his famous questions and make us think of answers for ourselves. Just like he does in class."

Every Monday Mr. C asks our social studies class cool questions about American history.

Today he had asked us to think about what the world would be like if Dr. Martin Luther King Jr. had quit. What if he'd never led the famous voting-rights march from Selma, Alabama, to Montgomery, Alabama, on March 21, 1965?

Mr. C explained, "Montgomery is the capital city of Alabama. The marchers planned to gather on the capitol building steps." Mr. C pushed up his glasses. They were always sliding down his nose.

"Montgomery is only fifty-four miles from Selma, but no one drove. Because they wanted to make a strong political statement, hundreds of people walked together. It took five days." He shoved his glasses back up. I considered buying him a tube of superglue.

"The March twenty-first walk was a great success. On the day they reached the capitol steps, twenty-five thousand people had joined the marchers. But it was also the third try. Before that day, many bad things happened and two other marches were stopped before the walkers even left Selma."

Mr. C closed his eyes for a minute. I think he was remembering something.

When Mr. C reopened his eyes, he said, "That third march changed America. Not long after, African Americans were given the freedom to vote."

Mr. C explained that when people can't vote, they can't help make laws. They can't get new people elected to government. Voting is an important freedom.

"Being able to vote means that you are truly free," he said.

I thought all Americans had been free and equal for a really long time. I was totally amazed. The year 1965 wasn't very long ago at all.

We learned that in 1964, after a lot of hard work by Martin Luther King Jr. and others, congress passed the Civil Rights Act that ended segregation. Mr. C said, "'Segregation' meant that people with black and colored skin were kept separate from people with white skin." I wrote down the definition of the word "segregation."

That faraway look came into his eyes again when Mr. C said, "Segregation was so strong in the southern states that there were separate areas for blacks and whites. They couldn't sit together in restaurants or at the movies. There were even separate bathrooms. Some for whites and others marked: 'Coloreds Only.'"

Usually Mr. C sits on the edge of his desk when he talks. Today he was standing up in front of the class. He was also usually messy on Mondays. But today his tie was tied and his hair combed. Because he looked so nice, I knew what he was saying was extra important.

"Dr. Martin Luther King Jr. was a major leader in the Civil Rights Movement. He helped abolish segregation." Mr. C went to the blackboard and wrote: "Abolish" means get rid of.

Next to the definition for "abolish" he wrote: "Civil rights" means equal treatment for all people.

I carefully copied the words into my notebook so I would never forget.

Mr. C went on to tell us that after the Civil Rights Act became a law, people were allowed to mix together in all places. But voting was still a problem.

Mr. C reminded us about the United States Constitution. "The Constitution is a document describing our national laws and how our government works. In the Constitution it is clear that every adult American citizen has the right to vote. No matter the color of his or her skin." He paused. "But blacks in the southern United States were often denied that right."

"I don't understand," Khoi Nguyen wondered. "If the Constitution said they could vote, why couldn't they?"

"Some white leaders still wanted segregation," Mr. C told us. "So they created new laws that prevented blacks from going into a polling place to vote."

I raised my hand and asked, "What kind of laws did they create?" I was surprised to hear that even if you had the right to vote, some people wouldn't let you. That seemed so mean.

"Well," Mr. C began, "some states and cities gave black people tests. If you couldn't answer the questions, you couldn't vote."

Mr. C explained that the tests were called "literacy tests," and lots of different cities had them. Then, he decided to ask Bo a question from one of these old tests. Since Bo's family is originally from Mexico, Mr. C told Bo that he would have been considered "colored." Bo's family would have had to take the test too.

"How many bubbles are there on a bar of soap?"

The question was so dumb, Bo wasn't even going to try to answer. He just shrugged.

Jacob started to laugh. "No one can answer that!" he argued.

Mr. C asked the class another literacy test question. "Can anyone recite the whole United States Constitution by heart?"

Zack raised his hand, but he was the only one who did. Zack was such a kidder. We all knew he was joking around.

There might be two or three people on the entire planet who have the whole thing memorized. I bet the president doesn't even know the entire Constitution by heart.

"See?" Mr. Caruthers told us. "They gave unfair tests, made people pay taxes to vote, and told them they could vote only if their grandfather had voted in 1861. These kinds of laws prevented Americans with colored skin from voting."

"Man," I said, letting out a big breath, "that stinks." I didn't mean to talk without raising my hand. I was so upset about the way people had been treated, the words just tumbled out of my mouth.

Mr. C wasn't mad at me for talking without being called on. He simply nodded in agreement. "It sure does, Abigail," he said with a small laugh.

Mr. C glanced over my head and noticed the clock on the classroom wall. "We have only a few minutes before the bell rings and we still have our 'what if' question to discuss."

He took a quick look around the room and asked, "What do you think the world would be like if Martin Luther King Jr. had quit and never led the successful voting-rights march from Selma to Montgomery on March 21, 1965?"

Ruti Takimora thought that some other black leader would have led the walk and America would still be as it is today. She reminded us that there were other civil rights leaders following the model of Malcolm X.

Matthew Abrams knew that there was a big difference between Martin Luther King Jr. and the followers of Malcolm X. Dr. King believed that there shouldn't be any violence when you try to change unfair laws. Malcolm X had also wanted voting rights, but he had taught that you should fight bad laws by "any means necessary."

Juan Garcia raised his hand. He was about to give his opinion when Shanika Washington started to cry. She had gotten totally freaked out at the thought of Martin Luther King Jr. quitting. She didn't want to imagine what her life would be like if she couldn't vote when she turned eighteen. It was too horrible to even consider.

Mr. Caruthers put his arm around Shanika. "It's all right. The question is just to get you kids thinking," he comforted her. "History is not going to change. I promise."

Then the bell rang. Class was over.

As we were collecting our books to leave, Mr. C asked Jacob, Zack, Bo, and me to hold back for a second. When we were alone, he secretly handed us a computer cartridge. It had a small picture of Dr. King on the front.

"Do you have the computer?" Mr. C asked me. Of course I did! It was Monday, after all.

"I need your help," he whispered. "Things have gotten too hard for Dr. King, and he's decided to quit. Right after school you need to make certain that Martin Luther King Jr. doesn't give up. He must lead the third march to Montgomery."

So here we were, ready to go to Selma, Alabama, in 1965. Stuck with a sleeping toddler.

"Okay," I said to Jacob, Zack, and Bo. "We can't babysit and find Martin Luther King Jr. at the same time. We need a plan."

Jacob put the computer and cartridge down on Mr. C's desk. "I think one of us has to stay back with Gabe while the rest of us go on to Selma."

I was bummed, but Jacob was right. Someone had to stay behind.

"I have a bad feeling about going," Zack said. "But even so, there's no way I'm staying here. I'd rather do almost anything in the universe than babysit Gabe. I'd eat live toads, roll in the grass with snakes, put my hand in a beehive and—"

"We get your point," I told Zack, cutting him off. "So Zack's going." I thought about Jacob and then quickly decided. "Jacob has to go. He's the only one who knows how to use the time-travel computer."

At that, Jacob looked down at the watch Mr. C had given him on our first adventure. "We have to hurry." He tapped on the watch face.

We needed to make a decision. Fast.

Bo read a lot and knew so many useful things, he really should go. Plus, Gabe didn't know him. . . .

"Okay." I sighed. "I'll stay and babysit." Sadness filled my heart.

The boys insisted they didn't know how they'd ever convince Dr. King without me. I was bold and curious. I always had a million questions—important questions that helped us on our adventures. But there was no other choice.

The boys said "Good-bye," and Jacob went to get the computer from Mr. C's desk.

It was gone.

We all turned just in time to see Baby Gabe slip the

cartridge into the back of the machine. The time-travel hole opened in the classroom floor. Green smoke oozed out and floated around the room. Gabe was holding the computer, standing at the edge of the hole. Giggling.

I quickly reached out and snagged the back of his little blue pants. Unfortunately, the waistband was elastic. It stretched. And stretched. And stretched.

He kept pulling forward, teetering over the hole. If I stepped a fraction of an inch forward, we were both going to fall in.

Bo grabbed me around the waist to steady me. Jacob put his arms around Bo. Zack held on to Jacob.

It was no use. With a quick turn of his head, Gabe sunk his teeth into my skin, biting me on the hand.

"Ouch!" I shouted, opening my palm in pain.

Just like that, Baby Gabe toppled over and disappeared.

"We've got to go get Gabe!" I shouted to the boys, motioning to Zack to grab the diaper bag.

It was my turn to break the sound barrier as I quickly leapt, following Gabe down into the hole.

As I fell through time, I distinctly heard Jacob call out, "That mini-monster better not have broken Mr. C's computer!"

3

Brown Chapel AME Church

We were in a big church. People were crammed in all around us. They were in the pews, standing in the aisles. We'd landed near the back, in an empty spot between a potted plant and the main doors leading outside.

Way at the front a group of black men stood near a table and microphone. They were taking turns giving speeches.

I stood up on my tiptoes and scanned the room. We needed to find Baby Gabe. Immediately. There was no sign of him.

"What are you doing?" I asked Bo. Instead of standing on his toes, Bo was squatting low, his cheek pressed to the ground.

"Checking for little feet," Bo answered. I thought that was very clever.

"Any luck?" I asked, looking down at Bo.

"Nope." He stood up. "I don't see him."

"I knew something like this was going to happen," Zack groaned. He was up on his tiptoes too. "I told you I had a bad feeling. I didn't want to babysit Gabe. But I didn't want to lose him in 1965, either!" Zack's voice grew louder when he said, "Let's just find Gabe and go home."

"You're going to let Martin Luther King Jr. quit?" Jacob challenged his brother. "I can't believe you're willing to walk away without even trying to find Dr. King and convince him."

"We have to take Gabe back to school," Zack argued.

Jacob got in Zack's face. "We don't have to go home after we find him. We can still do the job Mr. C sent us here to do."

"We can't keep Gabe in 1965," Zack said. "What if he gets lost again? Or hurt?" Zack held up the diaper bag. "I don't even have a Band-Aid. Plus, what if mom goes back to the classroom and sees that we're missing?"

"Stop worrying, Zack," Jacob said, his voice tight. "You're being a loser."

"I'm not a loser, you are!" Zack sneered, shoving his brother.

Jacob lost his balance, stumbling backward, nearly knocking over the potted plant as he fell.

Just then, a white man and a black woman came out of a side aisle. The man caught Jacob before he hit the ground. The woman caught the plant.

"Pushing does not lead to freedom," the man said sternly to Zack. "Fighting only leads to more fighting. Dr. King preaches nonviolence. We must swallow our anger and meet fists with love."

"That's good advice," I exclaimed, then boldly asked, "Who are you?"

"I am Rabbi Gerald Raiskin." He helped Jacob to his feet. "I came all the way from California to be part of the march to Montgomery. Jews. Christians. Blacks and whites. People of all colors and beliefs. We are gathered here at the Brown Chapel AME

Church to begin walking for the freedom to vote."

Rabbi Raiskin turned to Zack and insisted, "You must apologize to your twin."

"I—" It looked like Zack was going to apologize to Jacob, but instead he grumbled, "It's his fault. He called me a loser."

The woman looked back and forth from Jacob to Zack. Rabbi Raiskin introduced her as Mrs. Hepworth.

"Names can't break our spirit," Mrs. Hepworth told Zack. "We're stronger than that." She squinted her eyes. "So strong, we're willing to try to march all the way to Montgomery again."

Giving us a long hard look, Mrs. Hepworth asked, "Do you children know what happened this past Sunday?"

I shook my head. Mr. C said something bad had made the marchers turn back to Selma, but he didn't say what. It was clear from the expressions on their faces that Jacob and Zack didn't know either.

But Bo knew. He took a deep breath before saying the words, "Bloody Sunday."

I trembled. Something called "bloody" was definitely bad news.

"That's right, young man. It was Bloody Sunday." Mrs. Hepworth held out her arm and rolled up her sleeve. There were big lumpy, purple bruises all the way from her shoulder to her wrist. "Two days ago six hundred marchers left this church headed to Montgomery. But there were police and state troopers blocking our way. They wouldn't let us cross the Edmund Pettus Bridge."

"That's the big bridge that leads out of Selma," Bo added, helping to explain.

Mrs. Hepworth went on. "The troopers told us to stop. They gave us two minutes to turn around and go back into Selma." She lightly rubbed the bruises on her arm. "After only one minute, they attacked us."

"The police attacked you?" Jacob was puzzled. "I thought police were supposed to keep us safe."

"Police enforce the laws," Bo put in. "But like Mr. C said, the laws weren't fair." He rubbed his chin. Bo did that when he was thinking.

28

"Sixty-five people were injured and at least seventeen went to the hospital. It was lucky that no one died at the march on Bloody Sunday," Mrs. Hepworth told us.

I felt tears at the back of my eyes. All the people wanted was the right to vote. Hitting them was cruel and unfair.

"How come you didn't fight back?" Zack asked.

"Nonviolence means more than not striking back. It means having a different type of strength. It means having quiet courage. So I just let them hit me," she said proudly. "And I'd do it again if I had to."

I was brave, but Mrs. Hepworth was the bravest person I'd ever met.

She glanced over her shoulder at the front of the chapel and said, "Dr. King wasn't with us that day, but he's here now. Getting ready to lead our march."

"Where?" I said, popping back up on my toes. I could barely see to the front of the room.

Mrs. Hepworth pointed at a thin black man wearing a dark blue suit and tie. He was talking into the microphone. I couldn't hear what he was saying, but still, I got very excited.

I was ready to rush to the front of the room to talk to him. Now that we'd found Dr. King, it would be easy to convince him not to quit.

I tried to take a running leap forward, but Zack held my arm. "Gabe first," he reminded me. "We can talk to Dr. King after we find Gabe." The way he said it, Zack had changed his mind. As long as we found Gabe first, he was willing to stay in 1965.

But Jacob didn't trust his brother. "Promise me you won't snag the time-travel computer out of Gabe's hands and make us go home," he seriously demanded.

Zack held up three fingers. "Scout's honor," he said. Zack had been in Boy Scouts for three weeks the previous summer, before he'd decided to try swim team instead. "But you have to promise you won't try to talk to Dr. King before we find Gabe."

"Deal," Jacob answered. Bo and I agreed too.

For the first time ever the twins had worked out a

deal without fighting. This nonviolence stuff was great.

Zack asked Mrs. Hepworth and Rabbi Raiskin if they had seen Gabe. They hadn't. We figured that if Gabe wasn't in the church, maybe he was outside.

"Let's hurry," I said. "We'll find him and rush back to talk to MLK." I decided to call Martin Luther King Jr. "MLK" to save time.

"We gotta run," I said to Mrs. Hepworth. "Thanks for telling us about Bloody Sunday." I smiled and said, "I bet that in the future you'll get to vote. Voting is power."

Mrs. Hepworth smiled at me.

All of a sudden the speeches up front ended and the doors behind us flew open. People began pouring past. They kept coming and coming. We were caught up in the crowd and practically carried out the door. Down the church steps.

"There must be hundreds of marchers," I said in awe.

"Not hundreds," Bo corrected me. "One thousand

five hundred." I looked at him sideways. He shrugged casually. "I read a Martin Luther King Jr. biography. The book said that's how many people are headed out on this second march."

"Second march?" I asked. I felt a knot in my stomach. "But I thought we were here for the third march to Montgomery, like we'd talked about in class." I looked at Bo. "Isn't today March twenty-first?"

"Not if Bloody Sunday was two days ago," Bo answered calmly. "Bloody Sunday was March 7, 1965."

"This isn't the right date!" Zack complained, scanning the crowd.

Annoyed, Jacob muttered, "When we find Gabe, I'll—" I shot him an evil eye and reminded him to cool it, saying, "MLK preaches nonviolence."

"I'll ask him nicely what he did to Mr. C's computer," Jacob finished, shaking his head.

I laughed and replied, "That's what I thought."

We stepped aside and waited for a break in the crowd. We couldn't risk getting separated. As we stood there, I wondered why today's march wouldn't work out. Why would there be another march on March twenty-first?

I hoped it wasn't going to be another Bloody Sunday. Should we warn the marchers? I bet Bo knew, but I didn't have a chance to ask him.

"Look!" I suddenly shouted. "Over there!" I pointed into the crowd.

Somehow, Martin Luther King Jr. had gotten by us. We never even saw him leave the church. He was walking quickly, disappearing into the mob.

I panicked. MLK was getting farther and farther away. I wanted to run after him, but we'd made a promise to Zack. We were going to find Gabe first. As soon as we found Baby Gabe, we'd have to figure out how to catch up with MLK.

"Hey! Check it out!" Jacob was jumping up and down, waving his finger like crazy.

Just behind MLK, a black man had a small white boy riding on his shoulders. With my eagle eyes I could tell that the boy was wearing blue pants and a

bright red shirt. Something in his hands glinted in the sunlight. It was Mr. C's computer.

We'd found him!

Baby Gabe was being carried off, toward the Edmund Pettus Bridge.

4

The Edmund Pettus Bridge

It was a bridge like any other. A wide bridge over a river. Cars went by us, crossing out of Selma and following the sign marked EAST ROUTE 80.

Across the top rail, words read: EDMUND PETTUS BRIDGE.

Struggling through the crowd, we chased after Baby Gabe as he bounced happily on the black man's shoulders.

Zack might have been the fastest runner, but Bo reached Gabe first. By the time we caught up, Bo was already holding Baby Gabe in his arms.

"Good work," I said as we reached Bo. I lifted Baby Gabe from him and set the toddler on the ground.

Gabe held my hand, happy to see us. He looked up

at me and said in his tiny sweet voice, "Abby." The monster melted my heart.

"You better not have broken Mr. C's computer," Jacob said as he pried the time-travel machine out of Gabe's tight, sticky fingers. Gabe didn't want to let go, but Jacob managed to peel off his fingers one at a time.

"What did you say?" Zack asked Bo. We were super-surprised that Bo had spoken to the man.

Bo acted like it was no big deal. "I explained that the kid was my friends' brother. We were supposed to be watching him when he escaped." Basically all true.

"I recognized the man from a book. That's Reverend Ralph Abernathy. He figured the boy's parents were on the march. So he took Gabe along until he could find them," Bo explained. Then added, "I can't believe I got to speak to Reverend Ralph Abernathy. He's a civil rights hero."

We would have thanked Reverend Abernathy for taking such good care of Gabe, but he'd already hustled off into the crowd. Instead, we thanked Bo for his help.

"Having a little brother is a major pain." Zack gave Gabe a small pat on the butt. "I was so worried. All I could think about was what would have happened if we hadn't found him."

Zack didn't take a breath before adding, "Mom would be totally mad. Of course, we wouldn't know she was mad because we wouldn't be there to see her. We'd be trapped here. In Selma. In 1965. Forever. Plus, we'd have wasted so much time looking for Gabe that MLK would've quit. Blacks would never get to vote. Mr. C would be bummed. And—"

Zack was on a roll. I interrupted him when I started to laugh. He might have gone on with his list of concerns all day. Zack cracked me up.

When Bo and Jacob began to laugh too, Zack shook off the stress and stuck his tongue out at us. Gabe stuck his tongue out too. "Let's just say that finding Gabe is one less thing for me to worry about." Zack chuckled.

Now it was time to find MLK, so we charged forward into the crowd. Well, honestly, Bo, Zack, Gabe, and I charged forward. Jacob hung back, eating our dust.

"What's the deal, Turtle Man?" Zack asked when Jacob finally caught up. "You're dragging your feet."

Jacob didn't say a word. He flashed an angry glance at his baby brother and then slowly opened his hand. Lying in his palm was one of the four red buttons from the front of the computer. There were torn blue and white wires sticking out from the hole where the button had been.

"Gabe broke the computer?" I asked the obvious question.

"I knew he would," Jacob answered. "He's a destroyer. This is exactly why we usually hide the computer over at your house, Abigail." Jacob tried to shove the button back on, but it fell right off. "The teeth marks in the plastic make me think Gabe tried to eat the button right off the front."

I remembered how Gabe bit me when I tried to pull him away from the time-travel hole. "He does have sharp teeth," I admitted. Then I asked, "Can you fix it?" If anyone could repair a broken computer, it was Jacob.

Jacob didn't answer. He just stared at the wires.

"This could take a while," he said. "And I need a few tools."

Jacob checked his wristwatch. "We only have an hour and thirty-three minutes left." Reluctantly, Jacob slipped the broken button and the computer into his front pants pocket. "Let's find Dr. King." Jacob bit the inside of his lip. "We'll worry about the computer later."

We hurried ahead. We'd almost caught up to MLK when I noticed the police officers. They were blocking the bridge.

There were rows and rows of police as far as my eyes could see: men in blue uniforms and blue protective helmets, blue state-trooper cars, police on horses. They were all holding clubs and what looked like canisters of tear gas.

I got scared. Bo took my hand and said, "On Bloody Sunday the Reverend Frederick Douglas Reese said that the soldiers looked like a sea of blue."

I looked around. It was a sea of blue. And these police weren't here to help us march for freedom. No,

these police were here to prevent us from marching out of Selma. No matter what.

I remembered Mrs. Hepworth's bruised arm and wondered if I could be strong like her. Could I continue to march forward, not knowing if the police would hit me with their sticks? Voting rights were really important, but so was my health. If things got bad, would I run away or bravely stay?

And then I saw him!

Dr. King was speaking to a policeman who was slapping a club up and down in the palm of his hand. I was scared Martin Luther King Jr. was about to get hit.

Goose bumps traveled up my back.

I swear I could literally smell the danger.

5

Turnaround Tuesday

"Don't stress out, Abigail," Bo said. I have no idea how he knew what I was thinking. "It's only the second march. This group of walkers isn't going to cross the bridge. No one will get hurt today. The marchers will just turn around and go back home."

I felt relieved. And selfish that I felt so relieved.

Telling myself over and over that Bo knew it was a nonviolent day, I inched forward so I could hear what they were saying.

"Stop where you are!"

I froze.

"This march will not continue," the policeman told Dr. King.

Martin Luther King Jr. lifted his foot, like he was

about to take another step. My heart was pounding in my ears.

"Stop where you are." The man repeated his command. "This march will not continue!"

Martin Luther King Jr. lowered his foot. He nodded politely and smiled at the officer. "May we kneel and pray?" Dr. King asked in a gentle yet firm voice.

The officer agreed and the most amazing thing I've ever seen happened.

One thousand five hundred people—men, women, and children; black, white, tan, all shades of skin; Christians, Jews, and people of every faith— dropped to their knees in prayer.

Bo, Zack, Jacob, and I sank to our knees too. It took a little work and a few crackers, but we got Baby Gabe to squat down. Not quite on his knees, but close.

We all closed our eyes and listened to Martin Luther King Jr.'s prayer.

When the prayer was over, all the marchers turned around and headed back to Brown Chapel. Everyone was holding hands. Arms linked. Singing.

We shall overcome

We shall overcome

We shall overcome some day

The song filled me and gave me a big boost of energy for our mission.

I saw Reverend Abernathy in the crowd. This time he was carrying a different kid on his shoulders, an adorable little black boy about the same age as Gabe. The little boy grinned at us and waved his chubby hands. I waved back.

Martin Luther King Jr. almost passed us by again, he was walking so fast. We had to leap forward to catch up with him. It took us two steps for every one of his. Zack picked up Baby Gabe so we wouldn't lose him in our rush.

When I was close enough so no one else would hear me, I called out, "Dr. King, wait up! We came from the future."

Dr. King kept walking, but now he was also looking at me. "Really?" he asked, in a way that showed he didn't buy my story.

"I swear we did," I replied with as much sincerity as I could muster. "We know that when things get tough, sometimes people feel like quitting." I was out of breath from talking and trying to keep up at the same time. It felt like we were sprinting back to Brown Chapel.

Bo was also jogging by our side. "We hope that you will carry on with your dream, no matter what happens," Bo said, putting all his shyness aside, trying to keep up his courage.

Martin Luther King Jr. slowed down and led the five of us to a clear spot by the railing on the bridge.

"What do you children know about my dream?" he asked us quite seriously. "Only you, young man, can share the colored man's struggle." He nodded toward Bo. "The rest of you are free as birds. You've never had to sit in the back of the bus. Never been asked to leave a restaurant because of your skin. You've never faced unjust laws that won't let you vote."

"We—" I tried to remind him that we were from the future, so Bo had probably never experienced that stuff either. But Dr. King wouldn't let me speak.

He held up one hand to silence me. I respectfully held my tongue.

"I've experienced all that and more," he said. I noticed that his voice was getting softer. He sounded really unhappy. MLK took a cigarette out of his pocket and lit it.

Watching him suck in some smoke, I desperately wanted to tell him to give up cigarettes. Smoking was terrible for his health.

Bo saw my concern. He leaned over and whispered to me, "In 1965 no one knew how bad cigarettes were for you. It wasn't until later that the government announced that smoking causes lung cancer. And might kill you."

I was glad for the information, but I knew it wasn't the cigarette smoking that would kill Martin Luther King Jr. In a few short years Dr. King would be shot.

I felt really sad thinking about this great man's assassination. After we got the computer fixed and before we left town, maybe I'd try to give him a little warning.

Of course, our mission in Selma wasn't to save

MLK's life. Our job was to convince him not to give up his dreams.

"After you march to Montgomery," Jacob told Dr. King, "maybe the police will leave you alone and you'll be safe to—"

"No," Martin Luther King Jr. interrupted. "I'll never be safe. My house was bombed in 1956 by people who didn't believe in equality. Another bomb was found on my front porch in 1957. I get death threats every single day." He looked over the bridge at the blue green water rushing freely below. "And I've been arrested many, many times."

"Now my own supporters are angry with me." Martin Luther King Jr. went on, his words flowing like the river. "Many are mad at me for turning them around today. Listen."

We all stood quietly. People had pretty much stopped singing and were now grumbling to each other as they headed back toward town.

They were saying things like Martin Luther King Jr. was a coward. He'd led them to march and he'd turned them back. They needed a new, stronger leader to take them all the way to Montgomery. Martin Luther King Jr. should go home to Atlanta.

And then I heard a woman who was wearing a yellow coat and a matching hat tell her friend, "This day will forever be known as 'Turnaround Tuesday.'"

"Turnaround Tuesday," Martin Luther King Jr. repeated, sadly shaking his head. "Those officers would have beaten us if we had marched forward. It would have been another Bloody Sunday. I may have saved lives today, but the march itself was a big disappointment."

He let out a low gravelly breath. "I'm always traveling and giving speeches. I'm so worried about winning voter freedom that I have headaches and my stomach hurts. My mind is constantly spinning and I don't sleep well. I desperately need to rest." Martin Luther King Jr. took one last puff on his cigarette. "I quit."

6

The Future

"You can't quit," I told Dr. King.

"I just did." He stared out at the wavy water below the bridge.

"But there's a national holiday named after you," I insisted. "We remember all the great things you did. Most kids get a day off from school. All government buildings and banks are closed. There's no mail. And"—in case he cared—"there are big sales at the mall."

I stepped up next to him and stuck my face under his, trying to catch his eye. "The third Monday in January is always Martin Luther King Jr. Day."

Slightly interested, he turned his face to mine. "In the future, I'm a holiday?"

MLK let loose a loud laugh, a husky rumble from the very middle of his chest. After his laughter died down, MLK said, "You're fooling me."

I shot a look at Bo. Maybe he had a few facts in his head that would help.

"In Selma in 1965," Bo began, "fewer than three percent of the voters were black. But fifty-eight percent of the town was black." I gave Bo a big ol' thumbs up. "Forty years later voter registration in Alabama will be nearly the same for blacks and whites. Thanks to you."

MLK didn't seem to care. Not even when Jacob put in, "Your friend Jesse Jackson is going to run for president in 1984 and 1988."

"You sound like Bo," I told Jacob, with a little giggle.

"I wish I had a memory like Bo," Jacob laughed. "My dad told me about Jesse Jackson. And the dates stuck in my head." Jacob put his hand to his mouth and whispered, "But Reverend Jackson hasn't won. At least not yet."

"It doesn't matter," I replied. "I bet just hearing

that an African American ran for president will convince him."

It didn't.

"You have to lead the next march from Selma to Montgomery." It was Zack's turn to try. "If blacks don't get the right to vote, America will be a very different, and far less cool, country."

"I'm not leading the march," MLK said, as he lowered his eyes back to the water. He was staring so intently, it looked as though he expected something to happen in the river.

Baby Gabe was climbing up the bridge railing right next to him. I couldn't tell if Gabe wanted to talk to MLK or go for a swim. Before any of us could get to him, MLK wrapped his hands around Gabe's belly. With a quick lift MLK lowered the monster back to the ground.

"I have another interesting fact about the third march," Bo told us.

"It's worth a try," I said, putting up my hands. "Go for it."

Bo tipped his face up to MLK. "On March sixteenth

a federal judge by the name of Frank Johnson will issue a decree that you can safely lead the march. There will be no blood and no turnaround. Even the president of the United States will help out. He'll order the Alabama National Guard to protect the marchers." Bo rubbed his chin, thinking. Careful not to leave anything out.

"Ooh," I said suddenly, remembering something else we'd learned at school. "You can't give up, because last year you won the Nobel Peace Prize."

Martin Luther King Jr. raised his head and turned to look at us.

"I don't know where you got your stories, but don't bother trying to convince me," he said. "I quit. My decision is final." He raised his hands as if he were surrendering. "Let the followers of Malcolm X work for voting rights. I don't agree with their methods, and yet I say, let them try. If you want nonviolence, give Ralph Abernathy a chance. John Lewis. Hosea Williams. Pick anyone else. I'm finished."

This was harder than I'd thought it would be. It was a good thing we'd found Baby Gabe first. We were spending a lot of time trying to convince Dr. King to lead the walkers on March twenty-first.

In fact, Jacob looked at his watch and announced, "We only have sixty-three minutes left."

We stepped slightly away from Dr. King. He was leaning on the railing, watching the river again.

"Forget the words," Zack said. "It's time for some action."

"I like action," I told Zack. "What's your idea?" Of course, as I asked, I knew what he was thinking. So did Jacob. And Bo.

"The future," we all exclaimed at the same time.

"De foootre," Gabe repeated. I smiled and put my hand on his head.

I glanced over to make sure MLK hadn't moved. He was still pressed up against the rails, staring at the water.

Jacob pulled the computer out of his pocket and began to fiddle around with the broken button.

"So where can we take him?" I asked the boys.

Bo went first. "We should take him to the United States Capitol building in Washington, D.C., to see his old friend John Lewis. Mr. Lewis led the march on Bloody Sunday and was badly beaten. He would have marched today, but he's still in the hospital. In our time he's a congressman."

Bo's idea was good. By visiting John Lewis, MLK would see that there are a lot of African Americans who make laws for our country now.

I had another suggestion. "How about Atlanta?" Dr. King was from Georgia. "We could show him how much things have changed there."

"No," Jacob began, "we have to go—" He didn't get a chance to finish because Zack interrupted.

"Let's take him to—," Zack started, but Jacob cut him off.

"We have to take him back to school," Jacob said quickly, throwing all the words out at once.

"You didn't let me finish," Zack snipped at his brother.

"You didn't let me finish either," Jacob argued. "Besides, it doesn't matter what you think."

"What do you mean it doesn't matter?" Zack complained, narrowing his eyes to slits. "What could we possibly show him at school that would be useful?" There was an edgy tone to Zack's voice.

"I don't know," Jacob responded curtly. "How about black and white kids learning together? Playing together? Stuff like that."

"School's out for the day," Zack reminded Jacob, his voice tight. "All we can show him are empty hallways. Or kids sitting in Chess Club. Playing basketball. Cooking in Cooking Club."

I considered Zack's words, then replied, "Maybe your mom can show him a voting machine?" I thought that was an okay idea. Not perfect, but not horrible, either.

"Sorry I cut you off, Zack, but we don't have a choice about where to go," Jacob finally admitted. "I can't get the computer button to stay on. I can't change the settings."

"So," Zack said, thoughtfully considering Jacob's words, "if it still works, then pulling out the cartridge should take us right back to classroom 305." Zack took a calming breath and lightly concluded, "Well, then. I guess we're going to school after all."

The twins had agreed and without pushing or shoving or rolling on the ground! It was amazing. An attitude of nonviolence was sinking into the twins' thick skulls and sticking there. What a big difference!

"We'll figure out what to show Martin Luther King Jr. when we get there," I told them. "I guess we could always introduce MLK to Mr. C. Maybe Mr. C can convince him."

"I need to see Mr. C, anyway. I want some new wire to fix this thing," Jacob said. Then, he tugged the time-travel cartridge out of the computer.

Nothing happened.

"Um, Jacob?" Bo was obviously concerned. "Where's the hole?"

"Uh-oh," I gasped.

"Uh-oh," Baby Gabe repeated.

"Something's wrong." Jacob jiggled the cartridge.

There was no green, glowing smoke. No time-travel hole in the sidewalk. Or on the bridge. Or anywhere.

"Something unusual is going on down there,"

Martin Luther King Jr. suddenly exclaimed. He was still looking over the side of the bridge.

"Shoot," I cried.

"Scoot," Baby Gabe copied.

I didn't have to look over the bridge railing to know what was going on. By MLK's reaction we all knew exactly what had happened. The time-travel hole had opened in the water under the bridge. There was only one thing to do. And we had to act fast.

Since Zack had played peewee football for a week the year before, he was our coach.

He instructed the boys to move back. Farther and farther away from the railing.

I went to stand next to MLK. Baby Gabe was in my arms. Zack needed to use both his hands, so he gave me the diaper bag.

On my face was that same innocent look I'd shown Mrs. Osborne in the classroom. The one that makes you think nothing's up, when something actually is.

"Can you swim?" I asked MLK, pretending to be interested.

"Swim? Why?"

"Oh, no reason," I said as I ducked out of the way. With a running start, arms folded across their chests, the boys quarterback-tackled Dr. King—slamming into his back. They rammed him so hard, MLK flipped over the bridge railing and . . . stuck there.

His head was over the water. His belly was caught on the rail. His legs hung in midair. Dr. King was very surprised. And very mad. "What are you doing?" he demanded to know. "Help me up!"

I could see the green mist swirling below us.

"I'm so sorry to do this," I apologized to the great civil rights leader as I pushed him over the rail by his feet. And down he went.

Martin Luther King Jr. crashed into the river below. Only there wasn't any splash. The time-travel hole didn't have any water in it.

Jumping off a bridge was dumb. Super-dumb. But we didn't have a choice.

Zack took Baby Gabe from me, climbed the narrow railing, and leapt off the bridge. The two of them followed MLK down into the swirling mist.

Carefully, Jacob, Bo, and I helped each other climb up, and we swung our legs over the railing. The hole was starting to shrink. We didn't want to dive too far out and miss our target. Even though I could swim, I wasn't in the mood to get wet.

We leaned against the metal rail, balancing with our legs bent.

On the count of three we jumped.

And on four we landed, because time travel is really fast.

7

Election Day

We were back in the classroom with fifty-one minutes left on Jacob's watch.

Baby Gabe immediately went over to the wall and
tore down an American history time-line poster. He
sat on the floor and began to shred it. I loved the kid,
but he was making our job way harder.

Being almost two years old, Gabe didn't understand and started to cry when I took the poster away.
"What are we going to show MLK at school?" I asked
the boys.

"Nothing," Zack told me.

"We aren't going to show him anything?" I
scrunched up my face with the question. I got Gabe

some notebook paper from my backpack. He started to rip that up instead.

"Nope. We aren't showing MLK a single thing," Zack confirmed.

I was really confused. "Why not, Zack? Did you already convince him?" That would be terrific. Though I didn't know how Zack could have convinced MLK when we'd only been back at school for three seconds.

"Nah," Zack told me. "I didn't convince him. But you aren't going to either. He's not here." Zack waved his hands around the classroom. "Somehow, between the time we shoved him into the hole and the time we arrived—"

"He vanished," I finished. I sighed a deep breath. I scanned the classroom carefully. I even went to the supply closet and opened the door. After checking under Mr. C's desk, I asked, "Are we sure he even time-traveled to school?"

"He's around here somewhere," Bo said, crouching low to the floor.

We all gathered round to see what evidence Bo had discovered.

"Eeww." I gagged as Bo picked up a bent and crinkled cigarette. He tried to hand it to me, but I refused to take it. "Yuck."

Bo got up and tossed the cigarette into the trash. "It's all the proof we need," Bo declared. "It's so bad for you that not many people smoke nowadays. Martin Luther King Jr. is definitely at our school."

Jacob gave Baby Gabe a piggyback ride, and off we went.

MLK wasn't in the hallway, so we checked the cafeteria. Not there. He wasn't in the library. Or the front offices.

There was a lot of noise coming from the school gym, so we decided to check it out. To our surprise the room was full of voters.

People were everywhere—standing in lines.

There was a line for VOTER CHECK-IN. Another line for the voting machines. There was even a line of people waiting to get "I voted" stickers near the gym exit.

Lines snaked this way and that, all around the gym.

"Huh?" I didn't know what more to say. It was weird, strange, and completely odd.

We were totally confused and it only got worse when we saw Mrs. Osborne.

"Oh, good," Mrs. Osborne said, rushing up to us. "I'm glad you brought Gabe by. I wanted to check on how he was doing." She took Gabe from Jacob and gave him some kisses.

"Fine," I said. "He's doing fine." I was staring at her as if she'd dropped down from another planet. What was going on?

"You kids did such a good job keeping him out of trouble yesterday during History Club. I know you didn't want to babysit him again today, but I really appreciate it." She threw a glance around the gym. "You can see how busy it is in here."

Mrs. Osborne gave Gabe one last kiss, handed him over to Zack, and rushed off.

We watched her rearrange some red, white, and blue balloons on a table.

"It must be Time-Warp Tuesday," Jacob declared.

"Balloons, voters, long lines—all the evidence indicates that we've come back to school a day late."

"It can't be Tuesday," Zack responded. "What happened to Monday?"

"Gone," Bo answered simply. "No book I've ever read mentioned Election Day on a Monday." He looked around the gym. "National elections are always on Tuesday."

"Tuesday," Zack muttered. He set Gabe down on the gym floor. Gabe immediately headed toward the steps at the back of the gym. I snatched him up. He wiggled, begging to be let go. I sat him down by my feet, facing away from the stairs.

Suddenly, there was a loud noise at the other end of the gym.

Yelling. Shouting. Screaming. A crowd was gathering to watch whatever was going on. When I heard the words "You can't deny me my right to vote," I knew who was in the center of it all.

We had to stop Martin Luther King Jr. before he got arrested. Again.

I bent down to pick up Baby Gabe. He was gone. Again.

"Big problem," I told the boys. It was Selma all over. We had to decide: find Gabe or talk to MLK. Which should we do first?

There was so much noise coming from the far side of the gym, this time Gabe would have to wait.

"These people are withholding my constitutional right to vote," Dr. King declared. "Voting is my freedom as an American citizen."

When Martin Luther King Jr. saw Bo, Jacob, Zack, and me, he said, "They say I'm not registered to vote. And they won't let me register!" He complained, "See? This is exactly the reason I quit."

"We time-traveled, remember?" I tried desperately to explain. "It isn't because you're black. It's because you don't live here. They have no record of you registering."

"Since the Civil War phony laws have kept blacks from voting. You may say we have time-traveled, but as far as I can tell, nothing has changed!" Martin Luther King Jr. stormed out of the gym.

I started to rush after him, but Zack held me back. Zack said simply, "You promised. We have to get Gabe."

"That promise was made in Selma," Jacob countered. "In 1965. Not here. Today. This time we have to go after MLK."

And since they now understood the importance of nonviolence, the twins calmly began to discuss which one should be first: MLK or Gabe.

I thought they might talk about it all day, but then, thankfully, our favorite social studies teacher entered the gym. Yippee. Not only was Mr. C here to help but he was carrying Gabe on his shoulders. And Dr. King was walking by his side.

"Lose someone?" Mr. C asked us with a laugh. "Or two someones?"

I exhaled with relief. "We're having a rough day," I said, feeling exhausted.

"Make that two days." Zack told Mr. C how we had left yesterday and come back today.

Jacob explained about the broken time-travel computer. Bo added that it's been extra hard to convince MLK. Harder than we'd imagined.

"Plus," I put in, "we have Baby Gabe hanging around making trouble—or disappearing, making even more trouble."

Mr. C listened carefully and then asked Jacob, "How much time do you have left for your mission?"

Checking his watch, Jacob answered, "Forty-four minutes."

"Plenty of time," Mr. C said. "Let me help."

Jacob thrust the computer at him. "Will you fix it?" Jacob opened his hand to show our teacher the broken button.

"I'll deal with that in a minute," Mr. C said. "But first, I'll talk to Dr. King. When I saw him standing outside, I figured something had gone wrong. I bribed him to come back into school with me."

"Bribed him?" Zack was stunned. "Did you offer him money to come back to school?"

"No." Mr. C chuckled at the thought. "I promised him something better. I swore that if he came back with me, he could see a black man freely vote."

"Is it time?" Martin Luther King Jr. asked Mr. C.

"Yes," Mr. C answered. Mr. C pulled Gabe down off his shoulders and handed the mini-monster to Zack. "Don't let him out of your sight. Not even for a split second." We all agreed. There was no way Gabe was getting away from us a third time.

Together, we followed Mr. C as he took MLK to the line for voter check-in.

"First, you must register to vote," Mr. C told Dr. King. "Times are different now. You can sign up before the election at the post office, supermarket— practically anywhere. Or at some polling places, they let you walk in and register on Election Day."

We all got in line. "I've already registered," Mr. C said.

"Are you telling me that you can register to vote without the fear of violence?" MLK asked.

"Yes," Mr. C answered. "It's perfectly safe to register."

"When you vote, you aren't going to get arrested? Or lose your job? Have your house set on fire? Your life won't be threatened?"

"Thanks to your hard work, there's no danger at all." Mr. C took MLK by the arm and edged him forward as the line moved up. "On Election Day the volunteers make certain you are registered, and then you get to vote."

"There's no literacy test? No question about bubbles on a bar of soap? No poll tax? You don't need an ancient grandfather who voted? No one will block your way?" MLK sure had a lot of questions. No wonder I was beginning to like him.

"Nope." Mr. C gave his name to a volunteer and picked up a pen. "Simply sign the registration book and you can vote." He leaned over and scribbled his signature.

Check-in complete, we tagged along as they headed to the voting booth.

"The booths are mostly electronic now," Mr. C told Dr. King. "You touch the name on the screen to vote for that person. If the question is about a new law, you lightly touch the word 'Yes' or 'No.' The machine counts the votes and they get added up at the end of the day."

Mr. C went into the voting booth and closed the curtain behind him. A few minutes later he came out.

A volunteer gave Mr. C a little sticker that said "I voted." Proudly Mr. C put the sticker on his jacket, where everyone could see it.

MLK stared at the sticker, then exclaimed, "It's true!" He pointed at some of the different people standing in line. "In your time, America is a place where people of all ethnicities and nationalities can freely cast their votes. This is a very exciting discovery."

Dr. King took a long, relaxed breath. "A great weight has been lifted from my shoulders. Now that I've seen this, my head feels clearer and my stomach doesn't hurt anymore."

"Don't forget, you made this happen," Jacob reminded MLK. "Your determination and dream forced America to change."

"Are you convinced?" I asked Dr. King. "Can we go back to Selma now?"

"I'm definitely convinced that the future is a better place for colored people." Dr. King surveyed the room. "This is the world I am fighting for. I have witnessed my dream come true." He looked back at us and said seriously, "I want to stay."

"You can't stay. You have to go back. None of this will happen if you don't lead the march on March twenty-first." Bo was speaking firmly, determined to convince Dr. King.

MLK just shrugged and picked up from a table an official booklet about voting.

This was a disaster! And yet, Mr. C had the most enormous smile on his face. "Dr. King makes firm decisions," he said to us. "But that's part of what made him such a great leader. I think you kids can handle things from here."

"We still need your help," I said to Mr. C.

"I took him to vote. It's your turn now." Mr. C asked Jacob to show him the computer. From his pocket he pulled out a handful of tangled wires, a mini-screwdriver, five buttons, two batteries, and a pen. He separated out two long wires—one yellow, one blue.

Mr. C tucked the wires into the computer and then twisted them around the red button. The button wasn't exactly attached. It hung down, swinging back and forth.

"Go out by the playground and put in the time-travel cartridge." He handed Jacob the computer. Jacob grimaced at Mr. C's quick fix. It didn't look like it was going to work.

"You'll need to time-travel to another place before you go back to Selma," Mr. C told us. "Slip in the cartridge and get going. See what you see. Afterward, when Dr. King is firmly convinced, you'll need to switch the wires to finish your journey. When history is on track, take out the cartridge as usual, and hurry home.

"Good luck." Mr. C left the gym.

8

We Shall Overcome

It took some doing to get MLK to the playground. We didn't want to lie to him. Or promise he could stay in our time. Rather, we begged, and begged some more.

To our amazement the begging worked. MLK came with us but was muttering the whole time about how excited he was to start a new life in our world.

On the playground Gabe really wanted to go down the slide. Since he had nowhere to go and nothing important to do, MLK said he'd take him. Dr. King liked being in our time so much, we thought he should have fun for his last few seconds.

We let them climb the ladder while Jacob slipped in the cartridge. I winked at the boys.

MLK and Baby Gabe reached the top of the slide ladder. Sat down together. Pushed off together. And whoosh . . . They disappeared together.

The time-travel hole opened just like it was supposed to at the very bottom of the slide.

We jumped in right behind them. And landed with a thud on a beautifully polished white floor.

"I told you I was staying in your time," MLK protested. "I demand you take me back there now."

"No," Jacob said, stashing the computer in his pocket. "We came here to show you something important." With a sigh he added, "Though we're not sure what."

I turned to Bo, who had picked up Baby Gabe. "Do you know why we're here?" I asked him.

Bo looked around. "Well, we're in the United States Capitol building. I came here with my mom last summer vacation. It was interesting."

I'm sure it was interesting, but we still had no clue why Mr. C had sent us.

There was a crowd gathering to our left. We thought we should head that way. But we didn't know how to get MLK to come along with us. He was still muttering about how we'd forced him through time. Twice.

"We are beginning shortly," a man called out from the center of the gathering. He hurried over to us. The sound of his footsteps echoed in the large open room.

"Who are you?" the man asked us. He was wearing a gray suit and a tie. A special badge was hanging around his neck. The badge made him look very important.

"We are here to witness history," Jacob quickly answered.

"Well, if you got into the Capitol building through security, you must be invited guests," the man responded, not knowing we'd dropped in instead of coming through the door. "If you want to hear the president's speech, you'd better come with me now."

"Which president?" I asked, cutting in.

The man looked at me curiously. "President Lyndon B. Johnson, of course."

"Oh, of course," I repeated. "I was just making sure

you knew which one." I was totally embarrassed at sounding so dumb. But what was I going to tell him? I couldn't say that we'd just time-traveled and didn't know the date or who was president of the United States.

"We don't want to be late." The man reached into his pocket and pulled out six special badges on strings.

"Put these on." He handed us the badges. MLK took one. And the last one went around Baby Gabe's neck. The man never even asked us our names. And the weirdest part was that he didn't seem to recognize Dr. King.

Wearing badges, we all looked important.

We followed the man into a huge room. There were rows of seats, like a theater.

The man said, "All the nationally elected politicians in Washington, D.C., have come together for this key moment in American history." I almost laughed when he said, "It's too bad Dr. Martin Luther King Jr. couldn't make it today. I hear he's watching the speech on television at Dr. and Mrs. Jean Jackson's home in Selma."

Dr. King didn't say a word. He just turned and winked at us. Obviously, he wasn't mad at us for bringing him here anymore. Now he just looked curious. We still didn't know what we were about to see.

Whatever it was, I hoped that it would convince Martin Luther King Jr. to march to Montgomery.

Every chair in the place was full.

We were told that we could stand next to the stage, out of the way. And that we'd better not interrupt.

I was worried about Gabe. He had caused us so much trouble already. I wasn't sure we could keep him quiet. Bo set him down on the floor near our feet. Zack gave him all the crackers left in the diaper bag.

I took my foot and pressed it against Gabe's back. That way if he moved, I'd know before he disappeared. But Gabe wasn't going anywhere. He was too busy making an enormous mess—eating crackers, smearing them on his face, and eating crumbs off the floor.

An announcement was made and suddenly everyone in the room stood up, clapping. Even Baby Gabe got up. He grabbed on to my pant leg with his messy cracker hands.

A man walked slowly into the room, shaking hands with everyone he passed.

Bo's face was glowing. "That's President Johnson!" Bo was having trouble keeping his voice down. I though he might burst with excitement. "Lyndon B. Johnson was the thirty-sixth president of the United States."

The man who had given us the badges shot us an evil look, so Bo lowered his voice. Leaning over to Jacob, Zack, and me, he said, "Now I know why we're here. The date is March 15, 1965." Bo grinned and added, "Mr. C is a genius."

He could have told us more, but a hush fell over the crowd. President Johnson approached the microphone.

The silence was broken when Baby Gabe suddenly began to clap and cheer for the president. I panicked. We were going to get thrown out! No matter how many times I said "shhh," Gabe wouldn't stop clapping.

President Johnson paused, looking around for the source of the noise. His eyes focused on Gabe. He didn't seem to notice the rest of us standing there.

Taking a handkerchief out of his pants pocket, President Johnson crossed to the side of the stage, bent down, and wiped the crackers off Gabe's face and hands. "Much better," he said with a smile. Gabe quieted down after President Johnson cleaned him up.

Returning to his place in front of the gathered assembly, President Johnson said, "I speak tonight for the dignity of man and the destiny of democracy. . . . The Constitution says that no person shall be kept from voting because of his race or his color," President Johnson declared. "The command of the Constitution is plain. . . . It is wrong—deadly wrong—to deny any of your fellow Americans the right to vote in this country."

Bo leaned over and whispered to me, "After this speech President Lyndon B. Johnson will send a new law called the Voting Rights Act of 1965 to congress for approval."

"So." I considered Bo's words. "The Voting Rights Act made sure everyone followed the U.S. Constitution. No one would be prevented from voting. Ever again."

"Exactly." Scratching his chin, Bo looked down at Gabe's clean hands. "I always wondered why President Johnson started the speech at two minutes after nine instead of at nine o'clock." He laughed. "Now I know."

Bo went back to listening to President Johnson. He was waiting for something specific in the speech.

I looked at Martin Luther King Jr. I couldn't tell if he was convinced how important it was for him to march to Montgomery, yet.

"Wait. Wait for it," Bo whispered. "Don't take your eyes off MLK's face."

We didn't.

Scanning the room, President Johnson took a deep breath and let his words echo through the chamber.

"And we shall overcome."

President Lyndon B. Johnson spoke those words loudly and clearly. Those were the exact words to

the song that we'd heard the marchers sing on Turnaround Tuesday. It was the marchers' song about their struggle for the freedom to vote.

"We shall overcome," President Johnson repeated.

Bo didn't have to point it out. We couldn't help but notice. At those magic words there was a tear in Martin Luther King Jr.'s eye.

After the speech MLK took off his badge and set it on a nearby table. We put ours on top. Gabe's was slightly chewed and very slobbery.

"I'm sorry, kids," Dr. King said with sincerity. "I can't come live in your future."

I tried to look disappointed. "Gee, why not?" I asked, with a half shrug.

"Having seen that America will soon be a better place, I now have the courage to follow my dream. I will even endure my headaches, stomach pains, and sleepless nights for the cause of justice and freedom. It's time to go to Selma." Dr. Martin Luther King Jr. said proudly, "I have a march to lead."

9

March 21, 1965

After switching the computer wires, the time-travel hole opened and we jumped back to the Brown Chapel AME Church. If I'd thought it was crowded before, it was double-packed now. People were crammed in every corner.

I had two burning questions.

Question one: "What day is it?" I asked Jacob.

He looked at the computer. "March 21, 1965!"

So we'd skipped a few days in between. No matter. We were here, and Martin Luther King Jr. was ready to march.

Bo told us that the reason the church was so crowded was that three thousand people started this, the third march, together. But, he reminded us, by the time they reached Montgomery there would be twenty-five thousand walkers.

Question two: "How much time do we have?"

Jacob reported, "There are only seven minutes left on the computer."

The doors opened, and this time we were ready for the rush.

So was MLK. He stepped out into the bright sunlight at the front of the crowd. A group of marchers from Hawaii had brought Dr. King a lei, a necklace made of fresh flowers, to wear around his neck.

As we walked toward the Edmund Pettus Bridge, Ralph Abernathy came up beside us. He picked up Baby Gabe and tickled him. Reverend Abernathy was also wearing a lei.

After carrying Gabe a block or two Reverend Abernathy put him down and went to link arms with Dr. King.

A line formed. The important civil rights leaders—black and white, all colors and faiths—marched arm in arm.

Thousands of people followed.

All around us the marchers were singing "We Shall Overcome."

The tune sounded better than ever. My heart swelled with pride at all MLK had done for civil rights and voter freedom.

I was so awed watching MLK start his third and final walk to Montgomery, I forgot to watch Baby Gabe. I guess the same thing had happened to the twins and Bo because Gabe escaped.

"Not again." I sighed. I looked around us. There were people as far as I could see. And no sign of Gabe.

Our searching was interrupted by Jacob slapping his hips and screaming, "That monster!" Even with so much noise around us, his voice rang in my ears. Turns out he wasn't slapping his hips. Jacob was patting his pockets.

Whenever it was that Gabe had disappeared, he'd pickpocketed Jacob before he left.

Gabe was missing. And so was Mr. C's time-travel computer.

"I hope you like Selma in 1965," Zack said to me. "Because it's home now." He gave Jacob a look that could kill. "It's your fault he got away with the comput—," Zack began. He stopped midsentence. A large group of people marched by, singing with their arms draped around one another.

After they passed, Zack's words became softer and he calmly said, "Let's split up and go find Gabe."

"I'll go with Zack." Jacob put his arm around his brother's shoulders. Zack wrapped his arm around Jacob and they stood there ready for action.

"Forget it," Bo told us. He pointed at the side of the road. There was Gabe playing with a little black boy. It was the same boy we'd seen on March ninth, riding on Reverend Abernathy's shoulders after the turnaround.

The boy waved at us with the same excitement as before.

I waved back, noticing that they were playing with a small black toy. After a closer look I saw that it wasn't a toy. It was Mr. C's computer!

The little boy was holding it and . . . it looked like he was licking the front. No wait, he was biting the front.

Jacob ran forward. "Don't bite the button back off!" He snagged the computer out of the boy's hand. The boy immediately began to cry. His mother came over.

"You didn't have to upset him," she told Jacob.

"I'm sorry," Jacob explained. "This one"—he pointed at Gabe—"is my brother. The thing they were playing with isn't a toy it's—" His voice faded away as Jacob looked down at the computer in his hand.

Bo looked over Jacob's shoulder. "The kid fixed it," Bo said, totally amazed.

Sure enough, somehow the red button was now firmly in its proper place. A new set of teeth marks was in the plastic. Right next to Gabe's older set.

"It seems that the boy fixed it with his teeth instead of tools," I commented. "Weird."

"Really weird," Zack added. He picked up Gabe and held him close. "Well, I guess we won't have to live here after all."

We apologized again and thanked the woman. Her son was still screaming. I felt bad, but even though he'd fixed the computer, he couldn't keep it.

Zack looked into the diaper bag to see what he could give the kid. He pulled out Gabe's sippy cup. He handed it to the boy, who had never seen anything like it. While the boy turned the cup over and over, examining it, we hurried to catch up to Martin Luther King Jr. at the front of the march.

With fifty-four seconds to go we caught up with him at the Edmund Pettus Bridge. He was in exactly the same place he'd been turned around the last time we'd walked together. Exactly the same place the marchers had been attacked on Bloody Sunday.

"Are you sure they get to march all the way to Montgomery this time?" I asked Bo. Already I could see the line of police officers. Another "sea of blue."

"Positive," Bo said. "These police are different from before. This time the officers are here to protect the marchers, not to prevent them from marching. President Johnson himself ordered these troops to help." Bo knew what he was talking about. He always did.

As MLK and the walkers approached the officers, the policemen moved to the side. Out of the way.

Martin Luther King Jr. hesitated. With a quick turn of his head, he searched the crowd. We knew who he was looking for, so we all waved. MLK winked in our direction. That was all the thanks we needed.

None of us moved a muscle, not even Baby Gabe, as we watched Dr. Martin Luther King Jr. lead the march across the Edmund Pettus Bridge.

And as his feet touched the pavement on the other side, we knew he'd made America a better place for us all.

Jacob pulled out the cartridge and we jumped home.

10

Home Again

We were back in the classroom. Jacob checked the computer. It was Monday and club time was over.

"Thank goodness, everything is back to normal," Zack said, sighing with relief. "The computer is fixed, we're not stuck in Selma, Gabe is here with us, and it's Monday again." He was still holding Baby Gabe. With all the excitement of the day, or days, Baby Gabe had fallen asleep on our last pass through time. "All that and voter freedom, too."

"Watching the marchers cross the Edmund Pettus Bridge was amazing," I exclaimed as we went to get our backpacks. "I wish we could have walked the whole way to Montgomery."

"It was an unbelievable journey," Bo remarked as

Zack lay Baby Gabe back down on the blanket Mrs. Osborne had set up for his nap. "Hundreds of people walked almost eleven miles a day. For five days. They had to sleep in tents at night. It was cold. It rained. They met people along the way who didn't believe everyone deserved to vote. One day a helicopter flew over the march dropping hate letters."

Zack shook his head. "It's hard to imagine there was so much hatred in America. I mean, it wasn't very long ago." He sighed. "I totally understand why MLK might have wanted to quit."

"And yet," I said, "I bet they sang the whole way. They supported each other. The marchers knew their cause was right." I thought about Mrs. Hepworth's bruised arm. "Freedom was worth every single step they took. All the way from Selma, Alabama, to Montgomery, Alabama."

Jacob was about to say something more when suddenly the classroom door opened. It was Mrs. Osborne. Jacob thrust the time-travel computer behind his back at sonic speed. Again.

"Hi, kids," Mrs. Osborne said cheerfully. "Did you have a nice History Club meeting?"

"I'm not sure if you'd call it 'nice,'" Zack responded. "But it was successful. So that's good."

"I see that Gabe wasn't any trouble," Mrs. Osborne said, lifting her sleeping son off his blanket.

Jacob nearly choked. Zack started coughing. I laughed. And Bo rubbed his chin.

"I knew he'd be fine." As she picked up Gabe's blanket, Mrs. Osborne said, "If it's all right, I'd like to leave him with the four of you again after school tomorrow. We're expecting a big crowd of voters in the school gym. I need to be there to help."

Jacob nearly choked. Zack started coughing. I laughed. And Bo rubbed his chin.

"Great," she said, even though we'd never really answered. She turned to the twins. "I'll just gather my papers and meet you boys at the car."

"We need to go find Mr. C," Jacob told his mom. "We have something to give him." He kept his arms pulled back, time-travel computer safely hidden.

"Okay," she said. "Five minutes." Baby Gabe let out

a huge yawn and rubbed his eyes. "He's slept so much today. I can't imagine why he's still tired." She took the diaper bag from Zack and left the room.

We hustled out of the classroom too. The school gym was empty and quiet. It was almost spooky. But not nearly as spooky as the stairs at the back of the gym. We rushed down the steps two at a time, setting a new speed record for getting to Mr. C's laboratory.

"We're back," I said as we barged through the door. Mr. C was wearing a white lab coat and thick plastic goggles. He was peering through a magnifying glass and making adjustments with tweezers to a metal globe.

In one swift move Mr. C tossed a dirty towel over his newest invention. "Don't you kids knock?" he asked as he removed his goggles and slipped on his glasses.

Oops. I guess we should have knocked since we knew his new invention was top secret. We were just so excited to be back, we didn't want to wait.

I wondered what he was working on. "What are

you—," I started, but Bo touched my shoulder.

"No time," he told me.

"Oh, right," I said. We only had a few more minutes before the twins had to meet their mom.

Jacob handed Mr. C the computer while Zack began to fill our teacher in on our adventure. He told the story so quickly, major chunks of the tale were left out.

"So you convinced him to lead the walk on March twenty-first, after all?" Mr. C asked.

"Yes," I said. "Thanks in part to you."

He raised an eyebrow. "How did I help?"

"Well, you—" A photo on Mr. C's shelf caught my eye. I stopped talking and crossed the room. I picked up the picture and stared at it.

It was a small African American boy, about two years old, sitting on a man's shoulders. Waving to the camera. The man was definitely Reverend Ralph Abernathy. The boy was the little boy we'd met. The one who played with Gabe and fixed the computer.

I passed the picture to Bo. He handed it to Zack, who gave it over to Jacob.

"Is this you?" Bo asked.

"Yes." Mr. C nodded. "When I was two, we lived next door to Reverend Abernathy and his family. He was friends with my parents. During the marches, he carried me partway on his shoulders."

"You were there?" Zack asked. "At both marches?"

"At all three marches," Mr. C corrected. No wonder Mr. C had that faraway look in class when he talked about the Selma marches. He had been lost in memory! Real memories of Martin Luther King Jr. and 1965.

"Were you hurt on Bloody Sunday?" I asked.

"I was little and don't remember much, but I know I was near the back of the line," Mr. C told me. "I got lost when the crowd turned around and began to run. Other than being scared, no, I wasn't beaten that day." He paused. "My dad was, though."

Mr. C took the photo from Jacob and put it back up on the shelf. "Abigail, you said I helped you convince Dr. King to march. How did I do that if I was here the whole time?"

Turned out Mr. C had helped us twice! I laughed. We all did.

I winked at the boys while I told Mr. C, "Just don't forget to vote tomorrow, okay?"

"I'd never forget to vote," Mr. C told us with a grin. "It's my right."

"And voting is power," Zack added.

We had to go. Mrs. Osborne was waiting for the boys. Sometimes she gave me a ride home, but today I felt like walking. The whole way.

"Oooh," I said before we left the lab. "I forgot to warn MLK about his assassination." I couldn't believe I'd forgotten something so important.

"History is back on track," Mr. C told me. "It's sad that Dr. King will die so young, but think of all the good he did during his life."

I was proud they'd named a day after him. But we needed more than one day off from school to remember all the great things Dr. King did for America. Maybe we could take off a whole month? Or a year? I bet that even in a year we still couldn't begin to learn about all the good MLK had done.

We were nearly out the door when Bo turned back to Mr. C.

"I can do it, you know," he said. I had no clue what he was talking about.

"I had no doubt you could," Mr. C told Bo. "It wouldn't have mattered. You still wouldn't have been allowed to vote."

"Yeah," Bo said sadly.

I realized that they were talking about the literacy tests. Bo was telling Mr. C that he really did know the entire United States Constitution by heart. Bo always amazes me.

I said good-bye to the boys in the school parking lot.

Jacob and Zack ran off to their mom's van.

As Bo walked off to get his bike, I could hear him muttering to himself:

"'We the People of the United States, in Order to form a more perfect Union, establish Justice, insure domestic Tranquility, provide for the common defence, promote the general Welfare, and secure the Blessings of Liberty to ourselves and our Posterity, do ordain and establish this Constitution for the United States of America. . . .'"

The Third March for Voting Rights

On March 21, 1965, with protection from the president of the United States, Reverend Martin Luther King Jr. led the march from Selma, Alabama, to Montgomery, Alabama. In this photo of that important day, Dr. Martin Luther King Jr. is walking arm in arm with his chief aide, Reverend Ralph Abernathy.

Musical and Lyrical Adaptation by Zilphia Horton, Frank Hamilton, Guy Carawan, and Pete Seeger. Inspired by African American Gospel Singing, Members of the Food & Tobacco Workers Union, Charleston, SC, and the Civil Rights Movement.

A Letter to Our Readers

Hi! We hope you enjoyed Blast to the Past: King's Courage.

King's Courage is part fiction, part fact. We made up the time-travel part. But the story of Martin Luther King Jr. and the three marches from Selma to Montgomery is true.

Martin Luther King Jr. spent his life working for civil rights. He imagined a world where blacks and whites, Christians, Jews, and people of all backgrounds could live together in peace. This was his dream.

The first march for voting rights took place on March 7, 1965. The marchers hoped to walk all the way from Selma, Alabama, to Montgomery, Alabama. At worst the marchers thought they might be arrested. They never imagined the police would hurt them. We made up the character Mrs. Hepworth, but her story is true. Bloody Sunday was a terrible tragedy. There are many Americans today who can tell you about the bruises they got when the police stopped them from crossing the Edmund Pettus Bridge.

Martin Luther King Jr. led the second march. Rabbi Raiskin wasn't really there that day. He does exist, though, and he actually walked in the third march to Montgomery. Many grown-ups today know people who were part of the Selma marches. We know Rabbi Raiskin.

The fact is, Dr. King knew they were going to turn around on the second march. He just didn't tell everyone. A federal judge named Frank Johnson had told Dr. King that he couldn't walk until the marchers could be protected. Had MLK tried to cross the bridge that day, it would have been another bloody battle.

As far as we know, Martin Luther King Jr. never really quit. He sure had a lot of good reasons to, though. His house really was set on fire, bombs were found on his porch, and his life was threatened. He was arrested and spent many days in jail. He knew that what he was doing was right, but it was hard. He was under so much pressure, he smoked, had stomachaches and headaches, and didn't sleep well.

Six days after Lyndon B. Johnson's "We Shall Overcome" speech, Dr. King led the third march to Montgomery. And finally they made it! A few months later, in August 1965, the Voting Rights Act was passed into law. And all Americans were free to vote.

Sadly, Dr. Martin Luther King Jr. was killed on April 4, 1968. He never got to see the America he helped create.

If you want to learn more about the series or want to contact us, visit our Web site at www.BlasttothePastBooks.com.

Have a blast!
Stacia and Rhody